W9-AAF-178

The MASTER

and

The APOSTLE

The MASTER

and

The APOSTLE

JOHN POLLOCK

INSPIRATIONAL PRESS

NEW YORK

Previously published in two separate volumes:

THE MASTER: A LIFE OF JESUS copyright © 1984
(British edition), 1985 (U.S. edition) by John Pollock.
THE APOSTLE: A LIFE OF PAUL copyright © 1972
(British edition), 1985 (U.S. edition) by John Pollock.

Dialogue and other Scripture quotations are from the following
Bibles and New Testaments: *The Jerusalem Bible,* © 1966,
Darton, Longman & Todd, Ltd., and Doubleday & Company, Inc.;
New English Bible, Oxford University Press and Cambridge
University Press; *The Revised Standard Version of the Bible,* © 1946,
1952, 1971, 1973; *New Testament in Modern English,* © by
J.B. Phillips, The Macmillan Company and Collins Publishers;
Good News Bible, © 1966, 1971, 1976, The American Bible Society;
and *Holy Bible, New International Version,* © 1973, 1978, 1984,
International Bible Society, permission of Zondervan Bible
Publishers.

First Inspirational Press edition published in 1995.

Inspirational Press
A division of BBS Publishing Corporation
386 Park Avenue South
New York, NY 10016

Inspirational Press is a registered trademark of
BBS Publishing Corporation.

Published by arrangement with Chariot Victor Publishing,
a division of Cook Communications.

Library of Congress Catalog Card Number: 95-79187

ISBN: 0-88486-119-8

Printed in the United States of America.

Contents

I.

The MASTER

A LIFE OF JESUS

Contents

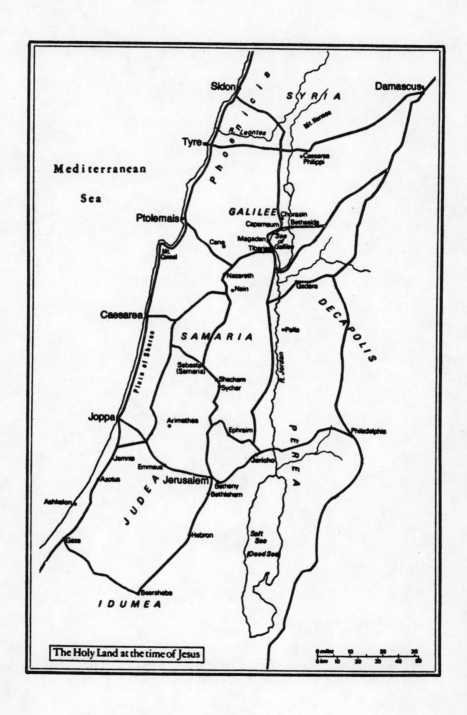

The Holy Land at the time of Jesus

Foreword

I count myself among John Pollock's greatest fans; his writings have had a tremendous impact on my life. In my early days as a Christian, I studied the Book of Acts using John's *The Apostle* as a commentary. His profile of William Wilberforce fueled my desire to emulate this great social reformer and biblical crusader of the nineteenth century; John's writings about the Siberian Seven made my heart beat as one with those of our brothers and sisters behind the Iron Curtain. John's body of work has contributed invaluable role models for the worldwide Christian community, by drawing upon the great classic stories of the heroes of the faith from the pages of Scripture and history.

But in this volume John Pollock has undertaken the greatest story of all. For in it he sketches, with love, faithfulness, and sensitivity, the life of the One whose mandates have compelled those he has profiled to live their obedient lives of faith: the Master, Jesus Christ.

In much the same way that the Gospels communicate the simplicity and power of our Lord's days on earth, John Pollock's narrative makes Christ accessible, alive, personal. For the Christian and the thoughtful nonbeliever alike, this book points the way to the Christ who lived among men, worked miracles in the dusty towns of Judea, shared God's power with a small band of ragged followers, and then took on the disgrace of death upon the Roman Empire's most degrading form of execution: the cross.

Pollock's depiction of that grisly death on our behalf points then to the victory and power of the event which transforms our lives today—the Resurrection.

So this book is a great recounting of the greatest drama of all time—and the grand paradox of God become a man, turning the ways and wisdom of this world upside down. John Pollock has faithfully depicted the person of Christ, faithfully adhered to his words; the reader cannot help but know Christ better after reading this book.

It's my prayer that this book will be used as a great tool, as have John Pollock's other works, evoking the Master, drawing others toward His love and light. It is that Light which still shines in the darkness, and can never be quenched.

CHARLES W. COLSON
Founder, Prison Fellowship,
Washington, D.C.

Part One

DISCOVERY IN GALILEE

One
COMPANIONS
OF THE ROAD

John had been aware of Jesus from his childhood. From snatches of talk between his parents, Zebedee and Salome, he knew that an element of mystery surrounded his cousin's birth; it was even rumored that Joseph was not Jesus's father, yet Salome spoke of her sister as a person of exceptional sweetness and purity.

Jesus had been born at Bethlehem, in the south, where Mary and Joseph had traveled from Nazareth because of the Roman census. When they arrived, every lodging was full and Mary thus had an experience more usual to the very poor: she gave birth to her firstborn in a stable and used a manger for his cradle. Then they had fled with the infant to Egypt to escape one of King Herod's atrocities and had not returned to Galilee until after Herod's death.

Since Jesus grew up in the hills at Nazareth and his cousins at Capernaum on the lake, the boys hardly met in their earlier years. The times were troubled. The revolt led by Judas the Galilean brought fighting in both their neighborhoods and afterward the grisly sight of men crucified at every crossroad. The land then became more tranquil and the two households could join the pilgrimage to Jerusalem for the annual Pass-

17

over festival the year both boys were about twelve. Joseph and Mary spread word that Jesus was missing from the pilgrim caravan on their journey home. They hurried anxiously back up the hilly, dangerous road and found him in the Temple, listening and asking questions of the scribes and rabbis, who were astonished at his understanding.

The boys had all received the usual education; they could read and write their mother tongue, Aramaic, and could talk a bit in the common form of Greek. They had learned the meaning of great passages in the Hebrew Bible and could recite phrases. But as the years of their youth and early manhood went by, occasional contacts showed that Jesus, a carpenter by trade, had an exceptional grasp of their ancient Jewish faith.

John's religion, on the other hand, was that of any plain Jew: its unending demands hedged and shaped his life and blurred his joys. He must attend synagogue every Sabbath, hear the prayers, and sit through the Scripture readings and the address, generally a compilation from commentaries and traditions. He must attempt to keep every jot and tittle of the Law of Moses, but John being high-spirited and rather tempestuous, knew how often he failed. Yet he could imagine no other way. It was rooted in history. John was proud to be a Jew and scorned the Gentiles who crossed his path.

These were too many. When John was in his early twenties, Herod the Tetrarch, ruler of Galilee, a client state under the Romans, built a new capital city above the lakeshore a few miles south of Capernaum and named it Tiberias in honor of the emperor and peopled it mainly with Greeks or Gentiles. Even nearer home, across the Jordan into the next client state, the ruler rebuilt and enlarged a sleepy fishing village and named it Bethsaida Julius, after Caesar. It became Greek rather than Jewish in speech and customs, but this had a happy consequence for John: two Jewish brothers, Simon and Andrew, who had been born in Bethsaida, moved to the more congenial Capernaum. They were burly and virile and became partners with James and John in Zebedee's fishing business.

Little did John and the other three fishermen realize that their lives would be intertwined with the carpenter of Nazareth. Zebedee was prosperous: he supplied fish to land-locked Jerusalem, so that John was known to the household of the high priest and to other notables; but Jesus' family at Nazareth was poor, for Mary was now a widow. The two households, the one on the lake and the other in the hills, drifted apart.

Then, in the early winter of A.D. 27-28 when John was turning thirty years of age, an extraordinary rumor swept the shores of the Sea of Galilee. A new prophet had arisen out of the Judean wilderness.

John, like all Jews, had clung to the age-old hope that one day the Messiah (or Christ) would come to rescue the nation. This hope burned low: the last prophet to foretell Him had lived nearly four centuries back. No word of God could be heard except ritual readings, veiled by the mutterings of scribes.

But now, from Jerusalem and its countryside, from Galilee and beyond the Jordan, crowds flocked to the barren lands where the river flowed into the Dead Sea, in a mass move-ment not seen in living memory. Farmers and vinedressers were free to go because that Jewish year (running from late March) was a sabbatical—the one in every seven when the land must lie fallow and the vines unpruned. Fishermen worked during a sabbatical, but when reports grew that this prophet was the forerunner of the Messiah, or was even Christ himself, John and his brother and their partners, Simon and Andrew, left their nets. They walked south, caught up in events which would link John's life forever to his cousin. No word had come about Jesus: he remained in Nazareth, apparently unmoved by the stir.

At a ford of the Jordan, John became part of a huge crowd listening to words of fire. "Repent!" cried the prophet, "for the kingdom of heaven is near." The man had a ruggedness about him. His camel-hair sackcloth, secured by a leather belt, marked him as an ascetic. And he insisted that he was only the forerunner foretold by the Prophet Isaiah: "A voice of one calling in the wilderness, 'Prepare the way for the Lord.'" Another and a greater was coming; and to escape his judgment they must confess their sins, repent, and be baptized in the river as a symbol of being forgiven.

When the Baptist ended each sermon, he strode toward the river's edge and stood in the shallows while hundreds pressed forward to take their turns. In Galilee, James and John may have seen the solemn immersion of a Gentile convert who went under the water to mark his entry into God's people, but no Jew was ever immersed. John did not hesitate. With his brother and their two partners, he waited under the sun until at last he stood before the Baptist. John the Baptist placed a strong hand on John, son of Zebedee, who humbled himself and bowed his knees in the muddy river until the rush of water sounded in his ears.

Toward the end of that winter, when the crowds were thinning, Jesus came from Nazareth, almost unnoticed, and was baptized after overruling the Baptist's protests. John did not see him or hear what happened. Then Jesus disappeared.

Nearly six weeks later the Baptist saw Jesus return, lean and sunburned and like a man who had emerged from a profound and costly experience which others could not share. The Baptist at once pointed him out publicly as the great one he heralded; but few took note of a young sunburned Galilean who did not fit their expectations. Next day John and Andrew were at the Baptist's side when he again pointed Jesus out. John recognized the cousin he had scarcely seen since boyhood, and the Galileans shyly approached Jesus.

He welcomed them to the booth where he stayed.

Jesus was thirty years old, much the age of John, and had a well-formed body and a strikingly handsome and open face, with a fringe of beard in the usual way. Instead of a towering judge with blazing eyes, they found him a man like themselves, with a harmony of gentleness and strength which so captivated them that Andrew immediately told his brother Simon, "We have found the Messiah!" Andrew hardly realized what his discovery implied, nor where it would lead them, but Simon hurried to meet Jesus. Jesus summed him up in a moment: "You shall be called Rock"—*Cephas* in Aramaic, *Petros* in Greek. Thus Peter received his name.

John and James and Andrew and Peter left the banks of the Jordan with Jesus. The Baptist encouraged their change of allegiance without trace of jealousy, saying: "He must become greater; I must become less." Jesus had collected two other disciples, Philip of Bethsaida and Nathanael of Cana, each profoundly impressed by their first encounter despite Nathanael's prejudice against anyone from Nazareth.

They set out together, climbing the pilgrim path to the eastern plateau; here they took the great road that ran south and north through a country more fertile and wooded than it would become in later centuries.

To the numerous travelers who passed them, they seemed a small party of disciples with their rabbi, a sight almost as common as a camel caravan or a posse of soldiers.

They spent the night at a roadside village. Leaving the great highway to descend again into the Jordan Valley, they walked on, in a glorious morning of friendship with no cloud of suffering on their horizon, and climbed into the hills of Galilee.

Then came the wedding at Cana of Galilee when Jesus turned water into wine. John wrote long afterward: "He revealed his glory and his disciples believed in him."

In after years John would dwell lovingly on their earlier days together and understand their meaning; but when Jesus returned to Nazareth John left him. For reasons unknown, there is a break in the story. During the winter of A.D. 29, one year after they had followed the crowds to the Baptist, the partners, John and James and Peter and Andrew, were back at their fishing; Jesus had returned to Nazareth.

In a sense, their friendship would need to begin again.

Two
THE AMAZING SABBATH

The Lake of Galilee sparkled in the spring sunshine which touched scores of sails as boats darted back and forth in trade or slowly trawled. Across the water, deep blue under a cloudless sky, the towns and villages of the eastern shore looked clear in the afternoon light, with the low hills behind them, well wooded in those years before the War of the Great Rebellion. To the north, the snow-covered summit of Mount Hermon showed hazily in the distance.

John had no eyes for scenery as he sat in the family fishing boat, drawn up on the barren stony shore, with his father and James and the hired men. John's mind was not on work either. They were preparing for the night's fishing, and James, as the elder brother, repeatedly rebuked him for tangling nets or missing a hole or ignoring seaweed which should have been washed away. John's thoughts were in a whirl. Jesus had come down from Nazareth, and John did not know whether to be glad or afraid.

First had come news that Herod had imprisoned the Baptist, silencing a mighty voice. Then travelers came into Capernaum with reports that Jesus was on the move and creating a stir wherever he went. At Nazareth they had flung him out of the synagogue. Elsewhere, they praised him and recounted his doings with awe. John had heard these rumors and tales as the spring days warmed up. On the lake at night, steering the ship or pulling in the trawl or jumping to his father's commands, he had thought long and hard. He wanted, yet dreaded, to see Jesus again. During the months of discipleship the previous year, John had remained his own master, despite growing admiration for Jesus, and had come and gone as he pleased. But he knew there might come a moment when he must pledge his allegiance forever, or go his own way.

He tangled a net again. James shouted at him.

Nearby, the other vessel of the partnership rested on the beach. Simon Peter and Andrew had prepared their deep-water trawls for the night and now stood in the shallows, stripped to their loincloths, adjusting a bell-shaped net to catch inshore fish.

Suddenly John heard a familiar voice. He looked up from his net. Jesus stood a few feet away on the shore, and behind him stood Peter and Andrew, their working clothes flung hurriedly over their burly near-naked bodies, their hair tousled and a look of adventure on their faces. Jesus' own face was shadowed by the usual flowing headdress to keep off the sun, but John could see that he smiled. His physique was slighter than that of the brothers, but his authority over them was plain. John realized by instinct that Jesus had summoned them to follow him. They had obeyed with a boyish zest which took no account of hazards ahead.

Jesus called out to James and John, "Follow me!" The moment of decision had come.

James flung down the net and leaped over the gunwale. John looked at a startled Zebedee and the hired hands. He thought of his mother, Salome, and knew she would approve. He delayed no longer. That night Zebedee took out the fishing boat without his sons.

Neither John nor Peter ever disclosed where Jesus took

them nor what he taught that first day when they were together again, but at this stage he did not wish them to abandon livelihood or home. Peter went back to his wife and family each night while Jesus probably was the guest of Salome. With Friday sunset came the Sabbath, to be kept strictly as a day of rest until sunset on the Saturday. No Jew might labor: the twinkling lights on the lake at night and the sails by day would be those of Gentile boats, working out from Tiberias, Bethsaida, or the eastern shore.

A stillness hung over Capernaum when John and James, their parents, and Jesus set out on Saturday morning down the black paved streets between houses of equally dark stone. They could hear nothing but the patter of feet from all directions. Jews must walk briskly toward their synagogue, as proof of eagerness for worship, and by law every man, woman, and child should attend. The dreariness of the services prompted neighbors to find an excuse, such as ritual defilement, which could release them without risk of punishment by the elders, but this Sabbath a larger crowd than usual converged on the new synagogue. This building had been built by the Roman centurion who commanded at the barracks above the town, a man who admired and supported the subject race which his brother officers despised.

Word had gone round that Jesus of Nazareth was in town and might be invited to teach. Jairus, the president or ruler of the synagogue, was indeed waiting outside to convey the invitation. Jairus owed his position to wealth and administrative ability rather than holiness, and he had no interest in Jesus except as a respected visiting teacher who might swell the congregation.

They entered the tall, cool building with its twin colonnades of ornamented pillars. In front stood the platform and the covered ark, which housed the scrolls. The women and small children took one side and the men and boys the other, and they all sat through the prayers and stood to recite their age-old testimony of faith in the one God. At last the *hazzan* (synagogue-keeper) walked to the ark, selected a scroll, and handed it to Jesus as he stood on the platform. Jesus unrolled it, and according to custom, he read the passage in Hebrew while the people struggled to follow a language they no longer spoke. Then he began his paraphrase and comments in their mother tongue, Aramaic.

John had heard Jesus preach and was not surprised that the congregation sat riveted. Other teachers would place before their hearers a long succession of obscure opinions by eminent rabbis until the original text lay buried. But Jesus ignored learned expounders of the past. Speaking with simplicity, he brought the passage alive and transformed it with new meaning on his own authority, "You have heard it said. . . . But I say to you. . . ."

They hung on his words. It was forbidden to exclaim aloud or interrupt a synagogue address, but John could sense their amazement, and that Jesus was making some of his neighbors uncomfortable with his insistent theme: "Repent! The kingdom of God is here, in your presence, at this moment. Repent and believe the Good News!"

Suddenly a great cry rang through the building. A man on one of the benches yelled in a high-pitched voice, throwing at Jesus the age-old phrase of challenge and taunt to an enemy, *"What have we to do with you,* Jesus of Nazareth?"

The people were horrified. They recognized the man's voice and wondered how he had slipped in, for by his staring eyes and strange ways they knew him to be in the grip of a demon, an unclean evil spirit, and should have been excluded from the congregation. He had defiled them by his presence and now was spoiling the sermon. They tried to suppress him: this rabbi from Nazareth might attempt a lengthy exorcism later but not here in the synagogue. Meanwhile, the man must be silenced.

But he yelled the more. "Jesus of Nazareth! I know who you are—the Holy One of God." Now he had added blasphemy, the people believed. They hoped the preacher would ignore him.

Jesus stopped. He looked in the man's direction and spoke in a stern, emphatic voice. "Be quiet! And come out of him at once!"

The man shuddered violently. With a loud shriek, he fell to the floor.

A few moments later the people could hardly believe their eyes. The man had picked himself up and now sat quietly with an intelligent look, which none had seen on his face for years. As Jesus resumed his sermon, the man listened, plainly unaware that he had made a noise.

When the sermon ended and the congregation spilled out, they could not contain their excitement. "It is something new," they were saying. "It is his authority which is amazing—he taught us on his own authority and not like the scribes." "Did you see his power over that demon? He told it to go and it obeyed; that is the most amazing of all."

Jesus slipped away. With John and James, he had promised to share the Sabbath meal at the home of Peter and his wife and Andrew. All over Capernaum delicious meals had been prepared the previous day to make the Sabbath delightful, and the women had nothing to do after synagogue but serve their menfolk. Peter's wife, however, was not at the synagogue because her mother, who kept house for them, had retired to bed with a fever, and she had stayed behind.

Peter hurried ahead while the others walked at the slow pace which traditionally symbolized sorrow that divine service had ended. The lake lay placid before them through a forest of the masts and furled sails of the larger ships riding at anchor.

When Jesus and his friends reached the house on the strand and entered the little courtyard which it enclosed, they found Peter and his wife in distress. She wrung her hands and brushed away tears as she told Jesus that her mother's fever had risen violently. And the meal had not been laid. Instead of the honor and pleasure they had intended to give him, he would sit down to their sadness and fear.

"Take me to her," said Jesus. They all went upstairs.

The old woman lay in a feverish sweat, already a little delirious. As Jesus bent over her, he seemed to John the very picture of physical well-being, to whom this fever was a personal affront, not to be tolerated in one of his friends.

Jesus said something which sounded like a rebuke, not to the patient but to the fever. He gripped her hand and helped her off the bed. She stood up. Her hot face cooled in an instant. Instead of tottering in a feeble convalescence, she was her usual brisk self and hustled them out of the room while she washed and dressed. She hurried to the kitchen. The men soon sat down to the happiest of meals.

Afterward, a stillness descended on Capernaum as every household rested until the sun dropped behind the hills in the west and the Sabbath was nearly over. Suddenly Jesus and his friends heard sounds of movement from neighboring houses and streets. John crossed the courtyard and looked out. By the light of the sunset, he was amazed to see the roadway filling with people limping or bandaged or coughing or fevered. Word had gone round of the incident in the synagogue, and a rumor was spreading quickly about Peter's mother-in-law. The pent-up misery of a country town was on the move. Sufferers might walk the short distance to Peter's house without desecrating the Sabbath, and since they had assumed that Jesus would never heal until it ended, because to heal would be to work, they had wanted to be ready. As darkness fell, men arrived with stretchers or with beds, not having dared carry one before sundown lest they be reported to the elders.

Jesus walked into the road. To John's astonishment, he healed the first cases by a touch or by a word. Soon his four friends were struggling to organize sufferers and keep off sightseers, both of which increased dramatically when patients whom Jesus had cured ran around the town spreading the news. Peter and John could recognize sick neighbors. Soon strangers outnumbered them because Capernaum was a dormitory for visitors to the healing springs beyond Tiberias, a city which pious Jews shunned for its defiling Gentile atmosphere.

Young men set up torches to light the scene. The crowd spilled over to the beach; some of the ablebodied even climbed the rigging of nearby ships to get a view. Compared with the multitudes who thronged him later, this crowd was small, but the noise sounded extraordinary; groans and pleas, the cries of epileptics foaming on the ground, shouts from those in the grip of evil demons, until Jesus silenced them with peremptory words which seemed to express equally his hatred of evil and his pleasure at the release of victims.

The scene left an indelible memory on those who were cured, and on sightseers. The centurion who had given the town its synagogue had hurried down from the barracks at the hubbub. Riot troops were not needed, but he stayed to watch, his military mind impressed by a sense that Jesus exercised power as representative of a mighty authority, which the forces of evil recognized and obeyed.

Another sightseer, variously named Levi or Matthew, saw it differently. Matthew at that time was a somewhat disreputable and unpopular character who did well for himself as collector of customs at the border outside the town. He had an excellent knowledge of the Hebrew prophets, however. This night scene reminded him of Isaiah's prophecy of the Suffering Servant: "He took our infirmities on himself and carried away our diseases."

John, keeping close to Jesus to protect him from the press of bodies, saw by his face how much it cost him. John was distressed for his Master yet excited by awareness of elemental, apparently inexhaustible power; and he was moved beyond words as he watched Jesus at work. John had seen him heal particular cases; tonight he healed all who came, and though neither John nor his friends described symptoms in the detail which they gave to some later incidents, John marveled at Jesus' compassion. Just as he had entered fully into the merriment at Cana, so now he became part of the suffering.

After the last patient, Jesus gave a quick smile to his friends, lay down on Peter's floor, and fell asleep. John walked home with James, climbed to his loft, and went to bed. But he could not sleep. His brain refused to rest as he tried to fathom an amazing man and extraordinary events. John knew nothing of a crucifixion, nor of finding an empty grave, nor of incidents to come in Jesus' life and stories from Jesus' lips which countless millions down the ages would learn at Mother's knee. He could not tell what Jesus would do, only that he had a purpose and seemed in command of events and of himself. There were majesty and mystery in his character; he must be far more than a carpenter or a cousin, yet he was approachable. John wanted to be with him and to help him, and never to leave again.

Suddenly shouts, far away at first, penetrated the deep sleep into which John had fallen. The voice of Peter roused him and he rushed to the window. Dawn had broken but the sun not yet risen.

"He has gone!" cried Peter from the street. "I came down at dawn. . . . People are coming to the door already. . . . but he has gone!"

Three
"BLASPHEMY!"

They hurried across the flat ground and climbed into the hills behind the town. As the sun rose to their right, they could see vessels returning after the night's work or hoisting sail to find the early morning shoals. Below, they caught glints on the spears and armor of soldiers parading in the barracks.

They passed fields which had been scraped from the poor soil. They scrambled up basalt rocks and beside the mouths of ancient caves. Peter had an instinct as to where they might find Jesus. John panted behind him with James and Andrew, and they climbed for nearly an hour, eating handfuls of raisins which John had taken from the larder. Then Peter stopped and listened. In quietness broken only by the cries of birds, they heard the voice of Jesus. With a glance at the others, Peter led them along the desolate hillside until they saw ahead a white figure against the basalt. They walked a little nearer, then stood transfixed.

Jesus was talking, apparently unaware of their presence. His face was lifted toward heaven and his knees were on the ground in an attitude of prayer; this was strange, for Jews always stood to pray. They were not surprised that he prayed aloud, because no man in the first century either read or prayed silently, or at least without using his lips; but Jesus was speaking to God with a familiarity which would have appalled them in anyone else. "Abba, Father," he prayed. Jesus had spoken the intimate term used by a child at home to a greatly loved parent; the liturgy addressed God formally as Father of the Children of Israel, but no individual Jew would dare call the Almighty Creator of the world "Daddy."

They eavesdropped. Jesus was asking his Father, in simple words, to bless sufferers he had healed. He offered himself for those yet to come. He spoke next of his close friends, one by one, until John realized how surely Jesus had probed their characters and failings and hopes; as Jesus prayed, John wanted to be like him in every way, and believed that this would be possible if only they kept together.

Jesus stopped praying. Rising from his knees, he turned to them and smiled. Pleasure at seeing them, forgiveness for their following him unasked, and for their eavesdropping were all in that smile, so that Peter was bold and exclaimed, "Everybody is looking for you!"

Jesus ignored the implied rebuke. And he did not turn back with them. "We shall go to other towns," he said, "so that I can preach the Good News. That is why I was sent." He began walking along the hillside in the direction of Chorazin, and because he had eaten nothing, they pressed the rest of their raisins upon him, and stopped to drink when they found a spring.

The next weeks were unforgettable, as they went from village to village and town to town. Jesus avoided "Greek" cities, nor would he return to Nazareth where his boyhood neighbors had applauded his preaching and then tried to murder him when he spoke home truths; but day after day he and his disciples walked the lanes and roads of Galilee. Sometimes they slept outdoors, but often a family offered welcome. Not having prepared for the journey, they carried no change of clothes, nor extra cloaks or sandals, and Jesus accepted hospitality and necessities as their due, but always with gratitude and courtesy.

When tired he was not cross. He never seemed to hurry yet never was lazy. His happiness, his endurance, unselfishness, and his peace of mind made every day a joy. John would never have believed that a man could be faultless, until he traveled with Jesus. Religious neighbors who boasted themselves as nearly perfect were insufferable, but Jesus made a delightful companion. Plainly, he felt the same pressures as his friends, yet always his reaction was right.

They noticed another most curious facet of his character, all the more surprising in view of his humility. When he went aside in the early mornings to some deserted spot where he could pray, and they escorted him and kept vigil a stone's throw off, they never once heard him confess sins or utter a prayer of penitence.

Whenever he entered a new place, he would ask to use the synagogue, whether a noble building as at Chorazin or little more than a shack in small villages; and because his fame had spread round the district and beyond, a crowd would gather at once.

On Sabbaths he took part in the liturgy. Often he would unroll the scroll of Isaiah until he found the prophecy which he had read out at Nazareth the day they had tried to destroy him: "The Spirit of the Lord is upon me, because he has anointed me to preach Good News to the poor. He has sent me to proclaim freedom for the prisoner and recovery of sight for the blind, to release the oppressed, to proclaim the year of the Lord's favor." When he ended his reading, all waited in intense silence to learn how he would expound the text. Jesus at once told them without apology or hesitation that the prophecy had come true as they listened: soon they saw proof as they brought him their sick.

One incident enlarged the crowds until they were nearly out of hand; yet it had filled his four close friends with horror at first. They were walking with Jesus toward one of the towns when they saw a man in rags and with an unkempt beard. They knew at once the obligatory signs—leper—and he should have shouted, "Unclean! Unclean!" to warn them.

The Greek word related to several skin diseases. Not all were as grievous or contagious as leprosy, but every sufferer was regarded as ritually unclean, and must avoid inhabited areas and distance himself from passers-by. The disciples drew back in disgust and fear when this one hurried nearer with his hideous bleached and flaking skin. He knelt down in the road less than a foot in front of Jesus and bowed his face into the dust in an attitude of abject humility and sorrow.

The disciples would have hustled him away before he could harm their Master, but they dared not touch the man. They were in a dilemma: unable to help, unwilling to run. They loathed the creature.

The leper looked up, covered with gray dust, which stood out against the whiteness of the infected skin. He pleaded, "Lord, if you want to, you can make me clean."

Jesus, who seemed unaware of his friends' fears or loathing, answered tenderly with unconcealed compassion, "Of course, I am willing!"

John had never known Jesus to heal a leper. John did not doubt his power nor, unlike the sufferer, his willingness; but John fervently hoped that Jesus would avoid contact, like the Prophet Elisha long ago, when he healed the Syrian general Naaman from a distance.

Jesus put out his hand and touched the man. The disciples were aghast. Not only had Jesus broken the religious laws and rendered himself unclean, he had endangered his health.

Jesus said, "Be clean!"

The Scriptures told how Naaman's flesh, when he obeyed Elisha, "came again like unto the flesh of a little child and he was clean." John had never expected to see such a thing take place before his eyes. As the disciples stared, the kneeling man's skin grew soft and took on its natural color. A look of intense gratitude spread across his face.

Then Jesus, so tender a moment before, spoke sharply to him: "Don't say a word to anyone!" Jesus ordered him to go to a priest for ritual discharge as a cured leper. He would take offerings and show his body and be pronounced clean. And he must stay silent.

The man disobeyed. He made the land ring with the story of his instant cure by Jesus of Nazareth. The sensation was enormous. Wherever Jesus went the crowds converged in such numbers that he could no longer preach in synagogues or even enter the towns, but must preach and heal in the pastures or on hillsides. At last he returned to Capernaum with his friends, very privately, early one morning before the town was astir.

Shortly afterward, John needed to revise profoundly his understanding of Jesus.

Dignitaries from Jerusalem had knocked at Peter's door. Their clothes, as well as their way of walking and speaking, showed them to be Pharisees—the "separated ones" who regarded themselves as the true guardians of Jewish religious purity, though many cared for outward display more than sincerity, and their ostentatious prayers at street corners were a byword. With these Jerusalem men came local Pharisees and some scribes, men who interpreted and upheld the Law of Moses in its every detailed requirement, but often were unpopular for refusal to help carry the moral burdens which they laid on men's shoulders.

Pharisees and scribes could ruin a man. Their appearance in Peter's courtyard sent a tremor through the household. Peter took the deputation to the upper guest chamber and told Jesus, who rested in his room, and they walked together, with John, along the narrow covered gallery which was the usual upper passageway of such a house, and entered the guest chamber. While the mother-in-law served refreshments, Jesus conversed with his formidable callers. They asked searching questions.

Their arrival had alerted the neighbors that Jesus was

home. Several entered the yard and sat quietly below in the shade of the gallery, ready to wait all day to hear him. They were soon joined by so many others that Peter looked out at the stir, and Jesus courteously told the Pharisees and scribes that he must preach. Since their purpose was to test his teaching, they welcomed the opportunity to listen and moved closer to the balcony when he stepped outside.

They heard the crowd's noisy welcome. Jesus leaned against the rails of the gallery, protected from the sun by its overhanging tiles, and began to preach. Peter and John stood near him, half listening, half nervously watching the scribes and Pharisees. Jesus' voice had a warm attractive timbre and even when modulated to address a small crowd in a confined space it carried well, until townsfolk in nearby streets hurried nearer and pressed into the entrance, pushing until the yard could contain no more. Latecomers jammed the entrance and spread across the roadway.

Jesus had preached in the shade for about half an hour when John noticed a sudden ray of sunshine on his Master's face. A moment more and the light increased and some dust fell to the floor. John looked up and to his astonishment saw tiles being lifted one by one until a space had opened over the gallery between the projecting eaves and the house wall. Jesus stopped. The crowd below and the disciples on the gallery watched, fascinated. Four brawny fishermen had been working unnoticed from over the low parapet which protected the flat roof of the house. They now lifted a pallet, secured at each corner with ropes, and let it down gently until it rested at Jesus' feet. On the pallet lay a misshapen man. He was not old, but his legs were drawn up stiffly at an unnatural angle, his arms lay rigid at his sides, and he looked up at Jesus with an expression of pleading and fear.

John realized at once what had happened. The four fishermen had intended to carry their paralyzed friend into the house and ask Jesus to heal him. Blocked by the crowd at the entrance, unable even to see Jesus, they had cannily gone down the street, begged permission to ascend to a flat rooftop and then had carried the man above the main block over each dividing parapet, until above Peter's. They could not dig through the beaten earth above the rooms without causing a cascade of dirt, but to remove the projecting tiles of the gallery was simple for sailors, who smiled with triumph as they saw their friend right beside Jesus.

Jesus smiled back, plainly delighted at their faith. Then he gazed down at the wreck of the man. Silence fell on the crowd as they watched from below. The Pharisees and the scribes leaned forward intently from inside the guest chamber. John waited. He had long abandoned any attempt to discover how Jesus penetrated a stranger's mind or could know his history.

Jesus spoke. "Son," he said, "your sins are forgiven you."

The Pharisees almost leaped from their places. They were appalled. Again, Jesus seemed to divine unspoken thoughts, for as John groped in his mind to understand what appalled them, Jesus turned and said to them: "Why are you thinking these things? Which is easier? To say to this paralyzed man, 'Your sins are forgiven you,' or to say, 'Get up, take your pallet and walk?' So that you shall know that the Son of man has authority on earth to forgive sins—" He spoke to the man again. "I am telling you now. Get up! Take up your pallet! Go home!"

The Pharisees and scribes gripped each other with amazement and anger as the man, his eyes fixed on Jesus, straightened one leg, then the other. He placed a once-rigid arm on the ground and stood up. Perfectly strong, he leaned down with a bemused expression and rolled up the pallet, ropes and all, then stretched himself. A broad grin of pure pleasure crossed his face. He took one step, another, and walked along the gallery as a great roar went up from the crowd, a shout of praise to God. "We have never seen anything like this," they were saying as Peter escorted the man downstairs into the yard. People made way for him, right out on to the street, to join his friends who had run and leaped across the roofs and down the way they had come.

The crowd broke up in excitement. But the Pharisees left without another word.

Afterward, John asked Jesus what these men had been thinking. Jesus looked straight at him. "They thought like this," he replied. " 'Blasphemy! This man blasphemes! Who can forgive sins *but God alone?*' "

Four
THE CUSTOMS OFFICIAL

John puzzled how one who was good and humble could claim to be God. John, Peter, and their brothers believed already that Jesus was the Messiah foretold by the prophets, but the prophets had not seemed to suggest that God himself, the Creator of heaven and earth, would come to his world; the Messiah would be a human being whom he anointed. Learned commentators even taught that several "Anointed Ones" might appear, for the Mighty King who would restore Israel's power and glory could hardly be the Suffering Servant too.

This was confusing to a fisherman, but not as perplexing as Jesus' announcement to the paralyzed man: "Son, your sins are forgiven." As the Pharisees saw, none can forgive sins but God alone, yet Jesus was sane; he was totally honest; moreover his implied claim to at least one of the attributes of God had been endorsed when the paralyzed man stood up and walked.

John did not try to resolve the dilemma. He wanted to stay with Jesus, to listen and watch; no one in the world meant more to him or, he was sure, to Peter, James, and Andrew. Jesus would make everything plain in time.

Meanwhile, fresh surprises were in store. One day they were threading their way along the road which led from Capernaum toward Bethsaida. A late spring rain had kept the listening crowds away, and now the weather was cloudy; Mount Hermon had disappeared, and the hills above the eastern shore looked distant. Jesus evidently had a purpose, though he had not disclosed it, for otherwise he would not have chosen the busiest route, where mule and camel trains befouled the paving stones and masters cursed the foot passengers whose bundles of belongings or merchandise got in the way. Drovers behind flocks of sheep and goats, and horsemen trotting or cantering on official business made the walk slow and a trifle hazardous. And all except officials were congealed into an impatient mass when the road reached the border customs post. Every bundle had to be unloaded, every sheep and goat counted; even clothing might be liable for tax.

At the head desk of the post sat Matthew, unperturbed by the noise, unaffected by the impatience and suppressed fury of those whose goods and persons he taxed. Like any taxgatherer or "publican" in Palestine, he was detested by most of his neighbors as an indirect agent of the occupying power, who made a comfortable living from the percentage he took for himself and from the bribes of those he passed unchecked. To the devout, he was an outcast, defiled by consorting with Gentiles and by too frequent handling of the pagan coinage with its image of Caesar. No one believed that a taxgatherer could be honest.

Jesus stopped at the customs post and watched. The expression on his face was not of disapproval so much as sympathy. He knew Matthew's interest in the Scriptures and especially the prophecies, knew of his presence when the sick had been healed during the evening of that Sabbath early in the spring. But the disciples grew restless: a publican was no fit companion for a man of God. The sooner Jesus continued his walk the better.

Matthew was absorbed in checking his underlings' work, in calculating and collecting. He took some time to be aware of Jesus. He looked up and their eyes met.

"Follow me," said Jesus.

After an almost imperceptible pause, Matthew decided to abandon his livelihood and ordered his chief assistant to carry on. Jesus turned back toward Capernaum, and there was almost a laugh in his tone as he told the disciples to welcome their new colleague, for their faces displayed a mixture of surprise, distaste, and admiration. They were surprised that Jesus should choose such a disciple. John knew himself to be a lusty young man with a hot temper, but he had not followed a disreputable profession nor consorted with men and women who broke the Law of Moses. Yet he admired Matthew's courage. When the fishermen had responded to Jesus' call, they had not lost their fishing boats, and had gone out on the lake several times since, but Matthew would be dismissed from the customs service forthwith. He had nothing left but savings.

John soon discovered that these savings were to help Jesus, in a glorious gesture before Matthew took the road as his disciple.

Matthew had been walking beside Jesus in front of their group, talking earnestly. Jesus had nodded, and when they reached the rather grand suburb where Matthew lived, they parted, Matthew to his home, the others toward Peter's house near the lake. Jesus told them to be ready in their best robes in time to return to Matthew's for dinner.

John had never entered the house of such a man, who to all good Jews was a sinner. Jesus, however, plainly felt no shame as they walked in, and John had already noticed the curious fact that any place which Jesus entered would soon reflect his character rather than its own. The house looked roomy and luxurious, with silk hangings and richly worked brocade on the couches—all bought, assumed John, by grinding the faces of travelers on the highways in Herod's name. Jesus had told the disciples as they approached the house that Matthew would sell everything, giving part to the poor and part toward supporting themselves as they walked those very roads in the months to come. If Matthew had a wife and family (which is uncertain), enough would be held back to keep them in simplicity.

Matthew bade them recline in comfort beside tables loaded with food. The friends he had summoned at short notice to enjoy a last banquet shocked John. There were tax collectors and customs officers from Bethsaida, Capernaum, and Tiberias, even a latecomer who in response to Matthew's messenger had hurried in from Chorazin, leaving his donkey lathered in sweat to recover in the shade of the garden behind; every one of these was a despised publican. Others were sinners who had cut themselves off from the synagogue by marrying Gentiles. In the shadows among the women, John thought he saw a prostitute; publicans certainly consorted with such, and Matthew probably had been no exception. Scarcely a man among his friends had not committed adultery, for they lived more like Gentiles than Jews. Some had doubtless worshiped in pagan temples.

Jesus received Matthew's lavish hospitality with enjoyment, and the hearts of those present went out to him. They listened to his words about repentance and purity and the kingdom which had come among them. Some became his followers, sensing that only by keeping near him would they resist the pull to a prostitute's bed or cease to rob the poor. Others looked wistful, thanked Matthew for the delightful banquet, and left. A few scarcely hid their contempt.

As the disciples came out into the street, while Jesus lingered inside with guests who sought his counsel, they were met by an angry group of Pharisees and scribes. News of the banquet had reached them as an almost unbelievable rumor that Jesus had not only entered the house of a man of bad repute but was eating with disgraceful companions. Since they had honored Jesus by allowing him to teach in the synagogue, his behavior reflected on their respectability. They threw a question at Peter and John: "Why does your Master eat with publicans and sinners?"

The question held menace, for a teacher who kept company with sinners could be silenced, might even be excommunicated, with his disciples. It held concern too, for some of the Pharisees were merciful men who cared deeply for their countrymen and believed that Jesus had a genuine gift for talking about God in a way that the simple and the poor could understand. If he cut himself from the mainstream of the nation's religious life, he would lose influence.

"Why does he eat and drink with taxgatherers and sinners?" they asked again. Jesus overheard the question as he came out into the street. He answered at once: "The healthy do not need the doctor! It is the sick who do. I have not come to call the righteous, but sinners." He threw in an apposite text and told them to go and learn what it meant.

He left them standing by the gate. Whether or not they held a learned debate on his answer, they soon showed that he had not met their complaint, for wherever the disciples went with Jesus in the next few days, some of this group shadowed them. The important men from Jerusalem who had gone back to report the incident of the paralyzed man would be returning to Capernaum shortly, and the local Pharisees wished to collect evidence on which a ruling might be made, whether to endorse Jesus or to throw him out.

A day or two after Matthew's feast, the Sabbath came round and Jesus taught in the synagogue. The scribes and Pharisees sat impassive, testing his every word for error. They followed him out afterward and dogged his steps when he led the disciples through the fields behind the town toward a secluded pasture, where he wanted to teach them privately before they went back together for the Sabbath meal. John and Peter reveled in the fresh spiritual horizons his sermon had opened, but being hungry they casually exercised the wayfarer's immemorial right to pull heads of wheat from the wheat crops. Harvest was near, for the late spring rains and sun had ripened the wheat fast in the low-lying lands beside the lake. The disciples husked the grain with their hands and tossed it into their mouths.

They heard a shout from behind. An angry Pharisee hurried up to Jesus and demanded, "Why do your disciples break the Sabbath?" It took a moment to guess the man's meaning. Then it dawned on them that he rated their plucking the heads of wheat as equal to the work of harvesting by sickle, one of the thirty-nine actions prohibited on the Sabbath.

Jesus promptly rebuked the Pharisee by citing an incident in the Scriptures, followed by two breathtaking statements: "The Sabbath is made for man, not man for the Sabbath!" exclaimed Jesus. Then, using the title with which he often referred to himself, he said, "The Son of man is Lord of the Sabbath too."

Seven days later when John went with his parents to the synagogue, he saw the Jerusalem deputation in town again, prominent on the benches reserved for rulers. Behind them sat the Pharisee whom Jesus had rebuked.

Placed where Jesus would notice him when handed the sacred scroll for the reading was a stranger disfigured by a withered hand. John suspected at once that this man had been brought from outside the town as bait with which to trap Jesus. John did not doubt his Master's power to remake a shriveled hand, whether atrophied as the result of accident or deformed from birth, but he realized at once why the man had been planted there: its healing would require a major work of reconstruction—on a Sabbath Day.

When the *hazzan* invited Jesus to the reading desk, the Pharisees leaned forward and watched closely, mentally waiting to pounce. The *hazzan* offered a sacred scroll. Jesus took and unrolled it, read a passage and began to expound as if a shriveled hand meant nothing to him. Suddenly he stopped. Looking straight at the man, he commanded: "Get up, and stand here in front where everybody can see you."

The man obeyed. A hush fell on the synagogue as the tension rose. The stranger's face expressed hope mingled with doubt and embarrassment. The Pharisees pursed their lips. Jesus turned toward them and in the unemotional tone of voice which rabbis used in debate, he put to them a question in debating form: "Tell me. Which is lawful on the Sabbath Day: to do good or to do evil? To save life or to kill?"

The Pharisees declined the debate. They stayed mute, but Jesus was angry. The anger threw into sharp relief the lovelessness, the hypocrisy, and narrowness of the religious leaders who cared for the letter of the Law but not for a crippled man. John could tell that the man mattered to Jesus, and that the hardness of heart of the Pharisees distressed him equally; if only they would open to Jesus, he could heal them too.

Every eye was now on the crippled man. "Stretch out your hand," ordered Jesus.

As the man stretched it out, a gasp of amazement passed through the congregation. No one ever described the process in detail, but all could see that a useless, shriveled hand had become strong.

Five
THE CALL
IN THE HILLS

The authorities banned Jesus from teaching in the synagogue for his flagrant breach of Sabbath regulations. They did not excommunicate him nor sentence him to be whipped, but they marked him publicly as in disgrace. Privately, they began to think of ways to murder him. Those who kept him company would lose their good names and perhaps their lives.

A few evenings later Jesus instructed Peter and John to pass the word that early next morning he would teach at a lonely spot above Capernaum. He went away by himself, ordering them on no account to follow him into the hills, while they visited or sent messages to all in the neighborhood who regularly sat at his feet. At first light they found that some had excused themselves, but seventy or eighty of the more eager were walking up the mountain, unaware why Jesus wanted them.

When the followers arrived at the chosen little plateau, John saw Jesus on a rock looking out across the lake below, which sparkled in the summer morning sun before the heat haze blurred the view. He seemed bathed in sunshine, but as they came closer, John realized that Jesus' face and eyes shone with an inner light; he must have spent the night in prayer.

Once they had gathered round him, Jesus explained his purpose. He was about to choose twelve men to work at his side, or occasionally to go elsewhere on his behalf and learn more than he could impart to crowds.

John's heart missed a beat or two as he waited to hear whether he would be one of the Twelve. First Jesus called out Simon Peter's name, and immediately, with a characteristic touch, put Andrew's fear at rest by telling him to join his brother. When John heard his own older brother named, his doubts dissolved, and a few moments later he was with James at Jesus' side. Jesus next called the friends of the walk to Cana from Jordan's bank, Philip and Bartholomew-Nathanael; then Matthew, and five more. Only one of the Twelve was not a Galilean. His name was Judas Iscariot, "the man from Kerioth," a town on the plateau to the east of the Dead Sea. Nothing about Judas gave a hint to the eleven others that the seeds of treachery were in him.

John was almost overcome by excitement, by feelings of privilege and gratitude, and a determination to be worthy. On the other hand, Jesus conveyed the unspoken sense that the privilege of having the Twelve was his, that each was a gift entrusted to him for their sakes as much as for his. John looked around at these eleven men who henceforth would be his everyday companions. Despite his affection for Peter and Andrew and love for his own brother, and the friendship which had already grown with most of the others, he could not help contrasting them with Jesus. Several might be taller or look stronger, but morally and in wisdom they could not compare.

There was little time for such thoughts. Someone called out that masses of people were crawling, as it seemed from that height, up the trail they themselves had taken in the early morning. Jesus began to walk down the mountain toward them immediately, as if to teach the Twelve their future attitude to fellowmen. The rest followed. He chose a level space on the hillside and waited.

No one, least of all John, could fail to be moved by the happiness of the people when they saw Jesus. There were not only Galileans; those from Judea and the coastal districts and the cities beyond the Jordan could be identified by slight differences in dress and speech. Young and old, poor and a few rich, men, women, and youngsters pressed close to Jesus, eager to touch him, to tell him of their sicknesses or to bring friends and relatives who needed care or relief. It was a scene which was becoming familiar: the pressure of the sick and the healthy; the selflessness with which Jesus helped them, and the indefinable energy which came through his touch. This time there was a difference. When he had healed all patients brought to him, Jesus instructed the Twelve to settle everybody on the grass, facing a knoll. The disciples from whom he had chosen the Twelve were to be in front.

He sat on the knoll, just as previously he had sat to teach in the synagogue, and then, his voice carried clear by the breeze to the confines of the crowd, he spoke the words which would echo round the world, through all ages, as the Sermon on the Mount.

"Blessed are the poor in spirit," he began, "for theirs is the kingdom of heaven. Blessed are those who mourn, for they will be comforted. Blessed are the meek, for they will inherit the earth.

"Blessed are those who hunger and thirst for righteousness, for they will be filled. Blessed are the merciful, for they will be shown mercy. Blessed are the pure in heart, for they will see God. Blessed are the peacemakers, for they will be called sons of God. Blessed are those who are persecuted because of righteousness, for theirs is the kingdom of heaven.

"Blessed are you when men insult you, persecute you, and falsely say all kinds of evil things against you because of me. Rejoice and be glad, because great is your reward in heaven, for in the same way they persecuted the prophets who were before you."

He continued with many practical exhortations. In the months to come, he would repeat what he said, sometimes varying his words, but this Sermon on the Mount would be remembered as the essence of all that he spoke on the theme of a disciple's way of life. They listened with strict attention, committing the words to memory. Since papyrus and parchment scrolls were owned only by rich men and the synagogues and the religious schools, Jews learned at their mothers' knees to memorize. A teacher's followers took pride in treasuring the teaching without changing it. Those closest, such as Jesus' own Twelve, considered it a point of honor to reproduce their Master's gestures and the very tones of his voice and his precise words.

It was easy to listen to Jesus, for he made his points with allusions to familiar things, such as salt which has lost its saltiness, or shining lamps, or a city on a hill, like Nazareth. Urging his hearers to keep their treasure in heaven, safe from hazards, he spoke of moths and rust, and thieves who break in and steal. In teaching against worry, he spoke of the wild flowers of springtime which neither toil nor spin: "Yet Solomon in all his glory was not arrayed like one of these."

As he continued, each listener saw in the mind's eye an angry worshiper, brought up short in the Temple by the need to make peace with a brother whom he had wronged; or a pompous hypocrite shouting out his prayers so that all should admire him, and hiring a trumpeter to advertise his gifts to charity. They all saw, with laughter, a carpenter trying to remove a speck of sawdust from a workmate's eye when he could hardly see for the splinter sticking in his own. And Jesus recalled to everyone's memory the anger and weariness of a hot walk when conscripted by a Roman soldier to carry his heavy load; a soldier had the right to compel a man to go one mile. Jesus surprised them by saying, "Go with him two."

Throughout his sermon Jesus contrasted natural attitudes with a life dictated by love, righteousness, and faith. To his hearers on that day, all of whom were Jews, or Gentiles following the Jewish way, it sounded a matter of emphasis: if they did as Jesus taught, they would really fulfill the spirit of the Law of Moses. But his words would be revolutionary when taught near pagan temples in Greek and Roman cities, or in faraway lands where for centuries, when Jesus first spoke them, men had followed the Buddha or Confucius, or had worshiped Hindu gods.

Libraries of books would be written relating to the Sermon on the Mount. Every phrase would be examined and expounded. At the time, as John listened closely with Peter and their friends, he could not fail to notice that the picture held before them of a perfect man was a self-portrait. The Jesus they knew, as no others yet knew so well, was meek and humble and merciful and a peacemaker; he loved his enemies and gave freely; he never worried about food or clothes or what would happen the next day. In effect, he was instructing them to be like him. But John understood himself well enough to realize that on his own he could not reproduce Jesus' character nor live up to the standards which he set; nor, John suspected, could a single one of the audience.

The only hope was to stay in Jesus' company, strengthened by his example, perhaps growing more like him, little by little. They were young men still, and the years stretched ahead. Had not Jesus just said, "Do not worry about tomorrow"?

John pulled back his thoughts, for the sermon was rising to a climax with a vivid story. "The man," said Jesus, "who hears my words and puts them into practice is like a wise man who builds his house on a rock," laboriously hacking and digging and sweating to lay the foundation, until at last he has his house. "The rains came; the river rose; the wind blew and beat against the house. And it did not collapse because its foundation was in the rock."

Then for everyone who heard the teaching and did nothing, Jesus painted a word picture of a foolish man who built his house with speed and ease by putting the foundation into the sandy soil above the riverbed. "The rains came; the river rose; and the winds blew and beat against that house—and down it came with a crash!"

Six
OUT OF
THE DEEP

While John listened enthralled to the Sermon on the Mount, a tragedy was unfolding below at the Capernaum barracks. Its commanding officer, the pagan centurion who had built the Jewish synagogue, was in despair because his household manager, his most trusted slave, lay dying in agony from a paralysis which almost prevented his breathing. This slave was not only valuable for his command of figures but a dear friend: a relationship often found in the Roman Empire where slaves could rise to important posts.

Physicians had failed. Time was running out. Suddenly the centurion recalled the night, after reports of an exceptional crowd, he had watched the sick being healed by Jesus. Jesus had impressed him as different from the wandering miracle workers and the quacks he had met in his army life. But the more holy the man, the less he would be willing to defile himself by entering a Gentile home or meeting a Gentile's direct request, or so the centurion believed from his observation of Jewish religion. He therefore sent a message to the elders of the synagogue which he had paid for, asking them to intercede with Jesus to save the slave's life.

This put the elders in a dilemma. They had excluded Jesus

from the synagogue and branded him as an undesirable character, yet they dared not deny a senior officer in Herod's service who was their own benefactor.

Hot from the descent but exhilarated by all they had heard on the mountain, the disciples were not a little surprised to find a deputation of elders welcoming Jesus to the town where they had tried to disgrace him. When they began to list the centurion's virtues, the irony of the situation could not be missed: the elders were begging a man they had rejected to help a man whom they despised, as a Gentile, whatever his generosity.

Jesus cut short their fulsome account. "I will go," he said.

As they all walked toward the barracks, a messenger must have run ahead to encourage the centurion, for another deputation met Jesus. Two or three of the centurion's friends carried an urgent message, which they gave word-for-word as from himself: "Lord, do not put yourself to trouble, for I do not deserve to have you under my roof. That is why I sent friends instead of coming to you myself. *Just say the word* and my slave will be healed! For I too act under authority. I have soldiers under me. I order one, 'Go!' and he goes, and another, 'Come!' and he comes. And I order a slave, 'Do this!' and he does it."

Though Jesus could penetrate the unspoken angry thoughts of scribes and Pharisees, he let himself appear astounded at the faith of a Gentile. He turned to the crowd at his heels and with delight in his voice said with great emphasis, "I have not found faith as strong as this, even among Israelites." Then he told the messengers to return to the pagan centurion who had seen, however dimly, that physical contact is not essential, since healing power derives from the Creator. Jesus sent him a direct assurance: "It will happen just as you believed it would." And he turned back toward the town.

Next day the district hummed with the news that the slave had recovered.

Despite the fact the miracle was performed after they begged Jesus to heed the centurion's request, the elders still barred him from the synagogue. The lakeshore became his pulpit. From cool early morning through the hot hours when Galileans normally sought shelter, and on into each evening, there seemed no end to the mass of ordinary folk from far and near who hungered to hear him. The Twelve and other disciples soaked up his words, while any casual traveler who stopped for an hour to listen would pass on the stories and sayings wherever he went, so that they spread from home to home, with excited accounts of how Jesus would interrupt his teaching to heal people. And this was happening in Galilee, despised by the orthodox and virtuous of Judea as a place of rough speech and bad habits, where too many Gentiles lived; a province of ignorance, compromise, and spiritual darkness.

Matthew summoned from his memory an apt reference from Isaiah about "Galilee of the Gentiles": " 'The people living in darkness,' " quoted Matthew, " 'have seen a great light; on those living in the shadow of death a light has dawned.' "

But Jesus' own family began to doubt his sanity. They had heard in Nazareth that he and his disciples neglected their meals because of the crowds; perhaps Salome herself told her sister, for Mary came down with his brothers to take him home for a rest. "He is out of his mind," they said. Mary wanted him to stop his work; his half brother James did not believe in him at all. They arrived one evening when he was back in Peter's house, still teaching the crowd in the courtyard.

The Nazareth family could not get through, like the paralyzed man's stretcher-bearers. Someone interrupted Jesus with a message. Jesus knew why Mary and James and the others had come, but he did not send the messenger back nor go out to meet them. Instead, he asked bluntly, "Who is truly my mother? Who are my real brothers? . . . They are here, sitting round me! Anyone who hears God's Word and does his will is my brother and my sister and my mother." He resumed teaching.

The implied rebuke, when conveyed to the family, hardened the opposition of James; much more would be needed before hostility turned to such devotion that he became the recognized leader of all in Jerusalem who called Jesus their Lord. But Mary quietly accepted it. Her mistaken mission had ended in a failure which she would never regret; the time came when she would leave home to help look after Jesus and his disciples on their travels, ensuring that they had enough to eat and time to eat it.

The incident emphasized the cost of following Jesus, especially to John and James, his cousins. They heard him say that if a man loved family "more than me," he was not worthy of him; that a man's foes would be those of his own household, that the choice might sometimes be so stark that loyalty to Jesus could seem hatred of father and mother. John had no doubt now where loyalty lay, even if his mother had tried to hinder. Pharisees might slander Jesus as in league with the prince of demons; religious leaders might scoff at him as a glutton and a winebibber, the friend of publicans and sinners.

Let them slander and scoff. Jesus was his Master, to copy, to support in whatever he planned to make men and women better in their ways as well as in their bodies. He brought great happiness. He had begun to curb John's hot temper and bring out the love and affection which lay beneath; to develop his mind, so that the fisherman would one day be the teacher and writer who could grasp profound truths and convey them in simple words. And beyond gratefulness for the influence of Jesus was an overriding desire for his company.

Yet fresh incidents showed how little John really knew

him. One night after Jesus had gone to bed, Peter suggested that the partners go fishing. Though Zebedee had continued his business with the hired hands, and Salome was generous, cash from a good catch would be welcome in both households; and Judas Iscariot, who had been entrusted with the money box of the Twelve, had been muttering.

The four partners slipped away to the shore and took the two smaller boats. Each pair rowed out in the darkness, raised sail, and began to trawl. After a while they pulled in their nets and found nothing. They tried every favorite inlet; they ventured into deep water; they changed from dragnet to casting net, and met nothing but bad luck throughout the short summer night. Not a salable fish came into either boat. Peter grew so exasperated that he scared away any last hope of a catch by shouting inquiries to John and James. This made them angry. The nickname that Jesus had given them, Sons of Thunder, was thoroughly appropriate.

The four partners returned to shore at dawn in a bad temper. Boats seemed heavier to push from the water, and nets were more tangled and weedy than they could ever remember. And then came the first of the crowd, back at a favorite spot in the hope of hearing Jesus. Peter pretended not to notice. He gloomily continued to wash his net: Jesus could get the people in order himself and do his preaching.

At sunrise came Jesus. Out of the corner of an eye, Peter could see that he looked tired. The crowd pressed on him as he stood on the beach and began to talk about God. Peter paid closer attention to the washing of the nets.

The crowd grew, pushing those in front; Jesus stepped back and his feet were in the water. Suddenly he turned, took a few steps and leaped nimbly into Simon Peter's boat.

"Simon," he called, and when Peter looked up from his nets at hearing the old name rather than the new, he saw a hint of a twinkle in the eye, as if Jesus knew what was passing in his mind. "Simon, put out a little from the shore, please."

Peter climbed in, took up the oars and rowed a few strokes. Jesus sat on a thwart and resumed his teaching, his voice carrying all the more because of the few yards of water between speaker and audience. And he had the gift of making each man, woman, and child in a crowd feel that the words came intimately to himself or herself.

When the sun had risen high from behind the hills of the eastern shore, Jesus stopped; many of his hearers had work to do and families to support. Yet many lingered until they realized that Jesus would say no more that morning. They then dispersed.

Jesus turned to Peter and Andrew. "Put out into deep water and let down your nets for a catch."

Peter replied, "Master, we worked hard all night and caught nothing." He sounded a bit annoyed at the suggestion, half ashamed by his earlier behavior. Then he added, "But since it is you who tell us, I will."

Peter pulled the nets into the boat. John and James splashed across to their own boat and pushed her afloat. Both partners rowed their vessels out into the lake, steering courses about a quarter of a mile apart. When they reached deep water, Peter threw out his dragnets. Before John could throw out his, he heard a cry. Peter's boat appeared to be swaying violently, and he was pulling in already, struggling with a huge haul, which here and there broke the net; fish were falling back into the water. Peter shouted to the men in the other boat, and they rowed across to take some of the weight. The boats began to fill with struggling fish until the water was almost over the gunwales. John and James had never seen such a catch. Peter and Andrew, sweat pouring from their bodies, looked equally astounded, while Jesus sat apart on a thwart, since no fisherman wants a landsman to interfere.

Suddenly Peter dropped the fish he was handling. He turned and threw himself down at Jesus' knees in a gesture of total submission. His enormous frame was trembling. "Go away from me," he cried, "for I am a man who is a sinner, Lord."

"Don't be afraid," replied Jesus. "From now on you will catch men."

John heard. He shared Peter's feelings, though his own cry as a sinner might have been, "Stay close all the time! Never leave me, Lord." Jesus had repaid their petulance by giving them the catch of the season, which would be the talk of the lakeside for years. And he had awed them by an affinity with nature far beyond their professional skill.

They reached land, heaved their boats on shore, handed the catch to Zebedee and his men, and vowed never to desert Jesus again.

Seven
"WHO CAN HE BE?"

Jesus was teaching from the boat. This time, when the early morning crowds pressed near him, he told them a story.

The fields behind had now been harvested and the earth was hard. Jesus took his hearers forward to the familiar scene when the autumn rains would have softened the soil, and each farmer went out with his bag of seed to scatter it, handful by handful, as he walked carefully up and down. Only when he had sown his whole field, including the path which the villagers had trodden across the stubble, and the hidden rocks, and the soil which weeds had invisibly seeded, would he yoke his oxen and plow it in; this was the immemorial way in Palestine, sowing before plowing. Jesus took the plowing for granted in his hearers' minds.

"Listen carefully," he said. "A sower went out to sow. In his sowing, some fell on the path and the birds came and ate it. Some fell on the rocky places. Here the soil was thin and it sprang up quickly because it had little depth; when the sun came up the shoots were scorched, and withered away because they had no root.

"Other seed fell where the thorns were, and they grew up

too and choked the shoots, and they never bore grain. And other seed fell into good soil and came up and grew and yielded a crop, increasing itself thirty, sixty, even a hundred times"—a harvest which evoked gasps of surprise from the listeners. Then Jesus rounded off his story with a challenge to solve its meaning: "Anyone who has ears, let him hear!"

The parable defeated all who heard it, whether those sitting or standing on the beach or those beside him in the boat. When the crowd dispersed to their daily work, Peter and John and some who remained on the shore begged for the key to the story. They also asked why he spoke in parables.

Jesus explained that he taught the horde of casual hearers by stories, and most of them would not understand the point: the meanings would remain hidden to any who did not genuinely want to know, for fear of having to turn from their old ways.

Those close to him, however, would be let into the secrets of God's kingdom. "Your eyes are happy and blessed because you really do see, and your ears because you really do hear. I tell you, and this is the truth: Many prophets and good men longed to see what you see but did not see it; and to hear what you hear and did not hear it."

Jesus gently suggested that the disciples should have seen for themselves the parable's points, and then he gave the explanation which would become so famous.

"The farmer sows the word," said Jesus. "The seed on the path is like those who hear the Word but do not understand, and the evil one snatches it away at once. The seed sown on rocky land is the man who hears the Word and receives it with joy; but he has no root and lasts only a short time—when trouble or persecution comes on him because of the Word, he gives up.

"The seed among the thorns stands for those who hear, but the worries and pleasure of life and the deceitfulness of riches choke the Word, so that it never ripens. But the seed in the good soil stands for those who hear and accept and understand the Word and produce a fine crop—thirty, sixty, or a hundred times more than the farmer sowed."

That day Jesus gave all his teaching by parables, as people came and went, and whenever he was alone with the disciples he explained the meanings.

By nightfall he was exhausted. Instead of going home, he told the Twelve that he would accompany them to the other side of the lake, a sail of some six miles. Peter and John prepared one of the larger vessels. As they boarded, John inserted the detachable rudder oar and stood ready to steer, and Jesus went to the cushion beside it, lay down, and fell fast asleep. His face immediately lost its lines, as John saw by the light of the stern lamp; Jesus lay as peaceful as a child.

The fishermen among the Twelve took the oars and rowed the first half mile, then Peter hoisted sail to catch a gentle offshore breeze. The night was overcast, but they could steer toward the faint lights of the eastern shore. The first hour passed uneventfully as they sailed into the center of the lake. Suddenly, however, the wind rose. A squall swept without warning out of the lower Jordan Valley. Peter pulled in the sail to ride out the storm, and John, exerting his strength on the tiller, was amused by the slight panic of the landlubbers like Iscariot, and Simon, the former Zealot or freedom fighter. A sudden violent squall was common on the Sea of Galilee, locked below its mountains.

A few minutes later fear gripped John himself. He had never known such a storm. The sea raged, the rain cascaded, the ship tossed like a cork, while wave after wave broke over them, soaking them to the skin and filling the bilge. John secured the useless tiller and joined the others. As fast as they bailed, the water rose faster, and since a storm was always followed by a heavy swell lasting several hours, which would prevent them making land, John's experience warned him of disaster. They might founder—a frequent fate of ships in ancient times. A few more buffetings by huge waves, and the timbers would start, and all their bailing be useless.

The storm showed no sign of abating. The wind displayed a ferocity which even to a sailor like John seemed malevolent and personal, as if some supernatural force had designed their destruction.

In their panic no one had remembered Jesus. Several then struggled to the stern. They were astonished to see him lying there wet, but fast asleep, as if in bed ashore on the quietest summer night. They shook him awake. "Master, Master, we're going to drown!"

Somebody shouted, "We are going to perish, for all you care!"

Jesus stood up. He faced into the wind, not even steadying himself by holding a rope or a timber. In the tone of voice he had used to the demon in the synagogue, he spoke sharply to the elements. "Quiet!" he commanded the wind. "Be still!" he ordered the waves.

For the next seconds the Twelve could hardly believe their senses. Wind and waves dropped instantly. Nothing could be heard except a gentle slosh from the water on board. The sailors among them were astounded that not even a swell remained of the storm. They were drifting in a calm.

Jesus turned to his bedraggled disciples all soaked to the skin. "Why were you frightened?" he asked. "Have you still no faith?"

He went back to sleep. They loosed the rudder and began to bail out, shaken and terrified by his power over nature. They asked each other: "Who can he be, that he gives orders to the wind and the waves, and they obey him?"

They had plenty of time to reflect. The great calm kept the sail useless, and they had to work the oars, as if in penance for their lack of faith, while Jesus finished his sleep. After rowing for half an hour or so, Peter handed over his oar to a landlubber and threw out a net to catch fish for breakfast. Dawn broke to find them blown off course by the storm. Jesus woke and told them to make for shore, where they could light a fire and broil fish.

Hills riddled with caves came down to the waterline. As the boat neared land, they could see on the slope a large herd of pigs kept by Gentiles; this was repulsive to the disciples; pigkeeping was forbidden to Jews. The swineherds had lit a fire and were cooking.

John steered toward a small bay with a narrow beach. Peter put the vessel close in and, with a short splash, ankle high, all of them stepped ashore. John wondered what Jesus intended to do after they had eaten.

Before he could ask, a horrible cry rent the early morning quiet. A huge naked man emerged from one of the nearby caves, which probably contained a tomb, and ran toward them down the slope, yelling and leaping over boulders. His hair was long and matted. He had cuts on his arms and legs and chest, and he held a sharp flint, whether to cut himself again or to attack them, they could not tell.

Jesus stood his ground. In a stern, powerful voice he shouted, "Come out of this man, evil spirit!"

The man ran on, straight at Jesus, then stopped dead; he threw himself to his knees, and in a voice to wake the dead, he yelled the ancient challenge: "What have I to do with you—Jesus, *Son of the Most High God?*"

Peter gripped John's arm. The creature knew Jesus' name; and he had addressed him in a way which none of them would yet dare use, whatever his private hopes and half-formed beliefs; and the man had challenged Jesus to battle. Naked, strong as Samson, he looked even more fearsome at close quarters, for an iron shackle from which a broken chain hung loose gripped each wrist; his ankles were bruised and raw, as if he had smashed and wrenched irons off them. The cuts on his powerful chest, the bloodstains, the tangled body hair, the staring eyes made him horrifying.

"What have I to do with you?" he yelled again.

Jesus, in a firm, even voice, said: "What is your name?"

In reply, though Jesus stood only a foot away, the madman

screamed: "My name is Legion, because there are so many of us."

Two thousand devils were destroying this man and challenging Jesus. One leap and Jesus would be crushed under a powerful torso while the stone and the shackles on the wrists could beat out his brains. Jesus had defeated the wind and waves. He was now at the mercy of a maniac; the disciples recoiled at the sense of evil and conflict.

Peter, the strongest built, took a step forward. Jesus gestured to him to stand still.

Looking straight at the man, Jesus spoke in an unforgettable tone which blended authority and compassion.

"Legion," he commanded, "come out of the man!"

The upshot was surprising. Legion spoke again, a little quieter but high-pitched: "Swear to God that you will not torture me! Don't banish us." Again and again Legion uttered the curious plea not to be sent away. At last he said, "Send us to the pigs; let us enter the pigs." His voice had the peculiar pitch of a man possessed.

The great herd of pigs fed in the browned grassland a little above the bay while the swineherds gaped at Jesus below; they never would have dared to venture close to Legion, the madman who snapped his chains when captured.

"Let us go into the hogs," cried Legion.

Jesus said something. The herd began to move. Two thousand pigs ran toward the sea, raced over the low cliff some twenty feet high, where the deep water of the lake had encroached on the slope, and here they drowned. The swineherds fled.

The disciples stood, shaken. Never in their lives had they seen a more dramatic lesson of the value of a human being. They recalled how Jesus had said that each of them was of more value than many sparrows, and that not one sparrow fell to the ground without the Heavenly Father's knowledge. Jesus knew what he was doing; if he had ruined the owners of the pigs and destroyed the livelihood of the swineherds, he had saved the sanity of a man.

John could see that Legion (whatever his real name) was different already. He was looking at Jesus with a smile. Then suddenly he realized that he was naked, and showed acute embarrassment. Peter ran to the boat and pulled out a spare garment, still a little damp but it would dry in the sunshine. Legion put it on gratefully. He helped them gather sticks to make a fire. But villagers were hurrying down, alerted by the agonized tale of the swineherds as they ran toward the town, which lay out of sight in a fold of the higher hills. Before Jesus and the disciples—with Legion—could finish eating their fish, they saw a dust cloud on the path from the town, as a string of riders on donkeys trotted to the bay; soon the pig owner and his neighbors and the local councilmen arrived.

"Go away!" they cried to Jesus. "Please go away!" They did not seem angry or heartbroken at the loss of the pigs, but frightened, especially when they saw the once-naked untamable man, decently clad, sane, and sitting on the ground beside Jesus.

"Go away! Go away!" they begged Jesus. Jesus did not try persuasion: he never seemed to press himself if not wanted. He stood up, beckoned to the disciples and made for the boat.

Legion was distraught. He ran after Jesus. "I want to go too. Please let me be with you always."

He would have become an unusual companion, a Gentile disciple before the time, and needing patient understanding as he rebuilt his life, across the lake and far from home.

Jesus looked upon him compassionately and spoke gently, his voice a contrast from the stern, powerful tones he had used when Legion had first appeared. "No," he said. "You cannot come with me. Go home. Find your family and tell them how much the Lord has done for you. Tell them how he had mercy on you."

Legion smiled back at Jesus, with the thought of home and family and a story to tell which would amaze them. As Jesus sat down in the stern of the boat, the disciples rowed from shore, and Legion, in Peter's spare coat, stood waving, with his neighbors gathered around, until his great frame grew small and they could no longer see him.

Eight
"IT IS TIME TO WAKE UP!"

A gentle breeze off the eastern hills gave good progress, but the morning was now well advanced and the heat kept Capernaum hazy until the vessel neared the harbor with the sun right behind her. Then they saw a crowd on the shore, visible beyond the masts and hills of ships already berthed, and another on the beach from which they had sailed the night before.

Peter trimmed sail. John steered toward a vacant berth at the quay. The crowd surged toward them, and when Andrew threw a rope, willing hands made the vessel fast. John saw at once that this was no casual welcome, for as Jesus stepped onto shore, the crowd parted and Jairus, president of the synagogue, identified by the rich linen of his summer tunic before they recognized his features, ran forward from the bench where he had waited in the shade. John's nerves fluttered, for Jairus was powerful and his presence might mean trouble; but Jairus dropped on his knees in front of Jesus, and when he looked up, his face under his headdress was ravaged by worry and grief.

"My little daughter is dying," he cried. "Please, *please*

come and put your hands on her so that she is healed and will live. Please, oh, please do this!"

The irony was rich. They had flung Jesus out of the synagogue, yet the elders had interceded for the pagan centurion; and now comes the president begging Jesus to heal his daughter.

Thoughts so unworthy were quickly killed by the distress of Jairus, and by Jesus' instant response. "I will come with you," he said. Jairus and Jesus set off together.

The people pressed behind and at their side, while more came running toward them. When they turned into a narrower street which took a shortcut toward the richer quarter, Peter and John and the others could hardly clear a path because everybody wanted to be nearest to Jesus. Suddenly he stopped and turned around.

"Who touched me?" he asked.

No one answered. He asked again. Peter replied, a trifle rudely, "Master, you can see they are all around and pushing you about. How can you possibly ask, 'Who touched me?'"

Jesus said, "Someone touched me. I know, because power went out from me."

He walked on slowly, looking around as if determined to find out who touched him.

Then a woman about thirty years old broke past John and fell on her knees. She trembled, yet wonder and joy, with a hint of fear, suffused her face as she poured out her story to Jesus. She came from a distant village, she said. For twelve years a continual flow of menstrual blood had rendered her ritually unclean, caused her to be shunned, and prevented a normal life. She had spent all her patrimony on doctors without success.

Hearing about Jesus, she came to Capernaum. She could not get near enough to plead with him. "But I said to myself," she told him, "that if I can just touch the fringe of his garment, I shall be well again. And I pushed my way nearer. And I touched. And I knew at that very moment that the blood had stopped and I was well! That's the whole truth!"

She seemed worried that he would tell her she had stolen her cure. Instead, he looked down at the woman kneeling before him, "Daughter,"—and his voice had a special tenderness—"your faith has healed you. Go in peace. You are free from your suffering."

Throughout their talk, Jairus had wrung his hands at the delay, and as if to justify his fears, he saw two or three of his friends elbowing their way down the street. They reached him while Jesus still comforted the woman. They spoke almost callously.

"Your daughter is dead," they said. "Why bother the teacher anymore?" There was contempt in their tone: he had healed the centurion's slave but this time had failed. They had disapproved of calling in the prophet of Nazareth.

Jesus put a hand on Jairus' arm and looked him straight in the eye. "Do not be afraid," he said. "Simply believe."

He beckoned to John, James, and Peter; not even Andrew was to come; he and the other eight must keep the people from following, and await his return.

Jairus led the way. Nearing Jairus' mansion, they heard women wailing and the sound of flutes; and entering the courtyard they saw that the professional mourners, with hair hanging down, had begun their dance of death. Wailing and clapping in rhythm to a lament played on the flutes, they moved slowly in a circle round their leader.

Jesus spoke sharply: "What is all this commotion and noise? The girl is not dead. She is asleep!" The mourners gave a loud cackle of laughter: each one of them had viewed the corpse. The grief-stricken mother, however, had come out of the death room on hearing Jesus' voice, and hope crossed her face as Jesus ordered the mourners and flutists to leave; his tone of quiet authority subdued them and sent them meekly into the street, leaving only relatives and close neighbors in the courtyard.

Jesus asked the parents to take him to their daughter's body and allowed no others except Peter, James, and John to enter the death chamber.

It seemed dark after the strong sunshine in the courtyard, but when their eyes adjusted to the shade, John saw the girl, who looked about twelve years old, lying on her bed in such peace that she might indeed have been asleep were it not for her pallor. The silent grief of the parents deepened the stillness. John felt that he and his brother and Peter were almost intruding, though grateful that their presence might support Jesus in whatever he had to do.

Jesus took her by the hand. A rather beautiful look crossed his face. Then he said what any mother or father would say to a girl when waking her up in the morning. *"Talitha koum! It's time to wake up, little girl!"*

The girl opened her eyes. She sat up and got off her bed. The parents clung to each other with amazement and joy and gratitude as she walked toward them and flung her arms wide in greeting.

Before they could thank him or fully take in what had happened, Jesus spoke briskly like a physician. "Give her something to eat!" Then, in contrast to his instruction that morning to Legion, he gave a strict order: "On no account tell anyone what happened"—an order which, in the excitement and relief soon to burst on the household and neighborhood, would be hard to obey.

Nine
A CONTRAST
IN COMPASSION

In the last weeks of summer, Jesus decided to take the Twelve into the hill country of Galilee. The days would be cooler, the crowds less, and he could train them for the future as they walked between the villages before they all went up to Jerusalem. Besides, the citizens of Capernaum and neighboring towns of the Sea of Galilee were behaving as if he had never come among them. They had brought him their sick, they had hung on his words, but most did not repent.

Before Jesus set out, he was summoned to dine with a Pharisee named Simon, one of those who had publicly disgraced him by banning his teaching in synagogues.

Such an invitation seemed strange until he crossed the threshold, with Peter and John, and found himself insulted. Simon pointedly refrained from giving him the kiss of welcome; no servant brought the usual bowl to wash street dust from his feet, and no drop of aromatic oil was sprinkled on his head.

Jesus appeared not to notice, though John thought he detected a twinkle in his eye as Jesus gravely joined the other guests already reclining at table. He was led to the couch beside his host, who at least had not put him at the lowest place, and ate what was brought and listened as Simon told him how he fasted twice a week, gave tithes of all he possessed, and was a most virtuous man.

Just then a woman came in from the courtyard holding a small jar. She stood behind Jesus as he lay on the couch and gazed at him. Though there was nothing unusual in a neighbor's watching a feast uninvited, Simon the Pharisee tensed. The woman was soberly dressed but she was lovely. As she gazed at Jesus, she began to weep. She knelt and allowed the tears to bathe his bare feet; then she shook her hair and began to dry his feet with her tresses and kiss them repeatedly. Undoubtedly, she was a woman of much experience with men, yet her actions were purged of suggestiveness. Her charms were so strong that John almost needed to remember a warning which Jesus had given, that a lustful look is equal to the act of adultery. But the woman was not making advances; plainly she had thrown her past behind her.

Suddenly she broke the neck of her little jar and poured its contents on Jesus' feet. Quickly a luscious scent filled the room. Whether the perfume had been given her by a lover or bought as an aid to her arts, she poured it with reverence.

Jesus had not moved, except to gaze back at her in a compassion and a love which neither condemned nor recoiled. Simon, on the other hand, bridled with distaste. His sneer disclosed his thoughts: that this man was no prophet or he would have detected a prostitute at once.

Jesus turned to him. "Simon," he said, "I want to tell you something."

"What is it, Teacher?"

"There was a moneylender with two debtors. One owed him five hundred, the other fifty. Neither had anything with which to pay him. So he canceled the debts of both. Which of them will love him more?"

"I suppose," replied Simon in a rather grudging tone, "the one who had the bigger debt canceled."

"You are right. Now, listen." Then Jesus publicly contrasted Simon's lapses in hospitality with what the woman had done: it was she who had washed his feet, who had given him kisses and anointed him. "Therefore, I tell you, her sins have been forgiven, for she loved much. Someone who has been forgiven little, loves little."

He looked with compassion at the woman. "Your sins have been forgiven."

Guests muttered angrily, "Who does he think he is, forgiving sins?"

Jesus ignored their mutterings. "Your faith has saved you," he said to the woman. "Go in peace."

Next day, John walked into the hills with Jesus and the others. As they went from village to village, Jesus showed his marvelous gift for speaking so that poor and rich, simple and wise, could understand him. He had acute powers of observation, as his parables showed. Naturally, he knew about carpentry and building; equally, he could make his points with stories about sheep and wheat farming, about vineyards and fig trees and pigs. He had a shrewd idea of trade and business so that he could tell of bad and good stewards, and moneylenders and tax men; he had observed the ways of the wealthy and of those so poor that a lost coin made a matter of utmost concern; he could describe scribes in flowing robes, judges and kings; burglars operating at night and highway robbers. Using word pictures and pithy comments, he could make truth plain, bring all heaven before the inward eyes of his hearers, and probe the ways of man.

He showed a compassion which came from the roots of his soul. He grieved to see men and women helpless and drifting and oppressed. His instinct was to bring immediate comfort and relief.

An unexpected incident near a town called Nain brought this out vividly. Followed by the inescapable crowd from villages recently visited, Jesus and his disciples approached the town gateway just as an equally large crowd left it. In the center four men carried a corpse. They were weeping, and beside them a woman wept even more. The two crowds met. When Jesus saw the woman, a spasm of pain crossed his face and he said, "Don't cry!"

He turned around and walked with her. Townsfolk explained that she was a widow; the corpse was of her only son and support, and they had been devoted to each other. He had died that morning. Burials always took place the same day, but she could not bear to see him go and had refused to allow them to wrap his face before they reached the graveside. Almost all the town came with her in sympathy.

Jesus stepped across to the bier. Those carrying it stopped. He said, "Young man, I say to you: *get up!*"

At once the man sat up and began to talk. Jesus turned to the mother and smiled. With a gesture that suggested the return of a prisoner-of-war or of someone ransomed from slavery, he formally handed the young man back to his mother.

A few weeks earlier Jesus had raised from the dead the daughter of Jairus, ruler of the Capernaum synagogue. John, James, and Peter had looked on, amazed. That had been in the privacy of a darkened room. At Nain they were in the open, and the people were awestruck. They did not shout nor laugh for joy; they stood and sang a psalm of praise. The town's patriarch voiced their feelings: "A great prophet has arisen among us." And a younger man echoed, "God has visited his people."

John, Peter, and the other disciples echoed those words too. But though Jesus spoke often of "the kingdom," he had not yet made plain whether he would create this kingdom soon and throw out the Romans by mobilizing his vast following or by supernatural aid; nor whether the kingdom lay far in the future. He spoke to his disciples as if the history of their race would reach its climax in himself. Sometimes he seemed indeed the Messiah foretold in ancient times, who would judge and purge; at other times he seemed perplexingly different, so gentle and willing to suffer.

The answers had eluded John. Then, in the next months from autumn through to spring, several events threw a flood of light; and the twelve months after that would show the truth to be far more terrible and glorious than anything John had imagined.

Ten
NO GOING BACK

After he had preached outside a town in the Galilean hills, large crowds pressed around Jesus. People brought him their sick, those who were lame, and others in distress. The Twelve worked, as always, to keep patients and suppliants in some sort of order.

In the midst of it, John noticed two travel-stained men whose rough clothes and ascetic faces set them apart as disciples of John the Baptist. At once he stopped what he was doing and asked for news of his old master, who languished in a dungeon in Herod's grim fortress of Machaerus in the wild country beyond the Dead Sea. The messengers said that Herod, when in residence, would question him and listen, and seemed in awe of him, but would not release him or put him on trial.

The men were in no mood for talk. They said they must speak urgently to Jesus, for their master had heard of his doings and wanted to ask a question. John maneuvered them through the importunate crowd until they reached him.

"Sir," they said, "John the Baptist has sent us to ask you if you are the 'Coming One'? Or should we look for someone else?"

If Jesus felt a pang of regret at the Baptist's doubts, he did not show it. Nor did he reply. Disciples of the Baptist had once asked why he did not fast or refuse wine or strong drink, and he had answered that no one wept or fasted in a bridegroom's presence, though they would when he was removed.

This time he went silently back to his work, so that as the Baptist's messengers watched, blind people saw again and the lame walked; others in the grip of madness or epilepsy or evil spirits became their normal selves; even lepers who had dared to mingle in the crowd were restored: it is sometimes forgotten that Jesus healed hundreds of sufferers whose stories were not recorded and would have healed more had they sought him.

Jesus gave the messengers time to gather evidence with their own eyes and from witnesses of earlier incidents. Then he told them to return and report, and to quote to the Baptist a passage from Isaiah's prophecy of what would happen when the Messiah came: "The blind receive their sight, the lame walk, lepers are cleansed, and the deaf hear; the dead are raised up, and the poor have Good News preached to them." Jesus added, "Happy is the man who has no doubts about me."

As the messengers left, Jesus praised John the Baptist as a prophet, and more than a prophet because he was the herald who had made men ready for the king. None greater than John had ever been born; "yet," Jesus told them, "he who is least in the kingdom of heaven is greater than he." The crowd, who listened intently as they sat or stood on the sunbaked earth, were left in no doubt that a new era had begun.

In a long sermon that afternoon, Jesus spoke of his sorrow that Capernaum and the cities on the lake, with their Pharisees and scribes, religious and learned, had not turned from their sins; if his miracles had been done in Gentile cities, or even in ancient Sodom, which was a byword for wickedness, the citizens would have repented and escaped judgment. At one point Jesus looked around at his humble audience of simple country folk and lifted his hands in prayer. "I praise You, Father, Lord of heaven and earth, because you have hidden these things from the wise and prudent and revealed them to little children."

Then came the climax of Jesus' sermon which would be quoted and pondered on and loved by humanity through all the ages to come. His eye had caught an ox cart, drawn by two yoked oxen; the driver had stopped and sat listening. One of the oxen was young, the other strong and experienced. The load was heavy, but everybody knew that when they moved again the young ox would find that the older took the strain and showed the way.

"Come to me," cried Jesus, "all you who are weary and burdened, and I will give you rest. Take my yoke upon you and learn of me, for I am gentle and humble in heart, and you will find rest to your souls. For my yoke is easy and my burden is light"—immortal words which, to John and those who knew him well, expressed the very heart of the man.

Soon afterward, Jesus took the disciples to Jerusalem for one of the great festivals. As was his way, he sought out the distressed. He went on the Sabbath to the Pool of Bethesda (or Bezatha), an ancient reservoir or tank with five porticoes, outside the city walls near the sheep gate. Because its water bubbled at intervals, Bethesda attracted the lame, the blind, and the sick in the belief that the first to enter after the water bubbled would be cured. Therefore, most were escorted by friends or relatives ready to act.

Jesus was unknown by sight. He walked in the porticoes and no one sought his aid. Suddenly the water bubbled. Uproar followed as escorts fought to get their patients into the pool. Jesus noticed an emaciated man of late middle age trying desperately by crawls and jerks to reach the water unaided, and then dragging himself sadly back to his pallet. Jesus approached him. The man had been an invalid for thirty-eight years, though John in relating the incident did not record how long he had waited at the pool.

"Do you want to get well?" asked Jesus.

The man answered in despair, "I have no one to help me into the pool when the water bubbles. While I am trying, someone always gets in first."

"Get up! Pick up your pallet! Walk!"

The man had neither sought aid nor shown faith; but he responded to the stranger's command at once. At the first movement, all weakness or paralysis disappeared. He rediscovered his strength, picked up his pallet, and walked away from the pool without a word of thanks.

None of the sick or escorts noticed, too intent on waiting for the next bubble in the pool. Jesus quickly left, followed by John and Peter. As they went down the street, John saw the man and his pallet out of the corner of his eye; he had been stopped by Pharisees, who were pointing at the pallet he carried on a Sabbath Day.

An hour or so later they met the man again, in the precincts of the Temple; perhaps he had come to offer thanks for his healing. Jesus knew that the illness of thirty-eight years had been the sufferer's fault, possibly as a consequence of fornication, and he warned him to cease sinning or worse might happen. The man did not take the warning kindly; he hurried away and shortly afterward a posse of Pharisees descended on Jesus to accuse him of incitement to Sabbath breaking: they had stopped someone carrying a pallet, they said, and he had now pointed out the person who had caused him to pick it up. Some of the accusers had been among the investigators in Galilee who had seen Jesus restore the withered hand in the synagogue on a Sabbath.

They immediately put him on trial, informally, in the Temple precincts, under one of the porches where debates were held. This debate might lead to formal arraignment: once again Jesus stood under the shadow of death, by judicial process or by murder in a back street.

John stood beside Jesus and marveled at his courage as he took up the challenge. His accusers demanded to know why he worked on the Sabbath. He answered by words which made them certain that he claimed to be equal with God, whom he called "my Father," an expression no Jew would dare to use. Not denying their interpretation, Jesus emphasized his relationship with God until no one present remained in doubt of his claim that his life and actions revealed the life and action of God. He claimed that he had power to give men life and that he, Jesus, would be their judge. He asserted that men should honor him exactly as they honored the Father. With strong emphasis, Jesus said, "Whoever hears my word and believes him who has sent me has eternal life and will not be condemned; he has crossed over from death to life."

His claims were uncompromising, forceful, and put him beyond retreat, being blasphemous delusion or fraud unless true. And since a man's testimony about himself was not valid, he cited as evidence John the Baptist's statements about him, and the witness of the miracles of healing and life which no human being had ever achieved before. The Father himself, he said, had spoken in witness, though the accusers had never heard his voice nor seen his shape.

He went on: "You search the Scriptures because you think that in them you have eternal life. They bear witness to *me!*" cried Jesus. Suddenly his eyes filled with compassion for his accusers in their emptiness and blindness. "They bear witness to me, yet you refuse to come to me to have life!

"I do not accept man's praise," he said. "But I know you. You do not have God's love in your hearts. I have come in my Father's name and you reject me, yet if someone comes in his own name you will accept him. You accept praise from each other but do not try to obtain the praise that comes from the Only One."

By now he had turned the tables. "Do not think I will

accuse you to the Father! Your accuser is Moses, on whom your hopes are set. If you believed Moses, you would believe me, for he wrote about me. But since you do not believe what he wrote, how are you going to believe what I say?"

They had no answer. They let him go. But he had signed his death warrant, however long it took to execute.

Eleven
TO MAKE HIM A KING

Jesus took his disciples back to Galilee. They did not go by way of Samaria, which Jews avoided when traveling at festival times, but down to the coast and then northward up the Great South Road built by the Romans. They turned with it into the hills. Jesus was heading for Nazareth, which he had not visited since his rejection and escape from murder before he had called John and the others from their fishing.

Throughout the journey, John walked under the spell of Jesus' answer to the Jewish leaders who had arraigned him, the speech in which he had stated his claims with authority, yet without histrionics or rhetoric. Yet neither John nor Peter nor any of them could force their lips to make open acknowledgment that this man who walked beside them, so like themselves though so different, was the Son of God.

They left the Great Road near Sepporis and climbed the few miles to Nazareth on a wet day of autumn rain and mist, to be welcomed by Mary without restraint. The formidable half brother, James, was more cautious, and the rest of the family still hardly knew what to make of the extraordinary events and stories which had surrounded Jesus for the past twenty months. On the Sabbath they all went to the synagogue. The ban of the Capernaum elders did not run elsewhere, and Jesus was invited to teach.

The townsfolk proved even less responsive than before. "Isn't this the carpenter's son?" they sneered, seeing him only as the local lad of earlier memories, whose relations were their neighbors. They had nothing against him, could recall no sowing of wild oats; indeed, they remembered his youth with affection and admiration. But they would not go further. Thus, the people of Nazareth dashed any hope that they would help him take his message to the surrounding countryside, or later would cross the seas on his behalf. Talking with his disciples in the privacy of Mary's home, he expressed amazement at Nazareth's refusal to believe in him, and his pain that their lack of faith frustrated his desire to help them. A blind man or two and a few sick sought him out and were healed, but Nazareth as a town turned its back on the one who would give them their only place in world history. John summed it up later in the matchless prologue to his Gospel, with a wider context: "He came to his own and his own did not receive him."

Rejected at Capernaum, Jerusalem, and Nazareth, he still had the Twelve. They might not fully understand, but they trusted him and he could trust them; when he led them away from his home to visit local villages, he disclosed that he would soon send them out on their own. Winter was coming on, when the crowds would not want to gather in the cold winds and the rain and hail or snow. This would be the season for smaller meetings.

First, Jesus trained them. He taught them what to do and to expect, both in the immediate short term and during the long years to come, when they would be hauled before kings and governors for his sake, be beaten in the synagogues, be forced to flee from one city to another. "Don't be afraid," he told them; and again, "I am sending you out as sheep in the midst of wolves. Be wise as serpents and innocent as doves."

What he had told them in secret they were to proclaim from the housetops.

They went out in pairs, John with James, Peter with Andrew, and the others paired as seemed best. Carrying out his instructions, they took no stick, no spare coat, nor money in their belts. When they reached a town or village, they asked residents for lodging; they accepted hospitality without offering any return except the privilege of aiding their work; but they refused to accept handouts of money, not even a penny. They avoided Gentile towns, nor did they enter Samaria, but went among the villages of their own Jewish people, and preached Jesus' message: "The kingdom of heaven is at hand." In some places they were rebuffed, and then, as Jesus had instructed, they turned their backs and at the town's edge, formally removed a shoe, and shook off the dust.

Jesus had said, "Heal the sick, raise the dead, cleanse the lepers, cast out demons." Not one disciple had ever done such things, though they had watched him often enough. John, conscious that away from Jesus he was nothing but a fisherman who had left his nets, went to it nervously. To his utter astonishment, when he placed his hands on the first sick person, he was at once aware of extraordinary power, as if Jesus himself stood by.

Jesus had told the Twelve where to meet him when the winter ended. But when the day came for reunion, and John and James took the last turn to join the trail to the rendez-vous, with a glimpse of Peter and Andrew marching steadily uphill half a mile in front, the whole countryside was in a ferment because of news from beyond the Jordan: Herod had beheaded the Baptist.

Jesus, they soon found, had already received details of the squalid events which had led to the execution. Herod, though a Jew, had celebrated his birthday at the fortress of Machaerus in a pagan manner, by a great banquet for his army chiefs, local governors, and all the high and mighty of the tetrarchy. His wife, Herodias, knew that the Baptist was chained in a cell below the banqueting hall. She loathed him for his courage in rebuking them when Herod had seduced her from his own half brother, Philip, and had long sought an occasion to destroy him. She now sent her daughter by Philip to dance before a tipsy stepfather and his guests. Salome danced in such a way that Herod promised on oath to give her anything she wanted. Her mother had told her already what to ask: "the head of John the Baptist on a dish." Herod was horrified, but a perverted sense of honor held his oath more sacred than natural justice or his admiration for John. And so, the great voice had been silenced by the heavy short sword of a guard. John the Baptist, the powerful moral influence, "the burning and shining light," was gone.

The people of Judea and Galilee were shocked and angry: the Baptist had been a voice of national resurgence. For Jesus, and for John and Peter, the Baptist's death was a deep personal sorrow.

There was no time for weeping or fond remembrance: the stirring throughout the nation had come at the same time as a stirring in Galilee caused by their own mission; before the disciples could give Jesus all their news as they walked together toward Capernaum, he was again the center of demanding crowds, coming and going, who made no secret of their conviction that Jesus was worth more than all his Twelve together. The following days were filled from morning to night, with time for only the most hurried of informal meals, or none.

Jesus was determined to give his Twelve a brief recess, when they could talk over with him their experiences and lessons in a restful, reinvigorating way. Early one morning before the town was astir, they all crept to the shore, enjoying the conspiratorial way in which Jesus gave the crowd the slip. They embarked in Peter's boat.

Rain had fallen for much of the night; Passover was only ten days away and the intermittent spring rains had come.

The mist rose from the water, though the day looked as if it would turn fine. Jesus sat in the stern at the tiller, and since the wind had dropped, all the Twelve took oars; landlubbers like Judas Iscariot had now learned the knack. Jesus had suggested they should go across the top of the lake, beyond Bethsaida Julius, to a rather desolate area where the land rose in steep green folds from the shoreline. Thus, they would not be spotted by people in the villages higher up; and many of these would be Gentiles who would not care.

Jesus did not want to make a straight course; by spending part of the morning on the lake, they could rest and be fresh upon reaching land. Thus, they passed close to the quay at Capernaum as they set out. None of them at the oars noticed a man staring at the boat; nor did they realize that he had recognized the profile of Jesus before the boat disappeared into the mist; least of all did they know the wild surmise that passed through this man's mind, and that he was rushing to spread the news of Jesus' arrival in the area.

The lake in the early morning refreshed them as the sun broke through the mist. Fishing vessels had put into shore after the night's work, and the carriers of merchandise and men had not come out; Jesus and his disciples had the Sea of Galilee to themselves. More than once they put up the oars and drifted while one after another put questions to Jesus or told him of encouraging or perplexing incidents. Sometimes they rocked with laughter at some memory; it was easy to be happy with Jesus. Then someone would recall a memory of the Baptist, and their great sorrow would come to the forefront and they wept; neither tears nor laughter seemed out of place in Jesus' company.

The sun grew strong. It was time to continue their day of rest in shade on a hillside. They rowed again, for the wind was offshore.

Their backs were toward the land and it was not until they reached shallow water and heard a great cheer behind them that the Twelve realized what Jesus in the stern had seen already. A huge crowd awaited him in the isolated place where they had expected to relax. The disciples turned on their thwarts in disgust and disappointment. Not only was the beach crowded, but they could see hundreds of men running toward the lake from the direction of Bethsaida; and had the disciples been high up instead of on the water, they would have seen that the road which led over the Jordan ford from Capernaum and Magdala and Tiberias was thick with men running.

John felt a spasm of anger that Jesus, who had seen the crowd, had not directed the boat to another beach; but once again this unworthy thought died when he turned and saw the compassion on Jesus' face. He also saw a slight hardening of the jaw, and as they stowed oars and jumped into the shallow water to pull the vessel on to the beach, he realized why Jesus' countenance had suddenly changed. This was no ordinary crowd. It was mostly male. Women and children, with their sick, had followed, but most of those who had run round the lake to meet Jesus were men and some were armed. They were not intending harm against Jesus: the mood was of excitement, of a desire for leadership, of a mass movement like a flock of sheep which would race wherever the bellwether went, if the shepherd were not there to control. The glint of the sun on steel suggested that some of the men hoped that Jesus would lead them at once to avenge the Baptist.

Jesus stood for a few moments surveying the scene. Then he walked at a steady pace inland, the men making way, and climbed to a little rise which formed a convenient pulpit to the natural amphitheater sloping down to the beach. The great crowd stood or sat noisily below him.

First, he ordered that any sick should be brought; he healed them, and this amazed and quieted the people. Then, with a gesture for total silence, he began to preach. With the land breeze carrying his voice, the people listened unwearied, hour by hour; it seemed that all thought of violence was stilled and that they would indeed "seek first the kingdom of God and his righteousness."

When the sun had moved into the west, Jesus stopped preaching. The crowd of several thousand were now very hungry. Some of the disciples suggested that he send the people into the surrounding villages to buy themselves food; but since they were in a desolate spot, where the few villages higher up could supply little, and since darkness would fall before anyone could reach the larger towns, this was a callous policy to urge.

Jesus rejected it. "You give them something to eat," he said, and John noticed again the twinkle in his eye, and was sure he wanted to test them.

Philip fell into the trap. "Two hundred *denarii*—eight months' wages—would not buy enough bread for everyone to have a bite. Are we to spend that amount?"

"How many loaves have you got here? Go and see."

The Twelve scattered to discover provisions among the vast number of people present, estimated at 5,000 men, plus women and children. But any who had hurriedly made up bags of food at the sudden rush after Jesus had long since eaten what they carried. John, Peter, Philip, and eight others found nothing. Andrew, however, met a small boy whom he probably knew, for the boy likely came from Bethsaida. The boy evidently had been on his way to bring supper to his father and brother keeping sheep on the hillside, and had been caught up in the crowd and had stayed to listen.

Andrew hurried to Jesus. "Here is a lad with five little barley loaves and two small dried fish—but what are they among so many?"

With a smile of thanks, Jesus took the loaves and fishes from the boy. Coarse barley bread was food for the poorest: three loaves, helped down by tasty morsels of dried fish, made one adult's meal, but Jesus had more than 5,000 to feed. Before the disciples could wonder what he intended, he ordered them to seat the crowd, many of whom had begun to wander around restlessly. Significantly, the people formed themselves into companies of fifties or hundreds, as if a military chain of command had been at work.

They all waited expectantly. Jesus held in his hands the five loaves and two little fish and looked up to heaven. He gave thanks as if he were the head of a household presiding at a feast. Then he broke up the five loaves. He handed broken bread to each of the Twelve, and pieces of the two dried fish, and ordered them to distribute the pieces among 5,000 hungry men, with their women and children.

Feeling a fool, but obeying Jesus without question, John walked toward a company of fifty or a hundred holding less than half a loaf and one sixth of a little fish. In a gesture of faith, he tore a generous lump from his half loaf, and a piece of fish, and handed the food to the first man in the first rank. When John looked down to see how to divide the remainder, he saw half a loaf still in his hand, and the portion of fish apparently undiminished. When he had fed the second man, he saw the same. With mounting excitement, he went down the line, tearing off larger portions. Thoughts raced through his mind of the wine at Cana of Galilee, and of Elijah's flour and oil which never failed in the famine long ago, as they often heard in synagogue; but Elijah had fed only himself and a small family, and Jesus at Cana had supplied a mere village wedding, whereas on this spring evening above the lakeshore, Jesus was feeding more than 5,000.

By now John and his friends were handing out almost all of a half loaf, and men were passing the pieces of bread down the line; still the supply did not fail.

No one went hungry. Before this extraordinary feast was over, many were taking more than they could eat, so that fragments were thrown on the ground. As John worked, power seemed to flow through his hands, and his heart leaped with the sheer joy of being part of this incredible creation; never had he felt closer to Jesus, although separated by rank upon rank of amazed and excited Galileans.

At last, at Jesus' order, the disciples gathered up all that was left on the ground, stacking twelve baskets in front of him. It was now almost dark, but the excitement of the people could scarcely be contained. Some were already drawing their swords, demanding that Jesus accept the throne usurped by Herod, and lead them at once, through the night, on a march of vengeance to overthrow Herod and his Roman overlords.

John felt himself beginning to be swept into a mass movement. When he looked at Judas Iscariot and at Simon the former Zealot, he could see the light of battle in their eyes. Then Jesus made a most unexpected move. He ordered the Twelve to return to the boat and to sail or row back to Capernaum; he would dismiss the crowd himself.

Such was his authority that they obeyed. Fears for his safety, regrets that he could not trust them, were extinguished. While the crowd watched, they walked meekly down to the shore. They heard afterward that Jesus had ordered the leaders of the incipient revolt to disperse their followers and that most had started back along the shore by the light of a nearly full moon while some had settled down where they were. Jesus had disappeared; he had been last seen climbing into the hills, and no one had dared to follow or to dispute his refusal to be made a king.

Meanwhile the Twelve had put out to sea. They hung about offshore for several hours, rowing up and down because they expected Jesus to signal to them that he wanted to come on board. About midnight they gave up and set course for the opposite shore. The breeze which had blown from the west during the afternoon had veered and they had to row without help of the sail. The farther they progressed toward the center of the lake, the more the wind stiffened and the waves buffeted the boat. The long day and its excitement and the lateness of the hour had sapped their strength, until even the hardiest sailor was in distress as he strained at his oar. Their memory of a miracle was washed out by the misery of backbreaking toil, though they faced the distant shore, still clear in the moonlight, where they had distributed the loaves and fish.

Suddenly one of them gave a cry. Then they all cried out in fear. Between them and the shore they saw a man walking on the water toward them, moving quickly despite the waves but on a parallel course. The apparition looked like Jesus. Terrified, they were certain that it was his ghost; he must have been killed by the mob: they should have ignored his command and stayed to save him.

The figure neared the boat. They cried out again.

Suddenly they heard Jesus' unmistakable voice above the wind and the waves. "Be brave," he shouted. "It is I! Don't be afraid!"

Peter apparently thought Jesus was going to pass them by. Impulsive as always, he yelled, "Lord, if it is you, tell me to come to you on the water!"

"Come!"

Peter, the experienced fisherman, who knew that the freshwater lake lacked even the partial buoyancy of the Dead Sea, left the boat. Amazed, the other disciples saw Peter walk toward Jesus. Then suddenly Peter lost his nerve. He began to sink, and they heard a despairing cry, "Lord, save me!"

Jesus stretched out his hand and gripped Peter. " 'Little-Faith,' why did you doubt?" they heard him say. The two were close to the vessel. Willing hands helped them and, as they climbed aboard, the wind dropped.

John, Peter, and the others were utterly astonished that Jesus should have reached them. They could no more understand how he walked on water than how he multiplied loaves and fish. They gaped at him.

Then one after another stumbled over the oars to fall at his feet. "You are the Son of God," they cried. "It is true! It is utterly true—you are the Son of God!"

But they hardly knew what they said.

Part Two

DEATH IN JERUSALEM

Twelve
THE MOUNTAIN

The great road Via Maris (Way of the Sea) bore a steady two-way traffic of camel caravans and donkey trains, of military detachments marching in the dust, of slaves and prisoners and strings of horses being led for sale. This was the road which Saul of Tarsus traveled a few years later on his way to Damascus, breathing threats and slaughter against disciples of Jesus: a journey which had an unexpected end.

In the high summer of A.D. 29, Jesus and the Twelve and a few other followers walked north on Via Maris. They could see the Golan Heights on their right and Mount Hermon far ahead, still with snow wedged below the summit despite the summer sun. Its coolness beckoned them from the heat which hung round the Sea of Galilee.

At the Ford of Jacob's Daughters, where Via Maris crosses the Jordan, Jesus turned off the Damascus Road onto a quieter route of Upper Galilee. They walked on, mile after mile, at a steady pace, through a city and round the western shores of the small lake into which the young Jordan flows after threading its way through the marshes.

When they were well into the hills, Jesus left the main road and they climbed upward. If anyone grew tired after traveling through the heat of the day, Jesus insisted on carrying his burden, though Peter tried to stop him and take it himself. The track became steep, but Jesus pressed on and upward until at length, as darkness fell, they reached the spot where one of the sources of the Jordan gushes out of the rock face, which the Greeks called the Springs of Pan, after the god of shepherds.

They slept where they were, for the summer night was warm even at that height. At dawn, as they woke, a pagan shepherd came up to the Springs of Pan and threw in a votive offering. When the sun rose, they saw in the distance the magnificent sight of the city of Caesarea Philippi, which Herod the Great had built and Philip the Tetrarch had expanded to make his capital; its newness was almost dazzling. High above stood Mount Hermon. Nearer, on a jutting rock to the left, they saw the white marble temple which Herod the Great had built to exalt the divinity of Caesar Augustus, though the region lay within ancient Israel.

In this setting where pagan myth, Roman power, and the lost glories of Israel were alike dwarfed by Hermon, Jesus taught the Twelve privately. As John listened while the hours sped by, he had a sense that Jesus wanted to draw them out and to make them face the deeper implications of discipleship; but before John could formulate his thoughts, Jesus turned to prayer. To be present when he prayed, in the intimate, unaffected way they knew so well, John felt was the greatest privilege of all, and when the prayer ended, a great peace held heart and mind. But Jesus did not resume his teaching. Instead, he asked a question, "Who do men say that I am?"

John was sure that Jesus knew the excited, puzzled, admiring guesses of the lakeside crowds, but several disciples repeated them. "Some say, 'John the Baptist!' "—the rumor that Herod Antipas, disturbed by his guilty conscience when he heard about miracles, had declared, that the Baptist must have come back from the dead.

"Others say you are Elijah!"

"Or the Prophet Jeremiah!" The popular explanation always involved the return to earth of a dead hero.

"What about you?" asked Jesus. "Who do *you* say that I am?"

In the fishing boat after he had walked on water, they had blurted out that he was Son of God. At Capernaum when many abandoned him, Peter had called him the "Holy One of God," but these were emotional responses to moments of crisis. Jesus now wanted a clear affirmation from which there could be no going back; and since lies and half-truths were impossible to utter in his presence, they must say what they believed, however absurd it might sound in the ordinary world of men and boats and fish markets.

John was still trying to frame words to express his personal certainty when suddenly Peter bounded toward Jesus. Looking as if an instant vision had blazed the truth into his mind, he cried: "You are the Christ! The Son of the Living God!"

Jesus looked at Peter with the utmost earnestness and authority. "Simon, son of Jonah," he said, "you are blessed indeed. For this was not revealed to you by man but by my Father in heaven. And you are Peter, the rock, and on this rock I will build my church, which hell itself shall never defeat."

Across the valley, the other rock, with its fine temple to Caesar, seemed to mock such a prophecy, but Jesus went on to promise, very solemnly, to give Peter the keys of the kingdom of heaven. All the Twelve knew that in a royal palace the king's most responsible servant carried the keys as a mark of his authority. Peter, carrying out God's directions, would declare the Gospel which loosed the sins of some while others remained bound. Then Jesus turned to the others and, to their astonishment, warned them all not to trumpet abroad who he was.

He led them away from the Springs of Pan and the Rock of Augustus. They spent the days after Peter's confession walking together in the foothills of Mount Hermon and near the villages of Caesarea Philippi. Jesus impressed upon them that the immediate future bore no relation to any dream they might have that he, as the Messiah whom every Jew awaited, would come swiftly to glory and power with his chosen companions in splendor at his side. He told them that they would be going to Jerusalem; that he would be abused, insulted, and maltreated by the elders and chief priests and the teachers of the Law; that he must be killed, "and on the third day be raised to life."

They did not take him seriously. Jesus repeated the teaching until at length they were left in no doubt that he did not speak in a parable but of what would happen.

Peter was horrified. The Christ, even if they must not reveal Jesus as such, would have unlimited power to prevent His own death. Besides, Jesus' moral goodness and beauty of character could not deserve death. Peter drew Jesus aside. They were near a village, and the crowds had increased, since his fame always caught up with him; and Peter did not want inquisitive ears to catch any hint that Jesus expected to be insulted and killed.

Once out of earshot, Peter spoke his mind. "Never," he said. "Never, Lord! These things shall never happen to you!"

Jesus walked on as if not hearing. Peter ran after him. "Never, never, never," he began again. Jesus turned, and Peter's words froze at the look on Jesus' face.

With such force that Peter trembled, Jesus rebuked him. "Out of my sight, Satan! You are a stumbling block to me. There is a smell of man about you, not the scent of God."

Jesus called the other disciples to gather round and beckoned all the people to hear, thus defeating Peter's intention of secrecy.

"If any of you want to follow me, you must say no to yourself and take up your cross and follow me!" John's heart chilled as he recalled the too familiar sight of a criminal, convicted by Roman law, struggling under a crossbeam toward a place of execution. John had seen a man stripped and iron nails hammered through his wrists or hands to the beam he had carried; screaming, he was lifted roughly on to the upright timber already in place and died slowly in fearful pain.

Jesus was speaking with unmistakable emphasis. "Whoever wants to save his life will lose it," he said. "Whoever loses his life *for me* will find it." It was no good if a man gained all that this world could offer, yet lost his own soul. "If anyone is ashamed of me and of my words in this adulterous and sinful generation, the Son of man will be ashamed of him when he comes in his Father's glory with the holy angels."

He dismissed the crowd and again led the Twelve into the foothills, where they camped the short summer nights under the cedars and spent daytime in seclusion while he taught them.

During the afternoon of the sixth day, while they all rested in the shade, John heard Jesus calling him by name. He called James and Peter too. Telling the others to await their return, he led the three along a rough track through vineyards to the higher pastures and up the ridge which climbs steadily northwest toward the summits of Hermon. They emerged from clumps of cedars to the region of scrub, then threaded their way easily through ravines on hard-packed snow.

They stopped to rest. The silence and the wildness and the isolation—since the coastal plain and the Jordan Valley were hidden by heat haze—made a perfect setting for Jesus to let his three closest friends into secret memories which they would not have understood before Peter's confession. He told them of the voice from heaven which he had heard as he came up from the Jordan water at his baptism: "You are my beloved Son. I am well pleased with you." This strengthened their conviction of who he was.

They continued their climb. The sun on the rocks and snow patches made the afternoon even hotter, and they stopped again by a stream which hurried down from the heights. Here, Jesus told of the arid wilderness of Judea where he had gone after his baptism, to be locked for forty days in a mental and spiritual battle. He spoke of temptation which John could barely comprehend, as all the evil that assaulted or deceived mankind converged: cruelty, lust, despair—whatever was contrary to the character of Jesus yet common to man.

It had mounted to a climax with three successive assaults. Toward the end of his long fast, Jesus said, he had become hungry. Some of the stones in that part of the mountains looked like loaves: they needed only the touch of God. The tempter said, "If you are the Son of God, tell these stones to become bread," and what he did in solitude for his own relief Jesus could do for others, swiftly meeting the physical needs of mankind and buying their adoration.

That was not his way. Jesus told of destroying the temptation by a quotation from Scripture: "Man does not live by bread alone, but on every word that comes from the mouth of God."

Next the devil had taken him to a high mountain. As Jesus told this on Hermon, the haze was lifting, and John could see the glint of the Sea of Galilee forty miles to the south and the Mediterranean to the west. Jesus had often spoken in parables, and nothing seemed strange to his three friends when he recounted how the devil had shown him in a flash all the kingdoms of the world and their glory, and had promised: "I will give you all their authority and splendor, for it has been given to me, and I can give it to anyone I want to. So if you will fall down and worship me, all shall be yours."

Again Jesus had refuted him from Scripture: "It is written, 'Worship the Lord your God and serve him only.'" Jesus refused to win the world as the devil's viceroy, making evil triumph forever.

John listened, enraptured. He had noticed the compassion of Jesus for men and women who suffered assaults of evil, but he never had conceived what Jesus had been through himself.

The third struggle had taken place on the pinnacle of the Temple, at the southeast corner above the royal colonnade, the pinnacle from which a blasphemer sentenced to death was thrown into the ravine. "If," said the devil to Jesus, "you *are* the Son of God, throw yourself down. It is written: 'He will command his angels to guard you carefully. They will lift you up in their hands so that you do not crash upon the stones.'" Jesus, the devil implied, would demonstrate that he was not a blasphemer and the people would flock to him. Above all, this would test his Father's love and care.

Jesus killed the temptation by yet another quotation, again from the Book of Deuteronomy: "Do not put the Lord your God to the test." Jesus had no need to test his Father's love: he was conscious of him always and clung to him.

Satan fled the field—for a time, said Jesus. Satan would return when the time was ripe, a prospect which dismayed the disciples listening on Hermon. But they believed their Master to be more powerful than all the powers of hell and took comfort too from his disclosure that he knew what it was to be tempted.

Evening was nearly on them. Jesus led them higher, almost to one of the summits, more than 11,000 feet above the Jordan. They sat on a broad ledge a little below an ancient ruined temple of Baal, where they were out of the breeze. The sun sinking into the Mediterranean bathed them in its glow; then darkness fell suddenly and the stars and a quarter moon appeared; in stillness and peace, heaven and earth seemed at one.

Jesus withdrew a few paces, lifted his face, and began to pray, sometimes silently, sometimes aloud. An hour passed as if in moments, and John wrapped himself closer in his cloak, determined to stay with Jesus in mind and heart all night if he wished, and James and Peter felt the same. But the climb up Hermon had been long. They were tired and had not eaten, and despite themselves they dozed, then fell asleep.

John was awakened by light. When he looked up, it was not yet dawn; the light came from Jesus as he prayed. John shaded his eyes, almost in terror, for Jesus' face shone like the sun, and his clothes were brilliant, dazzling white, like lightning. None of the three could find adequate words to describe the experience afterward: "We saw his glory." / "We were eyewitnesses of his majesty."

To their astonishment, Jesus was not alone. High on that mountain as the disciples became fully awake, they saw two resplendent figures speaking with Jesus. John listened as they talked; and he knew, without doubt, that the barrier between time and eternity had torn away, and that one was Moses, the long-dead lawgiver, and the other, Elijah, the long-dead prophet: John knew by the words they spoke, for he had never seen their portraits or sculpture, since images were forbidden to Jews.

The two patriarchs plainly regarded Jesus as their superior, yet he seemed to be drawing strength from them. They were talking about the way Jesus would depart from the earth. John, James, and Peter heard and understood the words but could no more accept the theme than they had accepted it from Jesus himself: that while yet young, Jesus would be disgraced and killed at Jerusalem like a common criminal, whereas Moses and Elijah had each gone to heaven gloriously, after a long life's work.

Suddenly Peter interrupted, blurting, "Lord! Let us make three shelters—one for you, one for Moses, one for Elijah!" He said it without thought. He was neither trying to preserve the moment nor reducing Jesus to the level of the patriarchs; it was Peter at his most impulsive.

Even as he spoke, they saw a cloud coming up fast, not the mountain mist before dawn but a cloud so intensely bright that the three disciples fell on their faces in terror. Instinctively, they recognized the cloud of glory which, at special times of divine revelation in the history of the people of Israel had veiled God's holiness from sinful man.

A voice irresistibly penetrated their consciousness: "This is My beloved Son, whom I have chosen; hear him."

John did not dare look up. He lay drained of strength and pride. . . .

John felt a touch on the shoulder. In familiar, comforting tones Jesus said: "Get up. Don't be afraid."

Dawn had broken. Jesus was alone. He now looked as they had always known him.

Thirteen
ON THE ROAD

Coming down the mountain, the three disciples—John, James, and Peter—did not share their thoughts, but John believed what Peter expressed, long afterward, that in their presence Jesus had received honor from God the Father by the voice and the glory. They had a story to tell that they believed would make every man worship their friend.

When they paused for a brief rest, Jesus ordered them not to give the slightest hint of what they had seen and heard, "until the Son of man has risen from the dead." They puzzled over his meaning yet obeyed his instructions, and during the next months suppressed the memory so effectively that sometimes they behaved as if they had never been present at his Transfiguration.

They continued their descent and emerged from the cedar forest. Below them, at the place where they had left the nine others, they noticed a crowd. When they were nearly down and plainly visible, a man of about thirty-five broke away and ran uphill toward Jesus and threw himself on his knees, his face a picture of agitation.

The man cried: "Teacher, I brought you my son. He suddenly screams and goes into a fit. He is deprived of speech and hearing. He is my only child, and the demon that has got into him is destroying him. I brought him to your disciples and they could not heal him."

Jesus sighed. "What an unbelieving and perverse generation!" he exclaimed. "How long shall I stay among you and put up with you? Bring the boy to me."

The boy walked normally until he reached Jesus, then fell to the ground and rolled about, foaming at the mouth.

Jesus asked how long he had been afflicted. "From childhood," the father replied. Then he described how the boy had frequently nearly burned to death or drowned. "But if you can, take pity on us and help us!" he added.

" 'If you can?' " echoed Jesus. "Everything is possible to those who believe!"

The father cried, "I believe! Help my unbelief."

The onlookers were now running to the place where the boy lay having a fit.

Jesus spoke sternly to the unclean spirit in the boy: "Get out, I command you, and never enter him again."

The boy shrieked and went into a convulsion, then lay inert. The onlookers began to murmur that he was dead. After a few moments Jesus bent down and lifted him tenderly to his feet. The boy opened his eyes, looked around, and smiled. Jesus handed him back, healed and normal, to the father. The people were astonished.

Jesus immediately led the Twelve away. "Why couldn't we do it?" complained the nine. Jesus replied that such a case could be healed only by fasting and prayer. He did not pursue the subject but began to emphasize once again that he was going to be betrayed into the hands of men, to be killed, "and rise again after three days." As they walked back to Galilee by the quiet bypaths which he chose, he taught them on this theme, but they could not grasp his meaning and were afraid to ask questions.

They seemed almost out of sympathy. Jesus was quiet and serious as if walking toward suffering, but the Twelve were bursting with self-importance derived from certainty now that he was the Son of God and they his chosen helpers. John and Peter kept their promise not to tell of their recent experience, but could not disguise their conviction that they would be vice-regents when he ascended the throne. An argument even developed as to who would be the greatest; fortunately, Jesus was walking a little way ahead and appeared not to notice.

They reached Capernaum and entered Peter's house to be welcomed by wives and families. Suddenly Jesus asked, "What were you arguing about on the road?" The disciples looked sheepish. Jesus sat down and made the Twelve gather round. "If anyone wants to be first," he said, "he must be the very last, and the servant of all."

Then he called one of the small children—perhaps Peter's youngest—and had him stand at his knees. Jesus put his arms round him and gently drove the lesson home.

"Whoever," he said, "welcomes this little child in my name welcomes me, and whoever welcomes me welcomes the one who sent me. For he who is least among you all—he is the greatest."

John tried to cover their shame by stressing their zeal. "Master," he said proudly, "we saw a man driving out demons in your name, and we stopped him, because he was not one of us."

John had merely floundered deeper. Jesus rebuked him again: "Do not stop him, for whoever is not against us is for us."

Soon afterward Jesus set out for Jerusalem with a determination which impressed all his friends that he was going toward the climax of his life. He turned away from the Sea of Galilee as if he would never see it again, and led the Twelve, with the large company of men and women who wished to accompany him, into the Galilean hills toward the direct route through Samaria. Theirs was a big caravan, all on foot.

Each evening, before they reached a village where they might camp or stay in homes, Jesus sent messengers ahead to arrange hospitality. At one village on the border, they came back rebuffed: it was peopled by Samaritans who refused pilgrims bound for Jerusalem.

John and James were standing with Jesus when the messengers reported. John was furious that his Master should be insulted. He and James, still puffed by their experience on Mount Hermon, wanted to vindicate him. "Shall we call down fire from heaven to destroy them?" he demanded, silently recalling how Elijah had saved himself when an evil king dispatched soldiers to arrest him.

Jesus turned and rebuked the brothers. His look pricked their pride and disarmed their violence yet assured them that he understood their love. He led them all to another village.

He seemed in no hurry to reach Jerusalem. The journey became a medley of memories as John looked back: He remembered the day, for instance, when they were nearing a village on the Samaritan border, and John heard men calling out, from a distance, in unison, "Jesus, Master! Have mercy on us."

Jesus had stopped. John had seen a group of ten unkempt outcasts, whose rags and long hair, and reluctance to come nearer, betrayed them as lepers.

Jesus called back, his voice strong and clear: "Go and show yourselves to the priests!" They ran off toward their own village while Jesus walked on. Some time later John heard the sound of a man shouting praises to God in an excited voice, and one of these long-haired outcasts pushed his way through the crowd, flung himself at Jesus' feet, and poured out his thanks. The ten men had been on their way to the priests, he said, when they became aware that they were healed. He himself had at once turned back.

Jesus noticed that this man was a Samaritan, and looking around he said: "Where are the other men whom I healed?

Has none of them returned to give God praise except this foreigner? Then he looked down at the grateful man kneeling at his feet. "Stand up and go; your faith has made you well."

In contrast, on another day a glib fellow ambled up to Jesus as he and his disciples walked along. The man announced dramatically, "I will follow you wherever you go!" Jesus was not impressed. "Foxes have holes and birds have nests," he replied, "but the Son of man has nowhere to lay his head." Nothing more was heard of the man.

Yet another day Jesus had risen early and gone a little way into the fields. John and the closest disciples had followed, partly to protect him but mainly to share the beauty and peace which they knew would linger as he prayed. The simple intimacy of his prayers highlighted their feeble struggles to reach God; when Jesus ended, one of them recalled how John the Baptist had given lessons in prayer to his disciples, and the disciple said to Jesus, "Lord, teach us to pray."

Jesus took the several disciples back to the whole company, then met the request. He told them to pray in these words:

> Our Father in heaven, hallowed be your name. Your kingdom come; your will be done, on earth as it is in heaven. Give us this day our daily bread. Forgive us our trespasses, as we forgive them that trespass against us. Lead us not into temptation but deliver us from evil.

Then the disciples repeated the teaching phrase by phrase after Jesus as they sat round him on the roadside. Posterity would call this—in reality the disciples' prayer—the Lord's Prayer—the single most quoted passage of all Jesus' sayings—words which, as the Christian faith spread across the world, would be prayed every day, year after year through all the centuries to come.

Jesus taught his disciples the phrases, but he stressed that God really wanted to know their detailed needs. With vivid stories he urged them to come boldly to their Heavenly Father. "Ask and it will be given you; seek and you will find; knock and the door will be opened to you. You fathers, if your son asks for bread, will you give him a stone? Or for a fish, will you give him a snake? . . . If you, who are evil, know how to give good gifts to your children, how much more will your Father in heaven give the Holy Spirit to those who ask him!"

One day he found in his audience many tax collectors who had grown rich, like Matthew before his call, by legalized extortion on behalf of the occupying power. Jesus showed at once that he did not ignore them because they were neither poor nor helpless; he welcomed them and accepted their hospitality. At this, the local Pharisees and doctors of the Law began to mutter. Jesus therefore addressed these first, putting the issue in the form of a parable.

"Suppose one of you," he said, "owns a hundred sheep and one gets lost. Does he not leave the ninety-nine in the open pasture and go after the one lost sheep until he finds it? And then he lays it on his shoulder and comes home rejoicing. He calls his friends and neighbors together: 'Rejoice with me. I have found the sheep which was lost.'"

He added a similar parable of a woman who lost a silver coin and swept until she found it and then called in the neighbors to celebrate.

After each story, Jesus drove home the point: "I tell you, there is more joy in heaven over one sinner who repents than over ninety-nine righteous persons who do not need to repent."

Then Jesus turned back to the taxgatherers and began the immortal story of the Prodigal Son, the young man who asked his father for his share of the inheritance and went to a far country and wasted his substance with riotous living. After he had spent all, a famine came and he was reduced to feeding pigs. Jesus continued:

"And when the younger son came to himself he said,

'How many hired servants of my father's have bread enough and to spare, and I perish with hunger! I will arise and go to my father, and will say to him, "Father, I have sinned against heaven and before you, and am no more worthy to be called your son; make me as one of your hired servants."'

"And he arose and came to his father. But when he was yet a great way off, his father saw him, and had compassion on him, and ran, and fell on his neck, and kissed him.

"And the son said unto him, 'Father, I have sinned against heaven and in your sight, and am no more worthy to be called your son.'

"But the father commanded his servants, 'Bring forth the best robe and put it on him; and put a ring on his hand and shoes on his feet; and bring hither the fatted calf and kill it; and let us eat and celebrate with a feast! For this my son was dead and is alive again; he was lost and is found!' And they began to prepare for the celebration."

Jesus rounded off the story telling of the surly elder brother, cross because the prodigal had been so warmly received, refusing to join the music and dancing to celebrate. The elder brother's character fitted the Pharisees and doctors of the Law who were listening, amazed that Jesus should speak of compassion rather than of wrath, of repentance, restoration, and joy.

This and other stories made the hours fly by and drew such crowds that people trod upon one another. Jesus balanced the parables by straight teaching, addressed primarily to his disciples. He condemned hypocrisy and did not hesitate to rebuke powerful religious leaders; he warned of coming judgment; he provided clear lessons for life in its every aspect in a harsh world; and he pictured a future when sin and crime and greed would have disappeared from the earth.

To John, this seemed only a dream, leaving intolerable longing, but the words were spoken by Jesus, whom he knew to be no empty dreamer but a man of action and purpose. John could not conceive of how all of this would come about, and neither did he understand Jesus' talk of being killed and coming alive again after three days. Once, in deep emotion, Jesus burst out with strange words: "I have come to bring fire on the earth, and how I wish it were already kindled! But I have a baptism to undergo, and how distressed I am until it is completed! Do you think I came to bring peace on earth? No, I tell you, but rather I came to bring division."

Neither John, nor other disciples, nor the people knew what Jesus meant. They sensed only that his face was set toward Jerusalem.

At last the band of travelers approached the final ascent from Jericho, a wild road, infested with brigands. Jesus made it the setting for his parable of the Good Samaritan later when a crowd gathered about him.

He told it because a lawyer put a test question to him: "What must I do to inherit eternal life?"

Jesus turned the question. He asked the lawyer what he read in the Law of Moses. The people listened intently as the lawyer recited part of the great declaration heard during every synagogue service: "Love the Lord your God with all your heart, and with all your soul, and with all your strength, and with all your mind." To regain the initiative, the lawyer added, from a different book of Moses, "*And* your neighbor as yourself."

Jesus replied, "You have answered correctly. Do this and you will live." The people tittered, for the lawyer had opened himself to receive a glimpse of the obvious.

He would not concede defeat. "And who is my neighbor?" he asked sneering.

Instead of embarking on a debate of the kind relished by lawyers and scribes, Jesus began a story. He told of a man who went down from Jerusalem to Jericho and fell into the hands of robbers. They stripped him, beat him, and went away leaving him half dead by the roadside. Several travelers came on the scene: First, a priest, hurried by on the other side

111

(lest he be defiled by touching what might be a corpse). Then came a Levite, one of the Temple singers and servants; he also thought it wiser to pass by on the other side.

The third traveler, Jesus said, was a Samaritan. The audience despised Samaritans and would expect no good of him. But, Jesus continued, the Samaritan "came where the man was; and when he saw him, he took pity on him. He went to him and bandaged his wounds, pouring on oil and wine." He put him on his own donkey and carried him to the nearest inn and took care of him, and on leaving next day the Samaritan paid the innkeeper to keep the victim until he had recovered.

"Which of these three," asked Jesus, reversing the lawyer's question, "do you think was a neighbor to the man who fell among thieves?"

"The one who had mercy on him," admitted the lawyer.

"Then go and do likewise," said Jesus.

The lawyer said no more.

Fourteen
A MAN
BORN BLIND

At the head of the road, hidden from Jerusalem by the flank of the Mount of Olives, lay the village of Bethany. When Jesus and his disciples stopped to rest after their climb, the Master was invited by one of the principal residents, a woman named Martha, to be her guest. He no longer had a large crowd at his heels because many of the Galileans had hurried ahead to the city for the start of the Feast of Tabernacles, the national thanksgiving for the harvests, held annually before the autumn rains.

Led by Martha and her sister, Mary, Jesus walked to their substantial home, with the Twelve following a little behind. Like all Jewish householders in the Jerusalem district who had the space, Martha and Mary had set up a tabernacle or booth of palm fronds adjacent to their home for the week of the festival, according to ancient custom. The booth opened to the garden. Martha showed Jesus to a couch in the booth and hurried off to supervise the preparation of the meal. Mary was about to follow when she noticed the Twelve gather round as if expecting Jesus to continue his teaching. She waited, and he began. Mary came close and the others made way for her, and she sat on the ground at his feet listening intently. She lost all sense of time. Suddenly Martha bustled out of the house and into the booth, interrupting Jesus. "Lord, don't you care that my sister has left me to do the work by myself? Tell her to help me!"

Jesus looked up at Martha, her brow knotted and her face flushed from her efforts, her sleeves were rolled up to the elbows. Then he looked down at Mary, absorbed and at peace. He turned back to Martha. His smile and the way he spoke took the sting out of his rebuke: "Martha, Martha, you are fretting and fussing about so many things, but one thing is needed. Mary has chosen the best part, and it shall not be taken away from her."

Martha smiled at Jesus, smiled at Mary, and went back inside the house without bustle. Evidently, she finished preparations less elaborately, for she soon brought out the meal to the booth, all grumbles forgotten. The sisters both served happily. Their brother, Lazarus, had arrived from Jerusalem, and from his first meeting with Jesus a warm friendship began.

Jesus did not remain overnight. He preferred to conform to the custom of pilgrims to the festival, from all over Palestine and countries far and near, and stay in one of the numerous temporary booths of palm fronds on the Mount of Olives. Next day he did not go into the city. As he had said in Galilee when his unbelieving half brothers taunted him to attend the feast in a flourish of self-advertisement, his time had not yet come.

John went to find out what people were saying. As he passed through the great walls and up into the magnificence of the Temple courts, he saw the smoke of sacrifices ascending from the altar. At festival time, and all through the year on a lesser scale, the priests killed bullocks, goats, or lambs offered by worshipers. Man's sins could be purged only by the shedding of blood; therefore, the innocent must die that the sinner might live.

By conversation with priests and nobles known to his

family, John learned that the unofficial decision to destroy Jesus, taken after he had healed the paralyzed man at the Pool of Bethesda, had not been rescinded; the rulers were watching out for him, since all males were supposed to appear at this festival. Among the crowds John heard plenty of gossip. Some said Jesus was a good man, others that he led the people astray, but no one dared refer to him publicly lest they be accused of being his disciples.

John reported his findings to Jesus, who still did not leave the Mount of Olives. On the fourth day of the festival week, he came into the city quietly and went to the Temple and sat down to teach under one of the porticoes of the great Court of the Gentiles. The court was noisy with merchants buying and selling and the bleating of sheep to be bought for sacrifice, but it was the traditional place for teachers who sought an audience.

Jesus soon had people gathered about him. Those who never had heard him were amazed. It was plain to most that he had not sat under any famous rabbi, for each school had its mannerisms, yet he displayed a learning which outclassed them by its simplicity, depth, and authority. Some among the crowd who knew that the Pharisees wanted to kill him were astonished that Jesus could speak freely. "Have they concluded that he is the Messiah?" they asked. Others scoffed at the idea because they knew that he came from Galilee, whereas, they said, the origin of the Messiah, or Christ, would be a mystery.

As he taught, Jesus made claims which aroused wrath. For instance, he said: "I am not here of my own accord, but he who sent me is true. You do not know him, but I know him because I come from him and he sent me." John saw several Pharisees lurch forward as if to seize him, only to stop as if some invisible power prevented them.

On the last day of the festival, the ceremonies climaxed with joyful processions of worshipers waving branches. Trumpets sounded. Priests poured out wine and water from golden ewers to symbolize prayer for rain. The people sang psalms of praise.

As the singing died away, Jesus cried out in a voice which carried right across the crowd and up to the curtained Holy of Holies: "If any man is thirsty, let him come to me and drink. Anyone who believes in me, rivers of living water shall flow from within him as the Scripture says."

John did not fully understand at that moment, nor for another seven months, but he realized that Jesus had stated unashamedly that he was the source of true spiritual life. His face and tones showed that he longed to draw all Jerusalem, and indeed the world, to himself.

Reaction was mixed, but Temple guards who were sent to arrest him stood open-mouthed in admiration, until John saw them clank away. He heard afterward that they had excused their disobedience by saying, "No one ever spoke like this man."

In the days after the Feast of Tabernacles, Jesus did not depart for the countryside with most of the pilgrims. His friendship with Lazarus, Martha, and Mary gave him a base of warm hospitality from which to face hostility.

The conflict between Jesus and the authorities grew more intense as he made claims which they could not ignore. They must accept them and acknowledge him, or suppress him by argument or force. No other prophet had made such claims for himself. One confrontation especially impressed itself on John. Jesus had gone again to the Temple. He led them to the Court of the Women, and took his seat under a portico near the trumpet-shaped offering chests, where a steady stream of worshipers came to drop in their Temple contributions and stay to listen to him. Pharisees were already there, shadowing him.

"I am the Light of the world," he taught. "Anybody who follows me will never walk in darkness but will have the light of life."

The Pharisees started to argue, but the more they tried to

refute or insult him the more firmly he held his ground. He assured his hearers that when they had killed him, "you will know that I am what I am. I do nothing on my own authority; I speak what the Father taught me. He who sent me is present with me. He has not left me alone, *because I always do what pleases him.*"

Jesus said it with such simplicity and authority, not as a boast but as a fact, that many believed in him. However, they would not go the whole way; when he told them that if they followed his teaching, "you will know the truth, and the truth will set you free," they retorted that as Abraham's descendants they had never been slaves. The religious leaders started to argue again. Jesus did not retreat. They were children of the father of lies, he said, and therefore did not believe when Jesus told the truth. He made an even stronger statement: "Which of you can prove me guilty of sin?"

They hurled insults at him: he was a Samaritan and demon possessed.

"I am not demon possessed," replied Jesus calmly. A little later he made the solemn declaration: "If a man keeps my word, he will never see death."

The leaders erupted with scorn. "Now we know you are demon possessed! Abraham died, the prophets died, and yet you say this! Are you greater than our father Abraham? Who do you think you are?"

Jesus parried the question. If he exalted himself it meant nothing; he replied, "My Father, whom you claim as your God, is the one who glorifies me. You do not know him. I do. If I denied it I would be a liar—like you. But I know him. I keep his word. Your father Abraham rejoiced to see my day. He saw it and was glad."

"What!" they said. "You are not yet fifty years old and *you have seen Abraham?*"

"In very truth," replied Jesus, "before Abraham was born, *I am*"—the sacred phrase which, in the Scriptures, God alone used. He had claimed to be God! They could bear no more. They rushed toward a pile of building stones to stone the blasphemer to death without trial.

Jesus slipped away out of the Temple.

A day or two later, a Sabbath, he was in the city with John, Peter, and a few of the others when they saw a blind beggar sitting by the streetside, well placed for the charitable on their way to the Temple. He was a man of about thirty, in rags, who called out, "Born blind, born blind."

One of the disciples voiced the traditional view of affliction as punishment, and with no regard for the man's self-respect, asked Jesus unfeelingly whom he thought had sinned, the man or his parents. Jesus replied that neither had sinned; the beggar was born blind so that a work of God could be displayed. The man lifted his head inquiringly as he heard Jesus say: "We must do God's work while it is day. Night is coming, when no one can work. While I am in the world, I am the Light of the world."

Jesus spat on the dusty ground, kneaded some mud with his saliva, and plastered the man's eyes. Two of these actions broke Sabbath prohibitions. He ordered, "Go and wash in the Pool of Siloam." Without hesitation the man seized his stick, left his begging bowl, and tapped away down the street for the long walk to the pool at the lower end of the city.

Next day the story was all over Jerusalem. The beggar had gone home that Sabbath from the Pool of Siloam, his sight restored, and his neighbors were astounded that he could see as well as they. They were even more astonished when they heard his story. They had him interrogated by Pharisees.

These met their match. The once-blind man surmised that they were less interested in the miracle than in obtaining the evidence against Jesus for breaking the Sabbath, and he was spirited, even saucy in his replies. After examining his parents, who were afraid to say much, they adjured the beggar to tell the truth, for "we know this man is a sinner."

The beggar refused to be browbeaten. "Whether he is a

sinner or not, I don't know. What I do know is: I was once blind but now I see!"

They started to question him again on the facts of his cure. He retorted, "I have told you once and you did not listen. Why do you want to hear it again? Do you want to become his disciples too?"

The Pharisees reviled him. He then had the audacity to lecture them, concluding, "If this man were not from God, he could do nothing."

The Pharisees suddenly became furious. "You were altogether born in sin," they said, and threw him out, so that he would not be allowed to attend synagogue. He risked formal excommunication, with all the social and material loss which would follow.

Jesus heard what had happened. He took John and others to find him; beggars who had been with the man could tell them where to look. When they met, Jesus asked him, "Do you believe in the Son of man?"

The beggar had never set eyes on Jesus, but with instinctive respect he replied, "Who is he, Sir, that I might believe?"

"You have seen him. He is talking with you now!"

"Lord," replied the man, falling at Jesus' feet, "I believe!"

The cure of the man born blind impressed Jerusalem deeply, but the miracle strengthened the resolve of the Jewish authorities to rid themselves of Jesus.

He spoke openly of his death: "I am the Good Shepherd," he said, in the course of a sermon which would remain among his greatest. "The Good Shepherd gives his life for the sheep." Later in the sermon he uttered an even stronger reference, though neither John nor any of the Twelve could fully understand or accept it. He had told his audience that he had sheep of other folds to bring into his flock. "They too must hear my voice, and there will be one flock and one shepherd. My Father loves me," he went on, "because I lay down my life, to take it up again. No one takes my life from me. I lay it down of my own accord. I have power to lay it down and power to take it again. I have received this command from my Father."

Some of his hearers reckoned him mad and not worth hearing. Others remembered the man born blind.

At last, in midwinter, when all Jerusalem was bright with lights to celebrate the recovery of the Temple from pagan defilement long ago, the Jewish elders demanded, "Tell us plainly. Are you the Christ?"

"I did tell you, but you do not believe," because they were not his sheep. "My sheep hear my voice and I give them eternal life. They shall never perish. No one can pluck them out of my hand." His questioners listened with mounting disbelief and fury, all the fiercer because Jesus spoke without rhetoric, as a man of integrity who cannot swerve from truth.

When he said, "I and my Father are one," they contained their anger no longer. They picked up stones to fling at him.

He stood still. "For which miracle are you stoning me?"

"Not for a miracle," they cried, "but for blasphemy! Because you, a man, make yourself out to be God!"

Fifteen
LAZARUS

With great sadness Jesus left the city and took his disciples down the steep road to Jericho and across the Jordan into Perea, which like Galilee was ruled by Herod.

Many came out from Jericho and the villages on the Jordan. They remembered vividly the Baptist's preaching in that very place and agreed that all he had said about Jesus was true. Others came down from Jerusalem. As the days passed, John saw more and more listeners believe in Jesus and range themselves at his side. John also kept open his contacts with Jerusalem, and men in high quarters warned that the chief priests remained implacably his foes, inflamed by reports coming up from Jordan. Jesus must avoid Judea.

Toward the end of winter a man pushed through the crowd after hurrying down the mountain road. He carried an urgent message from Martha and Mary about Lazarus. "Lord, your great friend is sick." Jesus at once shared this cry for help, already many hours old because of its journey. John was by now used to the impression that Jesus always knew more than anyone told him, but when he said, "This sickness will not end in death. It is going to glorify God by glorifying his son," none of the disciples could fathom Jesus' meaning.

He made no move. Since Jesus loved Mary, Martha, and Lazarus, John wondered whether Lazarus had recovered. Other disciples suggested that Jesus had healed from a distance, without touch, as he had done before.

Jesus spent much time by himself in prayer. Two days passed. Then he announced that they would go back to Judea.

"The Jews tried to stone you!" the Twelve objected. "Must you go back already?"

Jesus replied in picture language that they could walk safely because it was still daylight; night was coming but not yet. He said, "Our friend Lazarus has fallen asleep. I go to wake him."

When they supposed he meant natural sleep, Jesus dropped his picture language. "Lazarus is dead! And I am glad I was not there, for your sakes, because this is going to strengthen your faith. Come on, we must start."

"Let's go too," said Thomas gloomily, "so that we may die with him."

A day afterward, having climbed the road without haste, Jesus and his nervous disciples reached the edge of Bethany. They discovered at once that Lazarus had died four days earlier, before the messenger could reach them, and had been laid in his tomb by sunset.

Jesus sat down on a low wall. He would not enter Bethany; instead, he sent a message to the sisters by John, who heard the customary wailing as he reached their house. The three days of violent grief which began a month of mourning were over, but he saw furniture up-ended, hired mourners on the floor making loud lamentations, and neighbors and friends still coming in to offer condolences and then to join the wailing. Many prominent Jews had made the short journey from Jerusalem.

Martha was preparing food. She left at once, without telling Mary, who was inside among the mourners, and John ran with her. On reaching Jesus, she did not waste a moment in greeting, or in thanks for his coming, but unburdened her misery. "Lord, if only you had been here, my brother would not have died." The thought had haunted her and Mary the past four days. "But," she went on, "I know that even now, God will give you whatever you ask."

Jesus said to her, "Your brother will rise again."

She misunderstood. "Yes, in the resurrection at the last day. I know that."

He looked at her intently. He took her wrist, as if to prepare her for something that would test her faith to the uttermost. "Martha," he said, "*I* am the Resurrection, and the life. Anyone who believes in me will live even though he dies."

John could see this tremendous claim sink into Martha's mind: words which would be quoted all over the world in centuries to come, wherever a Christian's corpse awaited burial, heard first on the edge of Bethany under the Mount of Olives on a late winter's day. "The Resurrection is—*me*. Life is—*me*."

Jesus held Martha's gaze as he continued. "Anyone who lives believing in me will never die. Do you believe this?"

"Yes, Lord. I believe." And John heard her say softly what Peter had blurted out: "You are the Christ, the Son of God, who was promised to come into the world."

"Fetch Mary," said Jesus.

Without another word, dropping all protest at his delay, all her implied demand for action, she obeyed. John could not grasp any more than Martha what Jesus intended, but a little later he saw Mary hurrying toward them, her face wet with tears. Martha was beside her, and behind came a gaggle of mourners who had supposed that Mary intended to wail at the tomb.

Mary fell at Jesus' feet. "If only," she said through her tears, "you had been here, Lord, my brother would not have died."

The tears fell hot on his feet. The mourners held back,

wailing with simulated grief or weeping silently, heartbroken with the sisters.

John looked at Jesus and saw that he was moved to the depths. His body shook. A great groan came from far within, of sympathy beyond words and hatred of death and all that caused death.

"Where have you laid him?" Jesus asked.

"Come and see, Lord," replied the sisters, and led him toward the garden on the side of the hill. As they walked, Jesus wept. The sisters clung to him, drawing strength from his tears.

The mourners and the disciples followed. John heard a mourner murmur, "See how much he loved him." Others recalled the blind man in Jerusalem and wondered why Jesus could not have saved Lazarus.

They reached the garden. A great stone lay across the entrance to a cave set in the hillside. Again, Jesus groaned, his whole body moving, as if tensing for great spiritual and physical exertion.

"Take away the stone!"

"But he stinks, Lord!" cried Martha. "He has been there four days!" If Jesus wanted to enter for a last look, the stench of decay would be stronger now than the spices, for they did not embalm like the ancient Egyptians. She could think of no other reason for the command. Lazarus was beyond help; the Jews believed that the spirit hovered near the body for three days and then departed. Lazarus was dead indeed.

Jesus said, "Did I not tell you that if you believed, you would see the glory of God?"

Younger mourners heaved at the stone and shifted it. Jesus wanted it moved away, as if to emphasize that it would not be needed again. The cave ran into the rock face deep and high; at the burial the bearers had not needed to stoop.

Jesus lifted his eyes upward. "Father," he said. A stillness fell upon the little crowd; wails and weeping stopped. "Father, thank you. Thank you that you have heard me. I know you always hear me, but I am giving my thanks to help the people standing here, that from now on they may believe that you sent me."

Then with a loud confident shout, Jesus called, "Lazarus! Outside! *Come! Outside!*"

He waited. The silence could be felt. Then, from within the cave came the sound of a stirring. Tension gripped the watchers; John felt a cold fear crawling down his back. The sound grew louder, and fear disappeared with a mounting sense that God the Creator was greater than death, that with Jesus present anything was possible.

Not to their terror but to their joy they saw a figure shuffle out of the darkness. He came slowly into the sunshine, wrapped in graveclothes of unbleached linen, his head tied with the usual napkin. Yet there was a vigor and strength inside the bandages, a movement of muscle and limb which made John amazed that trappings of death should surround a Lazarus so obviously alive.

Disciples, sisters, mourners stood transfixed. Lazarus waited; for all his strength and health, he could not free his arms to release himself.

The voice of Jesus broke the tension. "Unbind him," he said, "and let him go home."

Then John knew that he did not dream, as Lazarus, Martha, and Mary fell joyfully into each other's arms.

Sixteen
THE LAST
APPROACH

Those whose sorrow had turned joy at Lazarus' coming back to life returned to Bethany like their ancestors returning from exile: "When the Lord turned again the captivity of Zion, then were we like unto them that dream. Then was our mouth filled with laughter and our tongue with singing. The Lord hath done great things for us, whereof we are glad."

As the sisters served the feast which Martha had prepared for a wake, Lazarus' vitality showed the strength of the new life flowing through his veins; no one doubted that Jesus, invited to the seat of honor, had the power to raise the dead. Prominent Jews rose in their places to acknowledge that he was who he claimed to be; wherever he went they would follow.

John, however, noticed that several distinguished citizens avoided the feast and saddled their donkeys. As he learned later, they rode as fast as the ascent would allow, then down into the Kidron ravine and up to the city, and did not dismount until they reached the palace of the high priest. Caiaphas was aghast at their eyewitness account. He summoned all Sanhedrin members at hand, including Nicodemus, a secret disciple of Jesus, who described it all to John afterward.

The deliberations were urgent and private, since formal meetings in the Hall of Polished Stones could convene only on certain days of the week. Jesus was a threat to their leadership. Opening the eyes of a man born blind was dangerous enough, but raising the dead would lead to a surge of popular support. Nicodemus heard his fellow members assess Jesus' motives and likely actions by their own. They convinced themselves that he would grasp at material power through a popular uprising against the occupying power, and as political realists they knew that this would fail. The furious Romans would destroy the Temple, remove the last vestiges of self-government, and crucify thousands of Jews.

The Sanhedrin debated what to do. Argument went round and round. Suddenly they heard the president's gavel.

Caiaphas spoke sharply and decisively. "You know nothing at all! It is much better that *one man should die* for the people instead of the whole nation perishing." He had a sound precedent in the case of a rebel against King David named Sheba. The royal troops were about to assault the town which sheltered him, and put its people to the sword, when the elders threw Sheba's head over the wall; the king's general lifted the siege and spared their lives. The Sanhedrin took Caiaphas' point. They began to discuss how to kill Jesus.

Nicodemus immediately sent a secret warning to Bethany. Jesus withdrew, first to an isolated village in the wild, rolling countryside some fifteen miles northeast of Jerusalem, alone with his disciples; then he crossed the Jordan to Herod's lands where the Sanhedrin's writ did not reach so effectively.

He resumed public teaching in the first days of spring, but his heart was in Jerusalem. When some Pharisees interrupted to say that Herod was out to kill him, Jesus refused to flee. He sent a message to "that fox" saying he would continue to work, "for surely no prophet can die outside Jerusalem." In tones of infinite sadness, he exclaimed: "O Jerusalem, Jerusalem, killing the prophets and stoning those who are sent to you! How often I have longed to gather your children together as a hen gathers her chicks under her wings, but you would not let me! Your house is forsaken. You will not see me again until you say, 'Blessed is he who comes in the name of the Lord.'"

Even as Jesus spoke, the scene was being set. Jews and proselytes were on their way by ship and caravan to reach Jerusalem for Passover. They came from Parthia and the Gulf and even a few from India; from Arabia and Ethiopia, from Spain and the far north African coasts; from Greece and Armenia; groups from all points of the compass took advantage of Roman peace and safe seas to converge on the Holy City. As the feast drew near, larger crowds from Galilee and every part of Palestine and Syria traveled the roads, until the 25,000 inhabitants of the city and suburbs were joined by at least 100,000 pilgrims. Whatever might happen to Jesus in Jerusalem would be reported throughout Palestine and in many parts of the world.

His relatives and friends from Galilee had started on the pilgrim route. At a camping place on the Great Road on the plateau beyond the Jordan, Jesus met his mother, and John and James met theirs. Mary and Salome brought other women who had looked after Jesus and his disciples during their earlier travels, including Joanna the wife of Chuza, Herod's steward, and Mary from Magdala, named by Christian tradition as the former prostitute who had poured the perfume on Jesus' head and had wiped his feet with her hair.

The Galileans comprised a large caravan of neighbors and strangers, including whole families. Word spread swiftly that Jesus of Nazareth had joined the travelers. Next morning, when they were striking their tents, John saw a young father shyly bring his small boy and ask Jesus to touch him for a blessing that would be a lifelong memory. Jesus put his hand on the child. Then other parents brought their children, including mothers with sleeping babies, until Jesus was the center of a nursery.

John, Peter, and several of the Twelve reacted sharply. Jesus had a long day's march ahead; he would want to teach the disciples as they walked, and all who gathered at the midday stop and the next resting place; he must not be jostled and fatigued by mere children. They began to shoo them away and rebuke the parents.

Jesus was indignant. "Let them come!" he ordered. "Do not hinder them!" He beckoned the children close and spoke to his disciples. "God's kingdom belongs to little ones like these," he said, a revolutionary idea, even to Peter and John who both loved children. "This is what I say to you: Anyone who will not receive the kingdom of God like a little child will never enter it." He took two of the smallest, one in each arm, and blessed them.

The disciples were abashed by the rebuke. But Jesus' indignation seemed honed to an even sharper edge by love for them no less than for the children, and John did not feel humiliated.

By now the caravan leaders had started the march. Families who had thronged round Jesus melted away with songs in their hearts. John brought Jesus his satchel and stick. Usually, Jesus not only had his own things ready but helped slow disciples get theirs; often he would have awakened them all with a cheerful word. This morning, however, the children had absorbed his attention.

Ready to start, Jesus stepped out and was about to get into his stride when a young man appeared; he wore a cloak of finest wool and a tunic of finest linen. His clothes were spotless despite the days on the journey; his fingers glittered with rings. Everything about him suggested new-made wealth and enterprise and authority.

He dropped to his knees and looked up anxiously. "Good Master," he said, "what must I do to obtain eternal life?"

Jesus turned the flattery. "Why do you call me good when no one is good except God alone?"

The young man did not answer.

"You know the Commandments," said Jesus, and ticked off five, all prohibitions: "Do not kill. Do not commit adultery. Do not steal. Do not bear false witness. Do not defraud." Then he added one out of sequence, most suitable for any young man who made money quickly: "Honor your father and mother!"

The rich man, still kneeling, answered that he had kept them all, since a boy. "What do I still miss; what must I do?" he urged.

A bystander who came from the same district murmured to John that the man had already built a synagogue, and thus had been elected a ruler despite his youth. Jesus was gazing at him, aware that he was so eager to do some great thing for his future, yet was blind to where his future lay. Suddenly Jesus bent forward, embraced him, and drew him up from his knees as if to call him to his side as he had called Matthew and Peter and John.

"One thing you miss," said Jesus. "If you want to be perfect, go away and sell everything you have and give to the poor—you will have treasure in heaven—and then *come, follow me.*"

The young man's face fell. He scratched his head. John could guess his thoughts. Gold and lands with their power and prestige and the means to do good as he wished would be out of his hands. Could he bear to strip himself of all he held dear?

The young man walked sadly away.

Jesus watched him, then turned to the disciples. "How hard it is for a rich man to enter the kingdom of God," he said.

John was amazed. Brought up to honor wealth as a sign of God's blessing, he could hardly believe his ears. It had been strange enough to learn that a little child may enter easily, but much more strange that a rich man could scarcely find the way. Jesus spoke again. "How hard it is, my children!" he said, and he used a well-known proverb to make his point. "It is easier for 'a camel to go through the eye of a needle' than for a rich man to enter heaven."

Peter muttered to John, "Who then can be saved?" Jesus directed at them all an intense gaze, until every eye focused upon him. He said, "This is impossible with man, but not with God. Everything is possible to God."

They started on the road again, settling into the steady pace which could be kept up mile after mile, but Peter would not drop the subject. After a while he said, "Look, we have left everything to follow you. What will there be for us?"

John shared Peter's feelings. But a shadow of grief passed over Jesus' face at their absorption in material reward. He stopped. John expected a rebuke. Instead, Jesus made a solemn pronouncement to the Twelve: "When all is made new and the Son of man sits on His throne of glory, you too will sit on twelve thrones, judging the twelve tribes.

"And there is nobody who has left home or brothers, or sisters or parents or children or friends for my sake and for the Good News, who will not receive much, much more in this life—houses, brothers, sisters, mothers and children and lands—and persecutions! And in the age to come, eternal life. But," he added, "many who are first shall be last, and the last first."

He walked on, and the Twelve closed up on him because he began a new story to show what the kingdom is like. As he talked, the spring flowers were showing, and they could see a field or two with the first shoots of barley, but he took their minds to hot days and the grape harvest, and told of a landowner who hired men early in the morning to work all day in his vineyard. They agreed on a denarius, a full day's fair wage. An hour or two later, he returned to the marketplace and hired more men, saying, "I will pay you a fair wage."

As the day wore on and the landowner assessed his grape harvest, he hired others. An hour before dusk, back again, he saw men standing around. Jesus made the scene come alive: "The landowner asked them, 'Why do you stand here idle all day?' They said to him, 'Because no one has hired us.' He said to them, 'You go into the vineyard too.'" Dusk fell— work stopped. The men came for payment. The owner, in an unusual move, told his overseer to pay first the last men to be hired. They received a denarius. The first group therefore expected more, despite having agreed on a denarius; but he paid everybody the same.

The men grumbled loudly. "These men worked only an hour," complained their spokesman, "and you make them equal to us who have worked all day in the heat!"

"Friend," he replied, "I do you no wrong. Did you not agree on a denarius? Take what is yours and go. Cannot I do what I like with my own money? Are you envious because I am generous?"

Jesus summed up his story. "So you see, the last shall be first and the first last."

The disciples walked on in silence for a while, digesting this new approach to the rewards of service. But soon they were talking again, asking questions, listening to more stories. Unlike an official rabbi, whose disciples followed meekly behind, Jesus liked to keep his beside him. When they reached the next camping place, he again allowed all the pilgrims to gather round. That evening no disciple dared shoo away a child.

Next morning they turned west and began the descent to the Jordan crossing and Jericho. Every step brought them closer to Jerusalem.

Jesus walked ahead. John quickened pace, intending to fall in at his side. Then he saw Jesus' face and dropped back, and not one of the Twelve dared obtrude. John became amazed at the intensity of the suffering. In the past months they had all drawn so close to Jesus that his feelings invariably affected them. Even the women and the other disciples in the pilgrim caravan sensed the atmosphere and were afraid.

After a while Jesus stopped and took the Twelve a little aside from the road. He made them sit round as they often sat when he taught. John's heart went out to Jesus; he wanted to share the horror and lighten the load.

But when Jesus spoke, his first words suggested no horror at all, but glory. "We are going to Jerusalem," he began, "and all the prophecies about the Son of man must come true." John knew the prophets; they prophesied glory for the Messiah.

Jesus' next words shattered the vision. "The Son of man is going to be delivered up to the chief priests and scribes. They will condemn him to death. They will hand him to the Gentiles, and *they* will mock him, insult him, spit on him, flog him, kill him." (His phrases sounded like hammer on nails.) "He will be crucified—"

Peter did not interrupt. None of the disciples understood. Jesus was alive, vibrant, young, good. John could not imagine him put to the torture and dying as a criminal; he had escaped murderous attempts and would escape them again, whatever his fears.

"—And on the third day he will rise again." Jesus spoke the words without flourish as a statement of fact, but John, James, Peter, and all of them did not know what he was talking about, despite their vivid memory of Lazarus' tomb.

John closed his mind to thoughts of crucifixion. He dwelt on messianic glory. He recalled Jesus' earlier words about coming into the kingdom. When the march resumed, John drew James aside and they walked together, talking in whispers. Jesus would achieve power in the land soon. They must stake their claim. When the caravan stopped for the midday halt, and fires were being kindled and cooking pots filled, they sought out their mother and outlined their plan. A little later Salome approached Jesus with her sons at her side. She knelt to ask a favor.

Through her lips, in the presence of their ten colleagues, James and John begged Jesus to promise them the seats of authority and privilege immediately next to him, to the right and left of his throne.

"You do not know what you ask!" cried Jesus, addressing James and John. "Can you drink the cup I am going to drink? Be baptized with the baptism I am going to undergo?"

His strange language did not make them pause. They replied confidently, "We can."

"You *will* drink. You *will* be baptized. But it is not for me to grant these places—they belong to those for whom my Father has prepared them."

The other disciples descended on James and John in indignation.

Jesus called them all to himself without raising the voice which had stilled the waves and summoned from the grave: one firm word and the Twelve stood around sheepishly.

He laid down a new attitude to leadership. They were not to be lordly like earthly rulers. "Not so with you; anyone who is ambitious among you must become the servant of all. Whoever wants to be top must be your slave—just as the Son of man did not come to be waited upon but to serve and," he added, "to give his life as a ransom for many."

They walked on together. None of them saw his meaning. They thought he had spoken in a parable again and was leading them to his triumph.

Seventeen
ROYAL ENTRY

Jericho, with its fine houses and Herod's disused winter palace, looked lush with palms and gardens and shade trees. Southward, the Dead Sea glittered in the sunshine; to the west rose the bleak Judean mountains. Jesus and his disciples approached Jericho by the road which skirted ruins of earlier cities. The neighborhood had become a camping place for pilgrims and many joined him. By the time he reached the first houses, he was the focus of a spontaneous welcome, with townsfolk out on the streets to see Jesus of Nazareth passing by.

As the road crossed the stream which flowed into the palace garden, they heard a cry above the hubbub: "Jesus, Son of David, have mercy on me!" Spectators shouted, "Be quiet!" but the voice came again louder, joined soon by another. "Son of David have mercy on us!"

Jesus stopped. "Bring him," he ordered. The crowd fell silent, and John heard someone at the roadside say, "Come on. Cheer up. He calls you."

The crowd parted, and John saw a blind beggar stand up and throw aside his cloak, a gesture of faith indeed, for he might not find it if he should return blind. Another blind beggar rose beside him, and willing hands guided them.

Jesus spoke with that tone of concern which John knew well. "What do you want me to do for you?" John reflected that it was a favorite phrase of his Master's, and never empty.

The beggars did not ask charity or a blessing. "Lord, we want to see," they said.

Jesus replied, "You *shall* see. Your faith has made you well."

He touched their eyes, and John was moved to the depths as he watched the impossible happen again. The two beggars blinked. They staggered a little, then leaped in the air with shouts of praise, which the crowd took up until the whole street echoed with the cry, "Hallelujah!"

The procession started again. The two men kept close to Jesus through Jericho and looked eagerly to left and right, shading their eyes in the sunlight, shouting their delight and their praise.

The triumphal walk was now well into the spacious new city, and the people lining the way stood thick on either side. Trees shaded the street, not in a formal avenue like a Roman highway but planted without design. Jesus passed into the shade of a sycamore-fig, an evergreen with short trunk and broad branches. Unexpectedly, he paused, looked up, and called out in a friendly tone, "Zaccheus! Come down quickly. I must stay at your house today!"

A face peered from the foliage. A stumpy little man scrambled down, his expensive clothes crumpled. He looked surprised, pleased, yet worried. Then he hurried ahead of the procession to make ready.

Townsfolk, on the contrary, looked dismayed. John overheard complaints and disbelief: "He is going to be the guest of a sinner!" John gathered that Zaccheus was taxgatherer for the Jericho district and, thus, in their opinion had insulted his name, which means "righteous." As chief collector of taxes, he held no official rank but had put in the highest bid and recruited subcollectors. The Romans required a heavy sum; the subcollectors wanted their share; his own wealth therefore depended on how much they could extort.

Among subject races of the empire, a rich taxgatherer like Zaccheus was even more of a pest than a tax collector like Matthew and doubly disgusting to Jews because wealth which was ill-gotten defiled all who it touched, except when received as charity. Therefore Zaccheus' company and delicacies were shunned by his neighbors. If he felt lonely, he had only himself to blame.

John knew this, and realized that Jesus had deftly faced the little man, who had climbed the tree to see him go by, with a choice: either to allow his guest to be defiled, or to purify his house by a true act of renunciation.

At length, Jesus, the disciples, and the crowd reached the elegant house on the outskirts of Jericho. John saw Zaccheus at the entrance with his family and household. Zaccheus bowed his welcome.

"Honorable Sir." He addressed Jesus in tones which all could hear. "Here and now I give half of all I possess to the poor." Since a formally expressed intention held almost legal force, no one doubted that he would carry it out, to disgorge his unfair gains and purify his house. He did more. "If I have cheated anybody of anything," he announced, "I will restore him four times the amount."

John noticed that Zaccheus had offered what the Law imposed on a rustler: restore four sheep for each one stolen. Jesus at once took up the allusion and addressed the crowd. "Today salvation has come to this home," he said. "And this man is a son of Abraham as much as you. For the Son of man came to seek and to save what is lost." John instantly recalled the parable. The Good Shepherd had found his lost sheep and brought him back to the fold. The ninety and nine must not shun him.

The Twelve enjoyed their stay. When they began the ascent to Jerusalem next morning, John and Peter shared with the others their pleasure that Jesus had called Zaccheus to be a disciple, because it disproved the strange talk about Jesus being crucified. There was no point in Jesus' calling disciples if he were about to die. Soon they were excitedly telling the Galilean pilgrims that God's kingdom was about to be revealed; Jesus would soon ascend the throne usurped by the Romans.

Jesus heard them. At the midday halt on the steep ascent, he told them a story about a nobleman who went away for a long time in order to receive a kingdom. Before leaving he distributed money to his servants to use on his behalf, and the parable turned on how faithfully and skillfully each discharged his trust before the king returned. Had the disciples ears to hear, this parable pointed them away from their excited expectations.

That evening they reached Bethany, shortly before the Sabbath began, and next day Bethany people joined together to provide a traditionally delightful Sabbath meal at the house of a neighbor known as Simon the Leper. Lazarus, strong and happy and a wonder to all, was an honored guest. Martha busied herself among the women who served. Mary, however, became again the center of an incident. This time it did not upset Martha but the Twelve.

Holding a pint-sized alabaster jar, Mary approached Jesus as he reclined at table. She broke the neck and poured a little on his head, then knelt and poured more over his feet. Fragrance filled the room and the house, stopping all conversation as guests and helpers recognized the scent of pure nard. This strong, delectable perfume came all the way from India, its cost reflecting the length of journey, yet Mary anointed Jesus with every drop in her jar and wiped his feet with her hair.

"What waste!" cried Judas Iscariot, the treasurer of the Twelve. "This cost a whole year's wages for a laborer. It should have been sold and the money given to the poor." The others agreed with Judas, though later, when he disclosed his true colors, they realized that he cared nothing for the poor and had pilfered the money box. They all began to rebuke Mary.

Jesus interrupted them. "Leave her alone. Why are you bothering her? She has done a beautiful thing to me. You will always have the poor and can help them whenever you wish, but you will not always have me. She has done what she could—*she has anointed my body for burial before the time.*"

A cold fear touched John's heart. Only a criminal's corpse could not be perfumed at burial. Foreboding silence closed John's ears to the prophecy which Jesus uttered: "Wherever the Good News is preached throughout the world, they will tell what she has done. She will never be forgotten."

John, however, forgot her soon enough in the exciting incidents which followed next afternoon. Jesus called John and James, and on his precise instructions they went up the hill to Bethphage, the neighboring village on the Mount of Olives. Exactly as Jesus had told them, they found a donkey tethered at a doorway, with a colt which had not been ridden. They began to untie them. Some bystanders demanded to know why, but Jesus had provided what sounded like a password: "The Master wants them and will return them quickly."

Whoever the bystanders were (perhaps Jesus had arranged it at the Sabbath Feast and they were a fellow guest's servants) this sentence satisfied them.

John and James started down the hill leading the donkey, with her colt trotting contentedly behind, until they met Jesus and the rest of the Twelve as they walked slowly up.

Jesus surprised them all by indicating that he would not ride the donkey but the colt. John saw the significance at once. Jesus was about to enter Jerusalem. Pilgrims traditionally made their entrance to the Holy City on foot, but Jesus would ride, thus showing that he did not come as a pilgrim. Formal entrance to the Holy City riding a beast on which "no man had sat" was the prerogative of a king. And when the king came on a donkey, not on horseback, he came in peace. Matthew quickly recalled the prophecy in the Book of Zechariah: "Behold your king comes to you, humble and riding on an ass, on a colt the foal of an ass."

John and James had shed cloaks as they hurried. In a spontaneous gesture, they threw these over the colt to form a saddle, scarcely noticing that they thus covered the darker hair on spine and foreleg which forms the shape of a cross. Jesus mounted. Up to that moment, he and the Twelve had had the lane to themselves, but suddenly it filled with people. Citizens of Jerusalem came out by ancient tradition to welcome pilgrim caravans, but this greeting to Jesus had an excitement of its own. The sensation created by his raising Lazarus had not died down during the withdrawal across the Jordan, and when word came that Jesus would enter the city, groups hurried toward Bethany, where they missed him and came pouring up the lane.

They shouted their welcome and pulled off cloaks and laid them in the road. John led the colt the first few yards, but it did not shy at the noise, or rebel at its burden, and carried Jesus up the hill.

They entered Bethphage, a village set in fields and olive groves yet no rural backwater but a suburb of Jerusalem, filled already with Galilean pilgrims who streamed out to join the procession. They cut branches, especially palms, from the trees shading the lane and threw them ahead of the colt to form a carpet of greenery, or waved them as they walked. The palm branch was a symbol of victory. Some members of the procession sang the traditional welcome from one of the "Psalms of Ascent," with its invocation, *"Hosanna* (God, save us), *Hosanna,* blessed is he who comes in the name of the Lord." Others adapted words to praise Jesus and shouted, "Blessed is the King who comes in the name of the Lord! Peace in heaven and glory in the highest."

The procession reached the Roman road, already packed with pilgrims nearing Jerusalem. Seeing Jesus, many burst into songs of praise and joy and recalled his deeds in Galilee, until the Mount of Olives rang again. John thrilled to be part of a royal progress.

Shocked Pharisees shouted above the noise, "Teacher, rebuke your disciples!" Jesus had always rebuked attempts to make him a king. This time he called back, as he rode the symbol of peace and humility, "I tell you, if these stay silent, the very stones will cry out."

The brow of the hill had prevented more than a glimpse of the city, the palaces on Mount Zion and the walls, but as the road curled round the northern summit of the Mount of Olives to begin the descent, Jerusalem burst into view a mile to the west, soaring majestically from the Kidron abyss toward the blue sky. Once again John caught his breath at its perspective of beauty: the rock face, scattered with tombs and monuments, then the walls, then the bright stonework and marble of the Temple and the palaces, then the gold of pinnacles and towers glittering in the strong sunshine. Jerusalem was indeed "a city of great magnificence and mighty fame throughout the world," made yet more marvelous to John because he escorted his Master and beloved friend.

Suddenly Jesus gave a terrible cry. John swung round and saw the colt reined in, and Jesus weeping as he gazed at Jerusalem. "Oh, if you, even you," he shouted, "had only known, this very day, what would bring you peace! But it is hidden from your eyes."

He began to utter a terrifying prophecy, describing Jerusalem, not as it now stood in its glory but as John would see it, to his horror, forty years on: the siege and the assault, the destruction and the fire, the thousand or more naked men nailed to crosses, while starving women and children were driven into slavery as the Romans rewarded rebellion and prolonged resistance. "They will not leave one stone upon another," Jesus mourned, "because you did not recognize the time when God came to save you!"

He touched his mount. All moved on.

They resumed their song. At the foot of the Mount of Olives, the stream of pilgrims merged with others from Emmaus and the north, and they pressed on together toward the northern gate which led to the city streets, with the Temple soaring above. Before they could reach the gate, a crowd poured out from within. By that instinct which sweeps an eastern city, hundreds had rushed to see Jesus enter. Pilgrims caught the excitement and inquired who came; Galileans already arrived gave the answer with pride: "It is Jesus, the prophet from Galilee." Judeans and pilgrims and Galileans struggled for a place as the procession neared the gate, with Jesus riding at the center of an adoring, vocal, palm-waving mob.

Roman sentries looked down from the walls on the seething mass. At Passover the garrison stayed on full alert, but none saw cause for alarm, for the noise and crowds were normal when half the world's Jews squeezed themselves into Jerusalem, as it seemed to a scoffing sentry. But Pharisees despaired. "What shall we do? The whole world has gone after him."

Eighteen
COURTS
OF THE TEMPLE

Next morning John was again approaching Jerusalem with Jesus, who this time was on foot, without a crowd.

The previous evening had perplexed the Twelve. After his deliberately royal entry, Jesus had not exploited the mood of the hour. He had not tried to seize political power or fan religious fervor. He sent the donkeys back to their owner, allowed the mob to fade away, entered the Temple, and saw what needed to be done; then, before darkness, he had gone quietly home to Bethany. In the morning, as Jesus led the way down the Mount of Olives by the steep path which he had avoided with the donkeys, and into the Kidron Valley, John wondered what Jesus had in mind.

They climbed out of the valley. As they neared the Shushan or Beautiful Gate of the Temple, they heard the bleating of lambs, lowing of cattle, and the cries of traders. Emerging from the gate into the vast Court of the Gentiles, they were confronted by the roar of an oriental market: a desecration which Caiaphas in his greed had established three years earlier, shortly before John had come to Jerusalem with Jesus after the wedding in Cana. He could vividly recall Jesus pulling out strands of his headdress to make a whip and driving out the cattle and sheep. His gesture had infuriated the authorities, who had allowed the commerce to resume.

Jesus now stood surveying the scene. Under the colonnades round the court sat money changers, since pilgrims must pay the Temple tax in a particular coinage. The open area, wide and long, was almost filled with flocks and herds, for during the seven days of the feast each worshiper must sacrifice 14 bullocks, 7 goats and rams, and 49 lambs: at the last Passover before the siege by the Romans more than 255,000 lambs would be slaughtered. Few pilgrims brought their own beasts, but the proper place for the market was the slope of the Mount of Olives and not the Court of the Gentiles; John saw Gentile "God-fearers," forbidden on pain of death to enter the inner courts, trying to pray amid the din.

Jesus watched and listened for a few moments. Then he filled his lungs, and in a voice which carried above the bleating and lowing, shouts of sellers, and arguments of the cheated, he called out texts from the prophets Isaiah and Jeremiah: "It is written: 'My house shall be called a house of prayer for all nations.' But you are making it 'a den of robbers'!"

With set face, he walked up to the nearest row of money-changers' tables and pushed them over, one after another. Coins clattered on the paving stones and rolled away. He upset the seats of the sellers of doves and drove flocks and herds toward the gate, calling out repeatedly the texts by which buying and selling in the Temple stood condemned. This time he made no whip. His righteous indignation was enough, backed by his reputation and the guilty consciences of merchants and customers, and the panic which swept through the crowd.

As the Twelve helped Jesus, John was impressed beyond all else by the expression on his face: not of moral force only but of love. John could feel the love which drove Jesus: love for God and his Temple, love for the cheated, love for the merchants and herdsmen who had been trapped into sacrilege by greed and custom, even love for the Temple authorities who had betrayed their trust. These were too amazed to intervene.

The Court of the Gentiles was emptying rapidly, leaving offal, spilled coins, and overturned tables. Jesus moved to the gate which led from the city. He stopped the flow of men and women who flagrantly used the Temple area as a shortcut to the markets. Priests and Temple police could hardly object to his upholding their own regulations. The court was now becoming quiet.

Suddenly John, recovering his breath, heard a different sound—a tap-tap of sticks, a shuffling of crippled feet. The blind and the lame were entering the Temple to find Jesus, and now John saw Pharisees throw up their hands in horror: they had ruled that the blind and the lame were excluded from appearing before the Lord in his Temple, and from offering sacrifices, though a few sat begging at the inner gates. Jesus, however, at once welcomed these outcasts and began to heal, so that lame men leaped and blind men saw.

Then came the boys and girls, an unforgettably touching sight, especially to Peter. They poured into the Temple despite being ritually excluded on grounds of decorum, and danced around Jesus. *"Hosanna,* God save the Son of David," they shouted, until chief priests and scribes were beside themselves. Commerce and shortcuts could be winked at, but for children to shout in the sacred courts affronted sanctity. Moreover their shouts acclaimed Jesus as King of the Jews. The officials were appalled. They rushed toward Jesus. "Do you hear what these children are saying?"

"Yes," replied Jesus. "And do you not know the Scripture: 'From the lips of children and babes at the breast, you have brought perfect praise'?"

To John his words sounded less a retort than an appeal in sorrow, not anger; as if he pleaded once more that the religious leaders should open their eyes to the truth.

They did not respond. He thanked the children and healed remaining cripples, then turned his back on his opponents and left the Temple.

Twenty-four hours later, on Tuesday morning, the Twelve again followed Jesus down the Mount of Olives, walking through the Garden of Gethsemane and across the Kidron and up under the cream-colored walls until they entered the Temple once more, to find that the flocks, herds, and money changers had not returned to the Court of the Gentiles.

Many people noticed Jesus' arrival and gathered round him, but before he could reach a shady portico from which to teach, he was stopped by a knot of chief priests, scribes, and Sanhedrin members, flanked by a few Temple guards, who evidently had awaited his appearance.

They demanded to know who had given him authority for his actions of the previous day. Their question held menace, since unauthorized behavior within the Temple precincts could be punished, and the guards might hurry Jesus away to be beaten.

He did not flinch. Nor did he answer. Instead he threw a question back. "The baptism of John: was it from heaven or men? Answer me that, and I will tell you my authority to do these things."

The question put them on the horns of a dilemma. They withdrew to argue the point while Jesus waited and the crowd relished the officials' embarrassment, for if they acknowledged that the Baptist's authority had been from heaven, they would have answered their own question: John the Baptist had hailed Jesus as Son of God and as Messiah or Christ, and Messiah could do as he wished in his Temple. "But," muttered the rulers, "if we say, 'From man,' the people will stone us. Everybody holds that John was a true prophet."

At last the rulers said shamefacedly, "We do not know."

"Then I will not answer your question either," replied Jesus. "I will not tell you what is my authority."

The crowd knew it instinctively. While the rulers' representatives retired to plot his downfall, the people settled down to listen. That day and the next Jesus sat for hours teaching. He was not addressing a multitude as in Galilee, when his voice had carried far and clear across a hillside or beach. He spoke intimately. The Twelve and the other disciples who had traveled with him, or had come to his side in Judea, listened in the shade of the columns—along with his mother and the other Mary, Martha, and Lazarus, Salome, and many whose names were never known to posterity.

Behind them, under the sunshine or the passing afternoon clouds, stood an ever-changing audience—pilgrims, citizens, priests, Levites—stopping a while on their way to or from the sacrifices or rituals in the inner courts. Some stayed until the shadows lengthened, others wandered off, busy with Temple duties or preparations for the feast.

He spoke frankly about the faithlessness and hypocrisy of the religious leaders and the coming fate of the nation. He drove home his warnings by telling vivid stories, such as his parable of the vineyard let out to tenants who not only refused the owner his share of the grape harvest but maltreated or even killed his collectors. Finally, he sent his only and dearly loved son, expecting them to respect him. Instead, they threw him out and killed him, "that his inheritance may be ours." As he listened, John knew that if the owner had no heir and took no action, the vineyard might legally lapse to the tenants; but he was not surprised at the reaction of the audience when Jesus put the question: "When the owner comes, what will he do to those tenants?"

"He will put them to death and let out the vineyard to others, who will give him his share at harvest."

Jesus looked squarely at them, and with an apt quote he warned solemnly that God would take away the kingdom from the Jewish nation and give it to others.

This was reported to the chief priests, who angrily resented

147

such an attack. Soon a posse of Temple guards clanked up to the fringe of the crowd as if to break it up and arrest him. They saw that the people hung on his words. Under orders not to risk a riot, they withdrew.

Then Jesus told a story of a king who had prepared a banquet to celebrate his son's wedding, but the important guests sent excuses, or beat up or killed his messengers. Therefore, the king ordered his army to punish them, and sent servants into the streets and lanes to bring in the poor, the lame, and the blind, both bad and good. Still there were empty places. "Go into the highways and hedges," he ordered, "and compel them to come in so that my house is full. None of those who were first invited shall taste my banquet."

As he continued his teaching, the audience grew larger, spreading into the area which previously had been cluttered by sheep pens. Then John saw one section draw back to let through a little procession of somewhat supercilious young men—students of a theology school, mixed with officers of Herod's army. They walked up to Jesus. One of them cleared his throat, and with little attempt to disguise insincerity, he poured out compliments: "Teacher, we know you are a man of integrity. You teach God's way in truth. You are not influenced by men, because you do not care who they are. Tell us your opinion: Is it right to pay taxes to Caesar or not?"

John held his breath. It seemed that now Jesus was impaled on the horns of a dilemma. If he said yes, he would be a collaborator. If he said no, the Pharisees who had sent the students and officers could denounce him to the Romans, who cared nothing for Jewish arguments, but would crucify a man for sedition. John could see no way out.

Without a pause Jesus replied: "Hypocrites! Why try to trap me? Show me a coin used to pay the tax."

A young man produced a coin. "Whose likeness and inscription is this?"

"Caesar's."

"Give to Caesar what is Caesar's and to God what is God's!"

The young men were amazed and abashed, and went away. Jesus' answer would be dissected, interpreted, expounded, and quoted without end, but the immediate effect was to spring the trap.

Opponents returned again and again. John found himself a listener at a great debate. On the one side he heard wily lawyers and scribes, self-important Pharisees in white robes, politically minded Sadducees, and students eager to prove zeal and verbal skill. On the other side sat Jesus, thirty-three years old, clear-eyed, holding himself well so that he was a delight to watch and hear, yet without pomposity, arrogance, or malice as he countered their thrusts.

They seemed determined to destroy him. Jesus might speak truth, but he looked frail against the weight of official opposition. John knew that the Sanhedrin itself numbered believers in Jesus who kept silent because of fear of the Pharisees. If they had ways to compel powerful men to keep silent, they could find means to silence Jesus forever.

Jesus appeared to ignore his danger, indeed to court it. He continued to state his claims without compromise; he did not hesitate to denounce the religious leaders in plain terms and thus to increase their fury.

Events mounted toward a climax. Huge, excitable crowds filled the city and the Temple. While Jesus taught, John heard the sound of Roman trumpets from the Fortress of Antonia which dominated the Temple from the northwest, and knew that Pontius Pilate, the Roman Governor, had arrived from Caesarea; he always took up residence during Passover, in case of trouble. Herod the Tetrarch was already at his own palace, but the two were not on speaking terms.

John felt the pressure of forces greater than he saw; he drew strength from Jesus' serenity but could not escape the sense of menace hanging over his head.

John did not understand what was happening, but a clue came when Peter tugged at his robe and pointed to Andrew and Philip escorting some Greeks through the crowd to meet Jesus. Afterward, John learned that the men had approached Andrew, who like Peter and Philip had been born in a Gentile city, and said they would like to see Jesus. Andrew, worried lest Jesus might dislike talking to Gentiles in the Temple, consulted Philip; then together they introduced the foreigners to Jesus.

With Greeks from a distant land standing before him, Jesus made a solemn pronouncement:

"The hour is come" he proclaimed, "for the Son of man to be glorified! Unless a grain of wheat falls to the ground and dies, it remains alone. If it dies, it bears much fruit."

He expounded the theme a little and then said: "Now my soul is troubled. And what shall I say, 'Father, save me from this hour'? No, it was for this very reason that I came to this hour."

Then he lifted his eyes and voice to heaven and said loudly: "Father, glorify your name!"

A sound like thunder reverberated round the court, though the sky was clear: "I have glorified it and will glorify it again."

John, Peter, and James all heard the voice, like the voice they had heard on Mount Hermon. The people said it was thunder.

Jesus spoke again: "That voice was for your sakes, not mine. Now comes judgment on this world; now the ruler of this world will be driven out."

His gaze held both Jews and Greeks. "And I, when I am lifted up from the earth, will draw all men to me."

John's heart chilled as he recalled Jesus' earlier words to the Twelve: "The Son of man will be crucified."

Nineteen
THE UPPER ROOM

Jesus had finished teaching on Wednesday afternoon and had walked up the steps into the court where only Jews might go: the Court of the Women. Ahead, the Levites were singing at the farther entrance leading to the Court of the Priests, which contained the altar and the slaughtering slabs. Beyond rose the towering marble building of the Holy Place, where the great curtain or veil of the Temple shut off the Holy of Holies, except to the high priest once a year.

Jesus sat down near the Treasury and watched as worshipers threw in coins. He saw a richly clad merchant shake a fat bag of gold into one of the trumpet-shaped offertory boxes. A pompous Pharisee strode up and looked around to make sure that someone saw how much he put in. Pilgrims passed by, casually throwing in coins, while several citizens looked resentful as they fulfilled their obligations. Then a little old woman, coarsely dressed in widow's weeds, hobbled up to a box. She stood a moment and bowed her head in prayer, with an expression on her face of devotion and pleasure. She fumbled for her purse and shook it into her hand.

All that fell out were two small bronze coins, the lowest in the Jewish currency, together equal to a quarter of a Roman copper. She took the two coins and reverently dropped them into the box and walked off with a light step, oblivious to being observed.

Jesus called the disciples' attention to the woman. "That poor widow," he said delightedly, "put more into the Treasury than all the others! They gave something out of their wealth, but she, out of her poverty, put in everything— all she had to live on."

He stood up and began to lead them out of the Temple, but the disciples were in a sightseeing mood and pointed out to Jesus the great stones of the buildings, some adorned with precious stones; and the magnificence of the pillars and arches, the stairways, and the gates of gold and pearl.

Jesus looked grave. "Do you see all these great buildings? The time is coming when not one stone will be left on another. All will be thrown down."

He remained solemn as they descended into the Kidron Valley and climbed the path up the Mount of Olives to his favorite place of prayer, the Garden of Gethsemane. He sat down and looked back over the city and his eyes filled with tears. John and James and Peter and Andrew talked softly among themselves, then went up to him. "Tell us, when will it all happen?"

In reply, Jesus began to prophesy at length, and they tried to understand. Sometimes he was describing in detail the terrible events of the coming Jewish War and the fall of Jerusalem. He talked too of even greater sufferings throughout the world which would be the prelude to his return in glory. As John listened, his mind's eye seemed to see in one view two vivid pictures of different historic climaxes, one behind the other, without being granted a clue to the length of time between. "Be ready, be on your watch," Jesus urged repeatedly. He warned them by straight talk and by parable how to prepare and to endure, and how to avoid being deceived.

John had listened in the synagogue to rabbis discoursing

on the end of the age: the prospect of world tribulation and a final judgment was not strange to any of the Twelve, but Jesus spoke differently from a rabbi, because he centered all on himself, the Son of man. He painted history as moving toward his own return in glory. Though the Father alone knew the day or the hour, they must never doubt that it would happen. Heaven and earth would pass away, "but my words will not pass away."

He ended on a characteristic note. The evening shadows were already falling across the city, which stood out in silhouette against the setting sun, when he told them one more parable. He likened the people of all nations to sheep and goats as they assembled before his throne for the last judgment. In Palestine their fleeces are superficially similar. Like a shepherd the king separates them, the sheep on his right, the goats on his left. The "sheep" are welcomed to their eternal inheritance: "For I was hungry and you gave me food; I was thirsty and you gave me drink; I was a stranger and you took me in; naked and you clothed me; I was sick and you visited me, in prison and you came to me."

The "sheep" are puzzled and ask, "When?" And the king answers, "When you did it to one of the least of these my brothers, you did it to me."

Then the king sentences the "goats" to punishment, "for I was hungry and you gave me no food, thirsty and you gave me no drink. . . ." The "goats" cannot remember starving the king or leaving him thirsty or naked or sick or in prison. But the king rejects the excuse: "Because you did nothing for one of the least of my brothers, you did nothing for me."

While the Twelve silently absorbed his parable, Jesus said quietly, "As you know, the Passover is two days away, and the Son of man will be handed over to be crucified."

He led his men back through the shadows to Bethany. They walked in silence, under the Passover moon, two days off the full; a cold fear, mixed with disbelief, clutched at John.

John slept fitfully that last night they would spend in Bethany—for the Passover night must be spent within the city walls. John feared for Jesus' safety and was relieved in the morning when Peter showed him two short swords. He was even more relieved that Jesus did not lead the Twelve back to Jerusalem but rose early and went to spend the morning alone in the garden on the Mount of Olives, hiding himself from listeners and opponents. The Twelve sat out of earshot, though Peter and John made sure that they could see him and be ready to spring to his protection. Away from the city, they felt he was safe; for though the authorities were unwilling to risk a riot by arresting him in the Temple, Jerusalem offered opportunities to murderers.

Judas Iscariot, as treasurer and administrator for the Twelve, left them soon afterward to buy their Passover lamb; every household or company of pilgrims must sacrifice and eat a living male, less than a year old. Time passed, and John wondered vaguely why Judas took so long, but suspected nothing.

Unknown to John, Judas made a detour on his way to the sheep market, to the high priest's palace. He approached furtively, then disclosed himself as an informer on Jesus of Nazareth, and was admitted at once: an informer was the chief priests' one hope of seizing Jesus without a riot.

Judas asked, "What will you give me if I betray him to you?" Judas had priced Mary of Bethany's nard at 300 small silver coins of the Romans. In the high priest's palace, they used a larger Greek coin worth three of these. They counted out thirty, less than a third of the value of Mary's nard. For these thirty pieces of silver, he promised to hand over Jesus quietly.

Every age has pondered the motive. John believed that Satan entered Judas Iscariot's soul. The most popular conjectures other than greed or jealousy are disappointment that Jesus refused to launch a rebellion; or a belief that if Jesus were arrested he would summon heavenly hosts to his rescue and precipitate his kingdom on earth.

Leaving the palace, Judas bought a lamb and carried it back to Bethany, where like thousands of other lambs in Jerusalem and the suburbs it spent the hours tethered in the shade within reach of grass or hay and water, not suspecting that its blood must be spilled at twilight. Judas joined his equally unsuspecting friends.

Early in the afternoon they all approached Jesus to ask where to prepare the Passover feast. Judas stood close, listening intently, but Jesus did not answer the question directly. He gave detailed instructions to John and Peter which, as they realized afterward, could provide no clue to Judas: Jesus did not want any interruption at his last supper with the Twelve.

They hurried away, fetched the lamb, and carried it to Jerusalem. As they entered they saw, exactly as Jesus had told them, a man marked out from the crowd by an earthenware water jar on his shoulder: women carried these; men carried wineskins. He led them silently through the streets and the partially filled ravine which split Jerusalem, and ascended to the upper city at the southwestern corner. John could see the Temple below to the east and Herod's palace to the west. The water carrier stopped at a substantial house.

They were greeted by the father or guardian of young John Mark, the future companion of Barnabas and Paul. Peter said, as instructed, "The Master asks, 'Where is my guest room where I may eat the Passover with my disciples?'" The host bowed, and escorted them, not to the common guest area but upstairs to a large room, quiet and already furnished with cushions and a low table.

Then they took the lamb to the Temple and joined the companies waiting their turn at the altars.

The great gates opened to the inner court. As they entered, John heard Levites chant and trumpets blow, while the fires and the smell of blood drove home to him again the age-old teaching that the sacrifice of an innocent on his behalf was the price of his eternal safety. When their turn came, John held the lamb while a white-robed priest held a golden bowl and caught the blood as Peter cut its throat. The bowl passed from priest to priest until the last of the line threw the blood at the altar's base.

Expert hands skinned the slain lamb as it lay on a rough frame between the shoulders of Peter and John; they removed the innards to burn them, taking care that not one bone should be broken. The disciples left the Temple to the sounds of trumpets, singing, and the bleat of lambs awaiting slaughter, and carried the carcass back to the home of John Mark. Rhoda the maid had an oven ready to roast it while they laid the table with bitter herbs and sauce, wine, unleavened bread, plus other requirements of a Passover feast.

Toward evening, shortly before the Passover began at 6 P.M., they heard Jesus and his ten other disciples ascending the stairs to the upper room. John gave him the kiss of peace with special affection, born of relief that he had passed through the city safely. Judas Iscariot, not knowing their destination, had not earned his thirty pieces of silver, and the unsuspecting John greeted him with the same warmth as he did the other disciples.

John had placed thirteen cushions in a horseshoe round the low table: three at the top, five on each side, leaving the bottom open for service. At Passover everyone must recline, not sit. Jesus took the head of household's place at the top, leaning on his left elbow in the normal way with feet stretched away from the table and his right hand free for food. John reclined on Jesus' right, immediately below him. Peter took the bottom of the table to his left, ready to fetch the roast lamb at the correct moment, but Judas hurried to the top to the other cushion next to Jesus—the chief guest's place (the guest reclining on the host's left must look down on him) which Judas regarded as the treasurer's privilege. A quarrel blew up later over precedence, but Jesus stopped it.

As they took their places, Jesus looked around at these special friends. "Oh," he cried, "how much I have longed to eat this Passover with you before I suffer, for I tell you I shall never eat it again until it is fulfilled in the kingdom of God." John did not understand.

Jesus stood up and began the supper by the time-honored ceremony of giving thanks over the first of four cups in front of him: "Blessed are you, Lord our God, King of the world, who created the fruit of the vine." The opening words of the Passover liturgy were familiar; but when he handed the cup to be shared round, and resumed his couch, he broke the familiar silence. "I shall never drink of the fruit of the vine again," he said, "until the kingdom of God comes." John still did not understand.

Before eating, the head of the household or company must ceremonially wash his hands. Jesus again rose from his place, but he did not place his hands in the basin. Instead, he removed his robe. John watched perplexed as Jesus pulled off his sleeveless tunic, woven from top to bottom without seam, and stood before them stripped to his loincloth like a slave. John never forgot the love and tenderness, the serenity on Jesus' face as he wound a towel round his waist, took the basin, and knelt down to wash Judas' feet. He wiped them with the towel, then moved to the next. Disciples watched in total silence as their Master worked as if he were their lowest slave.

When he came to Peter, Peter said in astonishment, "Lord, are you going to wash my feet?"

"You do not know what I am doing to you now. You will understand later."

Peter looked genuinely shocked and drew his feet back. "You shall never wash my feet!"

"If I do not wash you, you are saying in effect that you are not my follower."

"Then, Lord, not just my feet but my hands and my head."

Jesus shook his head. He reminded the Twelve that when a

man comes home from the baths he needs only to wash his feet. "And you are clean—but not all of you," he said as he dried Peter's feet.

John's feet were the last to be washed. John accepted the honor humbly and gratefully. Jesus put on his tunic and robe and reclined again on his cushion while Peter fetched the dish of lamb.

While they ate, Jesus taught them. The meat had been roasted enough to be easily handled, and they had segments of unleavened bread to sop up the gravy, They gave undivided attention to Jesus' words. He said: "I gave you an example. If I, your Master and Lord, washed your feet, you should wash each other's feet."

As the meal proceeded, Jesus followed the ancient Passover liturgy yet changed it by actions and words which sank deep into the consciousness, though neither John nor others yet understood. When Jesus rose, took bread, gave thanks, and broke it, he passed the pieces to them. "Take and eat. This is my body broken for you. Do this in remembrance of me."

When he lifted another of the cups of wine and spoke the words of thanks, he handed it to them. "Drink it, all of you. This is my blood of the new covenant which is poured out for you and for many for the forgiveness of sins."

Judas took the bread and sipped the wine with the others. Suddenly John saw their Master deeply troubled, just as he had been before the tomb of Lazarus. Jesus quoted from a psalm of David, "He who shares my bread has lifted up his heel against me." With great emphasis he declared, "One of you is going to betray me!"

John, horrified, stared at any disciple he could see. Jesus impressed upon them again that a betrayer sat in their midst. They became very sad and, not realizing that he referred to events that very night, they all searched their hearts whether they could ever betray. "Lord, is it I?" John asked, as the same anxious question came from almost every couch.

Peter caught John's eye and beckoned him to beg Jesus to

name the traitor. John carefully did so without attracting attention, by leaning closer against Jesus' chest without changing position. Jesus replied in a murmur, "It is he to whom I give this morsel when I have dipped it."

He stretched to dip a piece of food in the bowl of sauce. He offered it to Judas, a gesture of honor which opened a last route of repentance. Judas hesitated, muttering, "Is it I, Rabbi?" He could have stepped back from the brink, thrown himself on his knees, flung away the thirty pieces of silver secreted on his person, and confessed what Jesus already knew.

The moment passed; Judas took the morsel.

"Do it more quickly," said Jesus softly. Judas rose from his couch and walked from the room. John had a sudden urge to stop or denounce him, or rush to one of the two swords; but without Jesus' orders he did nothing. The rest thought Judas had been sent on some errand as treasurer.

Judas descended the stairs and went out into the night.

Twenty
THE GARDEN

With Judas gone, the atmosphere in the Upper Room became more intimate but not more relaxed. Jesus, still reclining at table, said immediately, "Now the Son of man is glorified, and God is glorified in him." John had looked forward eagerly to the glory of his Master all the time they had walked together toward Jerusalem. At last it would happen.

But Jesus dashed high expectations. He threw all eleven disciples into alarm with his next words. "Little children"— he had never called them "little children" before—"I will be with you only a little longer. You will look for me, but I tell you now what I told the Jews. Where I am going you cannot come."

John was horrified. He looked down the table to Peter and saw him shocked and dismayed, and he heard an anguished murmur from every couch. Before they could voice their protests, Jesus rose from his place. The head of a family or company usually addressed them at the close of the Passover feast, with questions interjected by his listeners. He began: "I give you a new commandment, *Love one another*. You must love one another just as I have loved you. That is how all men will know that you are my disciples, because you love one another."

John had heard rabbis and Jesus himself extol the great commandments, to love God and one's neighbor, and to love each other as intimate brothers, in the same selfless way in which Jesus had loved them; this would be a test indeed. Jesus, however, did not expound the theme because Peter interrupted. His mind was not on brotherly love.

"Lord," he demanded, "where are you going?"

Jesus repeated, "I am going where you cannot follow now. But you will follow later."

"Lord, why can't I follow you now? I will 'lay down my life' for you." John detected an echo of Jesus' story of the Good Shepherd.

Jesus looked at him. "Will you lay down your life for me? Believe me. Before the cock crows, you will deny me three times."

Jesus spoke to calm them. "Don't let your hearts be troubled. Trust in God; trust in me too." He was going to the Father's house to prepare them a room, and would return and take them there himself, to be with him. "You know where I am going, and you know the way."

Thomas interrupted. "Lord, we do not know where you are going, so how can we know the way?"

Jesus replied in clear, simple, unmistakable words which, in the years to come, John loved to ponder over and over again. "I am the way and the truth and the life," said Jesus. "No one comes to the Father except through me. If you really knew me, you would know my Father too. And from now on you do know him, for you have seen him."

Philip suddenly voiced the idea that was in the back of all their minds. "Show us the Father! And that will be enough for us."

"Have I been with you all this time, Philip," Jesus

answered, "and you do not know me? Anyone who has seen me has seen the Father. How can you say, 'Show us the Father?'" And Jesus pressed this home.

The Master reclined again on his couch, and all that he taught for the remainder of the evening had an unforgettable intimacy. Much of it John did not fully grasp at the time, partly because he could not realize that Jesus' crucifixion was less than twelve hours away, and partly because Jesus spoke prophetically about the future.

Listening carefully, John heard Jesus give a promise which seemed almost too good to be real: that when he went away he would ask the Father and the Father would send Someone to be with them always as counselor and comforter, the Spirit of truth, who would be none other than Jesus himself, but not in physical form. "I will not leave you as orphans. I will come to you. Before long, the world will see me no more but you will see me. Because I live, you also will live. On that day you will realize that I am in my Father, and you are in me, and I in you." He calmed their fears. "I leave you peace," he said. "It is my peace that I give you—the peace the world cannot give. Do not let your hearts be troubled. Do not be afraid."

At last Jesus told them that they must leave the Upper Room for what was coming, and as they rose from their couches he called them, with deep affection, "those who stood by me in my trials." He promised them special places and special work in his kingdom. Then he looked at Peter. "Simon, Simon," he said, not using the nickname "Rock," "Satan wants to sift you like wheat. But I have prayed for *you* that your faith may not fail. And when you have turned back to me, strengthen your brothers!"

Peter insisted: "Lord, I am ready to go to prison with you, and to death."

Jesus again warned solemnly that Simon Peter would disown and deny him before cockcrow.

He asked them all whether they had lacked anything when sent out on their own without purse or satchel or sandals.

"Nothing," they all exclaimed.

"But now, take a purse if you have it, and a satchel. If you have not got a sword, sell your coat and buy one!"

They showed him the two swords (common to be worn in the Roman world) which Peter and another disciple had unbuckled on entering the room. He said, "That is enough." But before they could understand what he had meant earlier about the swords, he froze their hearts by saying that a particular prophecy about himself must be fulfilled, "He shared the fate of criminals." John knew the quotation at once, from Isaiah's prophecy of the Suffering Servant: "He willingly gave his life. He shared the fate of criminals. He took the place of many sinners."

By now it was late at night. Led by Jesus, they sang the final psalm of the Passover liturgy, then went downstairs. John caught a glimpse of young John Mark, woken by their song, peeping from behind the curtain drawn across his sleeping place.

Jesus and his disciples walked quietly through the city in the light of the nearly full moon. As they passed the Temple's closed gates with the symbolic golden vine, Jesus taught them that they were like the branches and he the vine; they could do nothing cut away from him, but would bear much fruit if they remained part of him. He taught about God's love; and he said, "Greater love has no man than this, that he lay down his life for his friends. You are my friends if you do whatever I command you."

Grief began to overwhelm them as they walked. He told them that the world would be gleeful at his death while they mourned and wept. "But your grief will turn to joy! Now is your time of grief, but I will see you again; and you will rejoice and no one will take away your joy." John heard him again promising to come back, but in their sorrow none of them could grasp his promise.

By now they were looking over the Kidron ravine in the high moon near midnight. All households and pilgrim companies were still at Passover feasts, or asleep, and the city was still. Perhaps the cool air sharpened wits, for as he continued to teach, his words suddenly seemed startlingly clear. "I came from the Father and entered the world. Now I am leaving the world and am going back to the Father."

They all spoke at once. "You are speaking clearly! And not in parables. . . . We can see now—you know all things. . . . We believe that you came from God."

"Do you believe? A time is coming—it has come now— when you will all be scattered, each to his own home. You will all fall away. It is written, 'I will strike the shepherd and the sheep will be scattered.' You will leave me alone. Yet I am not alone, for my Father is with me."

Jesus said again, "You will all fall away, but," he added, "after I have risen, I will go ahead of you into Galilee."

At that, Peter repeated his earlier boast. "I will never deny you! If everyone does, I will not! I'll go to prison, to judgment for your sake."

"Truly, truly, Peter," repeated Jesus sadly, "this very night before the cock crows twice, you will deny me three times."

But Peter insisted vehemently, "If I have to die with you, I will not deny you." John echoed his words, and so did they all.

They walked on a little, then Jesus stopped. He waited until everyone was close to him and said: "I have told you these things so that in me you may have peace. In the world you will have trouble. But take heart! I have overcome the world."

As they stood around, he looked toward heaven and began to pray. "Father, the hour is come. Glorify your Son that your Son may glorify you. . . . The disciples lifted their hearts in prayer with him, awed by the intimacy with which he prayed for them and for all who would believe through them.

The prayer was long, but John did not notice the coldness of the night, for Jesus took them right into the warmth of God's presence. Jesus ended: "Righteous Father, though the world does not know you, I know you; and they know that you have sent me. I have made you known to them, and will continue to make you known in order that the love you have for me may be in them, and that I myself may be in them."

No one spoke as the disciples followed Jesus across the Kidron ravine to the Mount of Olives. They climbed a little way up the steep lane and turned into the olive Garden of Gethsemane, where he had often taken them. When they reached the stone shelter housing the oil press which gave the garden its name, he told them to sit down "while I go over there and pray." He beckoned Peter, James, and John to come.

As they walked beside him in the bright moonlight, John was appalled to see Jesus shuddering, in an anguish more intense than John believed to be possible. "My soul is crushed with sorrow, almost to the point of death. Stop here," he said, "and keep awake."

He went a stone's throw farther and fell to the ground, and John heard his agonized prayer. *"Abba,* Father," he cried, using that intimate term which John would never have dared use himself. He saw him kneeling against a stone, his head uplifted to heaven, his arms stretched out, his whole body convulsed.

The hour was late; they were exhausted, weighed down with sorrow. Peter took refuge in sleep, then James, then John.

A secret eyewitness and eavesdropper stayed awake: Mark, the valiant young man in the first flush of his strength, who had risen from bed and peeped from behind the curtain when the disciples left his home. With an instinct that Jesus might need protection, Mark had thrown the first garment to hand, a fine linen robe, about his naked body and had crept after the company undetected, waiting while they stopped, creeping into the garden, following Jesus to hide behind a rock as a self-constituted secret guard.

Mark was appalled by the sight and sound of a human being in agony. Jesus prayed, "O my Father, everything is possible with you. Take this cup away from me. Yet, not what I want, but what you want." Again and again came the cry, "Take this cup away." Mark listened and watched, amazed. Jesus was not simply pleading to escape torture, or distress and shame, or physical death in itself. Mark knew from the prophets and psalms that "this cup" meant the wrath of God.

At last Jesus rose from his knees and stumbled toward his three closest friends. John awoke, ashamed to find Jesus standing beside him. Jesus' anguish was now compounded by concern. "Are you asleep?" he said to them. "Could you not watch with me one hour? Stay awake. Pray! Pray, so that you do not fall into temptation." He added, gently, "The spirit is willing but the flesh is weak." John watched Jesus go back toward the stone, then sleep closed his eyes again.

Mark, from his hiding place, saw Jesus kneel down and heard him pray even more earnestly. Though midnight had passed and the night was cold, the body of Jesus poured with sweat; so great was the pressure on his heart that the sweat which fell on the stone was bloody. "Father, if you are willing, take this cup from me," he prayed again. As a follower put it years later, "He offered up prayers and petitions with loud cries and tears to the one who could save him from death." He knew that his Father would not force him; he could refuse, and leave the world as he had found it.

Jesus continued to pray. Mark, his own heart pounding, heard the words, "My Father, if it is not possible for this cup to be taken away except I drink it, may your will be done." Jesus rose from the stone.

A few yards away John awoke a second time to find Jesus standing beside them. They were speechless with shame. Jesus withdrew, and again sleep proved more powerful than loyalty, and they knew nothing of his further agony before his voice awakened them a third time.

Standing up guiltily, John saw by the moonlight that Jesus was weary, his face marked by suffering, yet at peace.

"Still sleeping and resting?" he said. "The hour has come! The Son of man is betrayed to sinners. Get up! Let us go! The traitor is upon us."

Twenty-one
"I HAVE CONDEMNED INNOCENT BLOOD"

With clank of arms, an approaching force drew nearer. Jesus went toward it. All eleven disciples, awakened from sleep, cowered behind him.

John saw soldiers and Temple police carrying flaming torches on poles, despite the nearly full moon, to hunt down their quarry if he fled through the trees; and lamps in earthenware holders in case he hid in caves. They passed the line of olive trees which marked the edge of the garden. Judas Iscariot detached himself from the soldiers. He strode up to Jesus and shouted, "Greetings, Rabbi!" and gave a disciple's customary mark of respect by kissing Jesus on the hand, only not once but effusively.

"Comrade," asked Jesus, "are you betraying the Son of man with a kiss?" Judas did not answer.

"Do what you came for," said Jesus.

Behind Judas emerged an excessively large body of Roman soldiers with swords, Jewish Temple police with cudgels, officials sent by the Sanhedrin, and a gaggle of servants and idlers who had stayed up late on Passover night. But when Jesus stood calmly awaiting arrest without a fight, they were nonplussed.

"Whom do you want?" he asked.

"Jesus of Nazareth!"

"I am," said Jesus. John, though in mounting terror, saw that the words literally made them stagger, for to the Jewish officials in front, with Judas beside them, Jesus had declared himself in that sacred phrase which God alone might use. His majesty of bearing underlined it and caught them off balance, and they fell back, stumbling into the soldiers behind.

Jesus repeated his question as they picked themselves up. Again they answered, "Jesus of Nazareth."

"I told you, *I am!* If you want me, let these men go."

A disciple shouted, "Lord, shall we strike with the swords?" Before Jesus could answer, Peter drew his short sword and struck out wildly, slicing off the right ear of a man whom John recognized as Malthus, a body servant of the high priest.

"Sheathe your sword!" Jesus ordered. Whatever he had meant when encouraging them to bring swords, he rebuked Peter: "Those who take the sword shall perish by the sword. Do you think I cannot call on my Father for more than twelve legions of angels?"—36,000 heavenly beings poised to rescue—"But how would the Scriptures be fulfilled, that it must happen this way? Shall I not drink the cup my Father has given me?"

Jesus stepped up to the shocked, bleeding Malthus who desperately held his ear to his head, and healed him. All the fight went out of Peter.

Jesus turned to the Jewish officials and chief priests. "Am I a brigand, that you come against me with swords and cudgels? Every day I taught in the Temple, and you did not touch me. But this is your hour, the hour of—"

John heard no more. He did not stand his ground when his colleagues' courage collapsed. Peter fled; James fled; Andrew fled; every one of the Twelve ran for their lives, except Judas.

The Roman officer was growing impatient. He gave a sharp

command. Soldiers seized Jesus and bound his arms tightly behind his back—brigand or prophet, what did a soldier care?

Someone suddenly saw young Mark. He had come to Gethsemane to protect Jesus, but the display of force and the flight of Peter, whom he had regarded as a rock, drained Mark's valor.

Hands grasped his linen garment. Mark shook himself free and fled naked into the night.

John recovered his nerve quickly. He turned back in time to see the soldiers march Jesus out of the garden and into the ravine. With newfound courage, John edged nearer in the darkness and followed them round the Pool of Siloam and into the lower city. He felt a tug on his sleeve and saw a shaken, irresolute Peter. Together, they went on, keeping behind the marching troops whose torches made shadows dance in the darkened streets. The procession crossed the Tyropoeon Valley and at last reached the high priest's palace on the farther hill, more than a mile from Gethsemane. The gates opened to admit police, servants, prisoner, and traitor, leaving the Roman soldiers to return to barracks.

John, being known to the high-priestly household, had no difficulty in joining the tail of the escort as they jostled into the courtyard. Peter did not dare enter. The gates clanged shut.

John saw Jesus, his arms stiff from the cord, being roughly escorted toward the wing occupied by Annas, the old man who had been high priest until deposed by the Romans fifteen years before; most Jews regarded Annas as equally high priest with his son-in-law Caiaphas, holding that the office was for life. They reckoned the shrewd and patriotic Annas to be still the dominant power.

When John saw where Jesus would be interrogated, he went back and spoke to the girl porter, who opened the gate to admit Peter. She looked at Peter as he crossed the flickering pool of light. Half recognizing him, she said, "You are not one of that man's disciples, are you?"

"I am not," said Peter.

Police and servants, cold from the night march to Gethsemane, had lit a charcoal fire in the courtyard. Peter crept near, trying to warm himself undetected. Behind him the girl stayed at the gate as members of the Sanhedrin, awakened by messages, arrived from their homes and hurried toward the great hall of the palace. John left Peter and quietly joined the priests and scribes watching the preliminary interrogation. He edged himself as close as he could to Jesus, who stood bound before Annas.

Annas was asking questions. Suspects should cringe before him and answer in tones of abject humility; Jesus, however, did not cringe, nor would he name his disciples nor provide information about his teaching. He had said nothing in secret, he replied, but had taught openly in synagogues and in the Temple; and John remembered that even when instructing in private, Jesus urged his disciples to shout from the housetops what he taught. He had nothing to hide. "Why question me?" was all he would say to Annas. "Question the people who heard me. Ask them what I told them. They know what I said."

"How dare you talk disrespectfully to the high priest!" said a guard, and slapped his face.

The welt showed up raw, but Jesus rebuked his assailant: "If I have said anything wrong, tell everyone here what it was. But if I am right in what I have said, why do you hit me?"

Annas suspended his interrogation, for a quorum of Sanhedrin members would have gathered round Caiaphas. Annas ordered the guards to march Jesus to the great hall.

Across the wide courtyard with its huddle of figures round a fire, and up low steps, they led him into the main building of the palace, and placed him under the light of torches flaming in the portico. Peter and those around the fire could see Jesus clearly. In front of him in the great hall sat Caiaphas on his judgment bench, flanked by elders of both Sadducee and Pharisee parties. Judas, the priests and the scribes, with John still unaccosted among them, gathered on one side.

No pleader or advocate rose to make a formal charge. John remembered what Nicodemus had told him, months earlier: Caiaphas was determined to see to it that Jesus would be put to death. But if this was to be done by judicial process, the Roman governor alone had power to impose a death sentence. Caiaphas and his friends needed grounds on which to secure conviction. They had retained witnesses, it seemed, and had summoned them when Judas told where Jesus might be arrested.

The witnesses now testified. They were important, for a bad case would be thrown out by the governor; moreover, John could see that Nicodemus and Joseph of Arimathea, though secret sympathizers, were alert for justice. As the night wore on and the shadows thrown by the moon altered shapes, John heard the witnesses, one after another, fail to substantiate their testimony, or admit to relying on hearsay, or contradict each other. The trial, if it could be called that, offered hope after all, since the governor heard cases at sunrise and time pressed. Jesus might be acquitted through lack of evidence.

Two more witnesses came forward. One deposed: "We heard this fellow say, 'Destroy this Temple made by human hands, and in three days I will build another, not man made.'" But the other witness recalled a different version of words spoken when Jesus first cleared the Temple, three years before. No charge could stick if the evidence was contradictory—unless the prisoner incriminated himself. Jesus had kept silent throughout the proceedings in the great hall.

Caiaphas stood up. "Are you not going to answer? What is this testimony that these men bring against you?"

All eyes turned on Jesus. He stayed silent.

172

Caiaphas said, "I charge you under oath by the living God: *Are you Messiah, the Son of the Blessed One?*"

"I am!" replied Jesus. He had not merely answered a question. He had again used the sacred phrase which, in the context, had one meaning only. He added, "And you will see the Son of man sitting on the right hand of the Almighty and coming on the clouds of heaven."

At that, the high priest solemnly tore his robe to express formal abhorrence of the mocking of the majesty of God. No further witnesses were needed. "You have heard his blasphemy, what is your verdict?"

They condemned him as worthy of death. Nicodemus and Joseph of Arimathea dissented but were powerless.

The high priest gave a curt order. The guards blindfolded Jesus, then spat at his face, and pummeled him with fists. Priests, scribes, and retainers ran forward to spit or strike, shouting, "Prophesy! Tell us who hit you," and thereby absolved themselves from being accessories to blasphemy. Flinching at the blows, John recognized that they were also submitting Jesus to a traditional test: according to the scribes' interpretation of the eleventh chapter of Isaiah, the true Messiah would be able to see blindfolded. John's mind clutched at the opportunity which Jesus was given to save himself. Jesus declined to take it; he stayed silent.

Yet at the moment when the Council was deciding that he was not a true prophet, his prophecy to Peter was fulfilled. During the trial of Jesus in the great hall, a lesser trial took place in the courtyard. A slave girl peered at Peter as he warmed himself. "This man was with him," she told the knot of servants and police sitting round the fire.

"Woman, I do not know him!" said Peter. A cock crowed outside the palace, but Peter was oblivious to the meaning. He moved away from the fire toward the gate where the girl porter had half identified him when John had brought him in. This girl repeated to bystanders her earlier belief that he was the prisoner's disciple (and therefore possibly dangerous). When the trial in the great hall was nearing its climax, one of those who had been in Gethsemane, a relative of the servant injured by Peter's sword, accosted him. The man said, "Surely I saw you in the garden. This man is certainly a Galilean—you are one of them!"

"Man, I am not!"

"But your accent gives you away!"

Peter denied with an oath and swore curses on himself if he knew Jesus, while across the courtyard came the shouts and the sounds of blows as they hit the blindfolded Jesus.

The cock crowed a second time. Peter glanced up. In the torchlight he saw the guards remove the blindfold. As the cockcrow died away, Jesus turned and looked straight at Peter. Peter remembered. The gate stood open. He stumbled out into the street weeping bitterly.

John saw him go; and a few minutes later he saw another of the Twelve go into the night, just before dawn. John had watched Judas during the trial. When Judas heard the verdict, his face contorted and he yelled, "I have condemned innocent blood."

An underling of Caiaphas retorted, "What do we care? That is your affair."

Judas threw the thirty pieces of silver on the floor and ran out of the palace.

Twenty-two
"AWAY WITH HIM!"

The Sanhedrin paused briefly until first light before condemning Jesus formally, because a judgment pronounced in the hours of darkness was invalid. Then they had him marched through the dawn the short distance to the palace built by Herod the Great which the prefect of Judea (the Roman governor) used as his praetorium when visiting Jerusalem. Herod had chosen the site of King David's citadel, on high ground adjoining the wall at the northwestern corner of the upper city.

John had no difficulty in following undetected among the priests, scribes, and household servants. At sunrise he was waiting with them, behind the prisoner and some of his judges, in the street of the Upper Market, just outside the wide, open forecourt known as the Pavement. It contained the raised stone *bema*, the tribunal where the governor sat to give verdicts, pronounce sentence, or issue formal orders with force of law. To one side stood the barracks. Ahead, through shady colonnades, were the audience chambers and halls where he heard cases and received deputations and entertained, and behind these a smaller yard led to his private quarters.

Pontius Pilate, the Roman knight from the mountains of southern Italy, who had been prefect of Judea for the past four years, had risen at his usual hour before dawn. At first light he had entered the public rooms to meet heads of departments, hear police reports, and receive petitioners, or transact other business. He knew that the Sanhedrin would bring before him a troublemaker, for he had authorized an armed detachment for the arrest, but no Jews awaited him; it was the Day of Passover, and strict Jews regarded all Gentile houses as ritually unclean. To enter would defile a man for seven days and would ruin his Passover celebrations. Pilate was not surprised therefore when a household slave reported that the Sanhedrin representatives had arrived with their prisoner but refused to enter the palace.

Pilate had learned through much irritation and bloodshed to honor Jews in minor matters. Soon after sunrise he went out to the Pavement, saw the prisoner and his accusers and stood beside the stone *bema* to put the formal question in Greek: "What charge do you bring against this man?"

They did not give a direct answer. Blasphemy was no offense in Roman law unless a man blasphemed the divine emperor, a crime silently committed by every devout Jew, but they hoped Pilate would dispatch Jesus by administrative decision, without trial, as a disturber of the peace. This was within a prefect's prerogative; Pilate had slaughtered Jews readily enough in his first four years. They therefore named no specific crime.

"If he were not a criminal," said the Sanhedrin spokesman, also in Greek, "we would not have brought him before you."

Since the prisoner did not appear to be the usual run of troublemaker, Pilate demanded details. They still hedged. "Take him yourselves, then," said Pilate, "and judge him according to your law."

"We have no right to execute," they replied.

Sometimes they stoned or strangled a man without being called to account, especially if a Gentile trespassed into the inner courts of the Temple; but as John now realized from what Jesus had warned, Caiaphas was determined that Jesus should die by the Roman capital punishment of crucifixion. When a man was crucified, whether on a standing tree near the place of his crime or, more usually, on a tree trunk erected at a crossroads or on a hill, he hung from the tree by nails in his palms or wrists and his feet, until he died a lingering death. Every Jew knew from Scripture that anyone hanged on a tree was cursed. If, therefore, Jesus was crucified he would die under a curse and be exposed as a false messiah. Were he stoned, his disciples might revere him as a martyr; if he hung on a tree they must abhor him or share his curse.

To have him crucified, the Sanhedrin needed to prove that Jesus was guilty of a crime against Rome. The spokesman threw before the governor somewhat incoherent charges of subversion; and that Jesus had urged nonpayment of taxes to Caesar; "and calls himself Christ, a king."

Pilate asked the prisoner to state his defense. Jesus stayed silent. His silence amazed the governor and clearly disturbed him: Roman justice disliked absence of a defense as much as lack of clear charges. Pilate seemed to hesitate, then he withdrew, ordering that Jesus be marched inside. The prosecution refused to defile themselves by entering too; Pilate had guessed correctly. He could question the prisoner without his accusers.

The interview would not be private; John knew that anyone willing to accept defilement could enter the audience chamber, and he at once mounted the steps and walked across the Pavement, mingling with Gentile hangers-on to stay near Jesus and listen. Pilate's questions and Jesus' answers, both in Greek, impressed themselves unforgettably on John's memory.

"Are you the king of the Jews?"

"Is this your own question, or have others told you about me?"

"Am I a Jew?" Pilate spoke in a tone of contempt. "Your

own people and the chief priests have brought you before me. What have you done?"

"My kingdom is not of this world. If it were, my servants would be fighting to prevent my arrest by the Jewish leaders. My kingdom is not here."

"Then you are a king?"

"It is you who say that I am a king." In words that opened new vistas of time and eternity if Pilate would look, Jesus went on: "For this I was born—for this I came into the world: to bear witness to the truth. Everyone who is on the side of truth listens to me."

"What is truth?" said Pilate. He did not wait for an answer, and the world has teased ever since over his meaning: whether he jested, or feared to pursue the subject, or had satisfied himself that Jesus was not guilty. A Roman magistrate was trained to seek out truth, but Jesus had placed a disturbing meaning on the word.

Pilate left him in the audience chamber and went out to the Pavement. "I find no case for this man to answer," he announced.

The Sanhedrin spokesman refused to accept the verdict. Their shouts reverberated across the Pavement as they cried out that Jesus had caused disaffection by his teaching throughout Judea: he had started in Galilee and now was here.

At the name "Galilee," Pilate pricked up his ears. If Jesus were a Galilean subject, he could be sent across to Herod Archelaus, the Tetrarch. Although an arrested man need not be returned to his own jurisdiction, as formerly, this could be done if a governor preferred. Pilate told the prosecution to lay the case before Herod. The accusers marched Jesus out of the audience chamber. John slipped out too, hoping that Jesus had caught sight of him and knew that one friend was near.

While they were on the way to Herod, Pilate went on with the next cases. The first two ended swiftly: two thieves were proved guilty of sedition. Pilate ascended the *bema* and pronounced sentence: "I consign you to the cross." Each robber was immediately removed to the barracks to suffer the first stage of the punishment—a violent flogging. Provincials were always executed on the day of sentence. No appeal lay open except for Roman citizens, of any race, who might appeal to Caesar. Nor might Roman citizens be executed by crucifixion: it was regarded as so cruel, slow, and disgusting a death that it could be used only for slaves and low provincials.

Pilate started hearing the third case. This soon developed complications. The brigand Barabbas, who had committed murder in a recent rebellion, was a popular freedom fighter or Zealot, and his friends had swarmed up from the stews of the lower city to watch his trial. They began to shout that Pilate should follow custom and mark the Passover by releasing one prisoner chosen by popular acclamation. They wanted Barabbas. Friends of Jesus also swelled the crowd; news of his arrest was all over the city. Some who had heard him in the Temple, along with fellow pilgrims from Galilee, had come to the Pavement and would shout for Jesus. The crowd grew every minute; the mass of Jews from every land, packing Jerusalem for the festival, included many who were avid for excitement.

Meanwhile, Jesus had been arraigned before Herod the Tetrarch. Sitting on a throne in his lesser palace, the superstitious Herod, who had admired John the Baptist yet killed him, showed pleasure at the opportunity to satisfy his curiosity about Jesus and perhaps to see a miracle. The prosecution hurled charges. Jesus declined to utter one word of rebuttal. Herod questioned Jesus, but he did not answer. Herod soon tired of the case, but whereas Pilate was perplexed, Herod took Jesus as a joke. The Tetrarch and his army captains turned Jesus into a king of the revels. They arrayed him in a gorgeous robe, made fun of him, and returned him, still silent, to Pilate.

As all stood again at the Pavement, it became obvious to John that Pilate more than ever wanted to release Jesus, whom neither he nor Herod had found guilty of a capital crime. Moreover, a messenger came from the private quarters and told Pilate that his wife, disturbed by a dream, urged him to have nothing to do with "that innocent man." But Pilate the judge was also Pilate the politician who did not wish to anger the Jewish leaders; they could make life wearisome or complain to Caesar. He decided to shift responsibility from his shoulders by acceding to the demand for the festival amnesty by popular acclaim. Conviction or acquittal by the people was not unusual in the Roman Empire, and he trusted that the vote would go to the right man; otherwise, Barabbas would resume his career of insurrection, murder, pillage of caravans, and nocturnal harassment of soldiers.

Neither prisoner had yet been formally condemned. Pilate mounted the stone *bema* and proposed to the crowd that he should have Jesus beaten, to teach him a lesson, and then released. The lictors would beat him with rods—the lesser form of corporal punishment, such as Paul and Silas suffered at Philippi. It was frequently ordered as a warning, or when a man was a nuisance to the authorities, and generally was administered in public to shame a man before his neighbors.

Pilate put the question. "Shall I release to you the king of the Jews?" They would first have to watch their king being beaten; the whole episode of kingship would fizzle out in absurdity.

Shouts came back from the crowd: "Not this man but Barabbas." Shouts for Jesus were drowned as the priests stirred up the people for Barabbas. The priests turned any confusion to Barabbas' advantage until the calls for his release grew overwhelming.

"What shall I do with Jesus who is called Christ?" asked Pilate

"Crucify him! Let him be crucified," roared the crowd.

Pilate hesitated again. The sole responsibility for life or for death was his. He sensed that to settle the case of Jesus by acclamation would now be a miscarriage of justice, yet he shied from an acquittal in the face of near riot. His contemporary, the Jewish philosopher Philo of Alexandria, described Pilate as "by nature rigid and stubbornly harsh"; yet when confronted with Jesus, he wavered.

Pilate saw another way out. As a first step, he ordered Jesus a scourging; to be beaten, not with rods but with the dreaded *flagellum,* which was the preliminary to crucifixion, yet could be treated as a sentence in itself or as part of the interrogation of a suspect. When the crowd saw what was left of him, Pilate reasoned, their sympathy should ensure acquittal.

Syrian soldiers briskly marched Jesus into the barracks. For interrogation, the victim was stretched with hands over his head while a clerk stood by to take down confessions or evidence between screams. But they led Jesus to a courtyard where a half-pillar, waist high, stood between runnels for washing away the blood: the pillar had been used twice that day for two thieves.

John saw it all, as he crept in among those who came and went in the palace. Near to tears, he watched the soldiers strip Jesus naked and bend him over the pillar, tying him so that back, buttocks, and legs were equally exposed. Two burly slaves stood ready, also naked. Each picked up a whip of three leather thongs on which had been strung lumps of bone, and standing on either side of him, they brought down the whips in turn with all their might, to cut through skin, nerves, and muscle. They lashed his shoulders and spinal cord, his buttocks and his thighs. Thongs curled round and cut his chest and ribs. A flogging with the *flagellum* could kill in itself if prolonged, or cripple for life; but a man to be crucified must be left the strength to carry the crossbeam to the site of his execution. The pain was atrocious. When, in after years, followers of Jesus were whipped for their faith, and were conscious of him at their side, they were comforted because he himself knew what they suffered.

Jesus did not cry out. With superhuman strength, he endured the pain in silence. This courage did not move the soldiers. When the flogging stopped and they unbound him and he stood in his blood, shivering from shock, cut and bruised from shoulders to calves, they mocked him. They found a military cloak, near enough in color to the imperial purple, for his nakedness. To John's horror, they fashioned a garland of thorns with spikes which aped a raylike crown of royalty, and thrust it down on his head, so that blood trickled from the temples. They put a rod in his right hand, then knelt before him and crowed, "Hail, king of the Jews."

All their hatred of Jews erupted as they seized the rod and hit him on the head, driving the thorns deeper into his skin. One by one soldiers came up to kneel, to rise and spit on his face, to slap him, infuriated by his silence, his refusal to revile back.

The horseplay stopped when the command came to return Jesus to the Pavement. During the flogging, Pilate had retired within. Now he emerged and the waiting crowd fell quiet. John, choking back his nausea and grief, hurried back too before he could be caught and locked away. He stood in the street and watched Pilate come forward to the edge of the Pavement to address the populace.

"Pay attention," said Pilate. "I am bringing him out to you, to let you know that I find no crime in him."

In total silence all looked toward the barracks. Out of the shadows, slowly and painfully, prodded by soldiers, came Jesus wearing the purple robe and the crown of thorns, his face defiled by spittle and marked by agony, the robe soaked in blood.

"Behold the man!" cried Pilate.

John's heart stood still. On the next moments hung almost the last hope that Jesus would be released and restored to his friends. Then he heard a voice from the crowd call out in a tone of venom, "Crucify!" The cry was taken up, "Crucify! Crucify!"

Pilate had miscalculated his hope of sympathy for the victim. He shouted back, but the tumult grew. John heard priests chant, "We have a law. And by that law he ought to die. Because he claimed to be the Son of God."

Pilate looked nonplussed and scared. He took Jesus inside again. This time the interview was private. John must have heard the details afterward, in happier times, from Jesus himself, and could visualize the scene.

The scarred prisoner, whose majesty seemed more potent than the blood and filth on his person, stood before the governor. "Where do you come from?" asked Pilate.

Jesus said nothing.

"Will you not speak to me? Do you not understand that I have authority to release you or to—*crucify* you?"

Jesus replied through his pain and swollen lips: "You could have no power over me unless it had been granted you from above. Therefore the one who handed me over to you has the greater sin."

Pilate came out on to the Pavement again, alone. John knew that one word from the governor would free Jesus. But the accusers roared, "If you release this man, you are not Caesar's friend! Anyone who claims to be a king opposes Caesar."

Pilate was trapped. If he did his duty and released Jesus, whom he had found innocent, his career might be ruined.

He ordered Jesus to be brought out again.

"Here is your king!"

"Away with him! Crucify!"

"Why, what evil has he done?"

"Crucify! Crucify!"

"Shall I crucify your king?"

"We have no king but Caesar!"

In a calmer moment, Pilate would have relished the irony of the most insolent of subject races proclaiming loyalty. All he could see now was the danger of riot.

He took his seat on the stone *bema* to give sentence for

treason. First, he ordered a bowl of water to be brought. The crowd quieted as they watched him solemnly wash his hands.

"I am not responsible for the death of this innocent man," he said, "It is your doing."

"His blood be on us." their spokesman shouted. "On us and on our children."

Pilate, as guilty of judicial murder as the Jewish leaders, released Barabbas and sentenced Jesus to the cross.

Twenty-three
THE LONELY HILL

Once again there was a pause. In the barracks, the soldiers prepared to crucify the three who had been sentenced. Outside, John waited, determined to be near Jesus to the last. Priests and scribes waited also to see their victim suffer, but the friends of Barabbas had carried him off to celebrate. A company of devout women of Jerusalem, whose custom was to weep and wail for those about to die and to ease their sufferings, came to the edge of the Pavement, ready for service.

On this Friday, April 7, A.D. 30 (the date in modern style which best fits the evidence), the sun was already strong when John heard a sharp command from inside the barracks. A moment later, a young, smart centurion emerged and stood on the steps of the Pavement to supervise the execution squad under his command. First came slaves carrying ladders, ropes, iron nails and hammers; the logs, about six feet long, lay ready for use as crossbeams. Rome ordained that every condemned man carry his own, and soon the two robbers with their flagellated backs lurched into the street under theirs. Each was prodded or beaten forward as necessary by the four soldiers assigned to crucify and afterward guard him.

John saw Jesus come into the sunlight with his four executioners. He wore his own clothes but no one had removed the crown of thorns. Across his shoulders lay a heavy beam which chafed the welts of the flogging and weighed down his body, weak from loss of blood and lack of sleep and food. After a few yards along the street, he staggered, then fell, the log pinning him to the ground. The centurion came up, fearful lest the prisoner die before he could be crucified. Then a soldier caught sight of a strong-looking fellow walking up the street, an African named Simon from Cyrene, who was coming into the city from the country. The centurion exercised his right to order any citizen to carry a load one mile and commanded him to take the crossbeam. Since later Simon's two sons, Alexander and Rufus, became members of the Christian community, the experience must have changed his life.

Relieved of his burden, Jesus walked steadily between his executioners. The devout women began their wailing and weeping, but Jesus turned and begged them not to weep for him. He warned them to weep rather for themselves and their children because of the miseries that would fall on Jerusalem.

Behind the women followed a small crowd: the priests who would witness the execution on behalf of the Sanhedrin; a medley of ghoulish spectators; and his friends and the sympathizers of those about to die. John had been joined by Jesus' mother. Mary was bravely determined to stay by her son in his last hours, however terrible the sight, and her sister Salome, John's mother, was at her side, with Mary Magdalene and women from Galilee. Peter in his shame was nowhere to be seen, but by his own statement long afterward he was "a witness of the sufferings of Christ"—unnoticed, far off, alone with his thoughts and tears. If any others of the

Twelve had begun to recover their souls, they find no place in the record. Judas was dead by his own hand.

The procession moved through the street toward the gate. Dogs ran between legs or scurried off yelping when a soldier kicked. John saw Jews about their daily business, and pilgrims sightseeing, who traditionally hurried out of the way of an execution squad, many turning faces to the wall to avoid so unpleasant a sight. But John saw Jews who wept when they recognized Jesus and joined in behind to support him.

Passing through the Garden Gate of the city, the executioners and those who followed moved a little way beyond the walls to where the ground began to rise to the western hill overlooking Jerusalem. They stopped on a rocky outcrop with contours which fitted its name, Place of the Skull (*Golgotha* in Aramaic, *Calvarius* in Latin). It was dominated by tree trunks erected for crucifixions, used again and again as men were taken down dead. Disused quarries close by made quick burials convenient, in the old workings. Calvary's one pleasant feature was the nearness of the gardens beyond, including one which belonged to Joseph of Arimathea.

The centurion made a brief inspection of the site and spoke to his sergeant, who barked an order at the two robbers. They dropped their beams, each before a tree trunk to left and right. The sergeant told Simon of Cyrene to lay his beam beside the tree in the center. The centurion had in his charge a placard about Jesus and wanted him, as the only prominent convict, to die between the others.

The slaves leaned ladders against the uprights and arranged ropes. The devout women now carried out their permitted charity. They handed to the executioners, to pass to their victims, the drugged wine which would deaden some of the pain. Beheading was comparatively painless and swift; crucifixion was slow and literally excruciating. John saw the two thieves gratefully swallow every drop of the drugged wine, but when a soldier brought a wineskin to Jesus, he tasted the mixture, shook his head, and handed it back with unfailing courtesy. John then took Mary, Salome, and the women to a spot where they would not be able to see or hear too closely what was about to happen. He left them there and returned. Determined to comfort Jesus, standing as near as the soldiers allowed, he steeled himself to watch.

While the other squads worked on the thieves, the four executioners laid their hands on Jesus and stripped him naked, even tearing away the loincloth portrayed in Christian art: the Romans did not vary their practice because circumcised Jews abhorred nudity, since shame, and affront to human dignity, were part of the punishment. A man was crucified naked whether Gentile or Jew.

Then they threw Jesus to the ground: they never took chances with a criminal, who might make a last desperate struggle to avoid his fate. John longed to plead with them to be gentle, knowing that Jesus would not resist, but the plea would fall on deaf ears; the men cared nothing that his back was torn and tender, or that his head was circled by thorns. Two soldiers stretched out his arms, a third pushed the crossbeam under them while the fourth pressed hard against his knees.

A soldier picked up a long iron nail and a hammer, knelt on one of Jesus' arms and poised the nail above the palm.

With a sharp blow on the nail, he drove it through his hand into the crossbeam. John clapped his hands to his ears, but suddenly realized that the involuntary reaction of Jesus' vocal chords to the shock and pain was not a scream but the cry *"Abba,* Father." Each blow increased the pain, and the second soldier had started on the palm of the other hand. From behind him, John could hear the thieves being nailed down, to screams and curses and obscenities, but Jesus did not scream; he prayed. In gasps and gulps, the words came clear between the hammer blows: "Father, forgive them. They know not what they do."

John marveled, and his mounting hatred of his Master's executioners began to turn, in spite of himself, to love. And the prayer would be answered; John recalled Jesus' words to the Father, "I know that you hear me always." The soldiers now callously piercing and soon to mock Jesus would one day seek him to accept the forgiveness, perhaps far away in another land (indeed, one may have provided the vivid closeup memories used by Luke in his Gospel).

At present, the executioners seemed unaware that their cruelty under orders had met with love instead of hate. They drove the nails home and wiped the blood from their hands.

One of them climbed the ladder. Others lifted the beam with Jesus nailed to it, and thus caused the most dreadful pain as jolt by jolt they hoisted him by ropes and secured the beam with cords to the upright so that his body's weight pressed down on a stout horn or peg projecting between the crotch. They crossed his legs, forced the feet against the tree, and drove a nail through each. Their experience of crucifying ensured that every nail went where it would stay in place.

The soldiers removed ladder and ropes and left Jesus to hang by the nails, his feet a little way off the ground. One soldier stood guard, and when John wanted to brush away the flies and stinging insects, he was ordered roughly away, and forced to watch impotently as the torture wracked his best friend. The blood which flowed from the nail wounds in hands and feet began to congeal, but whenever Jesus struggled for breath it would start again. John could only guess at the agony: the cramps shooting through inert arms and legs, the suppurating of wounds from the flogging and the thorns and the nails; the pitiless sun and the thirst, already raging from shock.

A soldier put up the ladder again and hammered to the wood above Jesus' head the placard handed him by the centurion to proclaim the name and crimes of the crucified in Aramaic, Latin, and Greek: *Jesus of Nazareth, the king of the Jews*. The Sanhedrin's witnesses at once objected, "He *claimed* to be king of the Jews." The centurion shrugged his shoulders and told them that any complaint should be made to the governor. Two chief priests hurried off to demand audience. When they returned after not too long an interval, they were angry. They told the others that Pilate had snubbed them. "What I have written, I have written," he had said, a snub even more terse since he spoke in Greek: *"Ho gegrapha, gegrapha."*

In their anger they threw pity to the winds and hurled insults at Jesus as he hung immobile on the cross. "He saved others but he can't save himself," they jeered. "He is the king of Israel! Let him come down from the cross, and we will believe in him. He trusts in God. Let God rescue him now if He wants him, for he said, 'I am the Son of God.'" Crowds who had poured out of the city and travelers on the highway took up the cry, and threw his own words back at him and taunted him. The soldiers who had sat down to share out his clothes as their perk, and toss for the seamless robe, mocked him with his title, sneering, "If you are the king of the Jews, save yourself!" The crucified thieves joined in the insults, as if to relieve their own agony and fury before their voices should lapse into croaks.

One of the two thieves, suffering the same physical torture as Jesus, must have observed, as John had, Jesus' patience as fresh pains shot through his nailed body, his refusal to revile those who reviled him, his quiet dignity in disgrace, even a touch of joy as if he could see beyond the lingering death to somewhere wonderful. This thief fell silent, but his fellow, after writhing again in an attempt to relieve the pressure on his pinioned hands, taunted Jesus, "If you are the Christ, save yourself and us!" His voice was now scarcely audible beyond the crosses, but the other heard and rebuked him. "We are getting what we deserved for our crimes. This man has done nothing wrong." Painfully he turned his head to the cross between them. "Jesus," he said, "remember me when you come into your kingdom."

Jesus mustered strength to turn his head. "Truly I tell you," he replied, "today you will be with me in paradise."

John's attention had been fixed on Jesus and only now did he become aware that Mary, leaning on his own mother Salome, had moved in from the spot where distance had blurred the harrowing sight of her son being nailed down and mounted on the cross. John supported her, and together they looked up at Jesus and saw in his face his love for Mary and gratitude for her courage and devotion, and John's. Tenderly, he gave each into the care of the other.

John held Mary close, and henceforth his home would be Mary's. But Mary would not leave the cross; they stood there, unable to grasp a thought except that Jesus hung in dreadful pain and would die. Grief, perplexity, and defeat had driven from their minds his words about why he must die and his promise that he would see them again. A little way off, not obtruding, stood Salome and Mary Magdalene and a few other close friends. Behind them, farther away and beyond those who reviled Jesus, were bystanders who sorrowed. They had sat at his feet and admired his words and deeds yet now had lost all hope; he hung dying on a cross, and their belief was dying with him, that he would redeem their land and people.

By now, after nearly three hours, the torture had worked its havoc on Jesus' body until he was an even more horrifying sight. The physical beauty which matched his goodness had gone; he was contorted, disfigured, despicable. Blood dripped from his hands and feet. Lips and face and limbs were blotched by sun blisters and insect bites. The stripes where the scourge had curled round his chest and stomach and legs showed vivid against his skin. His bones stuck out from the flesh.

At noon a new horror began. Darkness covered the land: not an eclipse of the sun, for this was the day of full moon. The strange loss of light which precedes an earthquake would have had a small part in it, but whatever its extent and physical cause, the untimely darkness quieted mockers, and increased the anguish of Mary and John, for Jesus seemed enveloped by evil. His face showed signs of a struggle more fearful than the pain from wounds or mockery—as if he were indeed under a curse while hanging on a tree, and looking into the abyss with a horror of a great darkness invading his soul, and loathsome all about him. An invisible weight bore down upon his shoulders. As time passed, infinitely slowly without movement of shadows, Mary and John clung desperately to each other, unable to help him. This was no joyous martyr's death: Jesus sank into sorrow to a depth beyond imagination. His grief was fearful to behold.

After three hours of darkness, Jesus gave a sudden terrible cry, startling in its strength and clarity: *"Eloi, eloi, lama sabachthani?"* Mary and John were appalled. He had cried, "My God, my God. Why have you forsaken me?" He had spoken the opening words of *Psalm 22,* but the force of his cry left them in no doubt that the question had been wrung with full meaning from the bottom of his being.

Soldiers and others who were not familiar with Aramaic shouted, "He is calling for Elijah!" A little later Jesus spoke again. "I thirst." A soldier soaked a sponge into their ration of wine vinegar, wedged it on a hyssop stick, and put it up to Jesus' lips and he drank. Other bystanders were callous: "Leave him alone. Let's see whether Elijah will come and take him down."

A few more minutes passed. The breath came in short gasps as if he were dying already, though a man crucified in the prime of life might take three days to die. John could hardly bear to look and was too broken to recall Jesus' words in his great sermon on the Good Shepherd: "No man takes my life from me; I lay it down myself. I have authority to lay it down and to take it again."

Suddenly Jesus gave another cry, its tone not of desertion but of triumph: "It is finished!" A moment later John heard him say, "Father, into your hands I commit my spirit."

Gently, Jesus bowed his head with its crown of thorns. A second later his body hung utterly still.

The ground shook in an earth tremor, strong enough to split rocks in the nearby quarries, while in the Temple, half a mile off, the great curtain which blocked the way into the Holy of Holies tore in half from top to bottom.

As the earthquake ceased, the darkness lifted. The executioners stood white and awestruck. The Roman centurion looked up at the corpse of Jesus and said, "Surely that man was the Son of God."

Part Three
GLORIOUS MORNING

Twenty-four
THE EMPTY TOMB

The body of Jesus hung stiff in the afternoon light. John would not have been allowed to remove it for burial because exposure, alive and dead, was part of the sentence of crucifixion. Very occasionally, guards left an execution too soon and a crucified man was removed by his friends, who might try to revive him, but the two and a half hours during which Jesus hung dead on the cross removed all hope. John could do nothing but keep off the scavenger birds.

Mary still refused to leave. The other women, engulfed by sorrow, withdrew a little way off, uncertain what to do. Priests and scribes walked away toward the city, many looking shaken; some even beat their chests in a gesture of repentance. To the left and right of Jesus' body, the two thieves feebly struggled for breath. The torture, exposure, and starvation had reduced them to little more than conscious corpses, yet a whole night might pass before they died.

An official messenger came up to the centurion. Pilate wanted to know if it were true that Jesus had died so early in his crucifixion. The centurion sent the messenger back with confirmation.

The corpse on the cross stiffened with rigor mortis. The thieves moaned feebly and struggled to force air into their lungs by lifting their chests.

About an hour before sunset, John saw a picket of soldiers. They carried spears and iron mallets, and when they reported to the centurion, John overheard that Pilate had agreed to a request from Caiaphas: no dying or dead bodies should pollute the high Sabbath of Passover by hanging outside the city wall. A soldier walked up to each thief, lifted a mallet, and with brutal efficiency smashed his knees and legs. Weak cries gave little indication of the searing pain, but death rattles followed soon, for when a crucified man could no longer put pressure on his legs, he lost the last power to lift his ribs and breathe.

The soldiers converged on Jesus. He looked dead; to make death certain, a soldier jabbed him in the side with a spear, causing a wound large enough for a hand to be inserted. John saw a sudden gush of blood and water. A plausible medical explanation is that an internal hemorrhage, caused by the flogging, had settled in the rib cage.

Hardly had the soldiers completed their work when Joseph of Arimathea and Nicodemus, with servants carrying bundles of linen and bags of spices, approached the central cross. The two Sanhedrin counselors had thrown off the secrecy of their allegiance to Jesus and had boldly asked Pilate for permission to remove and bury the body. On receiving the centurion's report, Pilate granted their request since they were men of rank in good standing; permission was seldom refused except in cases of high treason on the part of the criminal.

As the evening shadows lengthened, John watched, numbed with sorrow, the gruesome work of extracting the nails with iron pincers, lowering the rigid arms, and laying the corpse of Jesus on the ground. Then Mary swooned at last, and when the women had revived her, John took her away, walking in their grief through the city to the home of John Mark.

It was not until dusk, therefore, a few moments before Sabbath began, and Mary Magdalene and the other women reached the house, that John Mark heard what happened.

Nicodemus had brought spices in great weight, as for a king's burial. Joseph had brought unbleached linen to make a shroud and a napkin for the head. Jews did not gut a corpse as the Egyptians did, and the two eminent counselors and their servants, in their hurry to complete the burial before Sabbath, wrapped the body of Jesus unwashed, but with reverence. They carried it the short distance to Joseph of Arimathea's garden. Joseph had planned to be buried there himself and had hewn out a new tomb from the hillside which sheltered his vegetables and shrubs. Since Jesus had no family tomb in Jerusalem, nor was there time to look farther, they laid him in this rich man's grave.

Mary Magdalene and her companions, following at a distance, saw the burial party stoop to enter the tomb. Inside, a shelf had been hewn from the rock. The two counselors emerged; their men, sweating and straining, heaved into position the great boulder which blocked the entrance. The women saw it all, then hurried back to the city.

John, Mary, and the other women spent the night and day of Sabbath in mute despair. Their world had collapsed. Neither the ancient prophets nor the recent words of Jesus could penetrate their grief. Bereft of him, they had lost hope and purpose. No one had heart to attend synagogue or Temple, but friends who called to offer sympathy spoke of a city divided. Many held high festival while others were perplexed by the sudden condemnation and horrifying death of Jesus. No one, however, told them that Caiaphas had sent chief priests into Pilate's palace on a high Sabbath, thereby ritually defiling themselves, to warn him that the disciples might steal the body and then announce that Jesus had risen from the dead; "this last deception will be worse than the first." Pilate wearily allowed the priests' request to mount their own guard and to put a seal on the tomb, a task which broke the Sabbath.

Had the women known about the guards they might not have had courage to do what they did next morning: they knew only about the huge stone, and were worried how they should move it.

As soon as Sabbath ended at sunset on the Saturday, Mary Magdalene, Salome, and another Mary (whose two sons were also among the eleven disciples) hurried to the reopened shops and bought spices. Even if they knew how deeply Nicodemus had embalmed the body, they wanted to add their own fragrance to help offset the stench of decay and to honor Jesus' memory. They mixed the preparation during the night, the second since his death, then tried to sleep.

At dawn on the third day, Sunday, April 9, A.D. 30, while Jesus' mother slept in her grief, the other women crept out at dawn. John watched them go, and could imagine them as they walked as mourners through the wakening streets and through the city gate, which opened at dawn; averting their gaze as they passed the bloodstained crosses, and entering Joseph's garden.

John heard a knock at the door. The maid Rhoda let in Simon Peter. No one knew where he had lodged, though his wife was presumably among the pilgrims. The two men sat together in grief too deep for words while the sun rose and light flooded into the upper room. Soon came other knocks. One by one the Eleven, who could move freely now that Sabbath was over, with other close friends, converged on the house of happy memories to draw strength from each other's sorrow. None recalled past desertions: they were united in grief, wanting only to comfort Mary, his mother.

Suddenly there was a commotion below, and voices and a pounding on the stairs. Mary Magdalene, Salome, and the other Mary burst into the room.

"They have taken the Lord out of the tomb," cried Mary

Magdalene, "and we do not know where they have laid him!"

The women's account was so incoherent and amazing that the first instinct of John, Peter, and the others was to dismiss it as nonsense. No statement of a woman was highly regarded (it had no force in law) and no one noted too precisely what they said, nor unraveled seeming discrepancies afterward, so that their testimony went down into history unpolished and spontaneous.

They had entered the garden, they said, just after sunrise. They saw at once that the stone was no longer at the mouth of the tomb. Armed guards lay on the ground either asleep or dead: the women had not expected to see guards, but they expected to see the body of Jesus when they looked into the tomb. It was gone. While they tried to collect their wits, they saw a vision of angels, dazzling like lightning; but whether two angels or one, whether in the tomb or sitting on the stone, the women could not recall with clarity. They received a message that they were not to be afraid: Jesus was not there, he was risen; he would go to Galilee where they would see him; they must tell his disciples, "and Peter," at once.

They had left the tomb in confusion, shock, and terror and run back to the city, not saying a word to any they passed, and had come at once to the house.

A huge stone had been moved; guards like dead men; dazzling angels; empty tomb—it all sounded idiots' tales. But something had happened.

Peter and John put on their sandals and ran, as if for their lives.

John was fleeter of foot than the more rugged Peter, and once they were free of the workaday streets and through the gate, he outpaced Peter and reached the garden first. The guards were nowhere to be seen. John ran to the tomb. He stooped and looked in and as his eyes grew used to the dark interior he saw no sign of grave robbers. The linen shroud lay all of a piece, not in a heap like Lazarus' graveclothes after

201

Jesus had commanded "loose him," but as if the body had passed through it. He saw the head napkin nearby, which had been around the skull and jaw. It lay folded.

Peter ran up and went straight into the tomb. Then John entered. Without doubt, the tomb and the shroud were empty. John believed the unbelievable: he had not expected what he saw. He did not bring to mind any of the prophecies which Jesus had taught them from Scripture that the Christ would rise from the dead; but he believed.

Peter went out of the tomb very silent. John followed him. Together, they walked away from the garden, followed by two of the women. Mary Magdalene stayed behind, and they heard her beginning to wail again. As they entered the city gate, Peter said not a word. Nor would he return to Mark's home but went off to his lodging.

An hour or two later, while John was trying to focus his thoughts, and the others puzzled over the meaning of the empty tomb, Mary Magdalene came into the house again and ran up the stairs. Her face was radiant: "I have seen the Lord!"

They crowded round her. Her story was one more amazement on that amazing morning. She told how she had stopped her wailing to take another look into the tomb. Where Jesus' body had rested, she saw through her tears a dazzling vision, one angel at the head and the other at the foot.

"Why are you crying?" they asked.

"They have taken away my Lord, and I don't know where they have put him!"

Something made her turn around. Blurred by tears, she saw a Man: no angelic vision this time but a Man so normal and strong, in his early thirties, that she assumed he was the gardener.

She begged this Man to tell her where he had put him, "and I will carry him away."

"Mary!" said the Man.

She could not mistake the voice. She cried, "My own Teacher!" and fell at his feet. Jesus gently told her not to hold him, for he was not yet returned to the Father.

And now Mary Magdalene was bringing the disciples his message. He had called them his brothers and she reported that he had said, "I am returning to my Father and your Father, to my God and your God."

It was only a woman's word. Could she have received a vision? John yearned to see him with his own eyes and to touch him, if only for the second or two which Mary had been allowed, before Jesus returned to the Father.

Mary Magdalene's joy was not infectious; some of them did not believe her, including Thomas, who had to leave shortly afterward for affairs which would occupy him the remainder of the day, and two who left to journey to Emmaus, seven miles from Jerusalem, in the afternoon. They walked away sad and perplexed.

They had not been gone more than an hour when the door of the house opened and closed again and John heard a heavy step, which could be none other than Peter's, upon the stair. Simon Peter entered the room, and John saw at once that something very wonderful had happened to him. He was subdued yet happy; tears of joy welled in his eyes. All he would say was, "He has appeared to me." He never revealed a word of what passed between them. John, yearning more than ever to see him, recognized the true stamp of Jesus; he had appeared first of all among the Eleven, to the one who loved him yet had denied him.

Though Peter would not disclose private words, most of those present doubted no longer. Whatever the world might say, Jesus had risen from the dead.

During the later afternoon, they learned that Caiaphas and his officials had countered the rumors sweeping the city by circulating statements that while the guards slept, Jesus' disciples had stolen the body. The high priest's next steps might be to discover, arrest, and destroy the disciples so that they could not expose his deceit. They hurriedly bolted the outer and inner doors of Mark's home.

They talked much among themselves. The tomb was empty; Mary had seen him, and he had appeared to Peter and forgiven him; yet they did not know what to do next because the events of the day were beyond human experience. When at dusk Rhoda brought up a meal of broiled fish, honeycomb, and bread, they thankfully sat up at the table and ate. Joy was uppermost in their mood, but grief and surprise were close below.

They were interrupted by a knocking so loud that some feared that the Temple police had discovered them. They heard the doors being unbolted, and excited friendly voices. While the doors were locked again, the two who had gone to Emmaus came running upstairs and into the room. John guessed at once, but before he could speak someone called out to them. "It is true. The Lord has risen! He has appeared to Simon!"

In reply, the two travelers could not contain their own excitement. They had been walking along the highway, they said, trying to understand the events of the past days but unable to throw off their grief, despite the women's story, when a stranger overtook them and joined their conversation. He asked the cause of their sorrow. With their downcast eyes, they did not look searchingly at the face under the headdress, and when he seemed ignorant they told him about the death of the Prophet on whom all their hopes had rested; and of the women's discovery of the empty tomb; and of the dash by Peter and John, who "found it just as the women had said, but they did not see *him*."

The Stranger rebuked them. He called them fools and too slow to believe all that the prophets had spoken about the Christ.

Then he took them through the Scriptures, explaining passages in such a way that their hearts were strangely warmed until on fire. They reached Emmaus. The Stranger apparently was going farther, but with dusk falling they prevailed on him to stay at their house.

They prepared a meal, and it was then, when he took up the bread, gave thanks, broke it, and gave pieces to them from scarred hands, that they realized who he was.

Seconds later he disappeared: the Man whom they had taken as another foot traveler until the glorious moment of recognition had simply disappeared. They had returned at once to Jerusalem through the dusk and nightfall to bring their news. A stony road and the risk of robbers meant nothing to tired feet impelled by joy.

John had listened with the rest in silence. No shreds of doubt remained, but he yearned even more to see Jesus. Four friends at the least had seen him, yet not John.

They were all talking excitedly when they heard the unmistakable voice of Jesus: "*Shalom*. Peace be with you." They looked and he was there, standing at the table among them, even though the doors were locked. They had longed for him; but, taken by surprise, they were terrified, wondering if they were seeing his ghost. The shattered corpse of Calvary was alive, in normal health, wearing his usual clothes, with that smile they would never forget. Despite hopes and belief that he had risen, his unexpected coming threw them in turmoil.

He spoke again. "Why are you troubled? Why do doubts rise in your minds? Look at my hands and my feet. It is I, myself! Touch me and see. A ghost does not have flesh and bones as you see that I have!"

He held out his hands, and the holes made by the nails were plain to their eyes. He made them look at his feet; they saw where the nails had pierced. When they were still speechless with joy and amazement, and some seemed still to doubt, he asked for something to eat. They gave him some fish and honeycomb, and he ate.

He sat down. As they relaxed he looked around and taught them just as in old times.

He recalled how he had told them that the prophecies about Christ would be fulfilled in him, and he began to take them through the Scriptures, as he had taken the two on the Emmaus road, showing that Christ had to suffer for the sins of mankind and then rise from the dead and enter his glory. Scripture after Scripture had been fulfilled in detail, by men acting unawares, such as the soldiers who had not broken his legs but had pierced him, and the counselors who had buried him in a rich man's grave.

By now all those present were overjoyed. Jesus said again, *"Shalom.* Peace be with you," and told them that they would continue his work of bringing men the forgiveness of sins.

He did not stay with them. Nor did he reappear the next day. Thomas, indeed, when he returned to their company, even refused to believe that they had seen him.

Thomas told them that unless he could see the nail marks himself, "and put my finger where the nails were, and put my hand into his side, I will *not* believe." Nothing they could say changed his mind, and still Jesus did not meet any of them, nor confront his persecutors. Days passed; doubt gnawed a little.

On the following Sunday evening, they were again gathered, including Thomas, in the Upper Room, as if instinctively celebrating the Resurrection one week later. Expectancy rose high and was not disappointed. The doors were locked, yet Jesus joined them and their hearts leaped to hear his *"Shalom!"*

He beckoned immediately to Thomas.

"Put your finger here and see my hands," He said. "Reach out your hand and put it in my side. Stop doubting, and believe."

Thomas did not lift his finger, but answered, "My Lord and my God!"

Twenty-five
WITH YOU
ALWAYS

One afternoon later that April the Sea of Galilee sparkled in the spring sunshine which touched scores of sails. Across the deep blue of the water, the eastern shore showed clear, with the wooded hills behind. Mount Hermon's snow hung hazily above the horizon to the north. The scene looked familiar; time might have stood still since the spring day three years before when John had jumped onto the beach from his father's ship to meet Jesus.

This afternoon John, James, and Peter were walking up and down the foreshore restlessly. Sitting on tufts of grass behind were Nathanael and Thomas and two more of the Eleven, while the remaining four were somewhere in the town. In obedience to Jesus' instructions, they had returned from Jerusalem to Galilee, but he had not appeared to them again. Their lives seemed suspended between the past and an unknown future. The uncertainty bothered Peter, who still had not recovered his natural exuberance and went around like a man who knew he was forgiven but could not forgive himself. John, for his part, had a strong yearning to see Jesus and not to let him go.

As the sun moved into the west, Peter suddenly said, "I'm

going out fishing." The others leaped at the idea of activity; even landlubbers Nathanael and Thomas wanted to come. Peter, John, and James spent a happy hour preparing tackle and shortly before sunset the seven put out from the shore. They trawled all night and caught nothing: it was like the night before Jesus had preached from Peter's boat.

At the first sign of the coming dawn, they headed back to shore. When they were about a hundred yards off and dawn was breaking, they saw a Man standing on the beach; the light behind them was too faint to show who it might be. The Man called out to them, "Boys, have you anything eatable?"

"No," they shouted back.

He called out across the water, telling them to cast on the right of their boat, "and you will find." They did not hesitate: a man ashore could sometimes see a shoal invisible to those on the water. They cast a hand net. Immediately, they felt weight and found it already too heavy to draw in.

John knew at once by instinct. Hardly looking up at the figure on the shore, now clearer in the stronger light of full dawn, he said quietly to Peter, "It is the Lord!"

Peter had stripped to work the net. He seized his outer garment, wrapped it round him and jumped into the water and swam toward the beach. John worked the boat inshore, towing the net, and grounded the vessel.

As they jumped out, they saw a charcoal fire. The Man on the shore was cooking a few fish and he had bread too. He said, "Bring some of the fish you have caught." Peter, still soaking wet, climbed back into the boat. He released the net. When the disciples had dragged it onto the beach, they saw an enormous haul; they were astonished too that the net had not broken. Excitedly, they began counting, not merely picking out some to cook, and John never forgot the exact total: 153.

Then Jesus called them to the breakfast he had prepared. As they sat around the fire, the atmosphere was tense; there were no spontaneous greetings. No one dared ask their Host whether indeed he was Jesus: they knew, yet he had an aura about him, of life and power and timelessness, of purity, and a serenity beyond that which comes through suffering. Then he took the bread, broke it, and handed it round, and the fish too; and the tension broke at that characteristic touch of his serving them. When the sunrise flooded the scene with light and warmth, it reflected their joy.

They finished eating. Jesus turned to Simon Peter. "Simon son of Jonah, do you love me more than these?"

"Yes, Lord, you know that I love you."

"Feed my lambs!"

John was happy that Jesus should publicly restore his disciple, John's best friend; but Jesus immediately repeated the question, and when he received the same answer, he said, "Look after my sheep."

Then he asked the question a third time.

Peter looked sad beyond words that Jesus should ask a third time, as if to recall the threefold denial. Peter stood up and walked away, not in pique but in sorrow, and Jesus followed him, and John followed them both. Peter hung his head. "Lord," he murmured, "you know all things. You know that I love you."

"Feed my sheep," said Jesus.

Simon Peter lifted his head. Their eyes met, just as they had met in the high priest's palace less than three weeks before. Peter's sorrow vanished. He accepted the commission to be shepherd of God's flock: no sheep could stray farther than he had. Jesus then gave him a prophetic warning of the martyrdom which he suffered for God's glory thirty-one years later, and repeated the very phrase he had used on the same beach when the four partners had left their nets and the great adventure had begun: "Follow me!"

Several days later they both saw Jesus appear again, not only to the Eleven but to a great concourse of more than 500 believers who had come together somewhere in Galilee on Jesus' instructions. Here was the young man of Nain; and

Legion; and a man who once had a withered arm; and another who had been paralyzed, who had come with the four friends who had lowered his pallet through the roof. Cured lepers; once-blind men who now saw; Jairus and his wife and daughter; the woman who had touched the hem of the garment; the Roman centurion, his servant, and his whole household; and scores of men and women who had not been afflicted or distressed but had heard the message which Jesus had preached throughout Galilee. Few were elderly; when the Apostle Paul, who knew many, wrote about the incident some twenty-three years later, most were still alive.

Jesus' words to this company were not recorded, but shortly afterward, he came again to the Eleven on a mountain to which he had directed them. He told them that all authority had been given to him in heaven and earth. He commissioned them to go out and make disciples from all nations, baptizing them, and teaching them to obey all that he had taught: "And be very sure," he said, "that I am with you always, to the end of the age."

From that day onward, the Eleven knew that they were not only disciples but apostles, witnesses of his resurrection, who should begin to proclaim and spread his Gospel to every man, woman, and child throughout the world.

The weeks went by. He appeared to them again and again. Even his half brother James believed, the only opponent to whom Jesus appeared after his resurrection until he stopped Paul of Tarsus on the Damascus road. Caiaphas might speak of a stolen dead body; others might mock, or hint at hallucinations, but John, Peter, and their friends, and James the half brother, knew beyond a shadow of doubt that Jesus was alive, that he was the Son of God, the Christ.

He taught the Eleven more and more about the kingdom of God, and showed in detail how the Scriptures had prophesied plainly what had happened to him. Many matters became clear: why the innocent Jesus had been engulfed by sin as he hung on the cross; why the Baptist, when first pointing him out on Jordan's bank, had said, "Look, the Lamb of God, who takes away the sin of the world"; why the veil of the Temple, which blocked the holiest place, had torn from top to bottom the moment he had died. Jesus instructed them so clearly that Peter, who had been angry when Christ had foretold his crucifixion, learned fast to become a highly effective preacher and witness.

When Jesus ended each time of teaching, he left as mysteriously as he had come, but the apostles were excited at the prospect of seeing him again and did not sorrow.

After five weeks, Jesus told the Eleven to return to Jerusalem, with his mother and other friends. The next great festival, Pentecost, was two weeks away and the city was again filling with pilgrims, but John Mark's family opened their home and the apostles made the Upper Room their headquarters.

Jesus appeared to them while they were having a meal, and ate with them. This time he ordered them on no account to leave Jerusalem. "You must wait," he said, "for the gift my Father promised, which you have heard me speak about; for John baptized with water but in a few days you will be baptized with the Holy Spirit."

On the morning of the fortieth day after he had risen from the dead, Jesus appeared again to the Eleven. This time he led them out of the city by the route of vivid memories which they had taken on the night of His betrayal. As they walked, somebody put a question which the others backed, and thus disclosed that they had missed the point on a vital matter. "Lord, are you at this time going to restore the kingdom to Israel?"

He refused to be drawn. "It is not for you to know the times or dates the Father has set by his own authority," Jesus replied, settling the question so firmly that they dropped the subject and never again confused his teaching about the kingdom. He went on: "But you will receive power when the

Holy Spirit comes on you. And you will be my witnesses—in Jerusalem; and in all Judea and Samaria; and to the very ends of the earth."

They walked on. After they had crossed the Kidron Valley, Jesus did not lead them to the Garden of Gethsemane but higher up the Mount of Olives to a quiet spot, without idle bystanders, above Bethany. They stood around him. He gave no farewell, but blessed them in the old familiar gesture, and as he blessed them, his body rose from the earth; the cloud of glory, which had terrified Peter, James, and John at the Transfiguration, enveloped Jesus while they watched. This time it did not terrify: the scene was utterly peaceful.

Their eyes were riveted on the glory as it receded, when suddenly they saw two men in white, who asked: "Why do you stand looking into heaven, men of Galilee? This same Jesus, who has been taken from you into heaven, will come back in the same way as you have seen him go into heaven."

Then they knew that they would not now see Jesus in physical form, to touch him or eat with him or hear his well-loved voice. They turned back toward the city. But they walked with a light step, not sorrowing nor hopeless but with happiness, because he had ascended to be with the Father, and with a strong expectancy.

They reached Mark's home and climbed the stairs to the Upper Room and told Mary, Jesus' mother, and the other women and friends. All accepted that they would not see Jesus again, but the contrast with the days after his crucifixion could not be greater. Then they had mourned, and felt crushed by the finality of his death; now they rejoiced at the prospect of his promise. They knew themselves to be living through an interlude before the story of his life resumed, and they could only guess at what was coming.

The days went by in mounting excitement. The Eleven and those who knew and believed that Jesus had risen from the dead, a brotherhood of some 120 men and women, met together frequently, praising God in the Temple or filling the Upper Room until there was no space to sit on the floor. They spent time in prayer, remembering his words, "How much more will your Heavenly Father give the Spirit to those who ask him." They talked among themselves. Mary, his mother, could now tell them the story of his conception when she was a virgin, which would have seemed an idle tale indeed before he had risen from the dead. The apostles learned details of his nativity in Bethlehem, and about shepherds and wise men and all the matters which Mary had hidden in her heart until the time came to tell.

Nicodemus could reveal what Jesus had told him when he had gone secretly at night, during Jesus' first visit to Jerusalem after his baptism. It made sense now, that unless a man is born again of water and the Spirit, he cannot see the kingdom of God. And Nicodemus could quote words of Jesus which had mystified him, but now were plain: "God so loved the world that he gave his only begotten Son, that whoever believes in him shall not perish but have eternal life."

They came and went but were very close: Martha and Mary and Lazarus; Zacceus up from Jericho, bringing the once-blind Bartimaeus; the Jerusalem man who had been born blind; the great counselors, Nicodemus and Joseph of Arimathea; and the numerous party of Galileans. It was from these that they chose a successor to Judas. Peter told them that the choice must fall on one who had been "with us the whole time the Lord Jesus went in and out among us," from the baptism until his ascension. They selected two, and after prayer they took Matthias by lot to become the twelfth apostle, a witness to Christ's resurrection.

By now the broad street outside the Upper Room was becoming busier as Jews and proselytes from countries east and west converged on Jerusalem for Pentecost.

The feast day itself, which originally celebrated barley

harvest, was a time for national rejoicing, but for the brotherhood, when they came together early on Pentecost morning, it brought special joy as the seventh Sunday and fiftieth day since Jesus had risen from the dead.

Shortly before 9 o'clock, all 120 were at prayer and thanksgiving in the Upper Room. John was beside Peter. Suddenly an extraordinary noise like the sound of a gale roared into the room. Everybody looked up in awe. The place seemed ablaze, without smoke. Fire separated into tongues and settled on every head. As the flame touched him, John had an amazing sense of being filled with joy and peace beyond anything he had known; a power that almost lifted him. He could see that all the apostles, all his friends, both men and women were being filled; spontaneously, they began to praise God in loud voices and a torrent of words.

Above all else, John had an overwhelming, exquisite feeling that Jesus was in the room—not merely in the room but right within him. Jesus was back, as he had promised: "I will not leave you orphans," he had said. "I will come to you . . . We will come to you and make our home in you."

Jesus had kept his promise. The Spirit had come—the Spirit of God the Father, the Spirit of Jesus himself, and by his coming he made all things new. The old passed away. John was reborn. Peter was reborn. All felt re-created. John could see it on their faces.

Power, fire, joy. Down the stairs and into the street, they cried with joy, praising and laughing, testifying that Jesus was alive. Passers-by and neighbors ran together to see what it was all about. Soon a huge crowd of citizens and pilgrims packed the street, their clothes showing that they came from a dozen or more countries. Only when John heard what the people said, and their looks of astonishment, did he realize that he, Peter and James and the rest were using a battery of dialects and tongues that they had never learned or known before; pilgrims were hearing of God's wonderful works in their mother tongue.

Seeing the crowd, Peter ran back into the house and upstairs and out on to the flat roof. John followed, and the ten other apostles. Peter put out his hand for silence. Most of the crowd quieted but John heard mocking voices: "They're filled with sweet wine!"

Peter heard, and good-humoredly rebutted the claims. "It is only 9 in the morning!" he said. "No, this is what the Prophet Joel spoke about: 'I will pour out my Spirit on all people. . . .'" Then Peter preached a tremendous sermon. Listening, John could hardly imagine a greater contrast from the scared slink-away who had lied to a servant girl and denied Jesus, whom now he proclaimed to be Lord and Christ.

Peter spoke of Jesus, his miracles and goodness. He minced no words in reminding his hearers how they had delivered up Jesus to be nailed to a cross: *"But* God raised him from the dead . . . God has raised Jesus to life, and we are all witnesses of the fact. Exalted to the right hand of God, he has received from the Father the promised Holy Spirit and has poured out what you now see and hear."

Peter reached his climax, and John knew that Jesus spoke through him as surely as He had spoken to the crowds in Galilee or Jerusalem. "Let all Israel know for sure," proclaimed Peter, "that God has made this Jesus, whom you crucified, both Lord and Christ."

The sermon went right home. "What shall we do? What shall we do?" cried scores of voices from the crowd. Peter seized his advantage. John thrilled to hear him proclaim the Good News, that everyone who repented and believed could be baptized and receive the same Spirit which had been poured out on themselves. "The promise is for you! And for your children! And for all who are far off—for all whom the Lord our God will call."

Hundreds immediately wanted to be baptized. The apostles worked hard down at the pool, until they had counted about 3,000 new believers on that one single day. And, to the apostles' delight, each of the new believers experienced the same inward sense that Jesus was alive.

For John and his fellow apostles, that Sunday began days more glorious even than those they had enjoyed with the Master in Galilee. Then, they had been too often stupid, doubting, or disobedient. Now they were fellow workers with him in a new way. They realized that all the Lord Jesus had done and taught in Galilee and Judea was the start of what he planned to do through them and with them, and through those whom he added to their number day by day. John remembered his words at the Last Supper, that they would do greater works than he had done; and with him beside them, they were proving it as they preached and instructed and healed.

It was only the beginning. They would indeed be witnesses to him in Judea and Samaria and the uttermost parts of the earth: Peter would go to Rome, Thomas to India, John to Ephesus and Paul, unknown to them yet, and soon to be their persecutor, would become the hardest working and most traveled apostle of all, after the direct intervention of Jesus.

They knew they were still weak and sinful men. None could compare with Jesus. But the Spirit was making them more like him every day and teaching them. John found that soon he knew the Lord Jesus better than when they had walked together along the lanes of Galilee. He could talk to him more freely in prayer than when they had talked about their needs, worries, or confusions during the months and years when he went in and out among them. Jesus had not only risen but had ascended. He was at the Father's side interceding for them and pouring out his gifts. But he was at their side too.

Each believer, John found, had this sense of growing intimacy. The memory of a great man or a good man will fade with the years, but John already knew the truth that would be expressed a few years later in the immortal phrase: "Jesus Christ, the same yesterday, today, and forever."

And so John and his friends went out into the highways and byways, the cities and the countryside and crossed the seas to proclaim "the Word of Life, which we have seen with our eyes, which we have looked at and our hands have touched."

II.

The APOSTLE

A LIFE OF PAUL

PREFACE

One of the most frequently mentioned figures in history, whose writings are read by millions every day, is little known to this generation as a person. The name of Saint Paul the Apostle is familiar to all Christians, to most Jews and Moslems; he is quoted, argued about, attacked and defended. Yet even those who read his words and adventures with unfailing regularity have scant idea of what he was like—as I found for myself when my publisher suggested I write a life of Paul.

Many recall only one book about him: H.V. Morton's deservedly famous *In the Steps of St. Paul*. But that was a travelogue, not a biography, and written in the very different conditions of the mid-1930s. So the man or woman of today, whether Bible reader or not, misses the fascination of knowing Paul as Luke or Timothy or the objectionable Elymas knew him.

I felt therefore that it would not be impertinent for a biographer who has enjoyed the intense satisfaction of getting closer to those of whom he has written to approach Paul as I did my previous biographies: to accept the New Testament as I had accepted the boxes of letters and papers which had formed the source material of my other subjects, use it in the same way, and see what happened. A biographer develops a nose, a sort of instinct, and it was not long before I was struck inescapably by the credibility, the genuineness of the person who was emerging from the Acts of the Apostles and the Epistles taken as a whole. A convincing character, with a completely credible if astonishingly unusual story, was taking hold of me until I found more and more excitement in getting nearer the heart of the man. I have been familiar with the Bible since childhood, but now I was seeing Paul as if for the first time: his motives, aims, and priorities; what mattered to him, and to what he was indifferent; his attitude to his mistakes when he recognized them. And what he was willing to die for.

I began to learn his contemporaries' view of him. There have been plenty of opinions ever since. Nietzsche called him "One of the most ambitious of men, whose superstition was only equalled by his cunning; a much tortured, much to be pitied man, an exceedingly unpleasant person both to himself and to others." Farrar, the Victorian dean, portrayed him as loftily superior, disdaining mortal weaknesses above ordinary passions, a saint in cold marble. Basil Matthews made him a muscular Christian, a boy's hero. None of these Pauls resembled the man I was getting to know, both as my wife and I drove in a Volkswagen along the roads he had walked 2,000 years before and as I studied the New Testament and many other writings.

As any writer on Paul must, I have dug into the enormous and ever-growing mass of scholarship about him and his background, but since I write for the general reader I have not burdened the narrative with the arguments which led to my conclusions. In regard to the gaps in Paul's life, I have sought to introduce nothing that cannot be deduced from the evidence, and have aimed at inference rather than conjecture. There is a world of difference between inference and conjecture, and imagination must not roam at the cost of authenticity.

Paul lived about sixty-six generations back—just twice as long ago as the Norman Conquest. He has more than ever a contemporary interest. Recent radical theologians have attracted the popular press because they are exciting; Paul is far more exciting and radical. I have tried to make him and his amazing story freshly alive to those for whom he is nothing except the man who wrote the chapter on Charity; and to those who read him frequently, whether Protestant, Catholic, Orthodox, or the Jews for whom he had such unbreakable love.

When I had finished writing, I felt rather as when nearing the summit of a high mountain. You recognize other routes up; you realize how little you know of the terrain. Yet you get a grand view—of the mountain and of the world around.

But I have not got to the top. There are some unattainable crags, just below the summit.

Acknowledgments

I am extremely grateful to Dr. F.F. Bruce, Rylands Professor of Biblical Criticism and Exegesis in the University of Manchester, Dr. Frank E. Gaebelein, Dr. L. Nelson Bell and Sir Richard Barrett-Lennard, Bt., who very kindly read the typescript and made valuable corrections and suggestions.

My warm thanks to all who aided us on our travels in the Holy Land and other Middle East countries, and in Turkey, Greece and Italy; especially Dr. Wilhelm Alzinger of the Austrian Archaeological Institute, director of research at Ephesus; the Rt. Rev. Abbot Brookes, O.S.B., of Rome; Mr. Courtenay Edwards, motoring correspondent of the *Sunday Telegraph*, London; Mr. F.J. Parkhouse and Mr. J. Wilcox of Exeter; and Miss Louise A. Shier, curator of the Kelsey Museum of Archeology, University of Michigan.

Contents

Part One

HOLDCOAT AND TURNCOAT

THE EASTERN
MEDITERRANEAN
PAUL'S EARLY TRAVELS

One
FROM THE LAND OF
BLACK TENTS

The judges leaped from their places howling in fury. The Hall of Polished Stones, scene of grave debates and historic trials, reverberated to the baying of a lynch crowd, which rushed at the young defendant and manhandled him down the steps into the strong sunlight of the Court of the Priests. Across this wide, open space, down more steps, through court after court, Stephen was swept by the maddened crowd swelled by bystanders, worshipers and traders, until they had him out of the sacred Temple precincts into the streets of the Holy City.

No sentence of death had been passed, nor could be executed unless confirmed by the Roman authorities and preceded by solemn ritual to ensure justice to the last. Judges and mob cared nothing for that. When the northern gate was behind them and they reached the Rock of Execution, "twice the height of a man," they should solemnly have stripped him, and thrown him cleanly over to break his neck or at least to stun him, so that death by stoning would not be too unmerciful. Instead they pushed Stephen as he was, and his tangled clothes broke the fall and he staggered to his feet fully conscious.

The mob was shocked into reverting to forms of law. In a

229

judicial stoning the first stones must be aimed by those who had brought the charges. These witnesses therefore elbowed their way to the front, threw off their outer clothes, and looked around for someone to guard them. A young lawyer, panting from the race through the streets, stepped forward. They recognized a Pharisee from Cilicia in Asia Minor known as Saul among Jews and Paul among Greeks and Romans.

Paul watched approvingly as each witness picked up a heavy jagged stone, raised it above his head, and threw it to gash and maim the man below. Then Paul heard Stephen's voice. In pain but clearly, he spoke as if to someone invisible but close: "Lord Jesus, receive my spirit."

Stones showered as the mob scrambled to complete what the witnesses had begun. Stephen mastered his pain while blood gushed from cuts and bruises. He knelt down in an attitude of prayer. Paul could not miss the words that came with loudness amazing in a dying man: "Lord, do not hold this sin against them."

The next stone knocked Stephen flat. He lost consciousness. The mob continued stoning until the body became obscene.

Paul was born in a city between the mountains and the sea. The year was probably A.D. 1, but all early details are shadowy except his clear claim: "I am a Jew of Tarsus, a citizen of no mean city, of the people of Israel, of the tribe of Benjamin, a Hebrew born of Hebrews."

Tarsus was the principal city of the lush plain of Cilicia in the southwest corner of Asia Minor. The sea lay out of sight a dozen miles south. The Taurus mountains curved in a great arc some twenty-five miles inland, coming nearly to the sea on the west and marked to the north by gorges and cliffs which stood like rock fortresses before the snows; a magnificent background for childhood, especially in winter when the snow showed smooth on cloudless peaks.

The river Cydnus, narrow and swift, and usually superlatively clear, ran through the city. It flowed into the artificial harbor, an engineering masterpiece of the ancient world, where Cleopatra had stepped ashore some forty years before Paul's birth to meet Antony, while all Tarsus marveled at silver oars, a poop of beaten gold, and purple sails "so perfumed that the winds were lovesick with them." Here, each spring when navigation resumed and the mountain pass thawed, slaves unloaded goods of the Orient. The city grew full of noise, smell, and prosperous bustle. Caravans set off due north up the Roman road and crossed the mountains by the Cilician Gates, another feat of ancient Tarsian engineering, a crevice which had been chiseled wide enough for a wagon.

Tarsus was a fusion of civilizations at peace under the rule of Rome: indigenous Cilicians; Hittites whose ancestors once ruled Asia Minor; light-skinned Greeks; Assyrians and Persians; and Macedonians who had come with Alexander the Great on his march to India. After the carve-up of Alexander's empire, when Tarsus became part of the kingdom of the Seleucids who ruled from Syria, King Antiochus IV settled a colony of Jews about 170 B.C. They had rights and privileges, and a determination never to marry into those outside their faith and blood, whom collectively they called Gentiles ("Nations" or "Greeks"). Paul's ancestors probably were among them and may have sprung from an obscure town called Gischala in Galilee.

His father most likely was a master tentmaker, whose craftsmen worked in leather and in *cilicium,* the cloth woven from the hair of the large long-haired black goats which grazed, as they still do, on the slopes of the Taurus. The black tents of Tarsus were used by caravans, nomads, and armies all over Asia Minor and Syria. Of Paul's mother, nothing is known; he never mentions her, either because she died in his infancy or because of some alienation or because he simply had no particular occasion to do so. He had at least one sister. His father was a citizen or burgess of Tarsus and obviously wealthy, for in a reform fifteen years earlier, the rank of citizen had been removed from all householders without considerable fortune or property. Moreover, the family held the coveted title Citizens of Rome. At that period the *civis Romanus* was seldom granted except for services rendered or for a fat fee. Whether Paul's grandfather aided Pompey or Cicero when Rome first governed Cilicia or whether his father paid money, the Roman citizenship conferred local distinction and hereditary privileges which each member could claim wherever he traveled throughout the empire.

It meant too that Paul had a full Latin name which would have been threefold (*cf.* Gaius Julius Caesar). The first two names were common to all the family (in Caesar's case, Gaius Julius) but are lost because Paul's life story was first written by his Greek colleague and no Greek could understand Latin names. The third, the personal *cognomen*, was Paullus. He was given also a Jewish name at the rite of circumcision on the eighth day after birth: "Saul," chosen either for its meaning, " asked for," or in honor of the most famous Benjaminite in history, King Saul.

Saul was the name used at home and emphasized that the Jewish inheritance meant the most in early years. Gentiles were all around and the columns of pagan temples dominated the marketplace; Athens and Rome, Babylon, and Nineveh had combined to create Tarsus, and Paul was unconsciously the child of this Hellenic-Oriental world. In his youth it seemed remote, for although many Jews throughout the Mediterranean had been influenced by the Greek view of life, Paul's parents were Pharisees, members of the party most fervent in Jewish nationalism and strict in obedience to the Law of Moses. They sought to guard their offspring against contamination. Friendships with Gentile children were discouraged. Greek ideas were despised. Though Paul from infancy could speak Greek, the *lingua franca,* and had a working knowledge of Latin, his family at home spoke Aramaic, the language of Judea, a derivative of Hebrew.

They looked to Jerusalem as Islam looks to Mecca. Their privileges as freemen of Tarsus and Roman citizens were nothing to the high honor of being Israelites, the People of Promise, to whom alone the Living God had revealed His glory and His plans.

The school attached to the Tarsus synagogue taught nothing but the Hebrew text of the Sacred Law. Each boy repeated its phrases in chorus after the *hazzan* or synagogue keeper until vowels, accent, and rhythm were precisely correct. Paul learned to write the Hebrew characters accurately on papyrus, thus gradually forming his own rolls of the Scriptures. His father would have presented him with another set of rolls, on vellum: the Greek translation of the Old Testament known as the Septuagint, from which the set readings were taken in synagogue each Sabbath. By his thirteenth birthday, Paul had mastered Jewish history, the poetry of the psalms, and the majestic literature of the prophets. His ear had been trained to the very pitch of accuracy, and a swift brain like his could retain what he heard as instantly and faithfully as a modern "photographic mind" retains a printed page. He was ready for higher education.

Tarsus had its own university, famous for local students such as Athenodorus, the tutor and confidant of the Emperor Augustus, and the equally eminent Nestor, both of whom had returned in old age to be the most distinguished citizens in Paul's boyhood. But a strict Pharisee would not embroil his son in pagan moral philosophy. So, probably in the year that Augustus died, A.D. 14, the adolescent Paul was sent by sea to Palestine and climbed the hills to Jerusalem.

During the next five or six years, he sat at the feet of Gamaliel, grandson of Hillel, the supreme teacher who, a few years before, had died at the age of more than a hundred. Under the fragile, gentle Gamaliel, a contrast with the leaders of the rival School of Shammai, Paul learned to dissect a text until scores of possible meanings were disclosed according to the considered opinion of generations of rabbis, who had obscured the original sense by layers of tradition to protect an Israelite from the least possible infringement of the Law; and, illogically, to help him avoid its inconveniences. Paul learned to debate in the question-and-answer style known to the ancient world as the "diatribe," and to expound, for a rabbi was not only part preacher but part lawyer, who prosecuted or defended those who broke the sacred Law.

Paul outstripped his contemporaries. He had a powerful mind which could lead to a seat on the Sanhedrin in the Hall of Polished Stones, and make him a "ruler of the Jews." The state being a theocracy, in which religious and national leaders were identical, the seventy-one members of the Sanhedrin were equally judges, senators, and spiritual masters. The court was supreme in all religious decisions and in what little self-government the Romans allowed. Some of its members were drawn from the hereditary priesthood. Others were lawyers and rabbis.

Before Paul could hope to be a master in Israel, he had to master a trade, for every Jew was bred to a trade and in theory no rabbi took fees but rather supported himself. Paul therefore left Jerusalem in his early twenties. Had he been there during the ministry of Jesus of Nazareth, he would surely mention having argued against Him like other Pharisees; in later years he spoke often of the death of Jesus by crucifixion but never as an eyewitness. Paul probably returned to Tarsus to work in the family tenting business, and resumed the old routine: winter and spring in Tarsus until the plain grew steamy and malarial, then the summer city in the Taurus foothills. Winter or summer he would have taught in synagogue. A hint in one of his letters suggests he was strongly missionary-minded. Wherever Jews worshiped, Gentile sympathizers were admitted as "God-fearers." Pharisees like Paul urged God-fearers to become proselytes, full Jews: to submit to the simple but painful rite of circumcision, and thereafter to honor the ceremonial and personal demands of the Law in all its rigor. The burden might be heavy but the reward would be great as they earned the favor of God. Paul's father could take full and justified delight in this son who had followed in his steps as a Pharisee and had the intellectual force to reach the highest office in Israel.

Soon after his thirtieth birthday, Paul returned to Jerusalem—with or without a wife. He almost certainly had been married. Jews rarely remained celibate, and parenthood was a qualification required of candidates for the Sanhedrin. Yet his wife never is mentioned in Paul's writings. He may have suffered bereavement, losing not only his wife but an only child, for in later years, though he seemed impatient with women as a sex, he displayed gentleness toward individuals and an understanding of marriage which bely his being a misogamist; and he virtually adopted the young man Timothy as if to replace a son.

More likely his wife and family returned with Paul. In Jerusalem they could discharge the Law's more complicated and praiseworthy obligations and display zeal where it would be noticed. Paul could also combat the movement launched by Jesus of Nazareth. Tarsus must have heard echoes of the teaching and claims of the new prophet and strange reports of miracles; even a tale that He had risen from the dead.

Two
STEPHEN

Compared with the marble and gold terraces of the Temple, the synagogue in Jerusalem attended by Jews from Cilicia was small and austere, and cool despite the summer sun. The men sat on stone benches along the walls, beneath columns which supported the women's galleries. The elders faced the congregation. Near them stood a small platform and beside it the seven-branched candlestick and the veiled chest or "ark" for the Scrolls of the Law. Here the Law was read aloud and expounded by any whom the elders might invite. Paul accepted such an invitation as his due.

In Jerusalem there was no lack of candidates; he had to listen more than he spoke. One of those he heard was a disciple of Jesus named Stephen.

Stephen and Paul were probably much the same age—the Greek word translated "young man," with which the historian Luke introduces Paul, denotes a male between youth and forty. Stephen's birthplace is unknown, for Jews from Egypt and elsewhere used the same synagogue as Cilicians, but he spoke Greek as fluently as Aramaic. Both men were quick thinkers, powerful minds, able controversialists. No tradition remains of Stephen's physique, but though Paul is believed to have been short, he held himself well enough to stand out in a crowd. His face was rather oval with beetling eyebrows, and fleshy from good living. He had a black beard, since Jews scorned the Roman taste for shaving, and his blue-fringed robe and the amulet strapped to a turbanlike headdress displayed his pride in being a Pharisee. As he strode about the Temple courts, he disclosed arrogance inevitable in a man whose ancestors and actions made him feel important. He carried out faithfully the unending cycle of ritual cleansings of platters and cups and of his own person. He kept the weekly fasts—between sunrise and sunset—and said the daily prayers in exact progression and number. He knew what was due to him: respectful greetings, high precedence, a prominent seat in the synagogue.

His days were consumed by his legal career and grooming himself for heaven. No time was left for the poor, the lame, and the outcast. Deep down in his character lay a vein of compassion, but he believed that a good man should keep away from bad men: Paul would have approved the Pharisee who, on seeing Jesus allow a prostitute to wash His feet with her tears and rub them with ointment, took it as proof that the man could be no prophet. Jesus' immortal picture of the Pharisee and the publican (tax collector) who went up to the Temple to pray would have fitted Paul. Like that Pharisee, Paul was sure he deserved God's favor, despised others, and could have prayed: "God, I thank Thee I am not like other men, extortioners, unjust, adulterers, or even like this tax collector. I fast twice a week; I give tithes of all I get."

Stephen, on the other hand, spent much of his time in doling food and necessities to widows.

In the two years since the execution of Jesus, the holy city had become pervaded with those who believed that He had risen from the dead. Most were nondescript and poor. Many lived in communal groups and all of them shared their resources. When Greek-speaking disciples complained that widows were being neglected, Stephen and six others had been chosen to undertake routine daily distribution of food.

Paul was disturbed that a man of Stephen's academic caliber should demean himself in social concerns; and irked that, while his own affairs absorbed him, Stephen should go around bringing happiness. Men respected but feared Paul; they respected Stephen and loved him. When Stephen preached, Paul could not fail to discern the gulf between them: Stephen always turned the Scriptures in the direction of Jesus of Nazareth as the Deliverer or Messiah (or Christ, when Stephen used Greek) whom every Jew awaited, and proved his point by citing the evidence of eyewitnesses that, incredible as it seemed, a corpse had come to life again and climbed out of the grave. They had talked with Jesus in different places during the six weeks following His execution. Stephen did not claim to be an eyewitness, but he was sure Jesus was alive and he claimed to know Him.

Paul considered Stephen's arguments nonsense. The Christ had not come yet. And the way to God was fixed forever: a man must belong to God's chosen people the Jews, and try to obey the Law's every detail. When he sinned, forgiveness depended on the ritual slaughter of animals day after day, year after year in the Temple. Paul could not stomach Stephen's idea that the dying of one young man, by a common if degrading and revolting form of punishment, could blot out sins. As for the alleged resurrection, he pitied those who narrowed their lives to the following of a dead Messiah.

Paul felt no personal concern, knowing his own goodness, but he recognized Stephen's contentions as dangerous. Gamaliel had advised toleration; Simon Peter and other disciples of Jesus worshiped at the Temple and continued to obey the Law. But Paul saw, as Stephen saw, that the old and the new were incompatible; man was saved either by the Temple sacrifices and obeying the Law, or by faith in Jesus. The old must destroy the new or be destroyed.

Paul dedicated himself to demolish Stephen's argument by

the time-honored method of a public debate. The synagogue benches were filled; the elders listened gravely.

Paul and his supporters argued from the Law that since Jesus had been nailed to a tree He must have lain under God's curse and could not possibly be the Christ. Paul disposed of the Resurrection by the accepted explanation: the disciples stole the body. The alternative, that "the Resurrection" was an imaginative symbolism or myth by which believers expressed the spiritual survival and triumph of Jesus, was not open to him. The tomb was empty. Had the Jewish authorities known that Jesus' body lay moldering in the grave, they would have exhumed it and thus exposed a fraud.

Stephen in reply showed that Moses and the prophets, David and the psalms foreshadowed how the Christ, when He came, would not strut as a conqueror but allow Himself to be hurt, jeered at, murdered; and would rise from the dead. Stephen retold the story of that Passover two years before when Jesus died, and capped the case, once again, by quoting eyewitness evidence that Jesus had been seen alive after death.

Stephen won. The congregation voted him the honors, and some asked how to become believers in Jesus. It must have been then that Paul and his friends first had the sensation that they did not fight only Stephen, but a force they could not fathom. Luke states: "They could not stand up against his wisdom or the Spirit by which he spoke."

Paul's reaction to defeat, to judge by scattered reminiscences in his letters, was the very opposite of the advice he would give in old age: "The Lord's servant must not be quarrelsome but kindly to everyone, correcting his opponents with gentleness"; instead, Paul pursued Stephen vindictively, stirring enmity, dissension, and jealousy, insulting and deriding Jesus and restraining neither hot temper nor sarcasm, strong components in Paul's character. Stephen did not retaliate. The qualities men remembered of him were strength and charm; he could display indignation and scorn but keep them for more positive use.

Paul's party had a stronger weapon than insult. If they could twist Stephen's words to sound blasphemous, they could silence him forever by due process of law. They set about it in a way from which Paul himself would often suffer in after years—the tortuous and indirect. They did not call at the high priest's house to lodge a formal complaint. Instead, there was much coming and going in the narrower lanes of the lower city. Soon afterward, apparently spontaneous incidents blew the activities of Stephen into the public eye. His meetings were disrupted by violence until scribes and elders who had found no time for hearing him discovered that his suppression was urgent.

They took Temple guards, arrested him, and arraigned him summarily before the Sanhedrin while Paul and his fellow Cilicians remained in the background.

The seventy-one judges sat on great benches which curved either side of the President's place in the Hall of Polished Stones. At each wing a secretary wrote on papyrus, trying to keep pace with Stephen's speech. Facing the judges and behind the prisoner were court servants, lawyers, teachers, and candidates for the Sanhedrin.

Paul sat among them, riveted to his opponent's words. Stephen held the court spellbound from the president in his high priest's robe and jeweled breastplate to the youngest lawyer. They appeared gripped by the expression on his face, a blend of serenity and authority unusual in a man on trial for his life; and by his grasp of Jewish history as he delivered, extempore, a masterly analysis in answer to the charges. Paul never forgot the theme of that speech, and would use it himself in very different circumstances in a faraway land, while one phrase, "The Most High does not live in a man-made place," so engraved itself on his memory that it emerged even later when he was speaking below the Parthenon at Athens.

As Stephen continued, the atmosphere changed. Admiration gave way to annoyance. Uncomfortable memories obtruded of another trial in the same Hall two years before, and of that executed body which could not be found. Suddenly Stephen seemed to sense that his judges would not hear him out. Throwing caution to the winds, he asserted to their faces that they were obstinate hypocrites, who had betrayed and murdered their Messiah.

The learned judges snarled furiously. The prisoner's reaction was equally astounding. He ignored their rage. He lifted his head in a gaze above and beyond them, and they could hardly believe their ears when this young enthusiast, whom they sought to condemn for blasphemy, called out that he saw God, and that in the place of honor at God's side stood ''the Son of Man''—by which, as everyone knew, he meant the late Jesus of Nazareth.

Thus began the mad rush which ended with a smashed corpse in a pool of blood below the Rock of Execution. It was no accident that the witnesses threw their clothes ''at the feet of a young man named Saul''; they knew his responsibility. But he did not throw a stone. He watched and approved—and heard Stephen call out: ''Lord Jesus, receive my spirit. Lord, do not hold this sin against them.'' And Paul's sharp mind saw, and repudiated, the essence of the prayer. ''Lord, do not hold this sin against them'' meant, in Stephen's teaching, ''Lord, You took their sin on Yourself. May they believe in You, know You, love You.''

During the rest of the summer when Stephen died (probably A.D. 31) and throughout the following winter, the Jewish authorities embarked on systematic suppression with Paul as chief agent.

He charged like an animal tearing its prey. This was not the sad efficiency of an officer obeying distasteful orders; the heart was engaged; and the mind too, with the thoroughness of an inquisitor unmasking treason, until Paul's operations had reduced a vigorous citywide community to apparent impotence, its leaders fled or in hiding. He went from house to house, then held formal inquiries at the synagogues when the congregation assembled. Every suspect, man or woman, had to stand before the elders while Paul, as the high priest's representative, put to them the demand that they should curse Jesus. On refusal, they were formally accused but had the right to employ the time-honored formula: "I have something to argue in favor of my acquittal."

Thus, Paul heard the stories and beliefs of a cross section of those who called Jesus "Lord." Many had met Him in Jerusalem or had traveled to Galilee to find Him, and these would repeat His words. Again and again the same phrases, the same parables would come up in the synagogue court. Nor was Paul surprised, since every rabbi insisted that his disciples should grasp sayings word-perfect, reproducing the very tones of his voice. And the sayings, whether Paul wished or not, were at once stored in the expanding library of his retentive brain.

Some of the Nazarenes defended their devotion by recounting the influence of Jesus on their bodies, like the man with congenital blindness which Jesus had cured, who would have retorted to Paul as saucily as he had answered the indignant Pharisees after the miracle. Some had seen Jesus stumbling toward Golgotha or had watched Him die. Several insisted that they had seen Him alive after He was dead, not a wraith but vigorous—despite the scourge that had stripped the skin and laid the muscles of His back bare, and the shock, exhaustion, and exposure of a Roman crucifixion with its unavoidable finish by suffocation if death had not come already. Most of the accused, however, did not claim to be eyewitnesses themselves, but converts of those who were, particularly of Simon called Peter or "The Rock."

Again and again a nondescript disciple—poorly educated, uncouth, timid—would be hustled in front of the tribunal. After a few shy sentences, the man would be transformed: clear words, unashamed convictions, it was almost as if he were prompted. A few such prisoners would assert that they certainly were being told what to say. Oblivious of Paul's rage, they drew apt quotations from the countless sayings of Jesus committed to memory: "When they bring you before the synagogues and the rulers and the authorities, do not be anxious how or what you are to answer or what you are to say; for the Holy Spirit will teach you in that very hour what you ought to say."/"This will be a time for you to bear testimony . . . I will give you a mouth and wisdom, which none of your adversaries will be able to withstand or contradict."

Paul could laugh at that.

He helped throw many of these prisoners into dungeons. One or two may have been stoned: Paul seems to suggest this ("When they were put to death I gave my vote against them") but Jewish rights of capital punishment were strictly limited by the Romans. The majority were punished by public flogging, the "forty stripes save one" which was no sight for the squeamish. The courage of a few collapsed. About to be lashed, or after a few strokes, or when forced to watch a wife's or a husband's torture, they screamed a curse on Jesus as Paul required.

He remained unmoved as men—and women—staggered away with backs a mass of weals and blood. He was equally unmoved by the refusal of grown men to be humiliated by a beating in front of neighbors. It was said that Jews beaten in synagogue would almost die of shame, but these seemed to be glad, and some called out that they were praying for those who despitefully used them and persecuted them.

Toward the end of winter, news came that followers of Jesus who had fled Jerusalem were not cowed but propagating their doctrines wherever they went—in Samaria, with outstanding success, and northward to Damascus; to the Phoenician country beyond the Lebanon range; and even overseas. Paul went in a rage to the high priest. "Still breathing threats and murder," as his first biographer describes, he asked for official letters to the synagogues, authorizing him to arrest men or women who followed "the Way" and to bring them, roped or chained, for punishment in Jerusalem.

He suggested Damascus as first objective. Though the Sanhedrin's discipline extended to Jews everywhere, the Romans disliked disturbances; but Damascus, though Roman, had two large communities with a wide measure of self-government: the Arabs who owed allegiance to the Nabatean king in his rock capital at Petra, and the Jews. Paul probably intended to pursue and punish in Phoenicia next and then in Antioch, the great Roman capital of Syria. He had a lifetime ahead.

He left, as soon as traveling began in spring, at first light, not the sleepy dawn of northern latitudes but the strong luminosity of the Judean hills. He rode a donkey or possibly a horse as Michelangelo imagined, but not a trotting camel, though the small party may have led a baggage camel. They would have passed close to the place of Stephen's murder. If they took the direct route through Samaria, they passed through stony hills carpeted with variegated spring flowers, and early on the second day had a brief glimpse of the distant snows of Mount Hermon, which dominates the road into Damascus. On the fourth or fifth day, they came to the Lake of Galilee, and here the very stones on the hillsides cried out. The place was alive with memories of Jesus and no man could pass that way untouched. Paul would have met more people here than in Jerusalem who swore they had seen Jesus alive again, with scars on His hands and on His feet.

Paul crossed the upper Jordan by the Roman bridge and climbed the bare heights where, centuries later, the Syrian guns would bombard Jewish *kibbutzim* until swept away in the Six Days' War. He had knowledge now of what Jesus had done and said, even to the tones of His voice, of what He was like in appearance and character, this Man who had been only a few years older than himself.

Paul never suggests that as his little caravan came in full

sight of Mount Hermon, he weighed up factors for or against Jesus. Jesus had been a blasphemous impostor and was dead.

Three
DAMASCUS ROAD

On the last day of the journey of the caravan, Mount Hermon was dropping behind. Its peaks, still under snow, rose from brown foothills white with wild flowers, but the mountain no longer looked particularly high because they were too close under it to see the summit, and the Damascus plain itself is over 2,000 feet. Far ahead, below a bare craggy hill, lay the green of the oasis, encouraging them to plod on to journey's end rather than stop, as on other days, before noon.

Paul and his party walked, while one man led their donkeys roped together a little way to the rear. The road had emptied of country people making for market. Now and again they saw sheep or goats guarded by a small boy swinging his sling, or an occasional patch of cultivation where a man walked behind a rough plow, guiding his ox by a long goad or wand tipped with iron.

The sky was clear blue. Paul's memory is emphatic that there was no thunderstorm or violent wind, as some suggest who seek a natural explanation for what happened. He was not near a nervous breakdown or about to suffer an epileptic fit; not even especially in a hurry.

"Suddenly about midday a great light flashed from the sky

all around me . . . a light more brilliant than the sun, shining all around me and my traveling companions.''

Paul and the other travelers all fell to the ground. They were appalled by this phenomenon, not just a flash but light, terrifying and inexplicable. The companions seem to have stumbled to their feet. Paul remained prostrate. For him only, the light grew in intensity.

He heard a voice, at once calm and authoritative, say in Aramaic: "Saul, Saul, why do you persecute Me?''

He looked up. Within the center of light which blinded him from his surroundings he faced a Man of about his own age. Paul could not believe what he heard and saw. All his convictions, intellect and training, his reputation, his self-respect, demanded that Jesus should not be alive again. He played for time and replied, ''Who are You, Lord?'' He used a mode of address which might mean simply ''Your honor.''

''I am Jesus, whom you are persecuting. It is hard for you, this kicking against the goad.''

Then Paul knew. In a second that seemed an eternity he saw the wounds in Jesus' hands and feet, saw the face and knew that he had seen the Lord, that He was alive, as Stephen and the others had said, and that He loved not only those whom Paul persecuted but *Paul:* ''It is hard for *you* to kick against the goad.'' Not one word of reproach.

Paul had never admitted to himself that he had felt pricks of a goad as he raged against Stephen and his disciples. But now, instantaneously, he was shatteringly aware that he had been fighting Jesus. And fighting himself, his conscience, his powerlessness, the darkness and chaos in his soul. God hovered over this chaos and brought him to the moment of new creation. It wanted only his ''Yes.''

Paul broke.

He was trembling and in no state to weigh the pros and cons of changing sides. He only knew that he had heard a voice and had seen the Lord, and that nothing mattered but to find and obey His will.

"What shall I do, Lord?"

He used the same ascription as before, but all the obedience and worship and love in heaven and earth went into that one word, "Lord." At that moment he knew he was utterly forgiven, utterly loved. In his own words: "God who said, 'Let light shine out of darkness,' has shined in our hearts to give the light of the knowledge of the glory of God in the face of Jesus Christ."

"Rise to your feet," he heard, "and stand upright and go into Damascus, and you will be told there what you are to do." He had trusted. Now he had to obey—a humbling, almost trivial first order.

When at last he stood, he was blind. He put out his hand and groped until his companions, who had been frightened even more by hearing Paul answer the inaudible, began to lead him. The riding and baggage animals had caught up and the little caravan walked toward Damascus in awed silence.

Paul moved blindly into the unknown, yet he was not in darkness but in light: "I could not see because of the brightness of that light." Though blue sky and the road's yellow dust and the green of the nearing oasis were all snuffed out, they were not missed. Light suffused his blinded eyes, his mind. And as he walked, obeying that first command from his new Master, he made the first great discovery: Jesus remained beside him, not the form of a crucified, risen body, but someone invisible yet there.

They passed the stench of the caravanserai, quiet in the early afternoon, and went under the city gate into the broad, colonnaded Via Recta, the Street called Straight, which bisected the city. This too was comparatively still, for the shops and booths had not opened after the midday sleep, and private homes were shuttered against the sun. They reached the house of a Damascene named Judas, probably a substantial Jewish merchant, a suitable host for a representative of the Sanhedrin: the synagogue elders must have been expecting Paul, for even the Nazarenes knew he was on his way to persecute. Both sides lost sight of him. The escort delivered him and disappeared. He made no request of Judas but to be taken to the guest chamber—refusing even a meal—and left alone.

Time became meaningless. Paul heard the evening trumpet, next morning's cockcrow, the rumble of carts on the paving, shopkeepers shouting their wares, the distant murmur of bargainers, and the occasional bray of an ass. Then the stillness of midday. Paul lay on his bed, wide awake except for an hour or two of sleep, or knelt long at the bedside and then lay down again. He did not want human company, only to be alone with the Lord Jesus, as he now called Him. He soon forgot hunger and thirst. His entire personality was in mutation. He was being turned inside out as he let Jesus light the recesses of his soul.

"Saul, Saul, why do you persecute Me?" He could reply now in the words of David's psalm: "Have mercy upon me, O God, according to Thy loving-kindness: according to the multitude of Thy tender mercies, blot out my transgressions . . . Against Thee, Thee only, have I sinned."

Paul felt defiled and loathsome. He could have used the words in Augustine's *Confessions:* "You set me there before my face that I might see how vile I was, how twisted and unclean and spotted and ulcerous. I saw myself and was horrified." By the gauge of man's inhumanity to man—the Roman suppression of the two Jewish rebellions, or Nero's massacre of Christians after the Fire of Rome, or Hitler's "final solution"—Paul's persecution was trifling. But murder is always absolute to the awakened conscience of the murderer. Nor was it only murder and cruelty. He had blasphemed and insulted and persecuted the Lord, whose response had been to seek him out and show him a love which surpassed anything he had known. The more he bathed himself in this love as the hours flew by in blindness, the more he was broken down by the enormity of what he had done.

He had imagined he served God. He had supposed himself climbing into God's favor. He had set up his standards of goodness and compared himself with others and seen that he was good. But now, in contrast with Jesus, whose Spirit had invaded him, he knew his purity was a counterfeit of the inexpressibly Pure, the good deeds a parody of Goodness. He had been mentally and spiritually hostile to God, though honoring Him by mouth; he had been busy in evil, though punctilious in religious rites; he had been altogether estranged, fit for nothing but to crawl away as far as he could from the blinding light that was God.

Yet Jesus had grasped hold of him. Paul would afterward cite this among the cast-iron proofs of the Resurrection, however much men might scoff or call him a liar. God, incredibly, had raised the shattered body of Jesus from the grave so that He was alive and had confronted Paul, not to crush and destroy, not to revenge the blood of the persecuted but to rescue the persecutor and overwhelm him with love and forgiveness. Paul knew from the bottom of his heart that Jesus was the Messiah, the Christ, the Saviour of the world. This was not a conclusion of cold logic, though that must come. It went beyond intellect. He knew, because he knew Jesus.

And in knowing Jesus, he understood what had happened on the cross.

Paul in his pride and wisdom had rejected Jesus because no man could be hanged on a tree unless cursed. As he now faced his sin, he saw by irresistible intuition that Jesus indeed had carried a curse on the cross, but not His own; it was Paul's and everyman's. Each hour that passed in blindness at the house of Judas, each day for the rest of life, would unfold a little more of the breadth and length and height and depth, but the heart of the Good News was sure, now and forever: the love of Christ, "the Son of God who loved me and gave Himself for me." Paul could instantly be treated as a man who had never sinned, be welcomed with love and trust. The more he looked with blinded eyes at the brightness of the light, the more distinct grew the fact disclosed in that instant of time on the Damascus Road: forgiveness was a gift, entire and whole and perfect, because forgiveness was Christ Himself. It could not be earned; no human merit could outweigh human sin; but in having Christ, Paul had all.

He could have shouted aloud in the house of Judas what he would write in the unknown years ahead: "God has sent the Spirit of His Son into our hearts!"/"The mystery hidden for ages and generations but now made manifest is: Christ in you!"/"For to me to live is Christ!" Already he had an urge to pray: not just the formal prayers of the glorious Jewish liturgy, but the conversation of a son with his Father; in talking with Jesus, he talked with the Father, in worshiping the Father, he conversed with the Son. He told the Lord all that was in his heart. He interceded urgently; for those he had persecuted, especially those he had forced to recant and blaspheme; for the Damascus Nazarenes who awaited him in fear; for his Jewish friends and superiors.

With prayer came hunger—for the words of Jesus. Like a newborn lamb which before it can stand searches instinctively for its mother's teats, Paul hungered for knowledge of all Jesus had said and done. Until his conversion he had been indifferent to the words of Jesus. From the moment Paul had said, "What must I do, Lord?" he accepted Jesus' authority, and now it was of paramount importance to know what He had commanded, and promised, and warned, and foretold; His attitude toward those who hated and those who loved Him, all He taught about the Father and about Himself, His verdicts on every matter of human behavior and destiny.

Paul had yet another urge: to broadcast his great discovery. Yet he had to wait. The Master's command had been: "Go into Damascus and you will be told there what you are to do." Waiting, he heard the evening trumpet, and cockcrow, and the country carts, and then again the evening trumpet. At last, as he prayed, he was shown what would happen next.

Four
A MAN SURPRISED

In a bedroom of a smaller house off the Street called Straight, a middle-aged Jew lay between sleep and waking.

Ananias was an honored member of the Jewish community in Damascus. He was also a follower of Jesus Christ, and showed no surprise or hesitation when he heard a voice call: "Ananias."

"Here I am, Lord."

"Get up, and go to the Street called Straight and ask at the house of Judas for a Tarsian named Saul. He is praying! And he sees a man named Ananias coming in and laying hands on him so that he may recover his sight."

Ananias was aghast. His Lord must have made a mistake. Ananias probably had attended little meetings of Nazarenes, who at the news of Saul the Persecutor's approach had prayed that the Lord should rescue them, without, apparently, expecting their prayer to be answered.

"Lord," replied Ananias, "I have heard all about this man from many people, and the harm he has done to Your saints in Jerusalem. And he has authority here to arrest everyone who calls on Your name!"

The voice said, "Go, because he is My chosen instrument."

The Lord then confirmed and amplified His command.

At that, Ananias threw off the bedclothes and dressed.

As he hurried down the narrow lane past watercarriers already returning from the river, while the sunrise tipped the northern crags, he almost shouted "Hallelujah!" So the Lord's hand was not shortened. He had stretched it out to heal, and the wolf would lie down with the lamb as in the ancient prophecy. And he, Ananias the obscure, never heard of before or since, had been chosen to baptize Saul—it was the first example of a historical pattern that great ambassadors for Christ, however much prepared in other ways, are brought to their vocation by unimportant agents: Augustine hears a child's voice repeat, "Take up and read!" John Wesley listens to an anonymous Moravian reading Luther; D.L. Moody, wrapping up shoes in a store, pauses for a few words from his Sunday School teacher; Charles Haddon Spurgeon, sheltering from a snowstorm, hears a workingman in a snowbound minister's pulpit.

Ananias was at once admitted and soon stood by Paul's bedside.

He looked at a face which had passed through deep suffering into peace. The skin sagged where Pharisaic good living had been drained away by fast; lines grooved by ruthlessness were still traceable, the beard straggled, the eyes stared. Yet it was a face relaxed, as if Paul had looked at the worst and no longer feared it, had looked at the best and knew he was being remade in its mold.

Ananias laid his hands on Paul's head.

"Saul, brother," he began (and if he had to gulp a little at calling the murderer of his friends "brother," the gulp was swallowed by joy), "the Lord has sent me—Jesus who appeared to you on your way here—so that you may recover your sight and be filled with the Holy Spirit."

At that instant a film or rind, as it were, peeled away from Paul's eyes. He saw Ananias. And saw him clearly. George Matheson, the blind Scottish preacher and hymn writer

(1842-1906), liked to think of Paul as semiblind for the rest of his life, the effect of that three days never quite leaving him. But there are recorded instances of Paul fixing an opponent with his eye, or compelling an audience's attention by a look, in a manner impossible to the half-blind. Paul recovered sight instantly and completely.

Ananias discharged the rest of his orders: "The God of our fathers has chosen you to know His will and see the Righteous One, to hear words from His own lips, and you are to be a witness to all men of what you have seen and heard." Paul would hear more, he said, direct from the Lord Jesus, who would give him a glimpse of what would be involved in pain and hardship as they adventured together, not to Israel only but to the Gentiles, small and great, slaves and kings—to "all men" whom previously as a Pharisee Paul had despised and rejected.

Then Ananias spoke more words, delivered as from Jesus Himself: "I send you to open their eyes! To turn them from darkness to light, and from the rule of Satan to God, so that, by trust in Me, they may have forgiveness of sins and a place with those whom God has made His own."

The scope and implication of this commission left Paul speechless.

Ananias said: "What are you waiting for? Get up, and be baptized and wash away your sins as you call on His name."

Ananias helped him off the bed. Normally, the followers of the Way baptized by immersion in a river or stream, like John the Baptist, but Paul was weak after his long fast. They probably moved slowly out into the *atrium*, the garden court of Judas' house where there would have been a fountain; or Paul with his iron will may have insisted that he walk, leaning on Ananias, the half mile to the Abana River, which flowed outside the city's northern wall.

Never had trees looked fresher than these Damascus apricots and peaches, or water so clear as the Abana. The cream-colored stone of the city wall and gates threw back the sunshine and the sky was blue. Paul had been promised storms enough but at this time he could echo the nineteenth psalm: "The heavens declare the glory of God. . . . The sun like a strong man runs its course with joy."

Paul felt a physical well-being, all tension relaxed, his perception acute, his mind at peace. As he walked down the Street called Straight, which like all eastern streets was a medley of color and noise and movement, or turned into the spice bazaar or the metal workers' lane, he was in love with all mankind. Damascus, being a frontier city, drew a variety of types: Arabs and Jews, Parthians in their conical hats, the clank of Roman soldiers; Paul knew he was sent to them all—and to his own people, the Jews, for even they had barely a glimmer of what God was like except those who had seen Jesus.

That evening, with Ananias, Paul met the little knot of Nazarenes. Almost certainly a few who had fled from Jerusalem would have been among them, and a highly emotional movement came when those who had received floggings at Paul's orders gave him the kiss of peace and shared with him bread and wine in token of their union with each other and with Jesus, through His broken body and the blood of His cross, in the way He had taught on the night He was betrayed.

An even more extraordinary incident occurred next Sabbath at the most important of the numerous Damascus synagogues. The elders and congregation had no idea of Paul's conversion. He had not disclosed it even to Judas. They merely supposed he had recovered from indisposition and was ready for the work they had gossiped about since the announcement of his coming. The stricter members, as they took their seats, expressed pious satisfaction that heresy would be erased; the cruel had a pleasurable anticipation of possible bloodletting. The Nazarenes, however, who knew the affair would develop differently, were praying for him when the *hazzan* escorted him to the dais, still dressed like any Pharisee in blue-fringed robe with leather amulet on his turban, and handed him the scroll of the Law.

He read aloud the allotted passage, each inflection correct, and returned the scroll. In the moment's pause before he began to preach, he marveled at the Divine strategy by which, during the past centuries, synagogues had arisen in countless Gentile cities—ready for the day when under his leadership they should be the spearheads of a great crusade for Jesus Christ! If he had seen the truth, surely they would too. He and they had been set apart to spread the Good News of Jesus Christ among the Gentiles. And they would begin in Damascus.

Then and there he proclaimed: "Jesus is the Son of God." Paul charged in with the same vehemence and abandon that he had charged into his persecution. Words tumbled out as he told how the Lord had met him, that the Lord was alive again and loved them. And the reaction was not at all as he had expected. The worshipers were stunned and aghast. Far from being convinced, they were angry. This turncoat received as the high priest's representative had now declared himself the representative of Jesus.

Paul was taken aback. In the days that followed, he felt rather as Moses, who "thought his fellow countrymen would understand that God was offering them deliverance through him, but they did not understand." What is more, Paul grew impatient with the Nazarenes. He joined them each evening but few had memories of Jesus. They had a stock of His sayings which had been repeated by those who had known Him, but this could not satisfy Paul. He hungered for first-hand evidence. Yet he could not return to Jerusalem. Even if the apostles, who had known Jesus better than any, gave their confidence immediately, Paul must not risk the clutch of an enraged high priest, who would ensure his disappearance by strangling or lifelong incarceration.

Each night at the house of Judas or perhaps now at the

house of Ananias, he tossed on his bed frustrated, the glory from those days of blindness slipping away. At length he told the Lord he would leave it in His hands. Peace flowed back. No voice or light disclosed the next move, only a growing conviction that he must get away by himself, taking nothing but his scrolls of the Scriptures. It was not the apostles that Paul needed but Jesus alone: not a city but the wilderness.

The next move was simple. Damascus was the terminus of one of the great spice routes from the myrrh and frankincense country in southern Arabia and the Horn of Africa. The camel caravans returned with coins and goods of the Roman world. The son of an important trading house had no difficulty in obtaining passage.

Five
ARABIA AND AFTER

Somewhere in Arabia lived Paul's first convert, probably a young Bedouin in the wilderness of cliffs and wadis between Sinai and the great sand desert. It is inconceivable that Paul could suppress his discovery of God's love for the world; rather he shared his day's meditation each night by some camp fire, learning to simplify for rough illiterate camel men.

Preaching was incidental to his primary purpose. He went to Arabia to learn—from the Risen Jesus. Just as he claimed to have seen the Lord on the Damascus Road, so he always claimed to have been taught by Him directly: "The mystery was made known to me by revelation"; and he never ceased to wonder that God should have chosen for this an ex-persecutor, less than the least of all saints. It was not merely a matter of listening to a voice, whether speaking to his ears or his heart, but intense application of mind. The will and the emotions had been captured by Christ on the Damascus Road; in Arabia, Paul's thought was captured too.

Months drifted into years: winter storms, the spring when the desert was scented with flowers, the furnace of high summer; he was now lean and hard physically, his face burned dark by sun. Then, in the third year after his conversion, he was ready.

The sequence is obscure, the most likely being that he walked into the Nabatean Arab capital, Petra, through the narrow gorge familiar to twentieth-century tourists and took the earliest opportunity of preaching Christ in the synagogue of the Jewish colony. The uproar led King Aretas, who hated Jews, to order the arrest of the troublemaker. Paul fled Petra with a price on his head, his signal to leave Arabia. He must return to the mainstream, as Moses emerged from the desert to confront Pharaoh with God's demands, as the Lord Himself came out of the wilderness and entered the synagogues with the message: "The time has come; the kingdom of God is upon you; repent and believe the Gospel."

Paul, now in his mid-thirties, set out north to assume leadership of the great crusade in which the Jewish synagogues should become the spearheads of Christ. Jerusalem was still barred to him, for he could not expect the confidence of the apostles until he had proved himself, nor was he sure they yet realized that Gentiles, no less than Jews, were to be offered Christ. He therefore rejoined the caravan route and traveled northward with the spice and gold. Days before he came in sight of Damascus, Mount Hermon beckoned him across the barren plateau toward the place where Jesus had appeared to him on the road.

In Damascus, Paul's conversion could hardly have been forgotten, though many must have dismissed it as transient because he had blazed across the sky like a comet, briefly, and Ananias had resumed his gentle, slightly nervous policy of peaceful coexistence. Paul was welcomed immediately by the disciples, and on the next Sabbath entered a synagogue to exercise his right to expound Scripture. And like Stephen, he reduced the Jews to confusion by proofs that Jesus was Christ. Those who remembered his earlier visit were amazed at his growth in understanding and conviction.

Luke says he grew more and more forceful. He did not attack the unbelieving Jews, nor display the bitterness of a renegade toward former friends who refused to be converted, yet there may have been one element lacking in this early preaching: "If I speak in the tongues of men and of angels, but have not love, I am a noisy gong or a clanging cymbal. And if I have prophetic powers, and understand all mysteries and all knowledge, and if I have all faith, so as to remove mountains, but have not love, I am nothing." These words of twenty years later may contain an autobiographical echo.

Nevertheless he made disciples. And it was they who came to his rescue when Jews plotted to murder him.

The plot was hatched with oriental twistiness, the more necessary in that the local elders risked crucifixion should they attempt a killing inside the city. When a traveler from Petra mentioned the warrant out for Paul's arrest, they hit on the solution. The Ethnarch appointed by King Aretas under his treaty with the Romans to protect and punish Damascus Arabs would not extradite a wanted man except on a capital charge, nor arrest him within the walls for an offense committed across the border. Rather, his troopers patrolled outside the gates to keep an eye on the Arab King's subjects as they entered or left. In return for a bribe, he gave orders to seize Paul, carry him off, and slit his throat.

Paul got wind of it, whether from a Jewish or Arab sympathizer or because no secret is safe in Damascus. His disciples took him at night to a friendly family who lived on the city walls in one of the private houses with windows jutting some eight or ten feet above the ground. They found a fish basket, a large shapeless sack which folded round his body so that no casual observer would notice in the darkness that it hid a man. In the small hours they lowered him to the ground.

As Paul picked his way through vegetable gardens and fruit trees to strike the road out of sight of the troopers at the gates, his humiliation was complete. The crusade on which he had embarked so gloriously had come to a summary stop; the appointed leader was a fugitive already. Soon he became inwardly aware that he was not alone. He had been promised sufferings and rebuffs and they had begun and he had escaped lightly. He had been promised the unfailing presence of Jesus too. A phrase which, like a theme in a symphony, would sound again and again through his life, sounds over Paul's story that night: "Persecuted, but not forsaken."

As his spirits revived, the irony was not lost on him that the mighty Paul, who had originally approached Damascus with all the panoply of the high priest's representative, should make his last exit in a fish basket, helped by the very people he had come to hurt.

Paul decided to fulfill his ambition to make friends with Peter and learn all he could about Jesus. He retraced his earlier journey through Syria, Galilee, and Judea until once more he looked down from Mount Scopus and entered Jerusalem.

With a humility in contrast to his former attitudes in Jerusalem, and not always too evident in future, he did not immediately accost the apostles but sought out a gathering of Christ's disciples. And he was appalled to find himself cold-shouldered. "They were all afraid of him," writes Luke, "for they did not believe that he was a disciple." Some of them had suffered horribly from him, and though these had (or should have) forgiven him, his unannounced arrival was un-nerving. The report of his conversion had been followed by long silence. His recent activities in Damascus were too brief for news to trickle to Jerusalem, and he had left in such a hurry that he carried no letter of commendation. He might be a spy.

For a few hours or days it seemed he was rejected by both former friends and former enemies; a castaway, lonely, with nothing but Christ's promises and spiritual presence.

He was rescued by the man who later would become, for a time, his closest companion. Joseph Barnabas was a Cypriot. Being from a wealthy background, though of different tribes, the two may have had previous acquaintance. Barnabas was generous and much loved, a man of commanding presence with a gentle manner. His gifts lay in counseling rather than preaching, and he was skilled at discerning genuine faith and strengthening it: hence the Aramaic nickname the apostles had given him, "Son of encouragement." Barnabas took Paul aside, drew from him the whole story and knew it rang true.

Barnabas was an uncle or cousin of the young John Mark who stood in special relationship with Simon Peter as a spiritual apprentice or assistant; through Mark and Mark's mother Mary and because of his own qualities he had the ear of Peter. Nor did Peter hesitate to act on what Barnabas told him. In his impulsive, warm way, he and his wife asked Paul to stay in their home and at once opened their hearts and memories to him. Peter was Paul's age but a contrast in background and character. A bluff fisherman with a strong Galilean rustic accent, he was literate, as were most Jewish peasants of the day, and after three years with Jesus was well versed in the Old Testament Scriptures. He lacked higher education or the mental brilliance of Paul.

If Paul had persecuted Christ in His disciples, Peter had denied Him, and felt no superiority, though he bore already the scars of a beating for Christ's sake, while Paul, as far as is known, was unscathed. Both had been transformed by the Risen Christ, and this was the link which would withstand the stresses of dissimilarity and, in years far ahead, of dispute.

Paul spent much of the next fifteen days listening to Peter and questioning him. His attitude may be deduced from the similar attitude, in the next century, of the young Irenaeus, the future theologian, sitting at the feet of the aged Polycarp, who had actually known the Apostle John. Polycarp, writes Irenaeus, "would describe his conversation with John and with the rest who had seen the Lord, and he would relate their words. And whatsoever things he had heard from them about the Lord, and about His miracles, and about His teaching, Polycarp, as having received them from eyewitnesses of the Life of the Word, would relate altogether in accordance with the Scriptures. To these discourses I used to listen at the time with attention by God's mercy which was bestowed upon me, noting them down, not on paper, but in my heart; and by the grace of God I constantly ruminate upon them faithfully."

As Irenaeus implies, the Early Church had a strict test of teaching in the name of Jesus Christ; it must derive accurately from "eyewitnesses of the Life of the Word," those who had known Jesus personally, and it must be "altogether in accordance with the Scriptures," which to Paul and Peter meant the Old Testament. Paul himself refers to this test when he comments to the Corinthians, "I delivered to you as of first importance what I also received, that Christ died for our sins in accordance with the Scriptures, that He was buried, that He was raised on the third day in accordance with the Scriptures, and that He appeared to Cephas (Peter), then to the Twelve. . . . Then to more than 500 brethren at one time, most of whom are still alive. . . . Then to James. . . . Last of all He appeared also to me."

Paul had dug deep into the Scriptures in Arabia; and he claimed since the Damascus Road that he was an eyewitness of the Resurrection, and thus had authority as an apostle; but these fifteen days with Peter provided the essential foundation of knowledge of "the Life of the Word." Peter had been convinced by the character, actions, and speech of Jesus over a long period before He disclosed who He was. Paul wanted evidence that Jesus really had lived sinless, and to hear how love and purity had been demonstrated in this human life which he believed to be the one complete revelation of God Himself. He wanted as much as he could get of Jesus' sayings.

That the Early Church possessed an enormous fund of Christ's words and actions, far more than Paul could absorb in a fortnight, is reflected in the closing words of St. John's Gospel: "There are also many other things which Jesus did; were every one of them to be written, I suppose that the world itself could not contain the books that would be written." Paul could rely on the exact accuracy of all Peter retailed, for whereas writers and orators in Hellenic lands had already developed the art of paraphrasing and developing another man's words, the Jews had a rigid attitude to the sacredness of the actual quotation, a horror of tampering with tradition. A disciple could not blend his own ideas with those which he passed on as his master's.

What Paul received whenever he questioned those who had known the Lord, he would transmit. He spent many hours teaching in Antioch, Corinth, Ephesus—wherever he traveled. The fact that his letters never quote Christ's words directly—his single quotation occurs in an address in Acts, to the elders of Ephesus—is not an indication of ignorance. He needed all the limited space of a papyrus roll to deal with the specific situations which provoked the letter, and his readers knew Christ's words already from the oral teaching, to which Paul makes several allusions.

Just as his writing must have awakened echoes of this talking, so the Epistles awake echoes of the Gospels. Apart from the basic facts of the life, death, and resurrection of the Lord, Paul probably told converts, for instance, the parables of the Good Seed (echoed in his words about God's husbandry, to the Corinthians) and the House Built on a Rock. He came very near repeating in an epistle the Lord's statement about defilement, and the evil things that come from the heart of man.[1] When he wrote that the Philippian Christians shone "as lights in the world, holding forth the word of life," they would have remembered the Lord's words, "You are the light of the world. . . . Let your light so shine."[2] Paul repeats Christ on loving your neighbor; he tells of faithful stewards and how the laborer deserves his hire; he speaks of the new birth; and of the meekness, gentleness, graciousness, and humility of Christ.

All this would have been drawn in large measure from his conversations with Peter, which thus became a vital factor of preparation. In after years, when Paul preached with dogmatic certainty that the Gospel had an urgent claim upon every human being to the end of time, a hearer might have cried, "Paul, how can you be so *sure*?" He would have answered by referring not only to the Damascus Road and the revelations in Arabia, to the Old Testament and to the believer's own private proof—the Holy Spirit guarding his heart—but to the career and character of Jesus. Be imitators of the Lord, he would plead. Let the same mind be in you, walk worthy of Him; walk, like Christ, in love.

By his own recollection of this visit, Paul did not meet any of the other apostles "except James the Lord's brother," who though not one of the twelve and slow to believe in Jesus, had risen to leadership of the Jerusalem church. He does not seem to have told these two of his special commission to preach to Gentiles everywhere whether or not they worshiped at a synagogue. Peter had not yet even half-understood Jesus' order to make disciples of all nations, for the vision on the housetop at Joppa, when he argued with the Lord but afterward baptized the proselyte Italian centurion, lay in the future. James was firmly wedded to the Mosaic Law alongside his faith in Jesus Christ; Paul may have detected already the seeds of strife between himself and James and was wary. Or he could think it unnecessary for the present to raise awkward questions, since at this time he intended to work through the synagogues overseas, to stir congregations for Christ until they preached Him to the Gentiles. Besides, he had come to Jerusalem to listen, not to teach those who "were in Christ before me."

Though he spent long hours secluded with Peter in the cool of his home or walking together, deep in talk, on the Mount of Olives or in the Courts of the Temple where Peter could quote Jesus' sermons and describe miracles in the place where they happened, Paul never was a man to be happy unless active. Fully accepted now by the disciples, he "went in and out among them at Jerusalem, preaching boldly in the name of the Lord." He had no opportunity to travel around the

Judean countryside meeting disciples in outlying towns but "they heard it said, 'Our former persecutor is preaching the Good News of the faith which once he tried to destroy'; and they praised God for me."

Paul did not limit his preaching to circles where he had no compromising past. He went to the synagogues of the Greek-speaking Jews, his old haunts, and took up where Stephen had left off, using the very methods by which Stephen had infuriated him four years before, and aware that another Saul the Persecutor might be listening. He talked. He debated. And once again he provoked dissension: the man who longed to be the agent of reconciliation seemed to cause violent arguments wherever he went.

The dissension possibly rather upset the disciples, for between the departure of Paul breathing threats and slaughter, and the return of Paul preaching boldly in the name of the Lord, they had recovered peace and numerical strength. When Jerusalem became too hot to hold him, they were almost relieved.

Once again there was a murder plot. Once again it leaked out, and Paul was hurried out of danger. This time friends took him to the coast and sent him off to Tarsus.

Damascus. Jerusalem. His crusade had again come to a summary stop. But he left Jerusalem assured that he would not be forgotten. Barnabas knew all about Paul's dedication to evangelize the Gentiles. When the time was ripe, Barnabas would find him.[3]

Six
HIDDEN YEARS

The best years of Paul's life were slipping away between the Taurus mountains and the sea. It was the harder to bear because he cared so deeply that all men everywhere should hear and believe, yet during his later thirties and into the early forties when a man approaches his prime, Paul drops out of history. The story of this last major gap in his life cannot be pieced together with certainty. Fragmentary evidence suggests the outline, but it must be qualified with a large ''possibly'' or ''perhaps.''

He rejoined his family in Tarsus. His parents had served God with a clear conscience in the only way they knew, by keeping the Law. He began to tell them about Jesus Christ, who had fulfilled the Law, and the advice was not well received. Tension between father and son, understandably high since Paul's return with a ruined career, tightened yet further when Paul ceased to dress as a Pharisee or to observe the ceremonial rules; the fundamental moral law enshrined in Scripture was more absolute than ever but the Mosaic injunctions were not.

He does not seem to have flaunted this freedom. He established the principle, then conformed to the family and the neighbors' ways when this helped his supreme purpose: "To the Jews I became like a Jew to win Jews. As they are subject to the Law of Moses, I put myself under that Law to win them, although I am not myself subject to it. To win Gentiles, who are outside the Law, I made myself like one of them, although I am not outside God's law, being under the law of Christ." He became "all things to all men, that I might by all means save some. I do it all for the sake of the Gospel."

It was this determination to win Gentiles that angered his family most, not least because he broke out of their spiritual ghetto and explored Gentile ways.

In youth his mind had been closed, every prejudice of upbringing a disinfectant against pagan ideas. He now had an even more satisfying answer to the puzzles of human strivings and destiny. Paganism at its philosophical best would appear a guttering candle to a man who followed the Light of the World, and more usually it was idolatry, mixed with license; especially in Tarsus, where the homosexuality for which the city was notorious had ties with local religion. Certain twenti-eth-century scholars argued that Paul was heavily influenced by pagan ideas, especially the "mysteries" coming in from the Orient, and the fertility cults of gods who, to make winter lead to spring, "died" and "rose again"; but to make him appear to borrow, scholars had to depend on descriptions which dated from after his day, while rejecting evidence that later paganism parodied Christian features. Paul's most highly educated audience, at Athens, would certainly have recognized any pagan parallel if it existed, yet when he spoke of a Man who really rose again, they laughed.

His advice to converts throughout his career was: "Shun idolatry." Disgust at idols, however, strengthened his love for idolaters, and the man who once had kept Gentile neighbors at a distance, now listened to their problems, fears, and temptations. He enjoyed watching their games. Too old to compete in athletics, he probably joined in the calisthenics down by the river, stripping naked in the normal way, possibly boxing to harden his body for the tasks he was sure lay ahead and certainly striking up friendships. He studied Greek literature too, which in a strict Pharisee's household would be despised or abhorred. Though direct references in the epistles are scanty, he quotes Menander, Aratus, and the Cretan poet Epimenides. In the speech to the intellectuals at Athens, he uses an apt allusion from Aeschylus' *Eumenides* and another from Plato's *Phaedo*, and makes a tactful paraphrase from Plato's *Republic*.[4] Such examples, which a fuller preservation of Paul's oral teaching would have multiplied, suggest a well-read man.

This interest in Gentiles threw him into conflict with the elders of the Tarsus synagogue. Their particular accusations are not known; he could be disciplined for entering Gentile houses. He could be scourged for eating food forbidden to Jews, which he might have accepted when dining with friends; or for disobedience after a plain order from his religious superiors, the offense for which Peter and John were flogged in Jerusalem. Writing in A.D. 56, he mentions being punished no less than five times by the Jewish "forty stripes save one," yet none of this is recorded in Acts. Thus it is probable that he was whipped more than once in the hidden years at Tarsus. Scourging was regarded as the correction of a brother, purging his offense that he might resume a place in the family of the synagogue. The alternative was excommunication, to be flung out of Israel, a fate that Paul, regarding the synagogues as Christ's potential spearheads, would wish to avoid.

At a trial before the elders and brethren, he could now claim Christ's promise which he had ridiculed in his persecuting days: "Do not be anxious . . . the Holy Spirit will teach you in that very hour what you are to say." He turned the occasion to a testimony and awaited sentence, knowing that Christ had warned him personally, through Ananias, that he would suffer.

It was the duty of the judges to estimate how much corporal punishment, up to the prescribed thirty-nine lashes, the culprit could take. Paul's physique was such that he was awarded the lot.

Watched by the congregation, he was bent and bound between two pillars. The *hazzan*, possibly the same who had taught him as a boy, solemnly tore at his robe until his torso was bare. The *hazzan* picked up a heavy whip formed by a four-pronged strap of calf hide with two prongs of ass hide, long enough to reach the navel from behind and above. He stood on a stone and with one hand, using "all his might," brought it down over Paul's shoulder to curl round and cut his chest. Thirteen lashes were counted, while a reader intoned curses from the Law: "If thou wilt not observe to do all the words of this Law that are written in this book, that thou mayest fear this glorious and fearful name, The Lord Thy God, then the Lord will make thy plagues wonderful."

After the thirteenth on the chest the whipping was transferred to the back, thirteen hard strokes across one shoulder, thirteen across the other, cutting across weals already bleeding. The pain may be gauged by a description of flogging in early Australia from the autobiographical novel *Ralph Rashleigh*, for whom the first dozen strokes were "like jagged wire tearing furrows in the flesh, and the second dozen seemed like the filling of the furrows with molten lead . . . Sensations of intense and intolerable pain."

The synagogue elder in charge could stop the punishment if the prisoner collapsed or lost control of his bowels, but such mercy can have been exercised seldom, for the scourger was expressly indemnified if the victim died. Paul endured to the end, tasting not only the agony he had inflicted on others but the sharing of his pain with Jesus.

As he lay recovering in the family home (for despite their shame they were obliged to treat him as a son) or went stiffly about the tentmaking business, no doubt he reconsidered whether his stand was necessary. Should he not conform, repudiate Gentile friendships, stop teaching salvation through faith? His conclusion could have been expressed in the words he used a few years later when the issue had become more than personal: "Christ has set us free, to be free men. Stand firm then, and refuse to be tied to the yoke of slavery again."

The elders sought a fresh pretext to punish him, and this time may have invoked a vicious clause in synagogue law, that if a culprit breaks two prohibitions and is sentenced on each, "he must suffer the first, be healed again, and then be scourged a second time." Thus twice more, making three of the five scourgings he mentions, Paul stood stripped at the pillars, each stroke driving home the truth of Christ's warning to His disciples: "You will be *hated* for My name's sake."

In an age when brutal punishments were normal, Paul would have escaped much psychological damage, especially as he accepted persecution as a small price for the prize of knowing and serving "Christ Jesus my Lord." Physically, he was marked for life. A curious piece of evidence strengthens the probability that he was badly beaten in Tarsus. The second-century document from Asia Minor called *The Acts of Paul and Thecla*, a story invented by a presbyter who tried to pass it off as genuine and was unfrocked for the fraud, includes a description of Paul which may preserve the traditional memory of his appearance on the first great missionary journey: moderate height, rather bald with a long nose and beetling brows, and *bowlegged*. The "young man named Saul" who ran through the streets before the stoning of Stephen and stood out in the crowd would hardly have been bowlegged, yet this is a deformity common among men who have been severely flogged.

Whether or not the elders had him scourged yet again, there is strong probability that he was excommunicated from the Tarsus synagogue and that the tension in the family snapped. "Fathers, provoke not your children to wrath," Paul's exhortation to the Ephesians, may carry the memory of a final quarrel, when his hot temper was roused beyond endurance to betray "the meekness and gentleness of Christ" within him. Whether after violent argument or by his father's implacable decision, he was expelled and disinherited, reduced to apostolic poverty.

And what of his wife, if he were not a widower? In his First Letter to the Corinthians, he says on his own authority ("not the Lord") that "if any brother has a wife who is an unbeliever, and she consents to live with him, he should not divorce her . . . but if the unbelieving partner desires to separate, let it be so; in such a case the brother or sister is not bound. For God has called us to peace." No one can ever know whether these words arose from the memory of a loved wife who rejected Christ, refused to join her husband in Damascus, returned to Tarsus, and finally deserted.

Every advantage that Paul had gained by birth "I considered lost for Christ's sake. Yes, and I look upon everything as loss compared with the overwhelming gain of knowing Christ Jesus my Lord. For His sake I did in actual fact suffer the loss of everything, but I considered it useless rubbish compared with being able to win Christ."

Cast out of home, comforts, and position, Paul disappeared into the wild country of the Taurus foothills and here, in A.D. 41 or 42, possibly in the cave that used to be shown as "St. Paul's Cave," he had a "vision and revelation of the Lord" so sacred that he never referred to it for over fourteen years and then in guarded terms in the third person: "I know of a man in Christ who was caught up to the third heaven— whether in the body or out of the body I do not know, God knows."

Unlike Saint John on Patmos, who was expressly ordered to write down what he saw, Paul "heard things that cannot be told, which man may not utter." In the humiliations and pains of years to come, when he was discouraged or temporarily defeated, he had the undying memory of this glimpse of eternity. "Eye has not seen, nor ear heard," he could encourage his converts, "nor have entered into the heart of man the things which God has prepared for those who love Him." He was quoting these words from Isaiah, but he had perceived by his own senses that the prophet spoke the truth, and it put into proportion the worst that man or nature could do. "I reckon that the sufferings of this present time are not worthy to be compared with the glory that shall be revealed in us."

Nevertheless, his exuberance must not grow inordinate. "To keep me from being too elated by the abundance of revelations, a thorn was given me in the flesh, a messenger of Satan, to harass (*or* buffet) me, to keep me from being too elated. Three times I besought the Lord about this, that it should leave me; but He said to me, 'My grace is sufficient for you, for My power is made perfect in weakness.' "

The ingenuity of 2,000 years has been exercised over Paul's thorn or (literally) "stake for the flesh." Some supposed it severe sexual temptation, but he would have scorned the idea: Christ's Spirit would certainly master the works of the flesh in that sense. Others decided that he referred to the violence of opposition. The more usual and likely view is "a sharp pain in my body," "a physical handicap," but its nature remains obscure. Those who dismiss Paul's views and visions as hallucinations have argued that he was an epileptic; others have sought a clue in illnesses which may be deduced from the record, especially malaria, with its splitting headaches, and ophthalmia; or the trouble may have sprung from tissues and nerves torn by the beatings.

Whether intermittent or chronic, the thorn threw him more fully on Christ.

So, leaving his cave, this half-bald, bandy-legged man of about forty-one, weak but tough, alone and obscure, yet light of heart, set out to talk about Christ.

Part Two

ALWAYS
A LITTLE
FARTHER

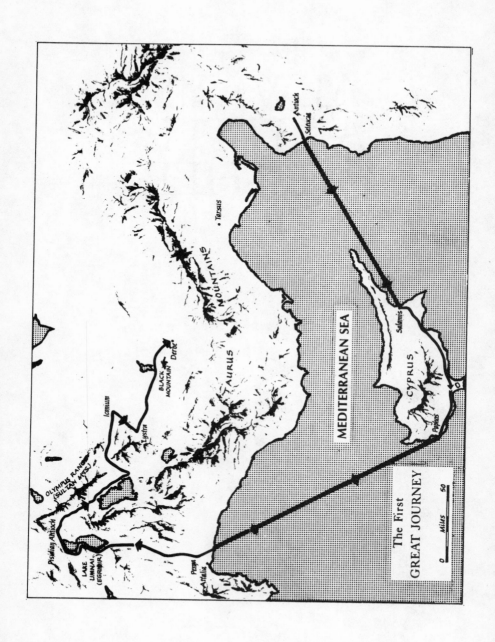

The First
GREAT JOURNEY

Seven
THE NEW ERA

In mountain villages and isolated farms, walking the trails through forests of fir and ash and up the ridges which led toward the high snows of Taurus, Paul founded little groups of disciples which were still active when he returned years later. Probably also he took a ship along the coast where land routes were poor, for the hidden years must include the three shipwrecks he mentions when writing in A.D. 56; after one of them "I was adrift on the open sea for a night and a day."

In this traveling he was a freelance. He always emphasized the importance of links between the churches of Jesus wherever they were, and of unity between itinerant evangelists and those who supported them, yet he was isolated from the apostles in Jerusalem and the main advances of the faith. He was lonely, too. He worked best with one or more companions; he seems to have had none from these country communities and if there were converts in Tarsus, Acts never mentions them: as Christ had said, "A prophet is not without honor, except in his own country and among his own kin, and in his own house."

Then Paul heard that a man from Syria sought him, and at last they met. Luke implies that Barnabas had a considerable search: "Barnabas went forth to Tarsus to seek for Saul, and when he had found him. . . ."

Barnabas brought important news. The faith had taken hold in Antioch, the capital of Syria. What is more, it had spread among pagans. Meanwhile Peter had undergone a remarkable experience with the household of an Italian centurion in Caesarea, a Jewish proselyte; Peter had entered rather gingerly after a direct order from the Lord, and the Holy Spirit came upon them as he preached. He told the brothers in Jerusalem who criticized him for entering a Gentile home: "If God gave the same gift to them as He gave to us when we believed in the Lord Jesus Christ, who was I that I could withstand God?" When, therefore, news reached the apostles that large numbers of non-Jews in Antioch had become believers, they selected Barnabas to investigate. He was delighted at what he found "and encouraged them all to hold fast to the Lord with resolute hearts."

Barnabas, who was unmarried, made his home in Antioch. Under his leadership, the church grew fast, and he wanted Paul to help him.

Antioch, the third greatest city of the Roman world, lay sixteen miles up the Orontes River, which flowed on through a barrier of hills to the sea. The city guarded the narrow plain which opened to the east toward the Syrian plateau, and was guarded itself from the south by the crags of Mount Silpius, with the citadel on the summit and below it a huge rock carving of a faceless human head, popularly supposed to be of Charon who ferried dead souls to the underworld. The city was a magnificent example of town planning and architecture, a testimony to the supremacy of Greek civilization enhanced by the Roman peace. Like all capital cities of the time it was an amalgam of splendor and poverty—broad colonnaded thoroughfares, the palace of the Imperial Legate, temples, the hippodrome where the novel *Ben Hur* places the chariot race; and mile upon square mile of overcrowded back streets.

Antiochenes had a rumbustious reputation, partly from their satirical wit and lively sense of the ridiculous but mainly because of a sex life which even ancient Rome rated excessive. Five miles south on the pass into the hills stood the extensive sacred Grove of Daphne, dominated by an enormous statue of the god Apollo, where hundreds of prostitutes gave their bodies to any man who cared to worship the goddess of love. Among the trees and temples lived also a human flotsam of escaped slaves, criminals, debtors, and others who had sought sanctuary.

Back streets and Daphne woods made fertile soil, and by the time Paul arrived the Antioch church reflected the racial and social variety of this crossroads of the East. He could plunge right in, preaching and gossiping the Gospel to pagans at the market, in homes, at the baths, in the dressing rooms of gymnasia and the hippodrome, knowing that there was already a warm, vigorous church life to welcome converts.

Believers used to meet (according to an early authority quoted in the sixth century) in Singon Street in the Epiphania district near the Pantheon, close under the carved head of Charon. They probably crowded into the house of a wealthy brother each Sunday, the day of the Resurrection which they called the Lord's Day, the Jews among them having already attended synagogue on the Saturday. Worship may have continued at all hours because slaves and the poor had to squeeze time from their labor. Antioch, which had scores of cults already, decided these people who had their own *ecclesia* or assembly and constantly talked about Jesus the Christ were not some new species of Jew; and thus coined the half-Greek, half-Latin term *Christiani*.

The church was rich in leadership. Besides Joseph "Barnabas" and Paul, there was Lucius of Cyrene, of whom nothing is known, and an elderly aristocrat named Manaen, a foster brother of Herod the Tetrarch who had executed John the Baptist and mocked the Lord Jesus and had lately lost his principality.

A leader named Simeon or Simon "Niger" was probably a Negro. And the evidence leans toward his being "Simon of Cyrene, the father of Alexander and Rufus," the countryman coming into Jerusalem whom the Romans had conscripted to carry the cross of Jesus; and that he had fled to Antioch when Paul made havoc of the church. His son Rufus emigrated to Rome. Paul in his letter to Rome long after sends greetings to Rufus, "an outstanding follower of the Lord, and to his mother, whom I call mother too," which suggests that he found a home and affection in Antioch with those he had hurt in Jerusalem.

Thus Antioch gave Paul home, friends, and work to heal the scars and strains of the lonely decade now ended. It brought him back to the mainstream of the Christian church. But it could not be more than a halt. He was sure he was not called to serve a settled if rapidly growing Christian community but to be an apostle, sent out to proclaim the Good News where the name of Christ was unknown.

The whole world waited. He itched to finish his slow apprenticeship and start as a master builder.

A group from the Jerusalem church visited Antioch and were received with delight, especially because they were prophets, who, like the Old Testament prophets, were recognized as able to reveal God's will about the present and, occasionally, the future. One of them, Agabus, stood up with the Spirit upon him and gave solemn warning of a coming great dearth of wheat. The Antioch Christians accepted this as a divine revelation and determined to hoard grain while the market remained normal, ready to send relief to Jerusalem where the unfertile hills would be hard hit by drought.

Most of the believers were poor. Each put into the famine fund what he could, week by week, and men were appointed to travel around the lush lands beside the great lake near Antioch, and up the Orontes, to buy grain wherever they could find it stored. Organizing this was after Paul's heart, for though his own work must be evangelizing and teaching, he would always show strong social concern; he was strong too for forging links between the Antioch church and Jerusalem.

In due course the harvest failed. Tacitus, Suetonius, and Josephus, the near-contemporary historians, record food shortages at this period. The severity of the famine in Judea is endorsed by Josephus' evidence that Queen Helena, the Jewish mother of a pagan king beyond the empire, bought grain in Egypt and figs in Cyprus to distribute relief in Jerusalem.

Barnabas and Paul were designated by the church to take the grain, probably in August A.D. 46. For this considerable expedition, Paul chose as an assistant a young convert of his own, Titus. The choice was deliberate. Titus was a pure-blooded Greek and therefore uncircumcised. If Paul could take him around in the heart of Judaism, he would have established the principle that a Gentile can be a Christian without needing to become a Jew.

They would have carried the grain by sea to Joppa and up by mule train, and thus, in the eleventh year after his last visit and the fourteenth since his conversion, Paul could again echo the psalmist: "Our feet shall stand in thy gates, O Jerusalem." The gates, however, had changed, for the Romans had made Judea a kingdom once more under Herod Agrippa I, nephew of the Baptist's murderer, and he had begun new walls to the north; the sites of the crucifixion and Stephen's death were now within the city. This Herod had recently arrested Peter and James, John's brother. James had been executed. Peter escaped by a miracle in answer to prayer. Herod had died suddenly and miserably at Caesarea shortly before Barnabas and Paul reached Jerusalem.

They handed the supplies to the church elders, for the apostles maintained the rule they had established in Stephen's day, of not entangling themselves in administration. The Antioch party were in no hurry to return and played a full part in the distribution of the grain to citizens of Jerusalem, not only to Jews who were Christians but to those who were not, though more and more were accepting Jesus as their Messiah.

But Paul had another, private task in Jerusalem.

He wanted to go over with Peter and other leaders "the Gospel that I preach among the Gentiles, lest somehow I should be running or had run in vain." If any detail in the revelations that had come to him, especially his conviction that pagan converts were not required to become Jews as well, conflicted with the words of Jesus and the attested narratives of the works of Jesus, then he was sure—as all early Christians would have been sure—that it was an aberration which could not have been taught him by the Spirit of God.

Taking Barnabas, he sought out Peter and arranged for a confidential discussion, together with John and the surviving James, the Lord's brother, who seemed the other foremost figures.

Paul was somewhat prickly about his status. He believed he qualified as an apostle as much as they, for like them he was an eyewitness of the Risen Christ; he had been personally commissioned to tell what he had seen and to preach the Gospel; and he had been directly instructed in Arabia as they had in Galilee and Judea. He was determined that no earthly leader should stand between himself and the Lord Jesus. He was relieved therefore to discover that these three appreciated his point and did not attempt to order him around. Indeed, they received him with utmost warmth, and found nothing that jarred on their knowledge of the Lord's teaching and actions when he had lived among them until the day of his Ascension. Paul's account of what God had done through him was plain evidence, they said, that he was assigned to the Gentiles just as Peter was assigned to the Jews. And they did not suggest that young Titus should submit to circumcision; Paul had needed already to be abrupt with a few Jewish Christians—he doubted the sincerity of their conversion and he hints that they had spied on Titus when he was undressed—who grumbled that an uncircumcised Greek was only half a disciple of Jesus. But now even James stifled his reservations.

The conference ended with handclasps, goodwill, and a settled policy that Paul and Barnabas should go to Gentile territories while the others worked in Palestine. The three Jerusalem leaders' sole request was that Paul, Barnabas, and their Gentile friends should always remember the Jerusalem poor, "which very thing I was eager to do." Paul's apprenticeship was over. He was accepted as an apostle.

He left to pray in the Temple. Here, the aged Simeon had seen the infant Jesus and offered his Nunc Dimittis, "for mine eyes have seen Thy salvation, which Thou has prepared before the face of all people; a light to lighten the Gentiles, and the glory of Thy people Israel." And now Paul had been chosen and acknowledged as an instrument in fulfilling the prophecy. His mind and soul were wrapped in praise and prayer. Though at forty-four he had little to show and might almost be counted a failure, the years ahead would be arduous yet glorious.

He still believed, as he had believed when he preached immediately after his conversion, that the worldwide church would be built on the foundation of the Jewish synagogues across the empire, each beaming Christ's light to city and countryside in the pagan lands around the Mediterranean. It seemed to him that the only way to begin was to inspire the Greek-speaking synagogues in Jerusalem. If he won these for Christ, the rest overseas would follow. At his early attempt in the previous decade, Jerusalem Jews had refused to listen because they rated him a turncoat. But the famine had opened their eyes and ears. Those who knew his past, how he had persecuted Christ's followers, knew now that he was an honorable, loving man who had brought his countrymen succor. Therefore the Risen Jesus he had seen, who had converted him, must be the truth and the way. Those in the synagogues would reverse their former verdict and accept what he told them about Jesus, and believe. The very fact that they knew he had persecuted the faith was his strongest claim to be heard.

Then, from Jerusalem, Paul would lead teams of Greek-speaking Jews and proselytes to the uttermost parts of the empire. They would be joined by pagan converts to carry the message of Christ yet farther. There would be one fold and one Shepherd.

As he mused and prayed, he lost all consciousness of the crowd of worshipers, of the din coming in from the outer courts, of money-changers and sellers of sacrificial pigeons and doves; he lost any sense of fatigue standing as the hours fled. He was conscious only of the Spirit of Jesus, the Lord Jesus, never absent, specially real whenever Paul's mind was uncluttered, and now more obviously present each passing minute. His heart was on fire. It was as if some atmosphere around him were thinning and the heat of God's love, of Christ's, burned in on his soul, unbelievable, precious.

And then it happened: "I saw Him."

As Paul recounted to a hostile audience years later almost at the self-same spot, "I saw Him there, speaking to me. 'Make haste,' He said, 'and leave Jerusalem without delay, for they will not accept your testimony about Me.' "

At that, Paul argued. As Ananais had argued, and Peter; arguing with the Son of God, who surely should see that Paul must remain in Jerusalem, that they would accept the word of a converted persecutor.

"Lord," he began, "they know that I imprisoned those who believe in You, and flogged them in every synagogue; and when the blood of Stephen, Your witness, was shed I stood by, approving, and I looked after the clothes of those who killed him—"

"Go! For I am sending you far away to the Gentiles."[8]

Eight
APHRODITE'S ISLAND

All winter after the return from Jerusalem a sense of an imminent new beginning possessed the Antioch church. At length, at a time of worship and fasting, there came a profound conviction of the Holy Spirit's will: "Set Barnabas and Saul apart for Me, to do the work to which I have called them." Then followed a solemn laying on of hands by the leaders in the sight of the church: the apostles would not be freelances but representatives of the Antioch Christians; the lowliest slave, the newest convert would have a part in the enterprise, talking to the Lord about them, wondering how they prospered, lapping up scraps of news that might trickle back from travelers who crossed their paths.

Barnabas and Paul were formally released from their local ministry. They went by boat down the deep, winding valley of the Orontes the sixteen miles to the sea, and round the bluff to Antioch's port of Seleucia, sure that they had been commissioned by God Himself, and that just as they were obeying the command of Jesus to spread His Gospel, so they had His promise, "I am with you always."

They had His words in their memories—and very possibly on papyrus. For they were accompanied by Barnabas' relative

John Mark, a young man with stumpy fingers and a terse way of speech, who had come back with them from his home in Jerusalem. He was their subordinate, yet an integral member of the team: Luke's term to describe his position was used in the Roman world for a "document handler." Mark may have already written down, at Peter's behest, a collection of the authentic sayings and doings of Jesus, and been sent by the Jerusalem church with the express intention of strengthening Barnabas and Paul, since they were to work among Gentiles, by public readings. And he could add priceless eyewitness testimony of the sufferings of Jesus if, as is generally supposed, he was the young man who had followed him in the Garden of Gethsemane and fled naked at the arrest.

The three missionaries shipped from Seleucia in the first days of the sailing season early in March A.D. 47 for the easy run to Cyprus, an obvious preliminary choice in that Barnabas was a Cypriot and the island had a substantial Jewish minority, large enough to raise a dangerous rebellion some fifty years later. There was also a big population of pagan slaves extracting the copper which gave Cyprus its wealth. The apostles landed at Salamis, the commercial center of the eastern half (near modern Famagusta), where they "proclaimed the Word of God in the synagogues of the Jews."

They next worked their way round the southern shore of the island, staying a short time at each town. If Paul thought that this method would not prove the best, he gave no sign, or else deferred to the preference of Barnabas, the acknowledged leader. For Paul, Cyprus could be no more than a prelude; the Christian message had been known there since the arrival of refugees from his own persecution fifteen years before, whereas he was determined to go "where Christ was not named." He was confident that the Lord would unfold a strategy. He had the strongest awareness, as his actions show, that the entire operation was in the hands of the Lord Jesus, who was no passive spectator but the invisible commander, ready to seize opportunities, recover from reverses, deploy

His forces as they gathered under His banner.

Barnabas possibly doubted whether the Word would be received by pagans; Antioch might have been a special case. Paul had no such doubts. Both awaited a sign.

They crossed low wooded hills, skirted the bay where, in Homer, Aphrodite, the goddess of love, emerged full grown from the foam. They avoided her famous temple at which prostitution, as in Daphne, counted for religious devotion, and came down to the Roman city of New Paphos, the capital and the best harbor on the Southwest coast. Soon, surprisingly, they received a summons to lecture before the august presence of the Proconsul of Cyprus, Sergius Paullus.

The palace of the Proconsul stood a little above the city. As Barnabas and Paul walked up the processional way on a late spring day, the sun gleamed on gilded gods above the granite palace gate and touched the helmets of the legionnaires, who raised spears in salute to honored guests.

Sergius Paullus had been Curator of the Tiber River before leaving Rome, and Luke is meticulously accurate in describing him as Proconsul, since by constitutional theory Cyprus belonged to the Senate and not the emperor, whose provincial governors were termed legates.[5] Sergius Paullus had a scientific mind: Pliny the Elder in his *Natural History* cited him as an authority. He had a taste for speculation and superstition too, as Barnabas and Paul realized when they saw among his entourage a notorious renegade Jew with the incongruous name of Bar-Jesus or "son of a savior," who purported to be a prophet of the living God but also, inconsistently, an astrologer, a wise man of the East (or *Magus*) who dabbled in the occult and could boast of the alternative name of Elymas, "Skillful" or "Sage."

Sitting on his proconsular throne in the spacious audience hall, a breeze gently blowing through the marble pillars, with glimpses of the deep-blue bay and the white town below, Sergius Paullus asked to hear what the apostles taught. Soon, according to a phrase in the very early but slightly expanded, "Western Text" of Acts, the Proconsul was "listening with much pleasure to them."

They were in full course, each adding to the other, when abruptly, in defiance of protocol, Elymas interrupted. He launched a venomous attack on them and their news, "trying to turn the Proconsul from the faith" with all the vigor of a man who sees his influence about to be overturned.

Paul stood it a few minutes, indignant, praying inwardly, struggling to master himself. Then he became aware of peace filling his mind, and fire, and knew for a certainty that the Holy Spirit had taken control.

Paul had a low flash point, a temper that could burst at times of extreme exasperation; but these next moments he was calm, his words the more terrible for owing nothing to temper. He saw right into Elymas, exactly what he was; Paul saw too the urgency of the situation, the struggle for Sergius Paullus' soul. The Roman officers of the entourage could not care how many gods a man worshiped, and had stifled a yawn or two before the sudden tension expelled indifference, but to Paul it mattered more than anything that Sergius Paullus should believe in Jesus; there was one truth, and if Elymas-Bar-Jesus perverted it, he must be judged. Paul cared nothing that he was about to risk his skin by exposing in the hearing of the quack's powerful protector this "son of a savior."

Paul fixed him with his eye. "You son of the devil," he began. "You enemy of all goodness, full of all deceit and every cunning, is it not high time you stopped making crooked the ways of the Lord?"

Elymas quailed. And Paul, totally in tune with the Lord of the universe, knew exactly what was about to happen. He could speak as a prophet, foretelling the immediate future. It was not Paul who was about to punish, but God.

"Look now! The hand of the Lord strikes: you shall be blind, and for a time you shall not see the sunlight!"

At once sight faded, then failed. Like Paul on the Damascus

Road, Elymas groped for someone to lead him by the hand.

Insofar as medical reason may be adduced, he had probably suffered a blockage of a central vein. If the Lord could open the eyes of the blind, He could touch a central vein; intervention to frustrate an opponent of His messengers is scarcely ever recorded, but this was for Elymas' ultimate good, as is suggested by Luke's precision of terms: "Instantly a *mist* and *darkness* came over him." Luke never uses words loosely, and he says plainly that Elymas did not go stone blind in a second: light faded before total darkness supervened. This detail could only have been provided by Elymas himself, presumably recovered and, at the very least, friendly to a Christian historian.

As for Sergius Paullus, he was astounded. No event could have more convinced an educated Roman used to authority that what he heard was not idle speculation but unique truth and power. When he "saw what happened, he became a believer, deeply impressed by what he learned about the Lord." He passes out of the story, for Luke was not writing a detailed history of the expansion of Christianity. But in the year 1912 the archeologist Sir William Ramsay unearthed an inscription in Anatolia which to his expert knowledge demonstrated that Sergius Paullus influenced his daughter to become a Christian; whereas his son, Governor of Galatia in the next generation, who probably was being educated in Rome at the time of his father's proconsulship of Cyprus, remained pagan.

For Paul and Barnabas, the incident was a sign that God would open a door to the Gentiles. And Barnabas joyfully conceded the leadership. He recognized that the Holy Spirit had fashioned Paul by background and training to lead them on, into the unknown.

Nine
INTO GALATIA

They set sail, Paul and his company, for another short run northwest to the coast of Pamphylia on the mainland of Asia Minor. And now at last they were truly pioneers. Pamphylia lay far west of any territory which Paul may have touched in the hidden years, nor had Christians been there or beyond.

Thus, in his late forties, an age when men settle to comforts and seek a firm base, Paul began his roughest travels. The task was immense. Against him stood the contemporary climate of thought, the great philosophies, the leading religions of the world. His ally was the age-old, unending human search for truth and security. In the first century as in the twentieth, some were devout, some superstitious, others were frankly materialistic, though in that age (as in India today) they paid lip service to the gods. Others, contemptuous of religion, believed only in Man. But at heart, when disguises were torn away and defenses broken, lay the same anxieties and hopes.

The ship sailed into the Gulf of Attalia. Leaving on the port side a great mountain, and the harbor of Attalia below cliffs where streams fell by waterfalls to the sea, she worked her way a few miles up the Cestrus River to the lesser harbor near the walled city of Perga, a steamy, inland center nestling beneath its acropolis. Paul had no intention of stopping. His urge was to press on; the work lay in the hinterland, beyond a barrier of mountains which faced them across the narrow plain, steeper and fiercer than the eastern Taurus near Tarsus, and more terrible than any hills known to the Cypriot Barnabas or the Judean John Mark.

Here Mark returned to Jerusalem.

Paul saw it as rank desertion. Mark's excuse has been variously guessed. Some think Paul had fallen ill of malaria, and made for the mountains to seek cooler air rather than from deliberate intent, and Mark was frightened. But he would hardly have left a relative in a strange land with an invalid. Another guess, that he considered they were exceeding their commission by going to the Gentiles, does not square with the undisputed fact that his Gospel was written primarily for Romans. He may have resented Barnabas' surrender of the leadership; he may have been a coward, or homesick, even lovesick. Whatever the cause, Mark's withdrawal left a wound in Paul which took years to heal.

Paul and Barnabas set off across the plain, where the dust rose in stifling clouds from the Roman Road, and next day into the mountains by steep gorges where the heat hit back from the gray rock. Chariots and carts were not expected on these gradients; the modern road uses hairpin bends, but the Romans laid theirs sheer up the pass, and the perspiration poured off walkers young and old. They entered a forbidding landscape of boulders and stunted pines. In Paul's era, between the peace of Augustus and the troubles of Nero, Roman roads were safer than at any time before, or afterward for a thousand years, but he was entering one of the few regions within the empire not fully tamed. Brigands and wild tribesmen made short work of lone travelers; the apostles must join a caravan.

Each night a huge fire would be kept alive and they all slept round it, their feet toward the heat. Paul would take his turn on watch, probably wrapped in a sheepskin. Before dawn they would break camp, eat olives and goat's cheese and, if cold, could drink mulled wine (tea was not known yet out of China, and even Arabs had not discovered coffee). They started before sunrise to use the cool of the day. The pace was a steady plod, and they walked with occasional halts until noon, expecting to cover about fifteen miles.[6] Then they cooked their meal, slept in the shade, oiled themselves in preference to washing, and did nothing in particular.

The journey was slow. Day after day on indifferent food in a high altitude did not encourage foot travelers to quicken the pace, lengthen the stages, or like horsemen, do another stint in the evening. The heat, the sudden drenching storms which flooded the gullies, the cold at night when limbs were stiff and old scars hurt, the danger of sudden attack—this first journey was one of the toughest. It must have been in Paul's mind when he recalled his hardships in the Second Letter to the Corinthians, and the sonorous English of the *Authorized Version,* like his original Greek, seems to echo the rhythm of the march: "In perils of waters, in perils of robbers; . . . in weariness and painfulness, in watchings often, in hunger and thirst, in fastings often, in cold and nakedness."

Paul would say in old age, "I have *learned* in whatever state I am, to be content. . . . In any and all circumstances, I have *learned* the secret of facing plenty and hunger, abundance and want. I can do all things in Him who strengthens me" (*or,* "I am ready for anything through the strength of the One who lives within me"). This secret was not learned at once. There may have been times when his endurance wore thin on this journey or when, later, he was hard put to control his temper at rapacious innkeepers.

But with the equable Barnabas by his side, he quickly became a good traveler, encouraging the weak or fearful in the company, laughing at difficulties. The Victorian biographer J.S. Howson thought Paul lacked a sense of humor. First-century Jews had little natural humor, yet a man who wrote so much about cheerfulness—"rejoice in the Lord always," "love, joy, peace," "make melody in your heart," "God, who gives us richly all things to enjoy"—could hardly have been morose. Joy was a release of Paul's conversion: not the hearty backslapping practical-joking humor of the Victorians, nor the cynical satire or the flippancy of twentieth-century mass media, just the gift of not taking himself or adversities too seriously.

Paul had his times of depression, even perhaps an inbuilt tendency to melancholy, but he got much fun out of life.

By now they were high up in the mountains and had crossed into the great province of Galatia, which stretched over much of central Anatolia. They filed down into more settled highland country, the caravans dispersed, and Paul and Barnabas continued by themselves. And so they came to one of the most beautiful lakes in the world, called Limnai in their day and Lake Egridir now. Hills all about them, a snow-capped mountain on their left and another, Mount Olympus, far ahead made a perfect setting for the extraordinary turquoise of the water.

For three days they walked on the path beside the lake. Wherever the hills stood back, each promontory and bay had a scattering of farms and cottages thatched from the reeds which grew offshore. The apostles easily found lodging, and probably they talked about their mission; they would not stop to tell it to passing wayfarers, for Paul liked to make for a definite field rather than scatter seed by the wayside, though the friendliness and spiritual hunger of their hosts, whether slaves or small tenant farmers, must have offered a hint of the astonishing developments to come.

At last they joined a branch of the great road from the far-distant west coast and turned the corner of the lake until it was lost behind the hills. Pressing on to reach their destination before Sabbath, they crossed a final low pass and saw, dwarfed by another mountain range yet proud in its temples and gates, the city and colony of Caesarea Antiochea, commonly called Pisidian Antioch.

Pisidian Antioch had been refounded by the Emperor Augustus as a Roman colony to keep the peace in the hills. It still had a frontier air and a touch, as it were, of Peshawar on the Northwest Frontier in the days of British India. Antioch, however, was better protected by nature than Peshawar, for below the southeastern wall, which would bear the brunt of tribal attacks, lay the deep, sheer gorge of the Anthios River.

Few remained of the tough old soldiers planted here by Augustus, but their descendants, together with the administrators of southern Galatia, were the aristocracy holding Roman citizenship, who despised the earlier Greek settlers forming a middle class, and the native Phrygians who did the hard labor. Pisidian Antioch, despite its name, lay in the district of Phrygia; Phrygians had brawn without brain. They were exported as slaves all over the empire so that "Phrygian" was almost synonymous with "slave." Paul and Barnabas, exploring the city, climbed the steps through magnificent arches which commemorated the victories of Augustus on sea and land, and walked in the square named in his honor and dominated by the white marble temple where the late emperor was worshiped with the local god; they could feel the arrogance of Rome and the bitterness of proud tribes conquered less than a generation before.

Antioch had its Jews, whose wealth and industry had earned Roman tolerance for their disrupting the economy by stopping work one day in seven. On Sabbath morning Paul and Barnabas entered the synagogue and sat down in the seats for visiting rabbis. After the prayers and readings, the synagogue rulers sent the *hazzan* with a courteous message: "Brothers, if you have any word of exhortation for the people, say it."

Paul stood up. He noticed at once that the congregation included not only a considerable number of local converts to Judaism but interested pagans or "God-fearers." With a gesture that stilled the murmur of anticipation, he caught the attention of everybody by an unusual opening: instead of following custom by ignoring the existence of God-fearers, he included them in his opening words: "Men of Israel and you God-fearers, listen!"

He began with a historical sketch closely modeled on Stephen's unforgettable defense. But whereas Stephen got no further than King David before the atmosphere grew so hostile that he broke off to accuse his judges, Paul was heard with complete attention.

From David's descendants, he told, "God has brought to Israel a Saviour, Jesus, as He promised." Still they listened. For the first recorded time in a synagogue, Paul had a sympathetic audience. He went on:

"Men and brothers, sons of the race of Abraham, and all among you who fear God, it is to us that this message of salvation has now been sent. For the people of Jerusalem and their rulers refused to recognize Him and to understand the voice of the prophets which are read every Sabbath day. Even though they found no cause for putting Him to death they begged Pilate to have Him executed."

He let the enormity of what had been done sink into their minds.

Then, in ringing tones, Paul proclaimed his fantastic good news: *"But God raised Him from the dead!"*

He talked about the resurrection of Jesus, its witnesses, how it had been foretold. Reaching his climax, he swept away the barrier between Jew and Gentile to include every person present in God's offer of free forgiveness: "Know therefore, *brothers*"—pagan God-fearers had never been called "brothers" before—"that through this Man forgiveness of sins is proclaimed to you and by Him everyone who believes is freed from everything, from which you could not be freed by the Law of Moses."

All over the synagogue Paul could see light dawning on faces, here a pagan, there a trueborn Jew, here a proselyte. He urged the need for personal repentance and faith in Jesus, and ended: "Beware, therefore, lest there come upon you what is said in the prophets: 'Behold, you scoffers, and wonder, and perish; for I do a deed in your days, a deed you will never believe, if one declares it to you.' "

As they went out, the congregation crowded round and begged for more next Sabbath. The synagogue doors were shut behind them, perhaps a little pointedly. Jews and proselytes followed Paul and Barnabas toward their lodgings. All that day and during the week the apostles were busy with individuals and groups and "urged them to hold fast to the grace of God."

The pagan God-fearers had scattered to their homes, scarcely daring to believe that faith in Jesus could bring immediate forgiveness and happiness without the necessity of circumcision and the rigors of the Jewish Law. They spread the news like wildfire. In the market, in the law courts, in the slave barracks at the Tribune's mansion, the word went round that these traveling preachers had a message that made sense of life.

When on the next Sabbath Paul and Barnabas reached the synagogue, they found an enormous crowd, Gentiles outnumbering Jews. Every seat was filled. Veterans and their families, Greek shopmen, Phrygian slaves stood pressed about the door and down the narrow street and into the Square of Augustus. Priests of the pagan temples looked on amazed at the size, quietness, and earnestness of the crowd, which ignored them and were interested solely in hearing, if they could, what the two Christians wanted to say. Only the higher aristocracy and their women folk held aloof.

In the synagogue the service never began.

Instead of warmly welcoming the largest congregation of their time, the rabbi, elders, and leading Jews were furious. They resented the response to Paul's message. What last week they had received respectfully they now repudiated root and branch, and the people who had flocked to learn about the power and love of Jesus heard His claims dismissed, His character traduced, His messengers covered with abuse.

Paul was not surprised; they only said what he had once said.

He did not mind being spattered with verbal filth. He could stomach even the blasphemies hurled at his Lord. But he was not going to be muzzled. Gentiles and Jews wanted to hear the message and no blind self-satisfied Jewish elder should hinder. The two missionaries stood up boldly (they risked being whipped for opposing lawful authority) and answered back: "It was necessary that the Word of God should be declared to you first. But since you reject it, and thus condemn yourselves as unworthy of eternal life, we now turn to the Gentiles. For these are our instructions from the Lord—" and Paul quoted the prophecy of Isaiah which Simeon had used in the Nunc Dimittis: " 'I have set you to be a light for the Gentiles, that you may bring salvation to the uttermost parts of the earth.' "

The apostles strode out of the synagogue followed by all the Gentiles, who were patently delighted, and many of the Jews. The crowds at the door made way for them, and they walked to the square and stood on the plinth of a statue. And there, to this great concourse of Galatians, Paul preached.

When he wrote his Letter to the Galatians he would remind them of it: " . . . before whose eyes Jesus Christ was publicly portrayed as crucified."

Ten
PROGRESS AND PERSECUTION

Shortly afterward, Paul fell ill, or so it seems. In his letter to the Galatians,[7] he wrote: "As you know, it was bodily illness that originally led to my bringing you the Gospel, and you showed neither scorn nor disgust at the trial my poor body was enduring; you welcomed me as if I were an angel of God, as you might have welcomed Christ Jesus Himself." Paul could not be referring to that first sermon in the synagogue, for the elders would never have allowed him to preach in a repulsive physical condition; they rated illness a divine judgment. On the other hand, Paul cannot mean he came to Antioch because he fell ill at Perga, for he would not be an object of scorn or disgust by the time he arrived: the grueling march must have killed or cured. He probably therefore means that he stayed much longer in the area than he had intended and that most of them heard the Gospel only because of this.

Until then, his strategy had been essentially mobile. In Cyprus he and Barnabas had preached in many places, staying briefly before moving on. At Pisidian Antioch, he was forced to stop. Several weeks of high summer passed while he lay sick; lack of mention in Acts is not conclusive, since Luke's immediate purpose in writing was to commend the Gospel to Romans, and he saw no cause to introduce subsidiary matters like illness which would offend a Roman reader. The Galatians, however, were not offended. New converts displayed a most un-Roman concern for the sick man. They showered him with love and care, wished they could pluck out their own eyes to replace his streaming, rheumy, and painful eyes. And all the time the Gospel spread.

Of the crowd which had heard Paul preach in the Square of Augustus, many believed. They showed immediate desire to share their discovery, so that faith in Christ leaped from man to man like some divine epidemic, not of disease but spiritual health. Barnabas had been hard-put to keep abreast of it. By the time Paul recovered enough for action, the openings throughout the district were far too many to permit him to abandon Antioch. Therefore, for the first time, he adopted the stategy by which he would thenceforth evangelize: settle in a center to reach a region, and reach it by the converts.

Even before he was well enough to walk, converts brought their friends to his bedside, and his Epistle to the Galatians gives retrospective glimpses of what he said. His entire message centered on Jesus Christ. Words used about Spurgeon by a contemporary could also apply to Paul: "The Lord Jesus was to him such an intense, living reality, he believed so in His nearness and presence and the wonderful love with which He loves us, that the hearer felt that he spoke out of living experience of what he had seen and heard." Paul could convey to a high degree the wonder and certainty of that recent event in history—the crucifixion of Christ for the sins of men; and the astonishing fact that "God raised Him from the dead," the phrase in Paul's synagogue sermon which probably he used again and again, for it comes in the letter as if familiar to Galatians.

And they heard and believed because, as Paul reminded them, the Spirit drove his words to their hearts. Pagans turned from the grip of the gods, "which are no gods," and

Jews turned from the grip of the Law and the pursuit of self-righteousness. It did not matter who they were, Gentiles or Jews, "for in Christ," Paul urged, "it is not circumcision or uncircumcision but the power of new birth."

The cost to Paul was immense. These were his spiritual children and the agony of childbirth (in a world without anesthetics) was the analogy he used to describe his concern and prayer and mental effort.

As soon as signs of a newborn personality appeared in young or old, he was prepared to let him be baptized, just as he himself had been baptized by Ananias a mere three days after conversion. Paul had strong views on changed character being the proof of genuine conversion. If the Spirit of Christ had come to a man, the "fruits of the Spirit" would appear: "love, joy, peace, patience, kindness, goodness, faithfulness, gentleness, self-control"; such things had been little known in Antioch, except stoical self-control among the upper classes. For a slave to be taught that he should no longer lie and cheat was revolutionary; more astonishing still was the slave's discovery that he did not now want to lie or cheat, and that he loved the owner whom he had resented and feared.

Paul knew well enough that each convert had a conflict, that the new nature did not eradicate the old, and he warned them, as his letter would recall, against "the kind of behavior that belongs to the lower nature: fornication, impurity, and indecency; idolatry and sorcery; quarrels, a contentious temper, envy, fits of rage, selfish ambitions . . . drinking bouts, orgies and the like." Such behavior was all around them, waiting to suck them back into the mud, but "if you are guided by the Spirit, you will not fulfill the desires of the lower nature." And so he worked hard to build them up in Christ. Their wish to pray was as natural as the cry of a newborn baby; he showed them how to pray. Their hunger for knowledge about the Lord Jesus was as sharp as in the newly converted Paul; he told them all he knew, and taught them, whether ex-pagans or Jews, to treat the Scriptures of the Jews as the Word of God explained through Christ.

None of this was in isolation. They had been born into a family; and—a radical doctrine to Paul's hearers—each member had equal worth.

The ancient world was shot through with hatred or contempt of one class for another. A man's color, race, or religion (except for Jews) mattered less than his current position; a Negro or a Scythian from the steppes could attain wealth, power, and Roman citizenship, but a conquered king's son, white-skinned, delicately reared, when taken into slavery became a disposable chattel whose owner might crack his skull in rage or have him whipped raw, for all the State or neighbors cared.

In contrast, Paul taught, and the Spirit proved it true to their experience, that "there is neither Jew nor Greek, slave nor freeman, male nor female; for you are all one in Christ Jesus." And so, as Barnabas and the convalescent Paul moved from one group to another, now in a rich Jew's home in the city, now in a Roman veteran's country estate, now in a Phrygian farmhouse, they would see master and slave, grandmother and youth, shopkeeper and soldier share the cup of blessing and break the bread.

In years ahead the Galatians would have their failures and falls, would nearly break Paul's heart; but in these first days as Christians, they had a tremendous sense of Christ's reality, His action and presence working in and through them. Each had a passionate concern to serve his neighbor and his Saviour by bringing the one to the other, being sure that trust in the Lord Jesus was the only entrance to the full life that began at once and came to fullness at death. Therefore, while still learning from the two apostles, the converts fanned out until, as Luke records, "the Word of the Lord spread throughout all the region."

Paul encouraged them. He expected the Spirit to turn "disciples," those who are passive and learning, into "apostles," active and proclaiming the message. He seems mentally to have upgraded true converts to the status of colleagues remarkably swiftly, and thus suffered almost exaggerated sorrow and deflation when any failed him.

Converts who were not tied by servitude pushed into the hills, and over to the great lake where the thatched cottages dotted the bays, and up into the high mountain range which divided the Antioch countryside from the central plateau. They preached the grace of God, and they knew that Jesus worked with them, for now and again they saw light dawn on a listening face. In a matter of weeks, a flourishing, expanding church sprang up. Since families often joined as one, there could be shallow faith mixed with deep, the tares among the wheat, but these days were like a springtime of spirit. Two goatherds watching the kids would talk freely about Jesus. Among the fishing boats on Limnai returning early with their catch, one would be seen to drop oars and its crew bow their heads in prayer. A woman meeting an acquaintance at market would discover that she too was a believer. A field slave on a great estate would find the last, worst hour before sunset more bearable and short because Christ was with him. The soldier on the wall at night above the gorge had a new song to hum.

Paul and Barnabas wished to stay until sure that the church could stand on its own. But after about two months in the city, when Antioch was frizzling in August heat and the dust irritated man and beast, a storm broke about their heads.

All this time the Jews who refused to believe in Christ had stayed passive. They could not attack directly because the apostles had withdrawn from the synagogue, nor would the city-colony magistrates hear complaints against law-abiding strangers. Yet the Christian influence widened and these Jews could bear it no longer. They therefore worked on two or three aristocratic women proselytes until their anxiety about the likely spread of disaffection among the lower orders grew as intense as their repugnance at Paul's teaching. In Antioch, as in all Asia Minor, pagan devotion to the Mother Goddess under her various names had left women a marked influence in the community. The proselytes' husbands, typical Romans whose religion was loyalty to the divine emperor, listened with respect to their wives, and decided that the new preachers were indeed nothing but vagrants up to mischief.

What happened next may be deduced from the brief guarded phrase of Luke and a reference by Paul in a letter written in old age.

Leading men of the city lodged an accusation, not with the provincial administrators, whose writ did not run in the local affairs of a Roman colony, but with the magistrates. The aim was to expel Paul and Barnabas, but expulsion always involved summary punishment: when the two were thrown into jail, they knew what lay ahead. Paul, however, was a Roman citizen; he may actually have carried a diptych on which his citzenship was recorded. He could certainly claim "Civis Romanus sum" and though expelled would escape a beating or indignities to his person. Barnabas, not being a citizen, would receive the full force of the law.

But Paul had no intention of escaping what Barnabas must endure, and he said nothing about his citizenship.

The next morning with a harum-scarum knot of petty thieves and recaptured slaves, the apostles were herded into a pen in the town square. The magistrates took their seats on the *bema* or raised platform. Behind them stood their broad-shouldered lictors, each holding his *fasces*, the bundle of rods strapped round an ax, symbol of the magistrate's authority in a Roman colony and the means of its execution.

The proceedings were public; many Christians watched sadly from the crowd. Paul and Barnabas, manacled, were pushed into the space below the magistrates. The case was soon heard and sentence given. A lictor stepped down. First Paul, then Barnabas, was pulled across to the waist-high whipping pillar. Their clothes were torn off them and thrown in a heap. Naked, they were bent over the pillar and tied. The lictor drew birch rods from his *fasces*. Then he inflicted punishment.

Afterward, the manacles were removed, the bleeding apostles dressed as their torn clothes allowed, and without opportunity to recover were escorted the mile or two to the colony boundary and thrust forth. Christians followed, along with unbelieving Jews, gloating at the success of the ploy. It was probably because of these that Paul and Barnabas drew themselves up and solemnly carried out the action ordered by the Lord Jesus in His instructions to His first messengers: "If any place will not receive you and they refuse to hear you, when you leave, shake off the dust that is on your feet as a testimony against them."

Eleven
STONED

Among the Christian converts who witnessed the beating were an elderly Jewess named Lois, her daughter, Eunice, who had married a Greek, and Eunice's son Timothy. Lois had believed first, then her daughter. Timothy, seventeen or eighteen years old, was Paul's "own son in the faith," one of those for whom he had suffered "labor pains" bringing him to new birth, a bond that never would be forgotten on either side. They were citizens of Lystra, the next Roman city-colony about 130 miles east, and evidently arranged to travel homeward at once with the apostles, who to Timothy seemed surprisingly cheerful in their pain.

Expulsion from Antioch did not affect freedom of movement beyond the immediate area. Paul and Barnabas may have lain up a day or two with Christians living beside the poplar-lined Augustan Way which ran straight over the low hills on the east of the city, to recover from the worst of the beating and to give final instructions. They found, to their delight, that far from being discouraged or fearful, converts were rejoicing, sure that the Holy Spirit would not forsake them, though His messengers must leave and that if Paul's punishment were the prelude to their own persecution, they would endure. With the Lord on their side, they would not fear what man might do.

So the little party set off on the Augustan Way, Eunice and Lois fussing a little about the half-healed weals and Timothy carrying their necessaries. Once they had covered two days' journey and were well into the broken country below the northern range, they had to stay at inns, which in the Roman Empire were usually brothels too, and Paul looked to the day when Galatia and all Asia Minor—and the world—should be dotted with Christian homes eager to put up Christian travelers.

On the seventh day's walk, their road forked, after rising from a narrow fertile plain beside another lake backed by the Taurus. Whether the women continued along the military road direct to Lystra or not, Timothy stayed with the apostles, who took the left fork through a pass and down to the ancient city of Iconium on the edge of the central plateau. The two apostles entered unheralded and unnoticed, but Paul took the first opportunity of preaching in the synagogue, and as at Antioch the effect was phenomenal. A large number of Jews and Greeks believed, so that from its first hours this second Galatian church was to Paul what a church should be: a union of races; born Jews or Gentiles, they were all one in Christ Jesus.

Jews who refused to believe that their promised Christ could be Jesus counterattacked immediately: "they stirred up the Gentiles and poisoned their minds against the Christians." While the converted were experiencing the new dimension which Paul called "eternal life," the unconverted were busily propagating tales that made the uncommitted shudder. Thus Iconium, with its dust and winds and the strange little twin peaks which stick up like pyramids, became the first place in the world to see on any large scale a pattern which would be repeated through history: if men and women begin to live like Jesus Christ, their enemies blacken their names: "Hated for their secret crimes . . . Convicted of haired for the human race . . . Men of the worst character and deserving of the severest punishment." The phrases come from Tacitus' near-contemporary account of Christians in Nero's reign yet are echoed almost precisely in Soviet propaganda against Christians in Russia today.

And as in modern Russia and ancient Rome, so in Iconium: the air of contention proved healthy for the Gospel of peace. Day after day, week after week, Paul and Barnabas, records Luke, "stayed on and spoke boldly and openly in reliance on the Lord, and He confirmed the message of His grace by causing signs and miracles to be worked at their hands."

Western theologians have sometimes dismissed that phrase "signs and miracles" or "signs and wonders" as a later gloss or as evidence that Luke believed old wives' tales, but it does not baffle Christians of Africa or the Orient. Nor will the sensitive Westerner who has slept in a tribal house in Upper Burma unknowingly near the altar to the spirits, or has confronted a witch doctor in the Congo, be disposed to doubt that Luke reported with his normal accuracy. The powers of evil may prefer sophisticated forms in the West, but the rest of the world is wary of dismissing "evil spirits" or "demons" as figments of imagination. And the "signs and miracles" at Iconium were probably instances of men and women finding, through Christ, sudden release from mental suffering, nervous illness, or conscious slavery to evil spirits. He was writing another chapter in the story that had begun in Galilee: "He healed many who were sick of various diseases, and cast out many demons."

Tension rose. The city split between those who followed or sympathized with the apostles, and those who hated them. Paul was frequently mishandled in the streets, yet he planned to winter in Iconium. Then, one day in late autumn, he heard that unfriendly Jews and Gentiles had won the ear of the district administrators, who were prepared to turn a blind eye to mob violence. He and Barnabas should be stoned, not by judicial process but like dogs.

They decided to flee. A stoning could be lethal. And public assault condoned by the authorities might provoke widespread persecution of converts. Though the apostles' flight would leave these to fend by themselves, Antioch had shown that a young church was ready to stand alone in Christ's strength sooner than its founders might expect. Therefore, with Timothy as guide, they obeyed the Lord's instruction, "When they persecute you in one city, flee to another."

Early next morning as soon as the gates were opened, they slipped south. It was obvious where to go: Lystra, the city-colony which lay out of Phrygia and into the neighboring Galatian district, Lycaonia, where Iconium magistrates had no jurisdiction. Lystra was Timothy's home. "You have observed," Paul would remind him long after, when they had trod many trails together, "my teaching, my conduct, my aim in life, my faith, my patience, my love, my persecutions, my sufferings, what befell me at Antioch, at Iconium, at Lystra, what persecutions I endured; yet from them all the Lord rescued me." By a forced march across the plain, with the distant abrupt lump of Black Mountain always on their left until they moved into the foothills of the Taurus, they covered twenty-five miles in the day. At last they saw the city of Lystra standing out above a shallow valley.

In front of the city, clear in the evening light, stood the Temple of Zeus, soon to be the cause of one of the most terrifying episodes in Paul's career.

Paul and Barnabas had not in the least lost ebullience or zeal through the troubles at Antioch and Iconium, and soon converts were out again two by two, taking the Gospel to little settlements which hugged the pools tucked here and there in the folds of the hills, and across the plain toward Derbe. These converts were mostly Greeks. If a Jewish synagogue existed, no trace of it remains in literature or ruin (Lystra has never been properly excavated) and the Romans, who spoke Latin here more than those in the colony of Antioch, were little interested. Lycaonians listened, for harvest was in, and they knew Greek, the trade language, though using their own tongue among themselves.

Few, however, had believed, until an extraordinary incident occurred in the sunshine of a winter's day. Close to Paul's favorite preaching spot in the forum was the squatting place of a congenital cripple, a well-known local character who had never been able to walk because he had no strength in his feet and whom friends carried each day to the colonnade. Paul was speaking of the Almighty God who raised Christ from the dead. His gaze ranged over the audience, some idly indifferent, others puzzled, attentive, or hopeful. Suddenly he noticed the cripple's face. He stopped preaching. His eyes bore right in. He knew without doubt that the man had faith to be healed not only in spirit but in body, and that the Power who had told a cripple in Galilee to take up his bed and walk waited to honor faith, Paul's and the cripple's.

Paul shouted: "Stand up straight on your feet!"

Instantly, the man leaped up, and walked. No hesitant, cautious prod of the toe but a leap into vigorous movement.

The effect on the crowd was electric. They began to jabber in Lycaonian, neither Paul nor Barnabas knew what, only that the entire audience buzzed with an intensely reverential excitement, and some of the young men had pushed out of the forum to run in the direction of the Temple of Zeus.

In Lystra's legendary past, as every child learned at his or her mother's knee, the supreme god Zeus and his messenger and herald, Hermes, had disguised themselves as poor travelers and sought shelter among Lycaonians rich and poor; and were turned away until they knocked at the door of an old peasant couple, Philemon and Baucis, who sheltered and fed them. The gods disclosed themselves, turned the inhospitable into frogs and the cottage of Baucis into a gold and marble temple which had stood outside Lystra since long before the Romans. Lycaonians had always looked to the day when the two gods should return, this time to be treated with honor.

And now it all fitted. Of the two wonder-workers who had come upon them, one was small and volatile and made many speeches: he was obviously Hermes (or Mercury in Latin). The other, tall, calm, speaking little in public but using his herald to convey his words, showed the marks of the supreme god Zeus (or Jupiter).[9]

The chief priest of Zeus hurriedly brought sacrificial oxen from the temple pasture and garlanded them with olive branches and colored wools, seized his knife, and with blasts on a horn proceeded toward the city, where crowds already were collecting in the broad space just within the gates. In the forum chanting, dancing Lycaonians surrounded the puzzled Paul and Barnabas. A procession formed. They were invited with deep obeisances to walk up the wide street toward the gate. Only then did the apostles realize, to their horror, that the chant proclaimed: "The gods have come down to us in human form," and that sacrifice was about to be offered to win their favor.

Instinctively, they tore their clothes, the Jewish reaction to blasphemy, and rushed up the street to implore the priest to stop. Paul clambered onto the sacrificial stone. "Men, what is this that you are doing?" he cried, his torn robe flapping in the breeze. "We are only human beings, no less mortal than you. The Good News we bring tells you to turn from these follies to the Living God, who made heaven and earth and sea and everything in them. In past ages He allowed all nations to go their own way; and yet He had not left you without some clue to His nature, in the kindness He shows: He sends you rain from heaven and crops in their seasons, and gives you food and good cheer in plenty."

It was touch and go. The priest hesitated. The crowd wavered, murmuring, fearful lest they anger a divinity, either their own idol or this Living God Paul talked about.

Just then strangers came on the scene: Jews by their dress, recognizable to Paul as antagonists from Pisidian Antioch and

Iconium who would have been trading in Lystra.

These men harangued the crowd. The murmurs swelled. With that terrifying suddenness of oriental mobs, the mood changed from worship to fury. A youth picked up a stone, took aim, and with a vicious flick caught Paul full face. In a moment, before Barnabas or his friends could protect him, he was under a shower of stones, on his jaw, the pit of his stomach, his groin, his chest, his temple. He fell stark and stiff, blood streaming from nose and eyes. The crowd dragged the body out of the city and melted quickly away before the Roman guards at the gate could identify individual murderers.

Converts who had watched appalled at the sudden assault formed a ring round the body, shocked and uncertain.

Paul stirred. With every muscle and nerve seared, head throbbing, stomach retching, he forced himself to stand.

Sympathizers helped him slowly through streets empty because the mob lay low for fear of civic action. They dressed his wounds, and next day, when every bone in his body cried out to rest, he set off with Barnabas. Though Paul may have been lent a donkey, the journey could not be anything but torture as they followed the road eastward along the line of hills a short way, then into the great plain, into the teeth of winter winds and occasional snow flurries, mile upon mile of featureless country with volcanic Black Mountain, like an island ahead, seeming little nearer each hour.

Across the boundary line of the native kingdom of Commagene they were safe.

For years experts wondered how Paul could have found shelter in Derbe when Lystra became too hot to hold him, since both were cities of Galatian Lycaonia and near together (whereas Iconium lay comfortably distant from Antioch, though still in the Phrygian district) but no one could discover Derbe's exact site. Then in 1964 it was finally identified; not, as had been supposed, on the near side of Black Mountain to Lystra but at Devri Sehri on the far side, the eastern, and thus across the border of the native state. It had been part of Galatian Lycaonia, even honored by the reigning Emperor Claudius, until ceded a year or two before Paul's visit with its more important neighbor Laranda to King Antiochus of Commagene, who ruled the territory between Galatia and Cilicia as a vassal of the Romans.

Here, the battered Paul found welcome, response, and recovery. Indeed, it may have been the people of Derbe—who still considered themselves Galatians since the transference of rule was merely an administrative convenience—that Paul had in mind when he wrote those words in his Letter to all the widely scattered churches: "You resisted any temptation to show scorn or disgust at the poor state of my body; you welcomed me as if I were an angel of God . . . You would have torn out your very eyes and given them to me."

The apostles made many disciples in Derbe that winter. While his iron constitution mended, Paul would not shelve his commission. The very scars on his body were a constant reminder of man's violence and sin. To him they were a symbol of the crucifixion too: he called them "the stigmata of the Lord Jesus," and the consciousness of man's need and God's love pressed on him almost to neurosis, one reason why he preferred to evangelize in a team. A colleague like Barnabas could comfort him in illness and keep him, when fit, from overstrain.

As the snow melted in the plains and foothills, and the winds dropped, the apostles left Derbe. They could have followed the trade route eastward to the Cilician Gates and reached Syria by Tarsus comparatively quickly. Instead, they turned back to retrace their route through the three cities which had despitefully used them. Though a new year meant new magistrates and the lapse of inhibitions imposed by the old, Paul and Barnabas were marked men. It required courage to face more stoning and beating.

On arrival at Lystra, they were enormously encouraged.

The church had not dissolved or ceased to grow despite problems and difficulties, persecution and hardships. The apostles did not hurry away, but "strengthened the souls of the disciples, exhorting them to continue in the faith, and saying that through many tribulations we must enter the kingdom of God." All the time they watched and sifted to discover whom among the converts should be entrusted with the oversight of the church. Paul had not yet defined the gifts of character required, but he and Barnabas believed they could tell whom the Spirit might be preparing, and were determined that each local church should be locally led, though no Galatian had long experience of Christ.

When the choice was made, the Christians set aside a day for prayer and fasting, closing with a solemn ordination, after which the apostles committed the new elders and their flock "to the Lord in whom they had put faith."

The two walked north. Plows turned up the brown earth in the patches of cultivation; blossoms were on the trees. They came over the brow and saw Iconium's twin peaks and rejoiced. To their right Black Mountain, topped with snow, reminded them that people were praying for them in Derbe.

After strengthening and ordaining in Iconium, they took the long march west. As they approached Pisidian Antioch, a plowman near the road might come running to greet them; soon men and women of different backgrounds jostled happily to assure Paul that what he had told them was true, in good days and bad: they had found for themselves that the Lord Jesus was all Paul promised, and more. The apostles had the excitement, too, of meeting many who had joined the church after they had left.

They stayed on in Antioch two or three weeks and at last turned for home. Beside Lake Limnai, where they had walked as strangers the year before, they had almost a triumphal progress. Each day a Christian family would escort them to the next Christian home. Sometimes they would be put on donkeys with foals following, or be rowed a stage on the water. At evening all the Christians in the area would gather in the home, with their children, and there would be the deepest sense of the Lord Jesus among them as Paul and Barnabas gave words of encouragement and advice, and then ordained elders.

Next morning they walked on, the lake so peaceful, the atmosphere so happy: "He leadeth me beside the still waters, He restoreth my soul." It was impossible to believe that disappointments were in store.

Twelve
"I OPPOSED HIM TO HIS FACE"

Christians of Antioch in Syria, as many as could, crowded into the open-air *atrium* of the large house in Singon Street whose owner was host to the church. Oblivious of the stench which arose from the city at the end of a hot day and of their own sweat as they sat shoulder to shoulder, Jew and Gentile, rich and poor, slaves and free had a single thought on this late summer evening in A.D. 48: Paul and Barnabas were back.

They had arrived unannounced like all but the most exalted travelers in the ancient world, by coaster of shallow enough draft to sail up the Orontes direct to Antioch, and had at once summoned their partners, the entire church. Their momentous report lasted far into the night, first one speaking, then the other, broken only by an occasional hymn of praise. They told the whole story from their arrival in Cyprus until finally they left Pisidian Antioch for home by walking back through the Taurus to Perga, where this time they stayed to give their message. They had continued along the plain a brief distance, then down the cliff to the harbor of Attalia.[10] They may have been wrecked at sea, for Attalia to Antioch was Paul's longest recorded voyage before the date when he wrote "three times I have been shipwrecked."

315

They had covered over a thousand miles on foot—sixty days entirely consumed in land travel—and as for the brutalities they had endured, some of Paul's scars were only too evident and his gait more bandy-legged and crooked than before. The emphasis, however, was not on sufferings and adventures but on "all that God had done with them." Above everything they stressed how He had "opened a door of faith to the Gentiles." Syrian Antioch had not been a special case: southern Galatia had proved beyond doubt that Christ offered Himself to all men.

Then Paul and Barnabas took their place once more as preachers and teachers in the ordered life of the Antioch church. Paul's desire was to thrust out farther, to the provinces of Asia and Bithynia, eventually into Macedonia and beyond, but he was willing to wait, recovering full physical strength and deepening his spiritual roots. And he had to wait longer than he wished.

Peter came to Antioch. A few weeks later he was followed from Jerusalem by Jews who had remained Pharisees though disciples of Christ. The subsequent controversy which rent the Antioch church and brought Paul into conflict with Peter was of crucial importance to the development of Christianity. Like many disputes which in retrospect proved turning points of history, the subjects might seem trivial to later ages: invitations to dinner, and a minor operation on the male organ. The issues, however, were profound: first, whether Christianity should be merely a variety of Judaism; and secondly, whether a man may be forgiven simply and instantly by trusting Jesus Christ, or whether such forgiveness is incomplete and conditional until he can show that he has worked faithfully and obediently to his life's end to do what is right.

When Peter came to Antioch, the only place in the world where ex-pagans were living on terms of complete equality with Christian Jews, everybody watched what he would do. His courageous words and gifts of leadership had made him the central figure of the early church; his willingness to shock

Jews by eating with the Roman Cornelius had opened the way to the winning of Gentiles. Yet at Jerusalem, where the disciples were primarily concerned to commend Jesus Christ to Jews, he had continued to observe Jewish laws including the normal segregation when eating. If, in the mixed community that was the Antioch church, he went off and ate by himself, he would give the strongest support to those who still believed that a pagan on becoming a Christian must accept Jewish ways and Jewish law, and thus that the new faith remained simply a liberal Jewish sect.

Peter, however, joined Paul and Barnabas in living like a Gentile, thereby ruining his status in the eyes of the orthodox Jews. He no longer observed the Mosaic fasts or taboos nor refused to eat with Gentile converts at the common meal called *agapē*—the "love feast"—which preceded the Lord's Supper. He thereby made plain that he believed as Paul did: no Gentile Christian need live like a Jew.

Then the Christian Pharisees arrived. Their words and actions were repudiated afterward, but they claimed to be traveling with the authority of the recognized local leader of the mother church, James the Lord's brother. They were shocked by the laxity of the Antioch church—and of Peter. They saw Jews eating with "sinners and Gentiles" (to Pharisees the words were synonymous), who thus were put on an equality.

They discovered that every Gentile believer had been excused the necessity, binding on all proselytes, of submitting to the rite of circumcision. At once they began a campaign: "Except you are circumcised according to the custom of Moses," they told converts, "you cannot be saved." Everybody involved in the dispute knew what they meant: "Except, after believing in Jesus, you become a proselyte by undergoing the surgical operation, and thereafter observe all the ceremonies and do the good works required by the Mosaic Law and keep ritually undefiled in addition to your trust in Jesus Christ, you cannot be saved; Jesus by Himself cannot fit a man for heaven." The implications of such an argument went far wider than the issue at Antioch which remained in the context of Jewish obligations. Paul saw that the Christian Pharisees' contention was totally at variance with a truth he had understood since Damascus and would expound fully in his letters later on: that self-righteousness, however expressed, is the rival and not the complement of grace.

The matter came to a head over the issue of ritual defilement. The advocates of "circumcision" argued their case so hotly and cogently that Peter stopped eating with Gentiles. Paul was indignant. Peter may have been swayed by representations that his actions in Antioch must severely embarrass his Jerusalem friends in their ministry to Jews, but Paul was sure Peter did not honestly believe the Judaizers were right; he conformed from fear of their tongues, or from a willingness to sacrifice principle for peace and unity. He was dissembling. Indeed, if there were any apostle walking crooked, it was not bandy-legged Paul but Peter.

Next, most of the Jewish members of the congregation followed Peter's example. Then Barnabas wavered—Barnabas who had taken Paul's part when the point had been discussed in Jerusalem during the famine visit, who had seen overwhelming evidence in Galatia that God remade pagans into full Christians. Paul resolved to speak out. This deep crack in the Christian church must not be papered over in order to preserve a spurious unity. The dispute was not about trivialities—the nick in the male organ, the invitations to dinner. The fundamental principle was whether anyone might be justified by faith alone.

Paul could not oppose Peter privately. The damage was public, the opposition must be public if the faith were to be secured for all men everywhere. The same instinctive courage that drove Paul to risk his skin by rebuking a bad man, Elymas, in front of the Proconsul drove him to risk his standing in the church by correcting a good man, Peter, the greatly loved and honored, in front of them all. Paul did not care. Though he saw himself in God's sight the least of all saints because he had persecuted, he considered himself in man's sight the equal of any apostle.

He chose an occasion before virtually the whole congregation. In the most public manner, he criticized Peter to his face using words that not only pilloried the inconsistency but emphasized the heart of the matter: "If you," said Paul loudly for all to hear, "a Jew born and bred, live like a Gentile, and not like a Jew, how can you insist that Gentiles must live like Jews?"

It was a moment when the church might split into factions and destroy itself. But the man who had wept when the Lord, at His trial, turned and looked on the disciple who had denied Him with oaths immediately accepted the justice of Paul's rebuke. Peter repented, and when the issue was debated again months later at Jerusalem, it was his strong support of Paul's position which gained the day. Nor did he resent Paul's intervention.

Peter returned to Jerusalem. That the question in dispute had been by no means trivial, nor fully settled, was shown by bad news which reached Antioch from Galatia.

Christian Pharisees—either those who had left Antioch defeated or, more likely, others who had hurried on through Cilicia—had been welcomed by the Galatians, had taught them "circumcision," and had met instant, widespread success. Paul's first missionary church, so promising and apparently healthy, had been swept into another gospel. Former pagans who had trusted Christ and rejoiced in being "new creations" were making their lives a misery trying to keep the Jewish Law.

As Paul cross-questioned his informants, he could see what must have happened in Galatia. These false teachers had first undermined his credentials by pointing out that he never had been a personal disciple of Jesus; he was the emissary of ordinary men from whom he had picked up his ideas, which held no more authority than other human opinions. His teaching had been good but incomplete. They then propounded what Paul had left out: circumcision and the keeping of the Law. The Galatians fell into the trap.

When Paul was among them, they had leaped at the offer of a grace that was totally free and gave them freedom. The old sinful life, whether of self-righteousness as Jews or of idolatry, lust, and fear as pagans, had been replaced by Christ within them, and all they wanted was to please Him by molding their lives in His pattern, by His strength. After He had gone, some of them fell back into grievous sin. They repented, but found themselves hard put to take literally that they could be utterly forgiven, cleansed, and healed, that no repentant, trusting Christian could ever be in disgrace with God or need earn a return to favor. Their natural instinct was not to depend on Christ's cross alone but on Christ and their own effort. The very simplicity of the Gospel was their stumbling block.

And now the new "apostles" who disparaged Paul taught that he was wrong and their natural instinct right; and by being circumcised and keeping the Law, they would have a bonus too in that they would no longer be persecuted by Jews.

Paul and Barnabas were appalled by the news from Galatia. Paul walked around Antioch in a confusion of emotions. He was indignant with the false brethren and astonished at the Galatians' speedy disloyalty to Christ. He was disappointed and hurt, for though he had grown a thick skin toward the malice of outsiders, Christian brothers who were false or converts who had failed bothered him.

Yet he had a yearning, a panting to help them, his little children, for whom he felt himself undergoing birthpains all over again. And because he loved them deeply, he determined to put them back on the right course. It was vital to them; it was vital to Christ. He could not bear the thought of Christ's agony on the cross being dismissed as secondary. He could not accept that an ill-defined or partial belief in Jesus was enough to make a man a Christian, even if that led to a more numerous, popular church. Nor could he tolerate teachers—whose spiritual descendants are much in evidence in the twentieth century—who used the name of Christ as an accolade on their own ideas of the nature of God.

All these emotions and desires exploded in a letter.

Thirteen
DEAR IDIOTS
OF GALATIA

Paul summoned the Antioch leaders so that his letter should carry the authority of the church which had sent the first missionaries to Galatia. He secured a roll of papyrus and a swift penman. With the leaders sitting around he began dictating urgently, rapidly.

"Paul an apostle—not from men nor through man, but through Jesus Christ and God the Father, who raised Him from the dead—and all the brethren with me,

"To the churches of Galatia:

"Grace to you and peace from God the Father and our Lord Jesus Christ, who gave Himself for our sins to deliver us from the present evil age, according to the will of our God and Father; to whom be glory for ever and ever. Amen.

"I am *astonished* that you are so quickly deserting him who called you in the grace of Christ and turning to a different gospel—not that there is another gospel, but there are some who trouble you and want to pervert the Gospel of Christ. But even if we, or an angel from heaven, should preach to you a gospel contrary to that which we preached to you, let him be accursed. As we have said before, so now I say again. If anyone is preaching to you a gospel contrary to that which you received, *let him be accursed!*" *The New Testament in Modern English* (Phillips) renders this, "Let him be a damned soul"—not too strong for Paul's phrase.

At this time Paul's character had a strong dash of controlled anger which could make him thoroughly alarming to wrongdoers, but righteous anger too easily leads to sin; in later years he grew to feel that fury was no weapon to be found in the armory of a Christian. When he wrote to the Galatians, however, the fire which burned within was allowed to scorch. This first letter sparked and flamed with no regard to sensitive feelings—or to literary polish. Paul knew it would be read aloud and seem to the hearers almost as if he were there, so that the force of his writing would be doubled by memory of his speaking, one reason why he always preferred to dictate.

What he was going to tell them he had previously taught them in person. This time he must make it even plainer. His passionate love for converts, his uncompromising devotion to truth drove him to wrestle mentally until his words could resolve with crystal clarity the key issue of the Christian faith—whether a man is forgiven through God's grace or his own merit.

Paul's first task was to establish beyond question his credentials as a messenger direct from Christ. He referred again, briefly, to the persecuting zeal of his early life, and how after seeing the Risen Christ he had gone, not to Jerusalem, but to Arabia. Truth had not been taught him by man but revealed by God, just as it had been to Peter. When Peter had blurted out to the Man Jesus: "You are the Christ, the Son of the Living God," he was told, as Paul probably had recounted to the Galatians orally: "Flesh and blood has not revealed this to you, but My Father who is in heaven"; in the same way Paul did not "confer with flesh and blood" but had received the message direct from God.

He continued the story up to the recent conflict with Peter and from there went straight to the crux: that a man is not justified (reckoned righteous) "by doing what the Law demands, but only through faith in Christ. . . . We have put our faith in Jesus Christ, in order that we might be justified through this faith, and not through deeds dictated by Law; for by such deeds, the Scripture says, no mortal man shall be justified.'' Paul, as he often did, illustrated the truth by his own case. The former Paul who had struggled to earn his way to heaven, had died: "I have been crucified with Christ. It is no longer 'I' who live, but Christ who lives in me; and the life I now live in the flesh I live by the faith of the Son of God, who loved me and gave Himself for me. I will not nullify the grace of God; if righteousness comes by Law, then Christ died for nothing.''

The order of words in Paul's original Greek makes him even more emphatic: "Christ I have been crucified with, but I live, no longer I, but lives in me Christ!'' His testimony has echoed down the ages as one of the most decisive passages in the Bible, beloved of Luther and Bunyan, opening the eyes of Charles Wesley.

His mind was on the Galatians. "O you dear idiots of Galatia who saw Jesus Christ the crucified so plainly, who has been casting a spell over you? I will ask you one simple question: Did you receive the Spirit of God by trying to keep the Law or by believing the message of the Gospel? Surely you can't be so idiotic as to think that a man begins his spiritual life in the Spirit and then completes it by reverting to outward observances. Has all your painful experience brought you nowhere? I simply cannot believe it of you! Does God, who gives you His Spirit and works miracles among you, do these things because you have obeyed the Law or because you have believed the Gospel? Ask yourselves that.''

He developed his argument of the essential weakness of the Law: that a man who attempts to earn acceptance by keeping it must do so totally, or be rejected. In contrast, "Christ bought us freedom from the curse of the Law by becoming for our sake a cursed thing; for Scripture says, 'Cursed is everyone who is hanged on a tree.' . . . If a law had been given which had power to bestow life, then indeed righteousness would have come from keeping the Law. But Scripture has declared the whole world to be prisoners in subjection to sin, so that faith in Jesus Christ may be the ground on which the promised blessing is given, and given to those who have such faith.''

All the time he was expounding, Paul's puzzlement and dismay at the Galatians kept breaking in: ''How can you turn back again? . . . I am afraid I have labored over you in vain. . . . You were running well; who hindered you from obeying the truth?'' His indignation at those who had corrupted his Galatians swelled into a thoroughly earthy expression: ''I wish those who unsettle you would mutilate themselves!''— which his readers would have recognized as a reference to the god Cybele's frenzied dancers whose climax was self-castration.

Paul realized that after all this the Galatians could be genuinely puzzled about the Law, since he himself had taught them to revere and learn from it. To explain its role, he selected analogies which would be easily recognized.

The Law was like a tutor exercising strict discipline during schooldays: Galatians who lived in cities knew the *paidagógos*, the slave who looked after a boy and took him to and from school: they were not expected to remain under him all their lives but be free. So, ''the Law was a kind of tutor in charge of us until Christ should come, when we should be justified through faith; and now that faith has come, the tutor's charge is at an end.'' The Law was a guardian: Galatians in the countryside, many of them slaves or tenants on great estates, knew that during the minority of an heir his guardians kept entire control; he must obey them as if he were a slave, although owner of all. So, the Law was the guardian of the world's minority. ''But when the term was completed, God sent His own Son, born of a woman, born under the Law, to purchase freedom for the subjects of the Law, in order that we might attain the status of sons. To prove that you are sons, God has sent into our hearts the Spirit of His Son, crying '*Abba!* Father.' You are therefore no longer a slave but a son, and if a son, then also by God's own act an heir.''

Paul could not bear the thought that these sons of God were slipping back into slavery, that they were chained to feasts, and fasts, and rules, and regulations. "Christ set us free, to be free men! Stand fast therefore, and do not submit again to a yoke of slavery.'' Over and over, he worked his argument, approaching it now from this angle, now from that, until the stupidest Galatian must see that submitting to circumcision as a religious duty, and trying to keep the Law, made nonsense of Christ's cross.

Only one law mattered for those in Christ Jesus: "Faith working through love.'' He emphasized the point. "You were called to freedom, brethren: only do not use your freedom as an opportunity for the flesh but through love be servants of one another, for the whole Law is fulfilled in one word, 'You shall love your neighbor as yourself.' ''

Paul's concern for the here and now, for man's behavior to man, glowed warm and strong, but he knew that the here and now turns sour unless behavior grows from the right root. He had warned the Galatians in person, and he warned them again that the lower nature, the "flesh,'' behaves in a way that cannot inherit the kingdom of God: "sexual immorality, impurity of mind, sensuality, worship of false gods, witchcraft, hatred, quarreling, jealousy, bad temper, rivalry, factions, party-spirit, envy, drunkenness, orgies, and things like that. But the harvest of the Spirit''—and his mind may have flashed to the rich earth of the uplands being turned by the spring plow—"is love, joy, peace, patience, kindness, goodness, faithfulness, gentleness, self-control; against such there is no law. And those who belong to Christ have crucified the flesh with its passions and desires. If we live by the Spirit, let us also walk by the Spirit. Let us have no self-conceit, no provoking of one another, no envy of one another.''

He was nearly done. One problem remained. He saw that those few who had resisted the false might feel smug toward those who had not.

"Brothers," dictated Paul, "if a man is caught in some offense, you, the spiritual ones, should put him right in a spirit of gentleness." (Did Paul feel he had been too harsh in the way he corrected Peter?) "Each of you think whether you yourself may be tempted. Bear one another's burdens and so fulfill the law of Christ."

With the addition of a few more words, the dictation was finished, a long morning of hard writing for the penman, hard thinking for Paul, close listening for Barnabas and the elders of Antioch. They may have broken off for a meal; then Paul made the penman read the entire letter. The penman reached again the very last words: "Let us not grow weary in well-doing, for in due season we shall reap if we do not lose heart. So then, as we have opportunity, let us do good to all men, and especially those who are of the household of faith."

Paul took the papyrus. There was still space on the roll. He seized a reed pen. "Look," he wrote, "at these huge letters I am making in writing these words to you with my own hand!" And while there was silence in the room after the long dictation, he scrawled with the pen, unable to leave the Galatians and their troubles: "These men who are always urging you to be circumcised—what are they after? They want to present a pleasing front to the world, and they want to avoid being persecuted for the cross of Christ. For even those who have been circumcised do not themselves keep the Law. But they want you circumcised so that they may be able to boast about your submission to their ruling. Yet God forbid that I should boast about anything or anybody except the cross of our Lord Jesus Christ, which means that the world is a dead thing to me and I am a dead man to the world. For in Christ it is not circumcision or uncircumcision that counts but the power of new birth. To all who live by this principle, to the true Israel of God, may there be peace and mercy!

"Let no one interfere with me after this. I carry on my scarred body the marks of my Owner, the Lord Jesus.

"The grace of our Lord Jesus Christ be with your spirit, brothers."[11]

Fourteen
A FRESH START

Since controversy continued, the Antioch church sent Paul, Barnabas, and several others to Jerusalem to seek a common mind about "circumcision" and finally settle the question.

They traveled by land, unhurriedly. In Phoenicia (modern Lebanon) and the hills of Samaria, where most of the local disciples were not pure-bred Jews and thus had been rated as only half-Christian, Paul and Barnabas brought joy by recounting all that had happened in Galatia. At Jerusalem the great welcome meeting contrasted strikingly with Paul's solitary first arrival, a convert cold-shouldered until rescued by Barnabas. Now the two friends, never closer, warmed to the atmosphere of love and encouragement as they told what God had done to create new Christians in a faraway land. But when the report ended, Christian Pharisees stepped forward. The old charge sounded again: "They must be circumcised and told to keep the Law of Moses."

The matter was adjourned for formal discussion. To resolve major disputes, the apostles with the elders, a considerable number, were accustomed to seek the will of God by studying the Old Testament and by recalling what Jesus had taught. On "circumcision," however, they had no clear word, the subject presumably being one which Jesus could not instruct them about until He had been crucified, had risen from the dead and left them, and the Holy Spirit had come. He had promised that His Spirit would lead them into all truth, and it was now their duty, as they met together, to find what He was saying. They seem to have followed the custom of the Sanhedrin by inviting junior members to give their opinions first, and the debate was long. Then Peter stood up. He had spoken no more than a few words when Paul's heart could leap.

"Brothers," said Peter, "you know that from the earliest days God chose me as the one from whose lips the Gentiles should hear the Word and should believe it. Moreover, God who knows men's inmost thoughts has plainly shown that this is so, for when He had cleansed their hearts through their faith He gave the Holy Spirit to the Gentiles exactly as He did to us. Why then must you now strain the patience of God by trying to put on the shoulders of these disciples a burden which neither our fathers nor we were able to bear? Surely the fact is that it is by the grace of the Lord Jesus that we are saved by faith, just as they are!"

He stopped. Not a word broke the silence until Barnabas—Paul had dropped tactfully to second place in the city where his friend had been a leader when he himself was still an enemy of the church—began in close detail to recapitulate the amazing happenings in Galatia. Paul took up the tale, and the hours fled as once more their epic narrative unfolded. Again no one argued.

At length, James, as president of the assembly, put into words what he conceived to be the general conclusion. James was a man of such devotion that long praying had made his knees as hard as a camel's, tradition says, and like Paul he had been converted by meeting, all alone, the Risen Jesus, his half-brother, whose claims he had doubted. James loved the Law of Moses and was held in high respect by non-Christian Jews, but he wished to obey his Risen Lord's will. He now saw that this will—if only they would all admit—had been made plain years before: when the Spirit had endorsed Simon Peter's action in entering the home of Cornelius. What Barnabas and Paul had since told, though it had swung the assembly, merely proved Peter's point. James rightly ignored them, and referred to Peter's speech which, he emphasized with a long quotation, was in accord with prophecy.

"My judgment therefore," he said, "is that we should impose no irksome restrictions on those of the Gentiles who are turning to God." Lest, however, the new freedom prove needlessly offensive to nonbelieving Jews, Gentile Christians should not eat meat which had been consecrated to idols before being sold in market, should not indulge in a pagan sex life, nor eat the meat of strangled animals, which was a prohibition imposed long before the Law, nor drink blood.

The Council's decisions were endorsed by the laity and elders of the entire Jerusalem church and embodied in a formal reply to Antioch and its daughter churches in the united Roman province of Syria and Cilicia, which disavowed those who had "unsettled your minds although we gave them no instructions." It paid generous tribute to "our beloved Barnabas and Paul, men who have hazarded their lives for the name of our Lord Jesus Christ."

Paul and Barnabas brought the letter to Antioch and all the Christians rejoiced. Two outstanding Jerusalem preachers came too and stayed on. As Judas Barsabbas and Silvanus, informally known as Silas, unfolded fresh meaning from the Scriptures the Antioch church went from strength to strength, and Paul and Barnabas sat at their feet. Paul never supposed that he had nothing to learn; even with young believers he expected encouragement to be mutual.

That winter, after Judas and Silas returned to Jerusalem, Paul's body remained in Antioch, but his heart and mind strayed more and more to Galatia. A desire swelled until it hurt, to know whether his urgent letter had solved their problems, whether they were progressing or failing. He spoke emphatically to Barnabas: "Let's definitely go back and visit our brothers in every city where we proclaimed the word of the Lord." Barnabas agreed, suggesting taking his relative John Mark again.

Paul demurred. He was not at all happy at having with them day by day the young man who had deserted at Perga. Barnabas felt Paul was wrong. He should give the lad another chance; Mark had the stuff of an evangelist in him if properly encouraged. Paul declined the risk. Hardships, disappointments, opportunities lay ahead, for he had no intention of stopping short in Galatia—he would press onward into the unknown. His team must be close knit, thoroughly reliable. He refused to accept Mark.

Feelings frayed. Luke does not hide the apostles' humanity any more than the Old Testament hides that gross human failing, King David's adultery. He describes the sharp argument by a Greek word which denotes violent anger and is the root of the English word "paroxysm." Whoever was right— Paul certainly needed a reliable team; Mark certainly made good, as Paul himself eventually would experience and acknowledge—they were both to blame for letting the dispute grow fierce. There must have been serious wrong in the situation which made the lovable, even-tempered Barnabas use angry words, and Paul had far to go before he could write, "Love is patient and kind. . . . Love does not insist on its own way."

Both insisted. It became obvious that their partnership must end.

Thereupon, Barnabas recovered his characteristic love of conciliation: he removed himself, sailing away to Cyprus with Mark. Paul chose Silas to replace Barnabas. Silas would bring the expedition an advantage in that he was a Roman citizen; when next faced with the prospect of a beating with rods, Paul could claim for them both "civis Romanus sum." But Silas had returned to Jerusalem. Paul could not wait with the season of travel already on them and much to do on the way.

He sent a message, never doubting Silas would respond, and set off alone: Luke is emphatic in saying "*he* departed . . . *he* went through Syria and Cilicia strengthening the churches." The "*they*" does not begin until after he has reached Derbe.

Thus in the spring of A.D. 50 Paul walked alone into the mountains northwest of Antioch and came down by the "Syrian Gates" to the splendid bay of Alexandria (Iskenderun), where probably he found one of the churches he wished to strengthen. He walked on along the undulating coastal plain, close to the battlefield of Issus, where Alexander defeated Darius the Mede 300 years before. He was lonely, rather lost without a companion, and the quarrel had aged him; he was now about fifty years old and the next letter he would write, later that year, reads like the letter of a man who has aged considerably since he wrote to the Galatians. But as he walked he could see the mountains of Cilicia ahead across the gulf where the Levant turns west to become southern Anatolia. He was coming home; though his family had repudiated him, the mountains were the mountains he knew as a boy.

Whether he stopped awhile at Tarsus or approached his family is not recorded. He spent time seeking out and encouraging congregations he had founded in his Hidden Years, and then joined the busy road over the Taurus through the Cilician Gates, probably early in May, for the snow is gone by mid-April from the pass and the slightly higher plateau just to the north, and into the native kingdom of Commagene. Across the wide plain with its volcanic outcrops he followed the Roman Road until at last he saw Black Mountain again and returned to his converts at Derbe.

Derbe was evidently the rendezvous for Silas if he had traveled direct from Jerusalem, possibly by sea to Tarsus and then up the safe and frequented road. Together they delivered the Jerusalem decisions, completed the work of Paul's own letter in healing breaches left by the "circumcision" dispute, and saw that once again the congregation was growing every day in depth and in size.

Paul took Silas on to introduce him at Lystra. Here too the church grew. And here, eager as ever, was Timothy.

Timothy was now about twenty-one. His faith and zeal were highly regarded by the Christians in Lystra and Iconium.

Paul invited him to leave his mother and grandmother and join the team, but he could not say when, if ever, Timothy would see home again. He thereby gained more than a substitute for Mark. He gained a dearly loved son, perhaps replacing the actual son who may have died in Paul's early married life, or if alive, had been irrevocably estranged with his mother by Paul's conversion.

Timothy was a complicated character. He had a weak stomach, looked very young, and was not a muscular Christian. Nervous, a little afraid of hardship though enduring it without flinching, he was tempted occasionally to be ashamed of Paul and the Gospel. But he was no weakling. Warm-blooded—Paul had to warn him to flee youthful lusts—and equally virile spiritually, Timothy became an able preacher who soon could be trusted with important missions on his own. From his pagan Greek father, evidently a man of culture and substance but now dead, he had inherited intellectual interests and an inquiring mind; from his mother Eunice he had learned the Jewish Scriptures, and from Paul had discovered their key. His one desire was to serve Christ: Paul was afterward to say that of all his fellow workers Timothy alone was totally without self-interest.

Eunice had brought Timothy up as a Jew before their Christian conversion, but he had not been circumcised; the father may have forbidden it to save the boy embarrassment in the gymnasium. Paul took him quietly to a surgeon and had the operation performed or perhaps he did it himself, since many rabbis had the necessary surgical qualification.

This action was not inconsistent with the attack on "those who would compel you to be circumcised." The offspring of a Jewish mother and a Greek father was regarded by Jews as a Jew, but if uncircumcised as illegitimate. In the Galatian cities, which would be Timothy's first field, his parentage was known and if Paul used an "illegitimate" Jew for assistant, he would hinder the work. He never inveighed against circumcision as a rite for Jews though holding it unnecessary; had Timothy been a Gentile, like Titus, nothing would have induced Paul to "circumcise him because of the Jews that were in those places."

After Timothy had recovered from the operation and before they left Lystra, a solemn ordination service attended by a numerous congregation set him apart, calling down the Spirit's gifts which his high vocation required. He confessed his faith publicly, boldly. A prophet, probably Silas, proclaimed in a memorable sermon that he would fight gallantly, armed with faith and a good conscience.

The Galatian trouble had convinced Paul that he must change his strategy.

His aim remained twofold: to win individuals to Christ; and to form churches which not only would endure without him but send out missionaries themselves to repeat the process, until all the world was Christ's. The Galatians, however, had stumbled after Paul left. He should stay in a center longer; not move from place to place as he had been forced to do in southern Galatia but find a city positioned to be the pivot of a widespread mission.

Ephesus, capital and principal port of the rich province of Asia, which included the entire Aegean coast of Asia Minor, was the obvious choice because it had a big population and was the focal point of roads and rivers giving access to the hinterland. Since all roads led to Rome, the main road from southern Galatia ran about 250 miles westward from Pisidian Antioch to Ephesus, where imperial messengers crossed to Greece and on to Rome. Paul, Silas, and Timothy would follow their route. When Ephesus and Asia were thoroughly evangelized, they could ship to Corinth and work all southern Greece. And from there to Rome.

Paul's attempt to reach Ephesus failed. They were very distinctly "forbidden by the Holy Spirit to preach the Word in Asia." It is possible that illness supervened, a fresh attack of Paul's "thorn in the flesh" accompanied by a conviction that he was not to evangelize Ephesus yet. Or they may have been turned back. They were sure that wherever God wanted them He would direct them, and if, like a shepherd directing his flock to better pastures by throwing stones, He hit them with setbacks they would not complain. However, adverse circumstances were often to be the means of guidance without Luke making a specific reference to the Spirit, and the probability is that Paul and Silas were forbidden by a definite word of revelation delivered by a Galatian Christian whom they accepted as a "prophet," just as the Syrian Antioch congregation had accepted Agabus' warning about the famine.

They continued to strengthen the churches in Phrygian Galatia. Then they tried again.

The other remaining province of importance in Asia Minor was Bithynia opposite Byzantium to the northeast—smaller than Asia but with two highly cultured Greek cities, Nicea and Nicomedia, and many Jews. They set off across the mountains above Pisidian Antioch and down into Asia, where the Spirit had not forbidden travel. The route led north mile by mile, day by day through midsummer, a tedious dusty road which had secondary status because it did not lead direct toward Rome, and wound from valley to valley against the lay of the land. At Dorylaion on the Tembris River, or at another town near the Bithynian border, they met a check. Official action is again unlikely, since they were private travelers unknown in those parts, unless civil disturbance in Bithynia had closed the frontier to all strangers. Luke uses the expression "the Spirit of *Jesus*[12] would not allow them" to enter Bithynia, which suggests a very distinct intervention, a vision of the Lord such as Paul had in the Temple and on the Damascus Road.

Disappointments soldered the missionaries together as no

easy success could have forged them, for a purpose not yet clear: the guidance showed only that they should not remain in Anatolia.

They turned west through Mysia, the northernmost district of the province of Asia. Their obvious course was to make for the coast, to the port of Alexandria Troas near the ruins of ancient Troy. From there it would be a short sea passage northwest to Macedonia, or longer and southwest to southern Greece, the province of Achaia.

Fifteen
ACROSS TO EUROPE

At Troas Luke slips into the picture. In the best tradition of historians he never thrusts himself forward and thus leaves his origins wide open to speculation. It is known he was a doctor: Paul calls him "the beloved physician," and he shows close attention to medical detail. He was plainly a Greek. Early tradition makes him a citizen of Antioch in Syria—the Western Text inserts a "we" into the description of the church in Antioch, while a further, if intriguingly circumstantial piece of evidence is Luke's odd lack of reference to Titus of Antioch despite his importance to Paul: it has been suggested that Titus was Luke's brother whom he did not wish to mention lest it seem family pride.

He must have met Paul, Silas, and Timothy at Troas by coincidence, for they had no prior intention of going there. He may have been traveling to or from the medical center of the ancient world at the Shrine of Aesculapius near Pergamum, not very far from Troas. Or perhaps he practiced at Troas, an emigrant Antiochene; a Christian whose spiritual ambitions, until he came under Paul's influence, had not yet advanced beyond a little local church formed as a footnote to personal faith. Another view is that he was a Macedonian and a pagan whom Paul converted at Troas. Whatever the truth, Luke, as he matured in Paul's companionship, grew to be a man of charm and compassion; quiet, unexcitable, watching the foibles of mankind with a shrewd, twinkling eye: his writings have delicious touches of humor. He cared especially about the downtrodden and despised. He was a friendly person, who used nicknames or diminutives when Paul retained formal names. Where Paul was the brilliant, original thinker, Luke was the careful scholar, investigating incidents and background with a physician's strict regard for accuracy. Paul's prose pours out like talk, in the language of the people. Luke's has literary grace and style, concise without being terse.

He had no doubt at all, after examining the case, that the man Jesus rose from the dead, was the Son of God and Saviour of the world. Luke had a vivid sense of the continuing, direct work of God among men and saw the Spirit's hand where some might see only changes and chances.

Paul accepted Luke gratefully. Indifferent health, wrestling against a constitution whose iron was mainly a matter of indomitable will, cried out for a personal physician. It says much for Paul's unselfishness that he would shortly be prepared to lose him for the sake of an infant church.

Luke writes, "They went down into Troas. And in the night a vision appeared to Paul; a man, a Macedonian was standing and beseeching him and saying, 'Come into Macedonia and help us.' When he had seen the vision, immediately we sought to go on into Macedonia, being utterly convinced that God was calling us to proclaim the Good News to them." There was a pause while they sought a ship, but when they found one, probably in the last week of July 50, the very winds seemed to approve. A strong south wind blew them in two days a distance which on another occasion, in reverse, took them five.

Luke loved the sea and remembered any incident whenever they sailed, but this was an unmemorable voyage, out by

Tenedos, the island where in the Trojan War the Greeks built their wooden horse; past the opening of the Hellespont or Dardanelles, with the Cape Helles peninsula shimmering in the afternoon heat haze across the deep blue of the sea. They rode out the night off the island of Samothrace and next morning could still run northwest before the wind, and through the strait between Thasos and the Macedonian shore.

They did not think of themselves as passing from the continent of Asia to Europe. The terms were in use, but the Aegean was Greek on either side. They had, instead, the excitement of approaching a new province, bringing them nearer Rome. They knew that beyond Macedonia they could reach Achaia and Italy, and the vast lands of Gaul, Spain, Germania, even the mist-bound island of Britain lately added to the empire: all save Rome untouched by the Good News. They were not bringing force of arms or a political program: just four men—and Another, invisible, who had known these seas and shores before Achilles or Agamemnon or Ulysses; who could demolish empires and cities by the breath of His mouth, but who had chosen to humble Himself and come to Macedonia as quietly, as weakly as, in the flesh, He had come to Bethlehem half a century before.

They landed the second evening at Neapolis (now Kavalla, the little tobacco port; in 1967 King Constantine fled from its airfield), a new harbor tucked close under a ridge of the Pangaean range, which they climbed next day with the broad Via Egnatia, one of the great roads to Rome. From the top of the pass they saw the city of Philippi. Beyond lay the narrow plain where the world's fate had been settled at the Battle of Philippi when Octavius (Augustus) defeated the murderers of Caesar. The city stood compact in granite glory on either side of the road, below an acropolis 1,020 feet high.

Philippi, named for Philip of Macedon, father of Alexander the Great, had become a Roman colony after the battle, and was a bustling center of military activity, the leading city of eastern Macedonia, though not the seat of administration; it was self-governing, a "little Rome" which used Latin for all official business. It had a virile, brisk, no-nonsense air, the streets full of muscular young legionnaries and hardbitten veterans and their families, proud of Roman eagle in forum and basilica. It was a place where Roman citizens were held in high honor.

Paul and his friends took lodgings. They saw idol temples but no synagogue, its absence showing that fewer than ten Jewish males lived in all Philippi. Paul's first stopping place in Europe therefore lacked his usual launching pad for the Gospel, and if any Jews or proselytes existed, they would worship on the Sabbath in the open air—outside the walls near the river for the sake of ritual ablutions. Early on Sabbath morning, therefore, Paul, Silas, Luke, and Timothy threaded their way past wagons with peasants coming into market and out by the northwestern gate built in honor of Augustus. They walked about a mile and a half under the shade of the finely arched trees down to the narrow Gangites River. A little way from the bridge, they found in a small grove some women preparing to offer praises and prayers, and here they sat down.

Very informally, they introduced themselves and made friends with the Philippians. One was a woman of substance, a Gentile God-fearer from Thyatira, a city in the district of Lydia in the province of Asia. She used the name Lydia and ran a business selling the rich purple-dyed cloth for which Thyatira was famous. Several of the other women were members of her household. At Sabbath worship, Paul told why they had come. He spoke of the Lord Jesus, how He had emptied Himself of His glory to be born as a mortal man, humbling Himself to die like a common criminal on a cross. He told of the resurrection of Jesus, and how to trust in Him. As Luke watched, he saw such understanding dawn on Lydia's face that he knew it was not through force of words alone. A miracle was taking place before his eyes: "the Lord opened her heart to respond to what Paul said."

This was clear to Paul too as soon as he talked with Lydia.

He baptized her then and there in the river. Several of her household who worshiped with her—the houseslaves and salespeople of a God-fearer would be given the Sabbath rest—were baptized too. Paul was content that they received Christ as best they knew; the One who had begun a good work in them would continue it.

Lydia said, "If you judge me to be a true believer in the Lord, then come to my house and stay."

Paul declined. He had a strong objection to their laying themselves open to the charge of being scroungers like the wandering philosophers of the day. It was true that the Lord had instructed His disciples to stay in the first house that invited them, for the laborer was worthy of his hire, but Paul preferred not to exercise the right. Lydia urged them until they agreed. Philippi was the only place where Paul accepted free board and lodging. It proved a good decision.

From the start the new church had a strong sense of partnership with the apostles. Young Timothy proved the genuineness of his vocation by the way he identified himself with the Philippians; Paul's own happiness, the aroma of peace about him, his delight in beauty of character and action, gave them an example they strove to follow as they shared the joy and the strength of God and worked together to pass on and defend the Good News. During the next days several slaves and tough young soldiers were baptized. They found new perspectives that transformed the drudgery of slavery or the hardship of soldiering because now they were, in Paul's words, "God's dear children, blameless, sincere, and wholesome, living in a warped and diseased world, and shining there like lights in a dark place. For you hold in your hands the very word of life."

The Philippian church, which retained a very special place in Paul's affection, did not expand spectacularly, yet its influence even in this first short period may be gauged from the gossip that spread rapidly across Macedonia: Paul and his friends were turning the world upside down.

Sixteen
FLOGGED IN PHILIPPI

Here in Philippi Paul thought he had found the city where they could stay for a time to dig deep foundations.

He went daily with the others to the riverside place of prayer. Being near the road, it could always attract an audience of wayfarers and citizens when Paul and Silas propounded and proved their Good News. One day, probably in August and about the twelfth day after their arrival, they were all walking down the Via Egnatia toward the river when they heard an eerie voice, oddly high-pitched, crying out behind them: "These men are slaves of the Supreme God and are announcing to you a way of salvation!"

Paul ignored the cry. Luke found that the girl was a slave, a "Pythoness" from Delphi or Pytho, the world-famous shrine of Apollo on the southern slope of Mount Parnassus overlooking the Gulf of Corinth. The Delphic Oracle was consulted by statesmen and ambassadors; a girl controlled by whatever strange force of evil lay at the back of it would be in much demand by men and women wanting to peer into the future. She was so valuable that she had been bought by a syndicate, not by an individual.

Next day the eerie voice cried again, "These men are slaves

of the Supreme God and are announcing to you a way of salvation." Paul again took no notice, though he was now more wrought up; he had no desire to be advertised by an evil spirit or demon, whether from Delphi or anywhere else. Jesus Himself had ordered demons to keep silent when they cried through the lips of those they controlled, "You are the Son of God!" Anyone who acknowledged Him at the word of an evil spirit would be a pseudo-disciple still under demon influence, and the last state of the man would be worse than the first. Each day the girl cried, Paul grew more worked up; there is no previous record in precise terms of Paul casting out an evil spirit, though the "signs and wonders" in Galatia would seem to imply this. The power of evil represented by Delphi was considerable. It is possible that Paul hesitated because he knew himself confronted by an enormity before which even he, who had seen the cripple of Lystra leap at the name of Jesus, was weak in faith.

On the third or fourth day, Paul and Silas were going to the place of prayer by themselves and had not reached the gate when again the high-pitched cry, the same words: "These men are slaves of the Supreme God and are announcing to you a way of salvation." Paul's disgust at the shameless exploitation of an innocent girl, at the parody of evangelism coming from her lips, boiled over. He turned and said: "I command you in the name of Jesus Christ to come out of her!"

The girl suddenly relaxed, lost her wild look, and spoke in a normal voice.

The syndicate of owners who had been leading her around were furious. They knew enough to see that she was no longer a medium. From a highly lucrative investment, she had been devalued into an ordinary slave girl good for nothing but scrubbing. As old soldiers they reacted to a tactical defeat by instant counterattack. They turned on Paul and Silas and shouted to the bystanders, a decisiveness which swung the crowd standing openmouthed at the miracle. Everyone began to yell and rush at the apostles, who found themselves propelled by brute force toward the center of the city.

In the forum, sitting on the *bema*, a judgment seat on the east side across from the gymnasium, with their lictors behind them, the elected magistrates of the colony had not completed the day's lawsuits and prosecutions when they were shocked to see a disturbance at the far end of the square: a yelling mob dragging two strangers who were thrust panting in front of the *bema*. As a threat to public order, this case, whatever it was, must be dealt with at once.

The slaveowners' case was in fact weak: the law took no cognizance of a medium losing occult powers through the influence of a third party; it is even doubtful whether damages could be recovered in a civil suit. But the slaveowners wanted revenge, a revenge which would hurt:

"These men are causing a disturbance in our city—"

The magistrates could see it was so, as the crowd yelled and pummeled Paul.

"They are Jews in the first place—"

That was bad. Jews always caused trouble, and Claudius had lately expelled them from Rome. A "Little Rome" should do the same.

"And they teach customs which it is not lawful for us to accept or practice, being Romans!"

That was worse. Magistrates were expected to suppress unauthorized religious practices lest they undermine public order, as these undoubtedly had. The case was clear. Every moment that the crowd continued yelling made immediate action more necessary; Roman discipline was collapsing and the magistrates would be held responsible.

Quite illegally, they never asked for a defense. The proceedings were in Latin. Paul knew Latin, yet had no opportunity to cry that both were Roman citizens, or if he did, none heard in the noise.

No formal sentence was uttered, merely a quick order to the lictors. The slaveowners looked on with grim satisfaction, the crowd quietened a little, as the lictors drew their rods. They stepped down, one to each missionary, and stripped him of all his clothes. When Paul's scarred, knotted back was exposed to the sun nobody had further doubts. They were thrown at the flogging posts. It is doubtful whether in the hurry they were tied; plenty of strong arms could grip either if he struggled. The lictors set to.

As the blood spurted from the cuts, the crowd roared. When a savage blow caught a vertebra and even a tough apostle could not suppress a cry, the people loved it. Paul and Silas fought the pain with prayer. The lictors urged on by the crowd swung their rods with a will until both backs were bloody. "The blows burnt like fire," writes modern martyr Pastor Richard Wurmbrand, who suffered rods frequently in Communist prisons. "It was as if your back were being grilled by a furnace, and the shock to the nervous system was great."[13]

The magistrates stopped it before either collapsed. They gave another order. The lictors half-pushed, half-carried the apostles up from the forum, across the Via Egnatia, to the prison built on and in the hillside below the acropolis, not far from the theater. The jailer, another veteran, was given strict instructions to guard them closely and assumed they were dangerous criminals who probably would be sent off to the provincial capital and end as galley slaves. He had them manhandled, still naked, across the main prison chamber where fettered thieves and small-time brigands awaited sentence, and through a low opening into a windowless cave. Here was a contraption used both for security and torture. Rough bars of wood were so placed that a criminal's legs could be stretched wide, held tight, and his wrists and even his neck gripped in various positions depending on how much pain the jailer wished to inflict.

Since this was merely a security matter, he had Paul and Silas thrown to the ground and only their feet clamped in the bars, leaving the rest of their bodies free. Their clothes were thrown in after them.

Outside, the sun dropped and set beyond the Pangaean mountains. In Lydia's house, Timothy and Luke had probably gathered the others to pray. There is a possible allusion to these prayers in words which Paul wrote to the Philippians from a later imprisonment, that he *knew* he would be delivered, through their prayers and the resources of the Spirit of Jesus Christ.

In the cave Paul and Silas lay side by side silent in a state of physical shock, the blood congealing, their muscles stiffening, unable to rest on their torn backs yet in acute discomfort when they sat upright. Their feet were numbed and the wooden bar pressed on their ankles. The clothes they had put round each other's backs could not stop the shivering, and they were forced to lie in their own excrement.

Sleep never came. Nor at first could they pray. When shock subsided and the pain eased, their minds sought an answer to the outrage, indignity, and injury that had engulfed them though Roman citizens in a Roman colony. There may have been depression, even a trace of resentment while each "*learned* in whatsoever state I am, to be content," until, as night wore on, any trace of spiritual or mental misery was assuaged, then overwhelmed by knowledge that in all these things they could be more than conquerors through Him who loved them; His arms had been under them when conscious awareness was impossible. He knew what suffering meant. They began to pray. As they prayed, prayers turned to praise.

Softly, a little brokenly at first, they started to sing. (Paul often writes about music and singing, and may have had a rich voice.) They were not singing to keep their spirits up; melody bubbled out of hearts for whom the Presence grew rapidly more real than aches, soreness, hunger, stench, and darkness:

> "At the name of Jesus
> Every knee should bow,
> In heaven, on earth, under the earth."

It is sometimes thought that Paul's great passage written to the Philippians from another prison, about the self-emptying of God the Son, His death and glory, was putting them in mind of a song they knew already. If so, it may have been improvised by Paul and Silas that night as their agony turned to joy, until the rousing climax rang out from the stocks:

" . . . And every tongue confess
That Jesus Christ is Lord,
To the glory of God the Father."

In the main chamber of the prison, the other dozen or so who lay chained to the wall heard the sound, each with his private misery as he faced possible torture, hard labor, or death. They had seen the raw backs of the men who had been thrown into the cave, yet now those two poor wretches were singing, and singing for joy. An extraordinary, infectious happiness, peace, and hope flooded the prison.

The jailer, in his house a few feet up the hillside, lay fast asleep.

Paul and Silas sang more. The prisoners listened. Suddenly the whole prison shook in a split-second earthquake. Earth tremors were common in Macedonia in summer, but this was a shake strong enough to throw the stocks loose in the cave, dislodge the iron rings which anchored the other prisoners' chains, knock the bars off the inner and outer doors and leave them swinging. And wake the jailer.

His inevitable reaction was to jump out of bed, seize his short sword and run into the unlighted courtyard. He saw the doors were open right through to the street. His prisoners must be gone and he ruined; his life was forfeit for theirs. Appalled but without a moment's hesitation, he chose suicide rather than public disgrace and execution. He drew his sword. The clink and the clatter as the scabbard fell to the ground sounded clear in the night. He heard a loud voice from the depths of the prison, "Don't injure yourself! We are all here."

By then he could see in the moonlight that Philippi stood. The earthquake had been entirely local under his patch of hillside. To a Macedonian, all earth tremors and quakes, small and great, were the touch of an angry god; this god had singled him out and the jailer was terrified. More amazing, the god had kept the prisoners from escaping and now came that strong voice from the cave, "Don't injure yourself!" The chastised Jews cared more for their jailer than for escape. The whole thing was beyond him.

Trembling, he shouted to his wide-awake, gibbering slaves for lights; every second's delay while they fumbled with pitch-pine torches was agony lest the god strike again. The jailer must have heard a smattering about why the two Jews were in prison, that they were servants of a divinity and talked about salvation.

The torches flaming at last, he dashed into the prison chamber behind a slave, and through to the cave. He saw Paul and Silas standing, filthy but serene. He threw himself at their feet. "Sirs, what must I do to be saved?"

"Put your trust in the Lord Jesus, and you will be saved, you and your household!"

By now his two or three slaves and the family had crowded into the prison chamber. The other prisoners, their loose chains clanking, pressed round the opening of the cave as eager as the jailer. And there Paul and Silas, with matted hair and backs stiff with dried blood, "spoke the word of the Lord to him and to everyone in his house."

The jailer then led them out. In the courtyard was a well or fountain where, helped by the women and slaves, he washed their wounds with his own hands. Immediately afterward, under the light of the torches, he was baptized and after him, all his family and slaves.[14]

After the baptism, the jailer took the apostles up to his house for a much-needed meal, "and he rejoiced with all his household that he had believed in God," so that when dawn broke, they were still sitting with Paul and Silas, asking more about Jesus, sharing together the incredible happiness that had spilled over and welled up within them.

Shortly after sunrise the lictors arrived at the prison with an order from the magistrates that the two Jews were to be released. Beating and a night in jail were sufficient summary correction; the whipped, disgraced strangers would of course leave. The lictors waited in the courtyard to conduct them to the city limits while the jailer, glad that the punishment was over, hastened into the house. It was nothing to the lictors where he kept prisoners provided he produced them when required.

"The magistrates have sent to have you released. So now you can leave this place and go on your way in peace."

Paul would have none of it. To the jailer's surprise and alarm he replied: "They gave us a public flogging, though we are Roman citizens and have not been found guilty; they threw us into prison, and are they now to smuggle us out privately? No, indeed! Let them come in person and escort us out."

This was a serious matter. The jailer did not doubt their word that they were Romans. Apart from his respect for them, no man would fraudulently claim citizenship and risk a capital charge. When the lictors reported the words the magistrates' pomposity quickly subsided. By the *Lex Valeria*, the *Lex Porcia*, and more recently the *Lex Julia*, a Roman citizen could not be beaten except for refusal to obey a direct order of a magistrate, and then only after full trial and formal conviction. By beating Paul and Silas publicly and uncondemned the magistrates had exposed themselves to complaint at Rome and to ruin. Worse, they could not know whether these outraged citizens intended to seek revenge or not. Safety lay only in abject servility.

The magistrates hurried across to the prison, entered the jailer's home, and offered humble apologies; to which Paul and Silas made no reply, knowing that the best protection for the young Philippian church was to keep the magistrates on tenterhooks. It was also a sure way of turning the other cheek and doing good to persecutors, for the magistrates might pay attention to the teaching of a church founded by Romans, and the lictors too.

With much public honor in front of the small crowd which would have followed the rush to the prison, the magistrates escorted the apostles out of jail, and begged as a favor that they leave the city to avoid the risk of another breach of the peace. Paul and Silas, perhaps with the jailer himself, went first to Lydia's house. Every Christian who could leave work ran there too, and praised God together and took fresh courage from all that the apostles told. It was too soon to ordain elders and presbyters, but Luke, much as he might wish to accompany his battered friends and patients, agreed to remain behind; he could set up a medical practice while shepherding the church.

Then Paul and Silas, with Timothy, took sturdy sticks and set off northwestward over the bridge and across the plain.

Seventeen
THROWN OUT OF THESSALONICA

A Jew bearing the Greek name Aristarchus went as usual to the large synagogue of the powerful Jewish minority in Thessalonica, the free city at the head of the Gulf of Thermae where the Governor of Macedonia resided. On this mid-August Sabbath the elders had invited a visiting rabbi to read and expound the Law. As Aristarchus listened in the sultry heat, he little knew that for this man's sake, in a few years' time, he would be manhandled by a mob, go two long journeys with him, be shipwrecked, and share imprisonment at Rome.

He could see at once that the man was unusual. He walked to the reading desk stiffly on rather bow legs and occasionally winced; this suggested recent severe physical pain. It had not soured him: his face had a sparkle, an attractive friendliness unspoiled by the beetling brows, yet he showed traces of nervousness when he addressed his audience, as if half-expecting them to hurt him.

This was less surprising when Aristarchus heard the controversial nature of the sermon. The stranger started with the set passage, then drew Scripture after Scripture to prove that the expected Messiah should not, as they had supposed, immediately refound the kingdom in Jerusalem, but should suffer and die—and come alive again. To Aristarchus, the stranger's copious biblical references made his point. When he talked of a man named Jesus who had been crucified recently; and when, without polish or style but with curiously compelling force, he told how this Jesus had risen from the dead, Aristarchus was sure, on the stranger's word, that it was so. "This Jesus whom I am proclaiming to you," the sermon ended, "*is* the Messiah!"

Afterward, the elders, if unenthusiastic, were polite and intimated that Paul should address them next Sabbath. Aristarchus and several others sought him out. Another member of the congregation named Jason invited him home with Silas and Timothy so that any who wished might meet them. There Paul and Silas told how they "had been treated abominably at Philippi, and we came on to you only because God gave us courage. We came to tell you the Gospel, whatever the opposition might be." Their walk of about a hundred miles along the Via Egnatia through two other important cities, Amphipolis near the lagoonlike mouth of the Strymon River, guarded by its ancient stone lion, and Apollonia on the shores of a lake, had restored their health; but when they came over the hills and down into Thessalonica, a conscious effort had been required to face the risk of further hurt as they proclaimed the Gospel. Paul therefore was all the more grateful that "when you received the Word of God which you heard from us, you accepted it, not as the word of men but as what it really is, the Word of God."

The first quality that impressed Aristarchus and the others at Jason's house was the genuineness of Paul and Silas, the integrity in their ways, and their words which shrewd merchants could recognize and respect. They had a mental cleanness about them, an absence of the tricks which strolling prophets used. They showed no interest in money or goods, only a touching gratitude for the friendliness of their hearers.

Paul's character might attract but it was his message that

convinced—a message rooted in fact. Paul offered no nebu-
lous fancies, nor asserted that only faith mattered irrespective
of whether Jesus' life, death, and resurrection were facts or
myth; his conviction of their truth was overwhelming. As
Aristarchus listened, he again sensed something more than
reason drawing him to believe and to commit himself to the
Jesus whom Paul preached. Paul was not surprised. He said
that this power was the Holy Spirit of God the Father—and
of Jesus. When Aristarchus, Jason, and several others from the
synagogue were converted, Paul refused any credit.

The courage and conviction of Paul and Silas bred courage
and conviction. Not only did converts assure fellow Jews that
Jesus certainly was the Messiah but they broke out of their
prejudices to tell pagan business acquaintances and the slaves
who carried their goods from the docks that he was the
Saviour of all men, until Jason's house, in a most un-Jewish
way, became the center of a movement which spread like
wildfire across the city. In a few astonishing days, "the church
of the Thessalonians in God the Father and the Lord Jesus
Christ," as Paul called it, had more Greeks than Jews, both
men and influential aristocratic women.

Again Paul showed his integrity. He refused to flatter.
When he spoke to inquirers, he made no attempt to disguise
his belief that the very roots of their lives were twisted, that
the little idols they worshiped in their homes and the classical-
ly beautiful idols which graced the temples were false gods,
impotent, dead. He did not accept these Thessalonians as they
were; he would have snorted, with a characteristic, "Perish
the thought!" ("God forbid!" in the *King James Version's*
paraphrase) at twentieth-century radical theologians who reject man's need for conscious acknowledgment of the Risen
Jesus of Nazareth as Lord and Christ.

And thus because Paul dealt honestly with the Thessalonians, and because his Gospel was grounded in facts of history
and came "not only in word but also in power and in the
Holy Spirit and with much conviction," he could rejoice

about "the welcome we had among you, and how you turned to God from idols to serve the living and true God."

Thessalonica stood at a strategic position. The city was near enough to Philippi for a sense of unity to develop between the churches; Paul was delighted when a messenger reached him with a gift of funds, for he had not stopped praying for his Philippians and was touched that they remembered him. Westward, when his work in Thessalonica was complete, the Via Egnatia could take him to the Adriatic and so to Rome. To the south, beyond the gulf, which from the harbor appeared nearly landlocked, he could see Mount Olympus, legendary home of the gods whom Christ had come to supplant. Few Greeks now believed that gods resided on Olympus, but their existence seemed nontheless real to those who worshiped them.

Beyond Olympus lay the plains of Thessaly and all Achaia or southern Greece; trading ships plied back and forth so that from Thessalonica the Gospel could soon "ring out," as Paul put it, wherever sea-faring Christians went about their business—to Corinth and Piraeus, to the Aegean islands, to Ephesus on the Asian shore.

Once again Paul thought he had found the city in which to settle down. He and Silas accepted Jason's house as their home but refused to impose themselves on his hospitality or to take free meals in other parts. "We did not accept board and lodging from anyone without paying for it; we toiled and drudged, we worked for a living night and day, rather than be a burden to any of you—not because we have not the right to maintenance, but to set an example for you to imitate . . . we laid down the rule; the man who will not work shall not eat."

Paul became a tentmaker again. Thessalonica is the first place in which he or Luke mentions his earning a living. On the first missionary journey all wants may have been supplied by Barnabas, for though Barnabas had sold his land and donated the proceeds to the Jerusalem church, this could have been as deliberate evidence of repentance since he was a Levite, and Levites were not supposed to own land, though many did. It does not necessarily mean he had reduced himself to apostolic poverty. He many have drawn an income from copper mines or other family business in Cyprus on which he and Paul had lived until the breach. But now Paul was without such private means.

All waking hours that he, Silas, and Timothy, whose trades are not specified, were not out teaching they worked, and as they worked they talked with converts or inquirers. Or they prayed for fellow believers. Paul is scarcely ever described in Acts as praying alone: only once does he withdraw by himself and then he is walking. Yet prayer is constantly mentioned in his epistles. It would seem that when traveling between cities the apostles spent part of their time in intercession as they walked. When settled in a city and at the loom, they again took to prayer, together or with converts, or each alone, the steady rhythmic actions of tenting and its kindred leatherwork providing the element of slight distraction to keep the mind from wandering.

Each Sabbath, Paul continued to preach, opening up the Scriptures, demonstrating their fulfillment in Jesus, debating after the liturgical service with those who disputed this conclusion. Always he rooted his argument in facts of history and experience and always, when he preached, a few more Jews and God-fearers would put his allegations to the test, to discover that they too met God.

All through the week Paul told Jews, proselytes, and pagans about Christ and strengthened the baptized. These would sit and listen, conscious of three loves blending in Paul: love for God, love for their neighbors, and especially love for them his "brothers and sisters in Christ." Paul brought a new concept of love, though he would say that it was God teaching them beyond any words he might impart. Where eroticism was in the very air, even in a city such as theirs not dominated by the cults of Apollo or Aphrodite, Paul used the new word *agapē* which Christians had coined to replace the debased word *eros*, and expounded a love that purified and transformed. Love at its highest and lowest was an urgent topic. Letters which Paul wrote back following his flight from Thessalonica disclose that the church included many young men and women. The men especially, virile and lusty, did not find it easy to allow Christ to control their sexual instincts. When they were pagans, they had thought nothing of seducing a friend's wife or fornicating with any girl who caught their fancy. Turning consciously from evil to faith did not always bring immediate awareness of how to please God in this matter.

Paul guided them precisely. "You know what instructions we gave you through the Lord Jesus," he would remind them in his first letter. "This is the will of God that you should be holy: you must abstain from fornication: each one of you must learn to gain mastery over his body, to hallow and honor it, not giving way to lust like the pagans who are ignorant of God."

Paul and his friends were not soothing an effete club of escapists but molding a high-spirited band who had lived all their days in a permissive society where sexual prowess was admired and its consequences could be exposed on hillsides. These men and women had given their allegiance to Jesus as king, given it so fervently that rumor in the city spoke of Paul recruiting for a rival to Claudius Caesar. They wanted to obey this King Jesus; His words were now their chief authority. They wanted to be like Him, though the old appetites surged in their veins together with the new. Paul strengthened and directed the new by making the most of their conscious desire to obey and to imitate Jesus. He told them what Jesus had said and done.

Nor did Paul confine himself to matters of present conduct. He told them of the coming kingdom when Jesus would return to earth to reign over all men.

Again he based instruction carefully on the words of Jesus. The letters to the Thessalonians, echoing this teaching, contain close parallels to the sayings of Jesus recorded by Luke and give some substance to the tradition—not highly regarded by biblical scholars—that Luke in making his Gospel wrote down what Paul preached. "Know this," Jesus had said, "that if the householder had known at what hour the thief was coming, he would have been awake. . . . You also must be ready; for the Son of man is coming at an hour you do not expect." Paul wrote: "You yourselves well know that the Day of the Lord will come like a thief in the night." Or again: "This we declare to you by the word of the Lord: . . . the Lord Himself will descend from heaven with a cry of command, with the archangel's call, and with the sound of the trumpet of God." Jesus had said: "They will see the Son of man coming in a cloud with power and great glory."[15]

Much of what Paul taught about the return of Christ was a puzzle to his hearers, just as the Lord's sayings puzzled His disciples at the time they were spoken, as ever since. The misinterpretations which the Thessalonians put on Paul's words would soon force him to define his understanding more clearly. He was convinced by Old Testament prophecy and the words of Jesus that the Lord would suddenly end the present age, with its lust, oppression, and crime, by returning bodily in majesty and power, but the details were obscure. And Paul's perspective was foreshortened. He looked for the Second Coming as a man reaching a mountain pass might look at the next snow-capped range: it seems only a few hours' march, though as he crosses the plain, the range grows no nearer but beckons him. So Paul walked on, forever expecting, hoping that his Lord might return at once, yet grateful for every new day which renewed the opportunity to tell men and women about the King who had come—and was coming.

Meanwhile, as Paul's letters also disclose, the three missionaries not only taught the Thessalonians in groups but took time and trouble with them "one by one, as a father deals with his children," encouraging and warning and sorting out the special problems of each. The three men gave themselves completely. And though it would have been easier to demand unquestioning obedience, they preferred to work gently, patiently, "like a devoted nurse among her babies," until Paul grew so personally involved in his converts that when the wrench came it was as if flesh were torn from his body. And it came unexpectedly.

By the fourth week he had ordained elders who were to encourage, admonish, and teach—and lead the church forward.

In Paul's view a church should not merely survive in its unfriendly pagan environment but advance. Christians should have nothing to do with a sad acceptance of harsh surroundings, bearing heavy crosses with uncomplaining gloom, cultivating an oppressive sense of sin. They were to be positive, doing good to each other, and to unbelieving Jews and pagans regardless of abuse or injury. "Rejoice everymore, pray without ceasing, in everything give thanks." No matter how adverse the circumstances, their way of life should be a rebuke to foulness and a spur to their neighbors to seek for themselves this new, extraordinary existence; Christians must outlove, outjoy, outthink, and always welcome those who opposed them.

Thus, the infant Thessalonian church became a mighty movement. Men were remade, relationships sweetened between masters and slaves, husbands and wives. But families were divided too and neighborhoods split. The new faith was discussed, praised, maligned. Paul was loved and admired by some, hated by others. Few stayed indifferent.

The climax came when unbelieving Jews could no longer contain their jealousy. They "recruited some low fellows from the dregs of the populace," writes Luke, "roused the rabble and had the city in an uproar. They mobbed Jason's house, with the intention of bringing Paul and Silas before the town assembly." Not finding them, the mob hustled Jason and some other Christians out of the house and forced them to the *politarchs*, the men responsible for law and order in a Macedonian city which was not a Roman colony.

The ringleaders shouted: "These men who have turned the world upside down have come here also, and Jason has received them. And they are all acting against the decrees of Caesar, saying that there is another king, Jesus."

The mob yelled for blood. The *politarchs*, however, showed a sanity very different from the hasty illegalities of the *strategoi* of Philippi. The charge disturbed them, for they must have known of the expulsion of Jews from Rome and its cause, which the early second-century historian Suetonius ascribes to their "indulging in constant riots at the instigation of one Chrestus," most likely a garbled reference to Jewish violence against Christ's earliest followers in Rome. But evidence of sedition in Thessalonica, of recruiting for a rival Caesar, proved scanty. Its alleged ringleaders were not even before the court.

The *politarchs* therefore adopted a cautious policy. They bound over Jason and his friends in a considerable sum which would be forfeit, and themselves arrested, if the strangers were seen again in the city.

Eighteen
THE FUGITIVE

Paul had no option but to flee with Silas at once. And if the prosecutors could contrive more incriminating evidence, soldiers might be sent out to bring him back.

When night fell, Christian brothers led Paul and Silas through the Arch of Augustus and on to the Egnation Way. Timothy remained but it is probable that a Thessalonian accompanied them as they walked quickly through the night to reach the broad river Axios by dawn. While they waited for the ferry, there was danger that horsemen would gallop up with orders to arrest them, but they passed over safely, walked on through the September morning as the haze enveloped the hills, then turned southwest off the Via Egnatia.

Had Paul stayed at Thessalonica as long as he wished, his probable next move would have been westward right along the Via Egnatia into the coastal province of Illyricum. Having evangelized there, he had hoped to cross the Adriatic to Rome. Rome at present was closed to Jewish travelers; nor did he want to leave the Thessalonians to fend alone, for despite his own teaching about the ability of the Holy Spirit to look after them, he was agitated lest these spiritual babies should weaken under persecution. He therefore chose the little town of Berea in the foothills of Olympus, well known as a summer resort and a refuge for exiles from Thessalonica, yet near enough for a quick return should the ban be lifted once the falsity of the charges was exposed. Paul hoped to be back for winter when gales blew round Mount Athos and snow blocked the Macedonian passes.

They reached Berea on the third day, a peaceful city in majestic surroundings looking down with a narrow view to the sea and up to the gorge from which a river emerged from the mountain. They found a synagogue where at the first opportunity Paul and Silas preached.

Their reception was friendly. The local Jewish elders showed no prejudice. Paul considered them, as Luke wrote, much more noble than those at Thessalonica in that "they received the message with great eagerness, studying the Scriptures every day to see whether it was as they said. Many of them therefore became believers, and so did a fair number of Greeks, women of standing as well as men." There was no need to seek neutral ground for evangelizing and teaching; the synagogue itself became the center of Christian faith. Unexpectedly, when Paul's heart was sore at expulsion from Thessalonica, this little hill town of Berea provided what he had longed for—a synagogue which became a spearhead for Christ.

Timothy arrived with the encouragement that despite persecution, for which Paul had forewarned them, the Thessalonian converts kept faith. Yet Paul worried lest they lose heart if it grew fiercer, especially when after about fifteen days in Berea all his plans were disrupted once again. Jews from Thessalonica, maddened by the news which had traveled swiftly back, arrived to make trouble. Seeing at once that the synagogue leadership had no sympathy with their fury, they began rousing the rabble to destroy Paul by riot or murder. The Christians of Berea felt his life hung by a thread and before riot could begin hurried him secretly out of the town and down toward the coast, leaving Silas and Timothy.

Paul longed to be in Thessalonica again and waited in the little port below Olympus while a messenger went to the city to judge whether this would be safe. He returned with bad news. As Paul wrote a few weeks later: "Since we were bereft of you, brethren, for a short time, in person not in heart, we endeavored the more eagerly and with great desire to see you face to face; because we wanted to come to you—I Paul, again and again—but Satan hindered us."

Winter was coming on. Paul could not wander around Macedonia waiting. The Berean brothers persuaded him to let them take him by sea to Athens. There he would be safe until his next steps became plain.

They took ship[16] down the Aegean past mountains famous in Greek myth: Olympus far back from the shore but clear in morning light, then Ossa which the Giants piled on its neighboring peak of Pelion in their attempt to reach heaven. For Paul, if his Berean friends pointed out Ossa and the forests of Pelion, the myth represented falsehood which Christ had come to supplant, and Christ was conquering even if His servants must flee. Next day they were in the long, narrow gulf separating Euboea from the mainland, and the ship had no need to shelter when night fell provided the winds were gentle. The following morning they rounded the point of Sounion dominated by the glorious marble temple of Poseidon, god of the sea, a center of worship and loyalty to which the sailors made prayers as they passed, its white-robed priests clearly visible in the strong light which is peculiarly Grecian. The temple seemed to mock the weakness of the battered traveler who watched from the deck with a different prayer in his heart.

As they sailed deeper into the Saronic Bay toward the port of Piraeus, Paul had his first distant sight of Athens—the pagan beauties of the Acropolis and the Parthenon, the marble of its great columns reflecting clear despite the intervening distance, its cool arrogance disdaining Paul's audacity.

The Bereans took Paul up the busy road from Piraeus

between the half-ruined fortified walls and through the double gate. They found him lodgings but he was restless. His heart remained in Macedonia. He fussed lest Christians had broken under the strain. He who had assured them so strongly that they would find Christ true and powerful whatever the malice of man, was nervous lest continuous and severe persecution should seem to disprove this, and they turn against both Saviour and servant. He had not yet reached the level of faith where he could leave the issue totally in God's hands.

"And so when we could bear it no longer, we decided to remain alone at Athens . . . When I could bear it no longer I sent to find out about your faith, fearing that the tempter might have tempted you and my labor might be lost." He persuaded the Bereans to hurry back home and tell Timothy that he must visit Thessalonica and encourage them to stand firm and strong in the faith and not be "unsettled by the present troubles." Then Timothy and Silas were to come to Paul at Athens as fast as they could.

To be left alone in Athens, city of idolatry and pagan philosophy, where the Jewish synagogue gave little welcome, was pain almost sharper than the rods of Philippi's lictors. Paul craved company and sympathy but the Thessalonians mattered more. For them, he was willing to endure an autumn of waiting.

Though worse was in store immediately, though the fiercest spiritual crisis lay several years ahead, the day when Paul waved farewell to the Bereans was one of the hardest in his life.

Nineteen
LAUGHTER IN ATHENS

The immense granite cliff topped with the Western world's most famous temples held the eye of Paul or any visitor to Athens by purity of line and color against the cloudless blue of the late September sky.

Paul was not blind to beauty, but if he took note of the exquisite forms of the Propylea and the Temple of Athene, Giver of Victory, or the Parthenon itself, he would not climb the hill to enter these centers of a rampant paganism. He knew that the gleaming statue of Athene was an object of worship, that the famous frieze that would become the Elgin Marbles represented religious rituals. Until Greek art should be stripped of religion its very loveliness strengthened Paul's repudiation.

He had not intended to evangelize Athens; he was without helpers and half-hoped to return to the Thessalonians; he needed rest. But as he saw the extraordinary number of idols on every side, he became more and more exasperated. Below the Acropolis, he walked in the busy *agora* or marketplace flanked by the chaste Doric magnificence of the Theseion and other temples where worship took place daily; even the city hall had its sacred fire. In the open space and under the *stoas* or porticoes, wedged together with statues of illustrious Athenians and wealthy Romans, were idols and altars of every divinity known or unknown. Yet this was the intellectual center of the world, where rich youths from every land in the empire were sent to complete their education by selecting a philosophy to their taste. The blend of shallow piety with philosophies that scoffed at the supernatural had created a flippant attitude which Luke takes off neatly: "All Athenians and the foreigners staying there spent their time in nothing else but telling and hearing whatever was new."

Paul's soul revolted at this misuse of human faculties, especially because, as his own words would show, he knew something of the long-ago intellectual splendors of classical Athens and of its search for truth. But when he unburdened himself in the synagogue, he met apathy; the Jews had written off their Greek neighbors and were content to treat them as lucrative customers whose moral and religious blindness were of no concern. He went therefore to work in the *agora*, where with his customary adaptability he became an Athenian to the Athenians by using the method of Socrates, engaging the strollers and bystanders in question-and-answer discussion. Socrates had been content to remain in one city, devoting himself to goodness as he saw it. Paul could not restrict himself to one city. No man in previous history had traveled so far or suffered so much to bring men truth; he could not stay still or silent while others remained ignorant of the Way, the Truth, and the Life. Every day he told all about Jesus and His resurrection, undeterred by lack of response.

This little man with bandy legs and quite unfashionable earnestness became sufficiently familiar to attract the attention of the two principal schools of philosophy. Stoics taught that people should strive, unafraid and proud, to accept the law of the universe however harsh, and should work toward a world state founded on reason. They believed that the soul survived the body; but their rivals, the Epicureans, did not. The Epicureans taught that happiness or pleasure was the highest good, which should be pursued unaided by whatever gods there be, but their idea had degenerated into: "Eat, drink, and be merry, for tomorrow we die." By Paul's day the disciples of each philosophy had lost much of their drive to make converts; a man's beliefs were his personal affair and philosophy had degenerated into an elaborate intellectual exercise.

Stoics and Epicureans listened to Paul, whom they took to be one of the usual scum of foreigners seeking patrons in Athens, and were amused. First, Paul kept emphasizing that he did not speak on his own authority, being presumably an intellectual bankrupt. Then instead of offering a rational philosophy, he sounded as if he were commending a divinity or two. The words *Jesous* and *anastasis* (resurrection) were frequently on his lips. *Jesous* sounded rather like the name of the Ionic goddess of health, especially as he linked it with the *sōter* (saviour) which to a Greek suggested a god who gave health of body and mind. As for *anastasis,* they had myths of gods returning from the underworld and this might be another. Yet Paul talked as if he referred to a real flesh-and-blood person who had been talked with, watched, and listened to, and then executed by crucifixion, which no one could survive. Paul seemed to be trying to persuade them this man had risen bodily from the grave.

"What *is* this gutter-sparrow trying to say?" they asked each other, using a typical slang word (literally a "seed-picker") for a rogue who picks up scraps from the gutter or hawks other men's ideas because he is too lazy or dull to have his own.

"He seems to be a herald for foreign gods," said others.

It all sounded like rubbish. And possibly dangerous to the morals of such Athenians who troubled to listen; though speech was free in Athens, there were limits. They decided that he must expound his views before the venerable Court of the Areopagus which had the right to expel unsuitable philosophers. They approached Paul good-humoredly and invited him to accompany them up the slope of the Acropolis and on to the small steep rock, the Hill of Ares, from which the Court took its name.[17]

As Paul stood on the Areopagus, on the white Stone of Shame reserved for the defendant (whether of a thesis or against a criminal accusation), the immediate background was filled by the pink-white marble of the shrines which man's religious devotion and incomparable architecture had raised on the Acropolis crag. At eye level, the Boule Gate below the summit; above it the twin Propylea, that dignified entrance to the sacred area, flanked by two temples. He could not see the Parthenon but over the Propylea the sunlight glinted on the shield, spear, and helmet of the colossal goddess Athene, a supreme example of human craftsmanship proclaiming the shape of the deity, while in the foreground, ready to listen, stood the heirs of Socrates, Plato, and Aristotle, of Zeno and Euripides.

The "prosecutor" stepped forward to the Stone of Pride, and with a grave courtesy that hid his amusement, addressed Paul: "May we know what this new teaching is which you present? For you bring some strange things to our ears; we wish to know therefore what these things mean."

A hint of menace hid in his words; Socrates had been sentenced to death for teaching strange doctrines, and although Paul was in no danger of hemlock, he might be expelled.

Paul was only too ready to talk about Jesus before so august an assembly. He felt in his element. Sometimes when addressing country folk and city slaves, he may have had to humble his intellect but here he could call up his knowledge of Greek thought and lead it higher. He was not in the least abashed. As a lawyer, he knew the Resurrection to be a thoroughly attested fact of recent history, for which only the seas between Athens and Palestine prevented him calling witnesses. As a converted sinner, he knew the existence of the Risen Christ to be self-evident. The Christian faith was not only more reasonable than any held by these philosophers, it was truth; with utmost confidence he could adapt himself to his special audience, approach them by their reason, tell them of the Resurrection, and lead them on from there.

He began tactfully and appropriately, using a rare word (translated "objects of worship") which would have awakened immediate echoes of the passage in the *Eumenides* of Aeschylus where Athene tells how the Court of Areopagus came to be instituted. Later he echoed Plato's reference, in the Tenth Book of the *Republic*, to the great Architect of the Universe who "makes everything which grows out of the ground and animates all living things." He also introduced direct quotations from the Cretan poet Epimenides and Aratus the Cilician, and a touch of Euripides. But the very way he used his Greek allusions showed that he rated their thought a feeble pale reflection of the God in the Bible of the Jews and in Jesus Christ. Paul was polite but most unsycophantic.

"Gentlemen of Athens," he began, "I see that in every way you are very religious, for as I passed along and looked at your objects of worship, I also found an altar with the inscription: 'To an Unknown God.' That which you worship without knowing—this I proclaim to you!

"The God who made the world and all that is in it, being Lord of heaven and earth, does not live in man-made shrines"—and Paul must have waved a hand toward the Acropolis while his mind flashed back to Stephen's use of that very phrase in his trial long ago—"nor is He served by man's hands as if He needed anything, for He Himself gives life and breath and all else. And He made from one stock every race of man to inhabit the surface of the earth, having determined and planned in advance the limits of their epochs and their boundaries. They were to seek God, if they might grope after Him and might find Him, though indeed He is not far from each of us, for in Him we 'live and move and have our being.' As some of your own poets have said, 'We are also His offspring.'

"As God's offspring, we ought not think that the divine is like an image in gold or silver or stone, a work of man's art and imagination"—and again his hand must have pointed toward the venerated colossus of Athene—"God overlooked these times of ignorance. But now He commands all men, everywhere, to repent"—("*all* men"? Several Areopagites would curl their lips at the idea of a philosopher, dedicated to the pursuit of truth, needing repentance. But Paul was warming to his theme)—"because He has fixed a day on which He will judge the whole inhabited world," the *oikoumene* which the Greeks talked so much about, "in strict justice by a Man whom He has appointed.

"He has attested this to all by raising Him from the dead—"

A guffaw broke the decorum of the assembly. A hubbub of voices and laughter interrupted Paul. They had heard enough. If he really thought that man can come to life again after he dies and the earth drinks up his blood, such folly proved him unworthy to be accredited a teacher among the wise of Athens. They said: "We will hear you on this subject some other time."

Paul knew that it was a dismissal. He withdrew, descending the rock with his back to the Acropolis. One Areopagite, Dionysius, followed him, determined to take literally the Council's polite words of prevarication and to hear more; for instead of an irrevocable fate fixed by a hostile universe, instead of the horror of the shade after death, which men feared though none should show it, Paul had said that eternity depended on a Person who had conquered death.

Dionysius became a believer. There was also an aristocratic woman named Damaris, who may have been a God-fearer who heard Paul at the synagogue; and a few more. But none of them seems to have been baptized, perhaps because of their civic positions or because their husbands kept them secret disciples. The first to be baptized in Achaia would be a household of Corinth.

Paul had to leave quickly. The Council had refused him license to teach, yet he declined to be muzzled. He moved onward, relying on Silas and Timothy to catch up with him.

Athens had rejected him. He could not know that his speech would go down to posterity beside the Funeral Oration of Pericles and the Philippics of Demosthenes as one of the great speeches of Athens. He could not know that whole books would be written about it or that in a few hundred years the Parthenon would become a Christian church; and that nineteen centuries on, when Greece after long suppression became once more a sovereign state, the national flag which flies beside the ruins of the Parthenon would be lowered to half-mast each Good Friday, and raised on Easter Day in honor of Christ's resurrection.

Part Three
NO ARROGANT APOSTLE

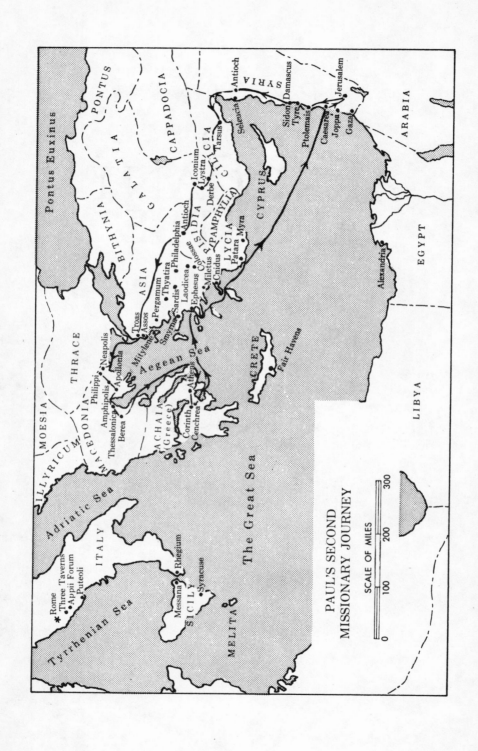

PAUL'S SECOND
MISSIONARY JOURNEY

SCALE OF MILES

0   100   200   300

Twenty
CITY OF UNBRIDLED LOVE

Across the Isthmus of Corinth, Paul passed slaves who portaged goods, and whole teams heaving and sweating under the overseer's lash to drag ships on rollers from one sea to the other. He walked through the port of Lechaion and up the slight incline to enter the walls of Corinth, capital of Achaia. "When I came to you," he told the Corinthians afterward, "I declared the attested truth of God without display of fine words or wisdom. I resolved that while I was with you I would think of nothing but Jesus Christ—Christ nailed to the cross. I came before you weak, as I was then, nervous and shaking with fear."

Encouragements came at once. While inquiring for a certain Christian tentmaker and his wife lately come from Rome, whom he had heard about from a mutual acquaintance or by letter, he met comments which convinced him that travelers from Thessalonica had already talked unashamedly about Christ. Then he discovered the tentmakers, probably in a typical open-fronted shop in a street near the Lechaion road, and was received with open arms, invited to make his home in their cramped quarters upstairs and ply his craft.

He had found two of the best friends he ever made. Aquila

was a Jew born in Pontus province on the southern shore of the Euxine or Black Sea. Probably he was younger than Paul and became an early convert when the Christian faith reached Rome by means which have never been precisely determined. His wife's name, Prisca, suggests with other clues that she was a Latin, and of a higher class than her husband. She might be known as the Lady Prisca but her unaffected simplicity and hospitable ways made it more usual to call her by the familiar "Priscilla." When Claudius expelled Jews from Rome because of "Chrestus," Aquila and Priscilla emigrated to Corinth, but until Paul came they had not seen themselves as missionaries.

The three of them went to the synagogue next Sabbath and Paul exercised his right as a rabbi.

Paul disclaims pretensions to oratory: "The word I spoke," he reminded Corinthians a few years later, "the Gospel I proclaimed did not sway you with subtle arguments; it carried conviction by spiritual power, so that your faith might be built not upon human wisdom but upon the power of God." There were Corinthians who rated him a contemptible speaker. Yet his preaching had a fine ring of assurance, every allusion crystal clear to his synagogue audience but the application startlingly fresh:

"Of legal righteousness Moses writes"—and Paul drew a text from Leviticus—" 'The man who does this shall gain life by it.' But the righteousness that comes by faith says"—and he began his main exposition, a passage from Deuteronomy—" 'Do not say to yourself, Who can go up to heaven?' (that is to bring Christ down), or 'Who can go down to the abyss?' (to bring Christ up from the dead). But what does it say? *The word is near you: it is upon your lips and in your heart.'*

"This means the word of faith which we proclaim! If on your lips is the confession, 'Jesus is Lord,' and in your heart the faith that God raised Him from the dead, then you will find salvation. For the faith that leads to righteousness is in the heart, and the confession that leads to salvation is upon

the lips. Scripture says''—and now Paul turned to Isaiah—
'' 'Everyone who has faith in Him will be saved from shame.'
Everyone! There is no distinction between Jew and Greek,
because the same Lord is Lord of all, and is rich enough for
the needs of all who invoke Him. For everyone, as it says
again''—and now Paul was on the Prophet Joel—'' *'Everyone*
who invokes the name of the Lord will be saved.' How could
they invoke one in whom they had no faith? And how could
they have faith in One they had never heard of? And how
could they hear without someone to spread the Good News?
And how could anyone spread the Good News without a
commission to do so? And that is what Scripture affirms:
'How welcome are the feet of the messengers of Good
News!' ''

Or were they? As Paul looked up southward from the
agora, the skyline was dominated by a mountain 1,900 feet
high and precipitous on all sides except the west: the volcano-
shaped Acrocorinth, visible on a clear day from Athens; and
above the rim of the mountain's saucerlike summit peeped the
great Temple of Aphrodite. The cult was dedicated to the
glorification of sex. One thousand girls were kept consecrated
to the goddess, and their processions, rituals, and individual
solicitude so aroused male devotees and set the tone of the
city that the ancient world described habitual fornicators as
"Living like Corinthians," a phrase coined by the early Greek
comedians and carried across to the new Corinth. In the city
itself, the archaic Temple of Apollo, which had been restored
by the Romans and stood behind Paul as he gazed at
Acrocorinth, also glorified sex as well as music, song, and
poetry, for Apollo was the ideal of male beauty. The temple's
inner recesses held nude statues and friezes of Apollo in
various poses of virility which fired his male worshipers to
physical displays of devotion with the god's beautiful boys.
This too set a tone.

Corinth was the biggest city Paul had yet encountered, a
brash new commercial metropolis founded in its current form

less than a hundred years earlier after a century in ruins. It squeezed nearly a quarter million people into a comparatively small area, a large proportion being slaves engaged in the unending movement of goods. Slaves or free, Corinthians were rootless, cut off from their country background, drawn from races and districts all over the empire and, except for the Jewish community, without natural groupings; a curiously close parallel to the population of a twentieth-century "inner city," the overcrowded materialistic heart of any great urban concentration, with the superficial difference that Corinthians masked their materialism, sexual appetites, and superstitions behind a cloak of religiousness. Paul had seen a Christian church grow and flourish in the essentially rural areas of southern Galatia and in the moderately sized cities he had found in Macedonia. If the love of Christ Jesus could take root in Corinth, the most populated, wealthy, commercial-minded, and sex-obsessed city of eastern Europe, it must prove powerful anywhere.[18]

He made converts—Stephanas whom he baptized with all his household, and Gaius a wealthy God-fearer with a large home; since "Gaius" is the first name this was most likely one Titius Justus whose house was next door to the synagogue. But progress was unsensational and the impact on pagan Corinth negligible, giving no indication of what would come. Paul was inhibited by the lack of his team and by the need to earn a living. He was impatient for the coming of Silas and Timothy.

When they arrived, his cup ran over. Closeted together for long hours above the shop, questioning Timothy closely, he learned to his relief that despite persecution the Thessalonian believers had not only endured with undiminished faith and love but were growing in depth and numbers. To Paul, who had fussed at Berea and Athens imagining calamities and failures, the news taught a lesson: that his Lord was perfectly able to keep those who put their faith in Him: "He who calls you is to be *trusted*."

He determined to express his love and gratitude immediately. "Timothy has just arrived from Thessalonica, bringing good news of your faith and love. . . ." It was probably Timothy's pen which scratched away as Paul dictated, perhaps sitting in the winter sunshine in Gaius' garden or out on the slopes of Acrocorinth looking across the Gulf of Mount Parnassus. "He tells us that you always think kindly of us, and are as anxious to see us as we are to see you. And so in all our difficulties and hardships your faith reassures us about you. It is the breath of life to us that you stand firm in the Lord. What thanks can we return to God for you? What thanks for all the joy you have brought us, making us rejoice before our God while we pray most earnestly night and day to be allowed to see you again and to mend your faith where it falls short? May our God and Father Himself, and our Lord Jesus, bring us direct to you! And may the Lord make your love mount and overflow toward one another and toward all, as our love does toward you. May He make your hearts firm, so that you stand before our God and Father holy and faultless when our Lord Jesus comes with all those who are His own."

The style of this First Letter to the Thessalonians reads quite differently from the exclamations Paul had thrown at the Galatians. Neither was elaborately composed in the manner of contemporary men of letters who used the epistolary form to publish their ideas, in carefully polished phrases, to cultured readers everywhere. Paul was writing for particular people and cared nothing if the style was "Pauline" or not. The Thessalonians had problems, Timothy reported. Christians had died already, possibly under the persecution, and survivors worried whether they would all meet again; certain church members were being idle, sponging on others while saying that to earn a living was unnecessary because of the Lord's imminent return.

Paul therefore applied himself to untangling the misconceptions and elaborations which had grown up around his teaching. At the same time, unconsciously, he gave an insight into his own character when he urged the whole brotherhood, to whom the letter was to be read aloud, how they ought to live. Since he loathed deceit, he would not outline a manner of life if he did not aspire to it himself. Thus by slight paraphrase, a portrait of Paul in the closing months of A.D. 50 may be drawn from the peroration of his First Letter to the Thessalonians.

Paul endeavored to live at peace with his fellow believers— not that there were many yet in Corinth. He rebuked the idle and careless, encouraged the fainthearted, supported the weak, and was very patient with them all. He took care not to pay back wrong for wrong but sought to help his fellowmen whether they were Christians or unbelievers. He was always rejoicing, he prayed constantly, and thanked God in every circumstance whether harsh or favorable, knowing that God as revealed in Christ particularly desired this. When others expounded texts or told him eagerly what they believed God had revealed to them individually, he did not crush them but tested their views, by Scripture and by the oral tradition of what Jesus had taught, and accepted gratefully every new insight which passed this test. He kept himself from every action or word which he knew was wrong.

His constant prayer, with full confidence, was that the God of peace would purify him and, in all the defilements of a pagan city; keep him sound in spirit, soul, and body, "without fault when our Lord Jesus Christ comes."

Timothy had brought another money gift from the Philippians. Paul could now temporarily abandon the loom and leather to devote himself to preaching, aided by Silas and Timothy. He concentrated on the synagogue, longing to see a nobility of spirit like the Bereans' which would create a firm base for advance among pagans.

But Jews who refused to acknowledge Jesus as Messiah reacted like those in Pisidian Antioch: "they opposed and resorted to abuse"—and the word Luke uses need not be limited to verbal abuse. Paul may have suffered once again a synagogue whipping, the "forty stripes save one," in the presence of Crispus the ruler of the synagogue and all the congregation. If so, there was a terrible irony in Paul's words when with bloodied back he picked up his torn clothes, drew himself painfully to full height, shook the clothes free of the synagogue's dust in a symbolic action which all recognized, and alluded to those words of Ezekiel by which a messenger is discharged of responsibility for the death of those who refuse his warnings. "*Your blood* be upon your heads!" cried Paul. "I am innocent. From now on I will go to the Gentiles."

His heart was as sore as his back. He longed that Jews and non-Jews should be one in Christ, a "new Israel"; Paul had nothing of the anti-Semite in him. He still hoped to win his "brothers according to the flesh" and it was for this reason, as well as the convenience and size of the house, and not because he wished to provoke and snub the Jews, that he accepted the offer of Titius Justus to make the house next door to the synagogue the place for preaching about Christ. And the first convert to be baptized, with his household, after Paul's withdrawal was none other than Crispus, the ruler of the synagogue. A man named Sosthenes took his place.

When the news that Paul had been forced out of the synagogue spread in the city, pagan Corinthians began at last to flock into the church, until early on any Sunday morning the lawn and mosaics round the fountain in the house of Gaius Titius Justus were covered by men and women, sitting separately, all eyes on Paul as he preached and on Silas or Timothy as they baptized afterward.

In Paul's mind, however, a seed of worry took root, that the pattern of previous cities was about to be repeated; rejection by Jews, progress among the pagans, fury from Jews, expulsion by mob violence or judicial process just when the Gospel gained a hold. The fear grew on him that he would never find a city where he might lay a spiritual foundation and build unhurriedly. One night as he sat late by himself in the upper room at Aquila's, when the city's noise had ceased except for the occasional bark of a dog or the metallic tramp of guards on their rounds, depression, which was one of the strands of Paul's nature seemed to gain the upper hand. He would never win another Corinthian to Christ and see the sparkle of new life in a Corinthian's eyes. And he dreaded the physical agony of another stoning or a beating with rods; the desolation of being flung out again with winter now on them, the seas turbulent, and nowhere to take his stiff, aging joints but the mountain trails of the Peloponnesus.

Suppose his faith was futile and Christ had never risen from the dead. Suppose the Presence was a figment of his imagination, and there was nothing, no one. He wanted to give up, stop preaching, take himself away to live quietly at peace, back to the Taurus, to Arabia, anywhere.

Suddenly he saw Him. As on the Damascus Road, as in the Temple, he saw Him, the Lord Jesus, and the unmistakable voice; quiet, reassuring. "Do not be afraid, but speak and do not be silent. For I am with you. And no one is going to attack you in such a way as to hurt you. For I have many people in this city."

Twenty-One
THE HOUSE OF GAIUS

Before dawn on the first day of any week during A.D. 51, several scores of men and women entered the house of Gaius next door to the synagogue. Since Sunday was an ordinary weekday for Jews and all days alike to pagans, the Christians met at an hour which even slaves could keep.

As Paul looked around in the growing daylight while they sang hymns to Christ and the Father, he could reflect that "Few of you whom God has called are men of wisdom, by any human standard . . . few of you are powerful or nobly born." One of the few was Crispus, former ruler of the synagogue, and another the ex-pagan Erastus, the elected city treasurer and probably the most substantial of the converts. Instead of the wise and powerful, God had chosen the simple and the weak, the base-born, the despised, to shame the world in its pretensions, "so that no human being might boast in the presence of God." Many slaves were free members of the church. Paul knew what some, whether black, brown, or white had been through: torn from home in forest, steppe, or mountain beyond the frontiers, hustled in gangs on a rigorous journey to one of the great slave centers; if young and healthy, put to hard labor in quarry or fields until their spirits broke, then shipped to Corinth, exposed naked for sale to good masters or bad. Their parents, wives, children were lost forever, unless chance threw them together again.

God had chosen even more unlikely raw material. Paul could mentally list the previous characters of some of his friends: fornicators, debauchees, and whores; he mentions homosexuals of both sorts, beautiful boys and the sodomites who used them; there were thieves, misers, swindlers, drunkards, extortioners, foul-mouthed slanderers, and of course idolaters. "But you have washed yourselves!" he would cry. "You have been consecrated, you have been justified through the name of the Lord Jesus Christ and by the Spirit of our God." The past was as if it had never been.

The stories converts must have told him privately would not only tear at his heartstrings but sicken him. As Henry Drummond, the Victorian natural scientist who wrote *The Greatest Thing in the World*, most famous of all meditations on Paul's chapter on love (1 Corinthians 13), said during D.L. Moody's evangelistic campaigns: "Such tales of woe I've heard in Moody's inquiry room, that I've felt I must go and change my very clothes after the contact." Paul must sometimes have stolen away to the remoter slopes of Acrocorinth where the scent of meadowsweet replaced the stench of garbage and offal, and the sight of the seas and distant mountains could refresh him while he prayed.

Corinth left him under no illusions about paganism. It was here, on another visit, that Paul wrote in the Letter to the Romans the diagnosis which precedes his unfolding of "God's way of righting wrong, a way that starts from faith and ends in faith." "All their thinking," he wrote in words unconsciously borne out by the evidence of contemporary pagan writers, "has ended in futility, and their misguided minds are plunged in darkness. They boast of their wisdom, but they have made fools of themselves, exchanging the splendor of immortal God for an image shaped like mortal man, even for images like birds, beasts, and creeping things. . . . In consequence God has given them up to shameful passions. Their women have exchanged natural intercourse for unnatural, and their men in turn, giving up natural relations with women, burn with lust for one another; males behaving indecently with males, and are paid in their own persons the fitting wages of such perversion . . .

"They are filled with every kind of injustice, mischief, rapacity, and malice; they are one mass of envy, murder, rivalry, treachery, and malevolence; whisperers and scandal-mongers, hateful to God, insolent, arrogant, and boastful; they invent new kinds of mischief, they show no loyalty to parents, no conscience, no fidelity to their plighted word; they are without natural affection and without pity. They know well enough the just decree of God, that those who behave like this deserve to die, and yet they do it; not only so, they actually applaud such practices."

To such people Paul preached the Gospel in Corinth. "First and foremost," he writes, "I handed on to you the facts which had been imparted to me: that Christ died for our sins, in accordance with the Scriptures; that He was buried; that He was raised to life on the third day; and that He appeared to Cephas, and afterward to the Twelve. Then He appeared to over 500 of our brothers at once, most of whom are still alive, though some have died. Then He appeared to James, and afterward to all the apostles. In the end He appeared even to me." Paul said his own spiritual birth was extraordinary—the strange word he uses could be translated "an abortion" or "abnormal"—"for I had persecuted the church and am therefore inferior to all other apostles; indeed not fit to be called an apostle." He emphasized his own meeting with Jesus on the Damascus Road; his detractors, indeed, said he lacked a fitting humility. He ignored them: Christ knew his weaknesses too well for the criticisms of others to matter, though they got a little under the skin. He went on drumming home the message. "Thus we preached and thus you believed."

And when they believed, they leaped out of their old existence as completely as Paul had leaped out of his. He analyzed for them what happened: "When anyone is united to Christ, he is a new creature: his old life is over; a new life has already begun." As soon as a man had this "new life," Paul expected him to talk about it, so that the Gospel spread with astonishing speed. At their assemblies, encouraged by Paul but with a strict eye to decorum, local Christians would expound and testify; again and again an unbeliever present would hear something that searched his conscience and brought conviction, and the secrets of his heart were laid bare, until in repentance and faith he cried, "God is certainly among you!" Day by day too in the marketplace and at the graceful Fountain of Peirene where Corinthians gossiped, in the gymnasia, perhaps even in the public baths, Paul led them in the work of an evangelist. Constantly, he would see the miracle of new birth, because "my speech and my message were not in plausible words of wisdom, but in demonstration of the Spirit and power, that your faith might not rest in the wisdom of men but in the power of God."

But though Corinthians were quick to believe and to evangelize, they were slow to mature. Paul had much that he wanted to teach them, and grieved that instead of strong meat which could form spiritual muscle and bone, he must feed them as it were on baby's milk, going over and over the simplicities of faith. Yet, if more slowly than he wished, they were undoubtedly displaying new characteristics and discernments which Paul said were gifts of the Spirit of the Father and the Son who was present among them, active if invisible, handing out different abilities to different people for the building up of His church.

In particular, many of the Corinthian Christians seem to have been entering on a novel and satisfying yet perilous experience: "speaking in tongues." The meaning of "tongues" or *glossalia* has been much debated, especially since its widespread revival in the twentieth century: the Pentecostals, growing faster than any other denomination in many parts of the world, owe their origin and much of their warmth and fervor to their use of "tongues," and similar spiritual discoveries have been made here and there in the major historic churches. Yet "tongues" remain the most puzzling of the spiritual gifts described by Paul, whether they are "tongues of men or of angels," whether a suddenly acquired fluency in languages hitherto unknown to the speaker, or prayer and praise in ecstatic utterance unrelated to a human tongue.

Paul welcomed the gift. But when the Corinthians abused it after he left, he had to stress the risks which, as the modern movement shows, are inherent wherever tongues are practiced. He warned that the gift of tongues is easily counterfeited, easily leads to excess. Those who do not possess it must never condemn as fanatics those who do, who in their turn must not despise as less spiritual the far larger number of Christians without the gift. The grave danger of a church breaking up into factions must be resisted. Speaking in tongues should always be accompanied by the parallel gift of interpretation, for the primary function of every spiritual gift was not to comfort its recipient but to build up, encourage, and stimulate the whole church. "I thank God I speak in tongues more than you all," said Paul. "Nevertheless, in church I would rather speak five words with my mind, in order to instruct others, than 10,000 words in a tongue."

The church was already an influence in Corinth—because of its new morality which neighbors could not fail to notice even when blind to its source.

The morality taught by Paul and demonstrated by his converts was in stark contrast to the old, permissive morality of the ancient world. It was unconventional: it showed a love of man irrespective of his race, showed forgiveness instead of resentment for wrong, joy instead of grim endurance of adversity or oppression. A slave no longer followed the proverbial maxims, "Love other slaves but hate your masters; love robbery and sexual lust; never tell the truth." Instead he sought by his behavior and prayers to win his master.

As at Thessalonica, there was a new conception of love. At Corinth it contrasted not only with the promiscuousness encouraged by the Aphrodite cult but with the homosexuality of Apollo. By sheer moral force, the Christians were introducing a completely different concept of love.

There were failures too, for the pressures on the young church were enormous. The right attitude to sex was inevitably a burning question to Corinthian Christians. Paul was so sure that misuse of sex damaged human personality, flouted divine law, and invited inevitable misery that he could not let his converts adapt their ethics to the situation in which they were placed. Nor would he clamp them in the legal strait jacket which was the Jewish answer; they must learn to live in Christ's freedom, by His strength.

Weak, few, absurd beside the power represented by pagan processions up wide steps and under huge columns of temples which looked as if they would flourish for a thousand years, Christians were surrounded by problems. In the meat market it was difficult to find joints other than from animals sacrificed to idols; purchase of this meat implied public recognition of the idol's divinity. Family or craft dinner parties were often held in temples, with the idol as host. In the theater a play was in essence a heathen ceremony, the stories generally were of gods and goddesses, and the performance bawdy; copulation on the stage was not unknown.

Small wonder that Paul would have to write in due course: "Let anyone who thinks that he stands take heed lest he fall. No temptation has overtaken you that is not common to all people. God is faithful, and He will not let you be tempted beyond your strength, but with the temptation will also provide the way of escape, that you may be able to endure it."

Twenty-Two
GALLIO'S DECISION

With churches already springing up in other parts of Achaia, Paul was about to leave Corinth on a local tour of encouragement when further excellent news arrived from Thessalonica. During the tour he could boast happily, according to his habit of spurring one church by lauding another, that the Thessalonians' faith remained steadfast under all persecutions and troubles. It leaped ahead, and their love for each other found more and more practical outlets.

They had problems and discouragements too and, on his return to Corinth, Paul composed with Silas and Timothy the Second Letter to the Thessalonians. Their sufferings, he told them, were making them worthy subjects of the kingdom of God, and when the Lord Jesus came back in glory the accounts would be squared; men and women who had utterly refused Him, spurned His Good News and hurt His people would not escape justice but suffer the eternal ruin of being "cut off from the presence of the Lord and the splendor of His might." In this he followed the teaching of Jesus, who never hesitated to warn those who rejected His love; Paul could not speak softly about a second chance in another life. He was not afraid to preach judgment, even if he would need later to amplify and clarify his thought.

Some of the Thessalonians had swallowed rumors that this "Day of the Lord" had come already, and were acting as though absolved from normal behavior. Paul begged them not to be "so easily confused" in their thinking or "upset by the claim." He reminded them briefly but vigorously of his oral teaching about the signs which must precede the Day, though part of what he wrote remains the most obscure of all Pauline literature, possibly because he veiled certain topical or political allusions in a code language to which his original readers had the key.

He was particularly concerned at the origin of the rumors, especially since one possible source was a "letter purporting to come from us." When Paul signed the letter he was now dictating, he took particular pains against forgery: "The greeting is in my own hand, signed with my name, *Paul*; this authenticates all my letters: this is how I write. The grace of our Lord Jesus Christ be with you all." Thus the Second Letter to the Thessalonians contains the earliest mention of forgery being used as a weapon to hurt Paul by confusing his friends. The forgers may have been the very Pharisees who had disrupted the church in southern Galatia until routed by the arrival of Paul's letter to the Galatians, and who now took a leaf out of his book. The forged letter was an indication that Jewish opponents were infiltrating the church to destroy it from within; Paul was to cross their trails frequently until they came near to achieving their aim.

Meanwhile, he urged the Thessalonians to "Stand firm and hold to the traditions which you were taught by us, either by word of mouth or by letter." He gave strict instructions that no one should be idle or a scrounger, but work for a living after the example of the apostles. Next he laid down a principle for the rebuke and recovery of recalcitrants in which he mixed firmness and love equally, guidance too frequently forgotten in the centuries to come: "If anyone refuses to obey what we say in this letter, note that man, and have nothing to do with him, that he may be ashamed. Do not look on him as an enemy but warn him as a brother.''

And then, almost casually, Paul concluded with a brief tremendous prayer which expressed his belief that the Thessalonian Christians could triumph above the harshest circumstance: ''May the Lord of peace Himself give you peace—at all times, in all ways. The Lord be with you all.''

In the course of this Second Letter, Paul made a personal request: ''Go on praying for us, that the Word of the Lord may speed on and be gloriously acknowledged, just as with you; and that we be rescued from wrong-headed and evil men, for not all have faith.'' Soon after the letter's arrival in Thessalonica, the prayer was answered at Corinth in a remarkable and decisive way.

During the early summer of A.D. 51, Sosthenes, who had succeeded Crispus as ruler of the synagogue, became a Christian. What is more, he retained his office, evidently agreeing with Paul that a synagogue was a natural sphere for Christian leadership. At that, the other principal Jews determined to break Christianity in Corinth. An opportunity came with the installation, on July 1, 51, of a new Proconsul of Achaia, Lucius Junius Gallio, whose two years' proconsulship has been dated almost exactly by fragments found in 1905 at Delphi. Gallio was the brother of Seneca, the great philosopher who was a high favorite of the Emperor Claudius. ''No mortal,'' wrote Seneca, ''is so pleasant to anyone as Gallio is to everyone.'' The Jewish leaders perhaps knew this reputation and hoped Gallio would be pleasant to them. They filed a prosecution against Paul.

When prosecutors, defendant, and their supporters ranged themselves before the raised open-air *bema* or judgment seat on the south side of the *agora*, Paul had the promise which had come in the vision at night, that no attack on him should prosper. Yet Gallio's decision would be supremely important, both to Greece, because he was governor of the chief province, and throughout the empire because of his influence at court. As much as any one man he could either stifle Christianity or, in Paul's phrase, cause it to "speed on and be gloriously acknowledged."

The Jews pursued their prosecution by arguing that Paul propagated a religion unrecognized by the State: "This man is persuading men to worship God contrary to the Law." Paul stepped forward. He was about to open his mouth in defense when Gallio stopped the case and addressed the Jews. Paul's legal mind would have grasped at once the enormous implication of Gallio's statement, for he took the Jewish charge about "the Law" in quite another sense than they had intended.

"If this were a matter of crime or grave misdemeanor," pronounced the Proconsul, "there would have been good reason for me to listen to you Jews. But since it is a matter of words and names and your own Law, *I do not wish to be judge of these things*"—a precise legal expression, by which a Roman magistrate exercised his discretion not to interfere where he ruled that no statute had been broken.

Before the Jews could appeal, Gallio gave a brief order which drove them from the judgment seat by the butts of military spears. The moment they were out of the precinct they got their own back. If Gallio ruled that this was a domestic matter, then they would act on his decision. They could not lay hands on Paul because he had withdrawn from their synagogue, but Sosthenes had not. They seized him, stripped him, and gave him the "forty stripes save one" in full sight of Gallio on the judgment seat. "And Gallio cared for none of these things." They were exercising their domestic right to punish those within their jurisdiction, just as he had ruled a few moments before.[19]

The proconsular decision left Paul and his converts free to preach where they wished with no danger of sudden assaults and imprisonments. Rome had become their protector.

Farmers and goatherds must often have seen a bandy-legged Jew, his black beard flecked with grey, his head well wrapped against the strong light, striding purposefully with a team of young men along the trails which wound between the course scrub, to reach some country town and receive a welcome from friends who had visited Corinth and heard the Gospel. The faith spread possibly even to Sparta and Olympia, and across the Gulf and up the slopes of Parnassus to Delphi itself. Almost certainly, Paul and the Corinthian church evangelized among athletes and spectators at the biennial Isthmian Games of A.D. 51, for his First Letter to the Corinthians sounds a distinct note of mutual reminiscence when he employs the metaphor: "You know (*do you not?*) that at the sports all the runners run the race, though only one wins the prize. Like them, run to win! But every athlete goes into strict training. They do it to win a fading wreath; we, a wreath that never fades. For my part I run with a clear goal before me; I am like a boxer who does not beat the air; I bruise my own body and make it know its master, for fear that after preaching to others, I should find myself rejected."

The long stay at Corinth crowned by the proconsular decision was one of the watersheds of Paul's life. Southern Galatia had proved his conviction that Gentiles could be full Christians. Corinth proved that Christianity could take root in a great metropolis and from there spread throughout a province. With the freedom won by the legal decision, it was obvious to Paul that his next objective must be the other great metropolis of the Aegean—Ephesus. After that, to Rome and beyond. But while his mind—and his commission—drew him to Rome, his heart cried, "Jerusalem!" He still yearned to preach in the city of his race; the words of the exiled psalmist echoed in his spirit, "If I forget thee, O Jerusalem, let my right hand forget her cunning. If I do not remember thee, let my tongue cleave to the roof of my mouth; if I prefer not Jerusalem above my chief joy."

He decided, therefore, to take a furlough and attend Passover at Jerusalem before settling at Ephesus. And because he remained a Jew, he determined to celebrate his return to the Holy City by a Nazarite vow—the vow of those specially set apart to the Lord under the old order—and let his hair grow for thirty days. Before sailing it would be cut, placed in a bag, and at the Temple he would solemnly cast it on the sacrificial fire.

In March 52, he was ready to leave at the opening of navigation. He had been based at Corinth eighteen months.

For the last time, he gathered at the House of Gaius with the Christians. He knew that backsliding and errors must emerge after he left; he may have had a shrewd suspicion of some of the forms these would take. But for the present all was unity, peace, and love as they met in the *atrium* beside the fountain under flaming torches, for the Lord's Supper conducted according to the tradition which had come to him through the earlier apostles from the Lord Himself: "that the Lord Jesus on the night when He was betrayed took bread, and when He had given thanks, He broke it, and said: 'This is My body, which is given for you. Do this in remembrance of Me.' In the same way also the cup, after supper, saying, 'This cup is the new covenant in My blood. Do this, as often as you drink it, in remembrance of Me.' "

Twenty-Three
ASSAULT ON EPHESUS

When Paul left Corinth, Aquila and Priscilla accompanied him to transfer their tentmaking to Ephesus. This seems to have been a deliberate decision of missionary strategy. While Paul took his furlough, they could prepare for his mission by making friends, and begin a business where he would earn his living.

Together, they walked down to Cenchreae, the Corinthian port for the Aegean, near the narrowest part of the Isthmus where in a few years' time the Romans would attempt to cut a canal by slave labor. Paul entered the synagogue, since he could not do so in Corinth, to discharge his vow by the ceremonial shaving of his head. After a night in the home of a believer named Phoebe, they took the ship through the islands of the Cyclades, beautiful in a wine-colored sea. Paul could enjoy it. Because Acts has no space for his personal feelings he has been considered indifferent or loftily superior to scenery. Yet he writes of the beauty of the stars, how one differs from another in glory; he was aware of the beauty of the human body and he notes how in the great houses he visited some of the vases and bowls were works of art, others merely useful. He was full of the psalms too and on a voyage like this could echo their phrase: "O Lord, how manifold are Thy works! In wisdom hast Thou made them all: the earth is full of Thy riches."

At length they entered the short Gulf of Ephesus which is now silted up. The modern visitor who stands on the shore with his back to the sea, then walks inland across the fields has much the view that Paul had as the ship sailed toward the harbor. On his left were the hills that separated Ephesus from the Gulf of Smyrna; on his right, Mount Coressos and part of the six-mile circuit of walls built by Lysimachus 300 years before, and the watchtower at the seaward end which would later be called Saint Paul's Tower. The ship rounded the point. The breakwater, which worsened the estuary's silting it was built to cure, was now on his left. As the ship threaded its way up the dredged channel, overcrowded with vessels, the city lay all around. Passengers' eyes were dazzled in the sunlight by the massed houses of calcar stone and the marble public buildings which filled the narrow plain and climbed steeply the hundred feet of Mount Pion ahead and the higher Mount Coressos to the right. Paul could see, cut from the hillside of Pion, the theater which would be the scene of one of the great incidents in his story. And on the alluvial plain to the north of Pion, at the foot of a smaller sacred hill, glittered the huge Temple of Artemis, one of the Seven Wonders of the World, burned down by the fanatic Herostratus the night Alexander the Great was born far away in Macedonia, but rebuilt to its former magnificence, a fitting crown for the "first and greatest metropolis of Asia."

Paul settled his friends, an easy task since Jews would always find a welcome from fellow Jews in a strange city. He then left Aquila and Priscilla and carefully did not associate them with his first approach to the synagogue, lest they be compromised should the elders reject him. On the contrary, the elders expressed interest in what Paul had to tell them about Jesus and asked him to stay longer in Ephesus. He declined, but when they came to the harbor to see him off on the pilgrim ship a day or two later, he said: "I will come back to you if it is God's will."

Paul seems to have traveled alone throughout this period of leave. The pilgrim ship took him to Caesarea. He went up to Jerusalem, one pilgrim among many. He kept the Passover and had an affectionate reunion with the Jerusalem church. It was now that he conceived a plan for raising money from all the new churches in Greece and Asia on behalf of the "poor saints in Jerusalem." Such a collection, put aside weekly with prayer, would unite these far-flung churches in a joint enterprise. It would also emphasize the honored position of the city where Jesus had been nailed to the cross, and be of distinct practical help because the Jerusalem church, lacking Gentile members, had less to draw on for charitable purposes, yet could not expect money from charities administered by the Temple authorities. Paul may have had a further hope. The money he brought them could be used not only for the aged and sick but to release some of the able-bodied to undertake missionary work in the East, such as he did in the West; at present the Jerusalem church was not particularly missionary-minded.

Paul did not stay long in Jerusalem but went down to Antioch through Galilee, where he met again many who had seen Jesus alive after His resurrection, and he heard of the death of others. The city of Antioch refreshed him. It was his home. For a man who would not rest when on the mission field, the city where he had taught for a year remained the one place where he could fully relax.

At the end of a short summer, Paul set out early in August 52 for his next term of service. He walked north and took the opportunity of brief but invigorating visits to his old haunts in southern Galatia, through Derbe, Lystra, Iconium, Pisidian Antioch, "strengthening all the disciples," and launching his scheme for the Collection. The Western Text then adds a curious statement which, if not authentic, catches Paul's feelings: "But when Paul wished, according to his own plan, to go to Jerusalem, the Spirit bade him return to Asia.'' Once again, his heart cried, ''Jerusalem!'' while his Lord directed him west. Therefore, he hurried back to Ephesus, taking the direct ''horse road'' over the uplands rather than the main trade route by which the cumbrous camel trains wandered down the valleys through the big cities of the interior. Before winter he was settled in Ephesus.

The first news Paul learned from Priscilla and Aquila was of a brilliant Jew from Alexandria named Apollos, whom they had heard in the Ephesus synagogue.

To their delight, he had begun to speak persuasively, intensively, about Jesus of Nazareth, describing accurately the broad facts of His life, death, and resurrection; Apollos, however, talked as if Jesus were a figure of history rather than Someone still at work in the world. The only baptism Apollos knew was that of John the Baptist, who had baptized men in token of their repentance because the kingdom of God was imminent and urged them to behave like penitents. Priscilla and Aquila invited Apollos home and filled in the gaps, until he learned the secret of the personality re-created by the Spirit of the Father and of Jesus. His teaching now became yet more urgent and persuasive, but he did not wish to stay in Ephesus; · his destination was Achaia. Priscilla and Aquila realized how valuable such a man would be in Corinth, and together with the little knot of believers who had already gathered round them gave him a warm letter of introduction. They could tell Paul how news had already trickled back from Corinth that Apollos ''was a great help to those who through God's grace had become believers. For with his strong arguments he defeated the Jews in public debates, proving from the Scriptures that Jesus is the Messiah.''

The aristocratic, motherly Priscilla and her husband certainly had not been idle during Paul's absence, but they had little conception of developing a church. They were primarily tentmakers, people who loved Jesus and shared the Gospel with their neighbors, whereas Paul was a full-time worker for Jesus who made tents to pay expenses. The limitations of Priscilla's activities are indicated by a curious discovery that Paul made.

As he walked about the pillared *agora* at the foot of Mount Pion or up and down the steep streets, with their sudden views of the sea, Paul was directed by someone who heard what he talked about, to a little group who seemed to believe as he did. He met them, some dozen men, evidently Gentiles, who were believers but rather in the manner of Apollos before he reached Ephesus. Their origin is a mystery, and even in so extensive and populous a city as Ephesus it is odd that Priscilla and Aquila had never come across them. Paul detected at once that their faith, though sincere, was lacking, and the question he put reveals what he thought important.

"Did you receive the Holy Spirit when you became believers?" he asked.

"But we have not even heard there is a Holy Spirit."

"What baptism were you baptized with, then?"

"John's baptism," they replied.

"John baptized with a baptism in token of repentance," Paul said, "and he told the people to put their trust in One who would be coming after him, that is, in Jesus."

They at once asked to be baptized into the Lord Jesus. Paul took them down to the river Cayster and not far away from the magnificence of the Temple of Artemis held a simple ceremony. After they had come up from the water, they knelt and Paul laid his hands on their heads, praying that each might receive the Holy Spirit. Immediately came an extraordinary release of power. It was like the Day of Pentecost in Jerusalem over again. They spoke in tongues, praising and proclaiming the glories of the name of Jesus, then told everybody they met about the truths which suddenly had become clear to them in the Scriptures they already knew. The whole atmosphere was heady with joy. Many years later the survivors read some words in Paul's letter to Ephesus and other Asian churches which must have recalled that day: "Do not get drunk with wine . . . but be filled with the Spirit, addressing one another in psalms and hymns and spiritual songs, singing and making melody to the Lord with all your heart, and for everything giving thanks in the name of our Lord Jesus Christ to God the Father.''

The dozen men, with Aquila and Priscilla and their converts, were already the nucleus of a Christian church when Paul went again into the synagogue to take up the elders' invitation. Regularly, for three months of that winter of 52-53, Paul (in Luke's words) ''spoke with utmost confidence, using both argument and persuasion as he talked of the kingdom of God.'' The Jews were more open-minded than those of Thessalonica or Corinth; they disputed but did not refuse to listen. Many pagans entered the synagogue for the first time and believed, and once again Paul saw Christ break down the dividing wall of hostility between Jew and Gentile.

Obdurate Jews, however, began to gain the upper hand. In early spring of 53, they abused Christ's way until constructive teaching in the synagogue became impossible. Paul withdrew, and all disciples, whether Jew or Gentile, withdrew with him, leaving many empty seats and a distinct drop in the offerings.

A spacious portico in the city gymnasium was offered Paul by a schoolmaster with the apposite name of Tyrannus (''Tyrant''), acquired perhaps as a nickname, though presumably he was now a convert and less irascible; or he may have been descendant of a ''tyrant,'' the honored ruler of a Greek city-state. He needed the portico for his schoolboys at the normal times for teaching, the cool of the day, and, according to the Western Text, Paul had it from eleven o'clock until four, the hours of heat and siesta when all Ephesus shut up shop; even slaves could come to hear him. Then Tyrannus and the boys returned in the remaining hours of light, two or three according to season, while Paul went off to private houses, rich or poor. As Paul would remind the Ephesians, ''You know that I kept nothing from you, that was for your good: I delivered the message to you; I taught you, in public and in your homes; with Jews and pagans alike I insisted on repentance before God and trust in our Lord Jesus." Nor was he ashamed of tears; he wept openly when men spurned Christ. Sometimes Paul would accept an invitation only to discover a trap laid by Jews who wanted to discredit him. He was equal to it. "They curse us and we bless. They slander us and we humbly make our appeal."

His chief work continued in the School of Tyrannus. Part of each session he would instruct converts. The letter to the Ephesians does not specifically remind them what he taught, as he reminded Galatians and Thessalonians, but it must contain echoes of the voice they heard as they sat in the shade of the portico during the heat of the summer days of A.D. 53: "Since you are God's children, you must try to be like Him. Your life must be controlled by love, just as Christ loved us and gave His life for us, as a sweet-smelling offering and sacrifice which pleases God. . . . Submit yourselves one to another, because of your reverence for Christ. Wives submit yourselves to your husbands, as to the Lord. . . . Husbands, love your wives in the same way that Christ loved the church and gave His life for it . . .

"Slaves, obey your human masters, with fear and trembling, and do it with a sincere heart, as though you were serving Christ. Do this not only when they are watching you, to gain their approval, but with all your hearts do what God wants, as slaves of Christ. . . . Masters, behave in the same way toward your slaves, and stop using threats. Remember that you and your slaves belong to the same Master in heaven, who treats everyone alike." Again and again he would emphasize, "Pay close attention to *how* you live. You used to be in the darkness, but since you have become the Lord's people you are in the light. So you must live like people who belong to the light."

Often he would take them into deep waters of Christian doctrine to help them mature in the faith, "reaching to the very height of Christ's stature." Those who were literate would scribble down on scraps of papyrus what he told them, especially the facts about the life of the Lord Jesus. As the months passed, a convert would acquire a whole stack of these papyrus notes and would sew them together. They could not conveniently be made into continuous rolls like the literary works in what was left of the famous Library of Ephesus (most of which had been removed to Pergamum before Roman times) but had separate pages. And thus the codex style, which would be universal for books in centuries to come, began in Ephesus and elsewhere simply as the form of Christian notebook.

Paul held classes like any other teacher except without charge. He also held open meetings when converts brought pagan friends. He began to acquire fame in the city. With converts, especially those who were indeed seeking maturity, a very special relationship grew up. The Ephesians knew him as a lovable man who brought out the best in those who followed him. Nor did they resent his constant call, "Imitate the way I live"; for he added, "as I imitate Christ."

Paul at this time was cheerful, the old tensions eased. The work was happy and Ephesus gave no hint of terrors to come.

Twenty-Four
THE NAME

Philemon, a landowner and slaveholder of Colossae, a small city far up at the base of a sheer mountain on the south of the Lycus near where it flows into a broader valley to join the Meander, came down to Ephesus to superintend the sale of his wool—for Colossae was noted for its glossy dark fleeces— and to worship Artemis at her temple. The temple at Ephesus was the largest building in the western world. The 117 Ionic columns, tall and slender, rose 60 feet and each weighed 15 tons; the column bases of the west portico had human figures sculptured life-size; and gold glittered inside and out. Behind the high altar stood the great Mother Goddess identified by the Greeks with Artemis, by the Romans with Diana, a black meteorite roughly carved in human form but with feet and legs fused together. Breasts by the score covered the torso as befitted the goddess of fertility, though the cult had not developed so fully the sexual extravagances associated with Corinth's Aphrodite.

Cities throughout the province of Asia had contributed to the building of the temple and were represented in the carefully graded hierarchy of virgins and priests. Pagans farther afield regarded it as the center of their worship. Thus religion joined with trade to bring a steady stream of visitors down the valleys of the Cayster and Meander from the interior, or along the coast from north and south. They traded, they worshiped, and returned with little silver or terra-cotta replicas of the image of Artemis to watch over their homes. Philemon, however, went back with a very different loyalty. He came across Paul and was converted. "You owe your very life to me," Paul would remind him long afterward when begging a favor for another convert.

Landowner and missionary became warmly attached, and Paul sent with him a mature, if recent Christian named Epaphras, a native of Colossae but a member of the Ephesian church. Back at Colossae, Philemon let his light glow brightly. His wife, Apphia, and their son, Archippus, probably still a youth and some but not all of their slaves were converted. Neighbors soon joined the church which met in their house. As Paul would write to them: "When the true message, the Good News, first came to you, you heard of the hope it offers. So your faith and love are based on what you hope for which is kept safe for you in heaven. The Gospel is bringing blessings and spreading through the whole world, just as it has among you ever since the day you first heard of the grace of God and came to know it as it really is."

Epaphras did not confine his witness to Colossae. He evidently traveled a time with Paul, who, when writing from prison in Rome, called Epaphras "my fellow prisoner in Christ Jesus." Probably, Epaphras spread the Gospel to cities near Colossae. A few miles northwest, on higher ground overlooking the broader valley, stood the twin cities of Laodicea and Hierapolis, the textile centers close to the petrified cliff of calcified stone which stands out like a white gash, visible for miles. Here churches sprang up, each with its own characteristics. The three were close, with much coming and going. In morning light, Colossians could look up at Laodicea and Hierapolis clear in the sunshine and perhaps pray for the Christians there. In the evenings, with the sun in the west, the twin cities in their turn could see across to Colossae below, and they too would pray.

The process at Colossae and the twin cities was being repeated throughout the province. By visitors returning from Ephesus, or by teams of converts going out at Paul's instigation, the Gospel spread to Smyrna, to the royal city of Pergamum perched on its high rock, to Thyatira the birthplace of Philippian Lydia. From each new center it reached out into the surrounding countryside. Luke did not exaggerate when he said that in the course of two years "all the people who lived in the province of Asia, both Jews and Gentiles, heard the word of the Lord."

Paul longed to go on a circuit to visit them everywhere; but too much was happening in Ephesus.

If Corinth was sex-obsessed, Ephesus, as Shakespeare says, was full of "dark-working sorcerers that change the mind." Magicians treasured scrolls of curses and spells and knew the grisly formulas to make them potent. ("It is a shame even to speak of the things that they do in secret," Paul told his converts.) They sold abracadabras written on strips of papyrus for wear next to the skin to cure aches and pains. ("Let no one deceive *you* with empty words," urged Paul.) It was famous for the study of the occult by those who boasted that they were in league with cosmic "principalities and powers," the superhuman forces of darkness.

Where evil went naked and arrogant, "God did extraordinary miracles by the hand of Paul." In Paul's estimation, workers of miracles and those with gifts of healing were normal in every Spirit-filled church, though less important than apostles, prophets, and teachers. Miracles are not recorded as usual in his own experience. Except for the healing of the lame man at Lystra and possibly (not certainly) the youth who at a later time fell out of the window at Troas, miracles are associated with Paul only at Paphos and Iconium where opposition was blatant, and at Ephesus. They can be no more explained than the miracles of Christ; they stand with His. The form of them at Ephesus, however, was precisely appropriate.

During early mornings, Paul was at his tentmaking and leatherwork in the close atmosphere of a small room in Aquila's house, a sweatband round his head and a cotton apron round his middle. Someone evidently begged him to come and lay hands on a sick or demon-possessed person. He could not go. But he knew that Christ was not limited to the hands of an apostle. If in Galilee he could heal without physical contact when faith rose strong enough, in Ephesus God could do "so much more than we can ever ask for, or even think of, by means of the power working in us"; for that power, as Paul would tell, "is the same as the mighty strength which He used when He raised Christ from death" and put Him above all principalities and powers. Christ was stronger than "any conceivable command, authority, power, or control," with a name "far beyond any name that could ever be used in this world or the world to come."

All this Paul told them. But these ex-pagans who had once worn abracadabras next to the skin needed a focus for weak faith. Paul tore off his sweatband and they took it and laid it on the patient, praying over him in the name of Jesus. He was healed. Many others begged similar aid, and Paul would send a convert, or Timothy who had now joined him, with a sweatband or an apron which he had used. Not that it was mechanical. Jesus in Galilee, when a desperate woman secretly and in faith touched the hem of His garment in the middle of a crowd, knew instantly that strength had been drawn from Him to stop her hemorrhage; so Paul paid heavily in spiritual energy for these Ephesus healings as he gave his whole self in prayer. A comment in another letter and another context suggests he had an exceptional gift for entering into the very presence and need of those, however distant, about who he prayed: "As you meet together, and I meet with you in my spirit, by the power of our Lord Jesus present with us. . . ."

It was the present Lord Jesus rather than the absent Paul of whom the patient and his friends would be aware. Each miracle was a meeting with Someone who could heal the whole man.

The news that men and women were really healed and evil spirits driven out spread like wildfire. Gossip swept the harbor and shops that Paul's sweatrags had a potency far beyond any abracadabra papyrus, that the name of Jesus was the best name of all. A strolling Jewish exorcist named Sceva, who claimed to be a high priest and operated a partnership of humbug with his seven sons, decided to add "the Lord Jesus" to his catalog of spells. The sons went around pronouncing it over clients. Nothing happened for a while. Then they entered the home of a demon-possessed man, stood around, and solemnly said in chorus: "I command you by Jesus whom Paul preaches—"

Before they could say, "Come out of this man," the patient interrupted. With beady eye and the strange voice of a body gripped by devilish forces, he said: "Jesus I know. Paul I am acquainted with. But *who are you?*"

And he jumped on them and beat up the lot, tore their clothes off them and threw them out of his house "naked and wounded."

The incident shook Ephesus. "All the Jews and Gentiles were filled with fear and the name of the Lord Jesus was given greater honor." What is more, it had a decisive effect on the young Christian church. Many believers publicly confessed that they had dabbled in magic and not broken clean. They said they wanted to put an end to the habits of darkness. "And a number of those who practiced magical arts brought their books together and burned them in the sight of all." As rolls of spells and rare cabalistic writings went up in smoke, including some for which magicians would have given high prices, public opinion reckoned that professional secrets worth the very considerable sum of 50,000 silver drachmae were destroyed.

The Gospel's swift advance provoked inevitable counterattack. How it came is uncertain. Paul's story enters a brief though vital period when facts are obscure. Luke turns very discreet. If he wrote Acts during the reign of Nero (A.D. 54-68) and especially if partly to aid Paul's defense in Rome, he needed to avoid angering Nero unnecessarily by any reference, however indirect, to a certain political event in Ephesus which impinged on Paul's affairs though did not affect his case. Paul had no such inhibition, but his epistles and a speech he made about Ephesus are equally tantalizing because his readers and hearers already knew what he had been through, and he was not writing autobiographically.

What happened must be pieced together from clues scattered around the New Testament and in secular history. Much depends on whether Paul wrote Philippians from Ephesus, not Rome, a theory which has attracted important scholars but will remain controversial to the end of time.[20]

A biographer has to decide between slowing to a halt here in a bog of conflicting possibilities which can never be resolved, or striding boldly across by a causeway of conjecture. I choose the second course and, without stepping aside to discuss all the alternatives, tell the story as I see it. Paul's next eighteen months unfolded somewhat as follows, though the tone of assurance in my narrative must not disguise that some of its conclusions are tentative and disputable.

The first counterattack came from unbelieving Jews. Knowing Gallio's decision in Corinth, they could not arraign Paul before the Romans for propagating an unlawful cult, nor apply domestic law since he had removed himself from Jewish jurisdiction. They thought up, however, a charge that could be fatal if proved.

By several decrees of Augustus and others, the Jews had secured imperial protection for money raised to support the Temple in Jerusalem; any tamperer, whether Roman official or private person, incurred the same severe penalties as for sacrilege against pagan temples. All Jews of the Dispersion were expected to pay the voluntary temple tax, and Ephesus, as contemporary evidence shows, was the forwarding center for collections from synagogues throughout the rich province of Asia. In A.D. 53 the treasurers at Ephesus noticed a decided drop and were not slow to appreciate the cause: many Jews in Colossae, Smyrna, Pergamum, and other cities were transferring their contributions to swell Paul's fund for the "poor saints in Jerusalem." Paul had not told converts to stop supporting the Temple and most lacked his conviction that Jewish Christians should not repudiate their heritage; those whom local synagogues had forced out because they followed Jesus Christ as a consequence ceased paying the temple tax.

The decline in funds showed how rapidly the Christian Way had spread among Asian Jews. It also offered Paul's opponents a fresh line of attack. They lodged a formal accusation of temple robbery before the Proconsul of Asia, Marcus Junius Silanus, alleging that Paul had misappropriated money which lawfully should go to the Temple of Jerusalem. Silanus, a member of the imperial family, and thus a cousin of the reigning emperor Claudius and of Nero, was an indolent man but upright; he could not ignore so serious a charge yet would neither hurry to hear the case nor decide it except on the evidence. He ordered Paul's arrest in the autumn of 53.

The slow process of taking evidence throughout Asia gave the prospect of a long imprisonment on remand. Being a Roman citizen, Paul was confined in reasonable comfort in a room of the Praetorian Guard at the proconsular palace. When eventually the case should come to trial, Paul could expect a horrible death if found guilty of such a felony. Unless he appealed to Caesar, he would be thrown into the underground dungeons until the next gladiatorial games at Ephesus, and then, as the last item on the program, he and other criminals, naked and with no weapons but their hands, would be driven with whips into the arena. At the opposite end, wild beasts, starved for two days to ensure that they should be both ravenous and furious, would be released from their cages and the fun would begin.

Meanwhile, his conditions were not oppressive. Timothy and other friends, including Priscilla and Aquila, visited him frequently. He was allowed to go about the city attached by a light chain to a soldier and to continue teaching in the School of Tyrannus for short periods. The pace of life slowed down, and he entered a phase when he was more than ever at peace. He had no sense of frustration and could say at last that he had learned in whatsoever state he was to be content. He had more leisure to pray. Long hours passed as his spirit joined friends far afield—in Galatia, Thessalonica, in Corinth from which already ugly rumors trickled in; and joined the Philippians, who by their prayers had shared his imprisonment at Philippi, brief but violent.

Paul prayed audibly. When he turned to his scrolls of Scripture he read audibly, for the ancients had not discovered the modern knack of reading with the eyes alone. But his prayers were not incantations; he talked quietly, reverently, to Someone present if invisible. Thus each soldier on duty, roster by roster, had an unexpected demonstration of the roots of Paul's personality. They were captivated, too, by his courtesy toward them, his patience and laughter and lack of resentment, his interest in their homes and backgrounds. They heard his conversation with friends and they noted curiously that when friends left he seemed conscious of Someone still in the room. Not surprisingly, the soldiers talked with Paul and thus the whole guard and the proconsular court quickly appreciated that his imprisonment had nothing to do with temple robbery but was for Christ. Before long there were Christians in the palace, and Paul's sentries became his companions in prayer.

On a more exalted level, the Asiarchs, the presidents, and ex-presidents of the provincial council,[21] who would not have stooped to attend teaching at the School of Tyrannus, were intrigued enough by palace gossip to send for him. Several

became friendly, a fact which would have an important consequence. In other ways too, Paul could recognize that "what
has happened to me has really advanced the Gospel." Most of
the local Christians, far from being intimidated, stepped forward to fill the gap. Paul found that his imprisonment gave
"most of the brothers more confidence in the Lord, so that
they grew bolder all the time in preaching the message without fear." And though the false Christians, whose activities
had dogged Paul elsewhere, hurried into Ephesus when they
heard he was confined, and began to set up a rival church
"meaning to stir up fresh trouble for me as I lie in prison,"
Paul did not mind. They could do little harm when he was
still around. "What does it matter? One way or another, in
pretense or in sincerity, Christ is set forth, and for that I
rejoice."

Paul was happy. Whichever way he looked, the future
shone bright.

Twenty-Five
THE HAPPIEST LETTER

A messenger arrived from the Philippian church. His name was Epaphroditus and he brought the sympathy of the Philippians in practical form, not only their assurance of prayers for Paul's release but another gift of money, timely because a prisoner had to pay for his lodging yet no longer could earn wages. Epaphroditus gave all the news, of Luke and the jailer and the rest until Paul longed to be again with them, and made himself Paul's servant, accepting the rough quarters allotted to prisoners' slaves. Then Epaphroditus fell ill and Paul sent verbal warning by a Christian traveler that the Philippians might never see their friend again. But he recovered and Paul determined to send him back.

Paul seized the opportunity of writing to the Philippians to thank them, and to promise them Timothy as soon as Paul's trial was over, to be followed—he was sure—by himself. Next day therefore Timothy's pen was poised to take the happiest letter Paul ever dictated.

"Paul and Timothy, slaves of Christ Jesus, to all the saints in Christ Jesus at Philippi, with the elders and deacons: Grace to you and peace from God our Father and the Lord Jesus Christ.

"I thank my God every time I think of you, and every time I pray for you I pray with joy because of your partnership in the Gospel from the first day until now, being sure of this, that He who has begun a good work in you will go on completing it until the Day of Christ Jesus—it is right for me to think this of you all, because I have you in my heart! . . . "

Words of love and encouragement flowed as fast as Timothy could write them down. Next Paul told how imprisonment had worked for the best and the future held no shadow. He admitted being in a dilemma—whether to long for acquittal and years of fruitful service, or for death and a yet more joyful release. His one fear was lest he might betray Christ publicly in the agony and humiliation of the arena. But their prayers and the inexhaustible strength of the Spirit of Christ Jesus would be decisive: "It is my strong expectancy and my hope that I shall never be ashamed but now, and always, I shall be full of courage so that Christ will be uplifted—whether by my life or by my death. For to me, *to live is Christ and to die is gain—*"

Timothy looked up. Paul had put into a brief, immortal sentence the intense conviction of them both and of so many others, whether in Ephesus, Philippi, or elsewhere: "To live is Christ and to die is gain." Timothy's pen put it on the papyrus. Paul was dictating again, thinking aloud: "I am not sure which I should choose. I am caught from both sides: I want very much to leave this life and be with Christ, which is a far better thing; but it is much more important, for your sake, that I remain alive—I am sure of this. *And so I know that I will stay.* I will stay on with you all, to add to your progress and joy in the faith."

He turned to practical affairs, urging Philippians to live in a way that commended the Gospel to neighbors and urged that they not be terrified by opposition. To make him really happy, they must be one in love and heart and mind, concerned about each other's needs, unselfish, unconceited. He warmed to his theme and, as was his way, moved effortlessly from mundane matters into a massive statement of Christian truth. Whether or not he was quoting a hymn that he and Silas had extemporized in the Philippi jail, his deep feelings expressed themselves, as on other occasions, in words that had the rhythm and clarity of true verse which no translation from the Greek can convey:

"Let this mind be in you
    That was in Christ Jesus,
Who being in the form of God,
Did not cling to His equality with God,
    But emptied Himself—
    Took the form of a servant
And was born in the likeness of men!

"And letting Himself seem a mere man
He humbled Himself,
Took the path of obedience,
    To death—
    Death on a cross!

"Wherefore God has highly exalted Him,
Granted Him a name above every name,
That at the name of Jesus
Every knee should bow,
In heaven, on earth, under the earth;
And every tongue confess
    That Jesus Christ is Lord
    To the glory of God the Father!"

The cell seemed full of music. The whole letter sparkled with golden phrases about Christ forged to emphasize or explain everyday concerns: "That I may *know* Him, and the power of His resurrection and the companionship of His sufferings." "I can do all things through Him who strengthens me." And, in thanking them for the sacrifice they had made to send money: "My God shall supply all your needs according to His riches in glory by Christ Jesus." The letter breathed affection for the Philippians which no distance could weaken and a joy no prison bars could quench. During the dictation, friends and soldiers wandered in and out and thus, in the chill of a late autumn evening as Paul and Timothy neared the end of their work, some of them were the first to hear words that have since warmed and heartened men and women in more than a thousand tongues: "Rejoice in the Lord always. Again I will say, Rejoice! Let your gentleness be known to all. The Lord is near: do not worry about anything, but in everything by prayer and supplication with thanksgiving, make your requests known to God. And the peace of God which passes all understanding, shall guard your hearts and minds in Christ Jesus.

"Finally, brothers"—and Paul's call to the Philippians lights up the furnishing of his own mind, for otherwise his words were humbug, and Timothy and the Ephesians would have known it—"Finally, whatever is true, whatever is honorable, what is just, what is pure, what is lovely, what is gracious, if there is any excellence, anything praiseworthy, fill your thoughts with these things. What you have learned and received from me, and heard and seen in me, do: and the God of peace shall be with you."

Paul's "finally," the second of the letter, did not bring it to a close; as in the letter of Galatia, if for a different reason, he was reluctant to break off his message to "my brethren dearly loved and longed for, my joy and crown." But at last he reached the farewells. "Greet every saint in Christ Jesus. The brethren who are with me greet you." Paul's Christian guards begged to be included, the soldiers of Ephesus to the soldiers of Philippi. So Paul added: "All the saints greet you, especially those of the Caesar household.

"The grace of our Lord Jesus Christ be with your spirit."

In the course of his letter, Paul had said: "I am not already made to send money: "My God shall supply all your needs according to His riches in glory by Christ Jesus." The letter breathed affection for the Philippians which no distance could weaken and a joy no prison bars could quench. During the dictation, friends and soldiers wandered in and out and thus, in the chill of a late autumn evening as Paul and Timothy neared the end of their work, some of them were the first to hear words that have since warmed and heartened men and women in more than a thousand tongues: "Rejoice in the Lord always. Again I will say, Rejoice! Let your gentleness be known to all. The Lord is near: do not worry about anything, but in everything by prayer and supplication with thanksgiving, make your requests known to God. And the peace of God which passes all understanding, shall guard your hearts and minds in Christ Jesus.

"Finally, brothers"—and Paul's call to the Philippians lights up the furnishing of his own mind, for otherwise his words were humbug, and Timothy and the Ephesians would have known it—"Finally, whatever is true, whatever is honorable, what is just, what is pure, what is lovely, what is gracious, if there is any excellence, anything praiseworthy, fill your thoughts with these things. What you have learned and received from me, and heard and seen in me, do: and the God of peace shall be with you."

Paul's "finally," the second of the letter, did not bring it to a close; as in the letter of Galatia, if for a different reason, he was reluctant to break off his message to "my brethren dearly loved and longed for, my joy and crown." But at last he reached the farewells. "Greet every saint in Christ Jesus. The brethren who are with me greet you." Paul's Christian guards begged to be included, the soldiers of Ephesus to the soldiers of Philippi. So Paul added: "All the saints greet you, especially those of the Caesar household.

"The grace of our Lord Jesus Christ be with your spirit."

In the course of his letter, Paul had said: "I am not already that city of unbridled love. Paul wrote a letter of advice which has not survived; and when Timothy set off on his promised visit to Philippi, Paul instructed him, young as he was, to go on afterward and sort out the Corinthians' muddle before Paul should return once more on his way to Macedonia.

Paul had not yet gone upcountry when Ephesus was stunned by the assassination of Proconsul Silanus.

Some weeks previously, Claudius Caesar had died, poisoned by his cousin and fourth wife Agrippina; they were both great-grandchildren of Augustus, and Claudius had adopted Nero, her son by a previous marriage, as his heir. As she intended, Nero was immediately proclaimed princeps or emperor. Agrippina feared that her cousin Silanus, who had as good a title in blood as Nero, would plot to avenge Claudius, avenge his own elder brother whose suicide Agrippina had provoked, and seize the throne by murdering both mother and son. To forestall this, she made Silanus the first victim of the new reign. At her orders the knight Publius Celer and the freedman Helius, controllers of the emperor's personal property in Asia, "administered poison to the Proconsul at a banquet," records Tacitus, "in a manner too open to escape detection."

Celer and Helius took over the province pending the arrival of a new proconsul, and proceeded to liquidate their enemies. No man, however unpolitical, who was reckoned to have been protected by Silanus could count life secure; and that included Paul.

His upcountry tour was thus shadowed by menace. When he and Sosthenes, the Macedonians Aristarchus and Gaius, and possibly Apollos traveled from city to city they suffered more than the hardships, heat, and fatigue of the road. They were not only in peril from implacable Jews, from worshipers of Artemis who resented conversions to Christ, although Paul never insulted the goddess; they had to contend with the contempt and ill will of petty officials anxious to shed their former loyalty to Silanus. "To this very hour," Paul wrote shortly afterward, "we go hungry and thirsty; we are clothed in rags; we are beaten (*or* knocked about); we wander from place to place, we work hard to support ourselves. When we are cursed, we bless; when we are persecuted, we endure; when we are insulted we answer back with kind words." They were looked on as scum of the earth; people felt well rid of them. But others listened. Doors were open, opportunities unlimited.

The tour ended prematurely because of more grave news from Corinth. Paul received a report that a Corinthian Christian had committed incest in a manner disgusting even to pagans in sex-mad Corinth; and this man had not been expelled from the brotherhood. Paul saw the church rapidly becoming a byword to the heathen. Then a letter reached him upcountry from the elders of Corinth seeking clarification of several matters he had discussed in the letter which has not survived. But they showed no compunction about the disgraceful state of affairs.

Corinth had never been long out of his mind. The hardships of pioneering did not blunt his responsibility for districts already worked: on top of everything else, he once wrote, "there is the daily pressure of my concern for all the churches." He now decided to return to Ephesus and devote the next days or weeks to the composition of a letter to deal thoroughly with the situation, and bring the Corinthians to a better mind before he visited them again.

Twenty-Six
"THE GREATEST OF THESE . . ."

When Paul arrived in Ephesus, several Corinthians awaited him, "Chloe's people," either members of a family or traders of a firm, to give him a yet more disquieting report.

Christians were suing one another in pagan courts, and the church was rent by quarreling. Some boasted they were "Paul's party," others that their loyalty was to Apollos, some were "Peter's men," whether converts of an unrecorded visit or merely using his name. And one or two boasted that they owed nothing to any apostle: "I belong to Christ." With quarreling went arrogance, as if they were superior in the eyes of God and man; and there were other faults until Paul wept. There could be no greater contrast between the happy letter to Philippi and the pain he faced in writing to the Corinthians, "with a greatly troubled and distressed heart, and with many tears, not to make you sad but to make you realize how much I love you all."

Corinth was displaying the paradox at the heart of Paul's activity. For him, the aim and the possibility was every Christian morally and spiritually perfect in Christ; yet in each church human weakness marred, false teaching confused. Christ had warned it would be so, for He wanted the love of free men, not puppets on a string, but Paul took it personally and rather hard when his converts preferred dissensions to unity, self-advancement to service, half-love to full devotion despite Christ's willingness to give every fine quality and all strength.

Paul settled down to dictate to Sosthenes an expression of gratitude and faith astounding in the circumstances, then went straight to an appeal for unity: "Is Christ divided? Was *Paul* crucified for you? Or were you baptized in the name of Paul?" He was glad he had baptized nobody himself except Crispus and Gaius; he added as an afterthought the household of Gaius but could remember no other. "Christ did not send me to baptize but to preach the Gospel, and not with eloquent wisdom, lest the cross of Christ be emptied of its power." Paul pressed the point and emphasized, as if to lift the whole discussion at once to a higher plane, the stark contrast between the world's philosophies, which seek goodness by the application of human thought and effort, and the Gospel which philosophy and common sense regarded as ludicrous: "God in His wisdom made it impossible for men to know Him by means of their own wisdom. Instead, God decided to save those who believe, by means of the 'foolish' message we preach. Jews want miracles for proof and Greeks look for wisdom. As for us, we proclaim 'Christ on the cross,' a message that is offensive to the Jews and nonsense to the Gentiles, but for those whom God has called, both Jews and Gentiles, this message is Christ who is the power of God and the wisdom of God."

The foolishness of God was wiser than men, the weakness of God was stronger than men. By the time Paul had unfolded a long argument, he had made plain that no man could discover God by force of intellect. Had Paul known what marvels of knowledge would emerge in the next 2,000 years, that the human mind and anatomy were infinitely complex, the universe so vast that the earth spun as a mere grain in space, he would have said the same, and considered it ironic that the more men discovered the insignificance of their planet the more highly they would rate themselves, the more sure that they could explain all without God. They knew nothing. "The wisdom we speak is the wisdom of God, secret, hidden, which God prepared for our glory before time began; which none of the rulers of this age has known, for if they had known they would not have crucified the Lord of glory. . . . The man who is merely natural does not receive the things of the Spirit of God; they are ridiculous to him and he is not able to know them because they can only be understood by a spiritual man. 'For who,' " Paul quoted from Isaiah, " 'has known the mind of the Lord? Who can instruct him?' But we have the mind of Christ."

Having forced the Corinthians, when his letter should be read aloud, to face the rest of it on the plane of the spiritual, not the merely human, Paul disposed of the question of party spirit fairly rapidly by showing that each apostle or messenger was a servant in the Lord's field—"I planted, Apollos watered, but God gave the increase"—or a workman building His temple. As for the arrogance that went with party spirit, "None of you should be proud of one man and despise the other. Who made you superior to the others? Didn't God give you everything you have? Well then, how can you brag, as if what you have were not a gift?" Paul slipped into irony that ran close to sarcasm, "You are rich already! Without us you reign as kings!" In contrast, the apostles were like despised criminals who were sent last into the arena to die. "We are fools for Christ's sake, but you are 'wise in Christ.' We are weak, but you are strong. You are held in honor, but we in disrepute," and he described the rough treatment on his missionary tour. "I am saying all this," he added, "not just to make you ashamed but to bring you, as my dearest children, to your senses." He would soon be with them and deflate the arrogant. "What do you wish? Shall I come to you with a rod, or with love in a spirit of gentleness?"

By now, when he seems to have stopped dictating until at

least the next day, it was clear that this letter would be longer by far than any he had written to date. It might also be his last, were he to be engulfed in the political storm which threatened Ephesus. It bore therefore the aspect of a testament.

He knew that his writing held equal authority with his speaking, the authority of an apostle and of a prophet, as truly commissioned to convey God's word as was Isaiah or Jeremiah. His opponents rated this conviction boastful but, he would tell the Corinthians, he had nothing of which to boast: "I am the least of the apostles, unfit to be called an apostle, because I persecuted the church of God." As an apostle and prophet, he must give them the word of God. Like Isaiah or Jeremiah, however, he must speak to the immediate condition of his hearers, and when he contemplated what to say in correcting Corinthian abuse of sex, he suffered uncertainty. In this letter to Corinth, and in no other, he is ready to admit that one or two of his judgments lack the authority of a clear ruling given by Jesus, and though Paul believes he interprets the Spirit's wisdom he will not go beyond the phrases, "But in my judgment . . . and I *think* I have the Spirit of God." The very uncertainty underlines Paul's profound belief that his writings had the same authority which impelled his predecessors, using a different form, to cry, "Thus saith the Lord."

Like them, he had a hard message. With utmost distaste, he had to look at apostasy and uncleanness and root it out. The Corinthian church must expel the incestuous man and send him back to the world where Satan reigns. Paul's actual words, "Consigned to Satan for the destruction of the body, so that his spirit may be saved on the Day of the Lord," caused confusion in the centuries ahead, and were misinterpreted to justify the burning of heretics; but Paul's concerns were equally the purity of the church and the good of the offender. When, later on, he heard that the punishment had been effective, he was almost afraid lest he had been too ruthless. "Something very different is called for now," he wrote in his next letter. "You must forgive the offender and put new heart into him; the man's sorrow must not be made so severe as to overwhelm him. I urge you therefore to assure him of your love for him by a formal act."

And they must all flee fornication.

To the church in a Corinth dominated by the sexual license of Aphrodite's temple Paul determined to stress the importance of sexual purity. "Every other sin that a man can commit is outside the body; but the fornicator sins against his own body. Do you not know that your body is a shrine of the indwelling Holy Spirit, and the Spirit is God's gift to you? You do not belong to yourselves; you were bought at a price. Then honor God in your body."

He agreed with those who in their letter had asked if it were not better for a man never to touch a woman. Anxious to conciliate the ascetic group within the church (possibly those who called themselves "Christ's party") and to preserve unity, he admitted his preference in the present distresses, and because the Lord would return soon, for an unattached state like his own; but he refused to let them think marriage or sexual relations were sinful in themselves. Nor must married couples suppose they would serve God better if they separated. Paul's words on chastity, fornication, and marriage, the subject of endless discussion and commentary ever since, have left him with somewhat of a reputation as a woman-hater, and he certainly betrays traces of impatience with woman as a sex. Yet a close study shows his acute awareness that in all consideration of sex, in its dignity and beauty as much as in its abuse, man and woman matter equally. Indeed, he takes a view exactly opposite to those in later ages who condemned a "fallen woman" while condoning the man provided he were discreet. Paul's condemnation is reserved for the man.

In his discussion of relations between man and woman, the keynote is his desire to help rather than to harass: "I am saying this because I want to help you. I am not trying to put restrictions on you. Instead, I want you to do what is right and proper, and give yourselves completely to the Lord's service without reservation." The good of all and the glory of God were the decisive factors, and equally when he turned to problems such as whether to eat meat which had been consecrated to idols before being sold or served. In another long, careful discussion, he showed that Christians were free to do as they liked, but such freedom must never hurt others. An idol was a mere piece of wood or stone, yet pagans—and many a new Christian convert—thought otherwise. If therefore the butcher, or the host, should make plain that the meat had been offered to an idol, the mature Christian should refuse it, not for his own conscience's sake but others, lest the weak brother or the pagan suppose the Lord Jesus is on supping terms with gods and goddesses.

"Whether you eat or drink, or whatever you are doing, do all for the honor of God: give no offense to Jews, or Greeks, or to the church of God." Paul told them that he tried to be helpful to everyone at all times, to meet them halfway, to please them, "not anxious for my own advantage but for the advantage of everyone else, so that they may be saved. Imitate me, then, just as I imitate Christ."

When he dealt with their questions regarding the form and order of a Christian church, sorting out their aberrations, correcting and criticizing but praising where he could, his aim was to urge them toward building up the church and not selfishly to please themselves. They should recognize that they were Christ's body "and each of you a limb or organ of it." In a physical body there were different functions, each indispensable to the other. "If the body were all eye, how could it hear? If the body were all ear, how could it smell? . . . God has combined the various parts of the body, giving special honor to the humbler parts, so that there might be no sense of division in the body, but all its organs might feel the same concern for one another. If one organ suffers, they all suffer together. If one flourishes, they all rejoice together."

In the same way, God had distributed gifts in the body of

Christ, the church: first and highest, apostles; then, prophets; next, teachers, workers of miracles, healers, helpers, and administrators, speakers in tongues, and interpreters of tongues. And some were appointed to very humble functions and should thereby be honored, not despised.

Paul said that all should aim at the higher gifts. Then he added: "And now I will show you the best way of all."

Days had passed in dictating, each passage in the letter needing deep thought and prayer. Paul had covered many subjects, propounded hard sayings, and passed through many emotions. Much of his teaching had related to the theme of love, the problems caused by Corinth's obsession with *eros*, sexual love. He now wanted to leave them with a true understanding of that higher, peculiarly Christian love which the disciples termed *agapē*. If he could convey the meaning of this kind of love, they would indeed have an example to aim at, a way by which to live.

His mind turned to all he knew of the Lord Jesus, both from the traditions of the life lived in Palestine and from the daily companionship of the Spirit of Jesus guiding and training through the years. "Imitate me as I imitate Christ," Paul had told the Corinthians. Somewhere in Ephesus or in the hills overlooking the sea, alone with his Master, Paul looked once more at Perfect Love. He could perceive Him only dimly, as if through a colored glass or reflected in a metal mirror, and longed for the day when he would know the Lord Jesus as fully as the Lord knew him.

The Lord Jesus—patient and kind; never jealous, not possessive, envying no one. Not boastful nor anxious to impress; not arrogant, proud, or haughty, nor giving Himself airs. Not rude or discourteous. The Lord Jesus did not insist on His own way, pursue selfish advantage, claim His rights. He was not touchy or irritable or quick to take offense. He did not brood on injuries, bear a grudge, or show resentment; He did not gloat over other men's sins, feel pleased when others went wrong, nor did He condone injustice. Instead, He was gladdened by goodness, delighted in it, and always took the part of truth. Yet He was slow to expose, could overlook faults. There was no limit to His endurance, no end to His willingness to trust, no fading of His hope.

With the face of Perfect Love filling his mind, Paul resumed dictating, to deliver the best known of all his works, a prose poem which, besides its profound spiritual value, entitles Paul to rank among the greatest masters of literature. Numerous translations have unfolded shades of meaning; every generation finds apposite words to express the Greek, yet the English language has few finer passages than the rendering of the thirteenth chapter of First Corinthians in the *King James Version*:[22]

"Though I speak with the tongues of men and of angels, and have not charity, I am become as sounding brass, or a tinkling cymbal. And though I have the gift of prophecy, and understand all mysteries, and all knowledge; and though I have all faith, so that I could remove mountains, and have not charity, I am nothing. And though I bestow all my goods to feed the poor, and though I give my body to be burned, and have not charity, it profiteth me nothing.

"Charity suffereth long, and is kind; charity envieth not; charity vaunteth not itself, is not puffed up. Doth not behave itself unseemly, seeketh not her own, is not easily provoked, thinketh no evil; rejoiceth not in iniquity but rejoiceth in the truth. Beareth all things, believeth all things, hopeth all things, endureth all things.

"Charity never faileth; but whether there be prophecies, they shall fail; whether there be tongues, they shall cease; whether there be knowledge, it shall vanish away. For we know in part, and we prophesy in part. But when that which is perfect is come, then that which is in part shall be done away. When I was a child, I spake as a child, I understood as a child, I thought as a child; but when I became a man, I put away childish things. For now we see through a glass darkly;

but then face to face: now I know in part; then shall I know even as also I am known.

"And now abideth faith, hope, charity, these three; but the greatest of these is charity."

Twenty-Seven
AFFLICTION IN ASIA

One major Corinthian problem remained. Some of them said that Christ's blessings were for this life only: no life after death, no resurrection into eternity.

As Paul thought out the best words to demolish this doubt which infected Christians, it looked peculiarly pertinent to his own situation. The storm clouds were gathering fast. One by one those whom Silanus had favored or protected were murdered or thown into jail. Paul knew his turn might come; he faced death daily, stood in jeopardy every hour. It was like the thunderclouds he must often have watched from the city walls high up on Mount Coressos at the turn of the season, black and threatening, deepening each minute but giving no indication whether the torrential rain would pass by or drench him. "A wide door for effective work has opened to me," he told Corinth, "but there are many adversaries." His opponents watched their opportunity to spring.

If he became a mangled corpse, a mess of blood and sinew to be pushed off the arena floor and piled in a cart while slaves sprinkled sand ready for the next item, was that the end?

Paul saw that the question was bound up with the resurrection of Christ. The two were mutual. He therefore reminded

428

the Corinthians that he had taught them categorically, as a first and foremost component of his Good News, how Christ had not only "died for our sins" but had been "raised to life again on the third day," at Passover time in Jerusalem twenty-five years ago. He listed the witnesses who had seen Him, "most of whom are still living." He reminded them that he too was a witness of the Risen Christ, how meeting Christ had revolutionized Paul, so that "I worked harder than any of them, though it was not I but the grace of God which is with me." If he and the other witnesses were proclaiming Christ as risen from the dead, "how can some of you say that there is no resurrection of the dead? But if there is no resurrection of the dead, then Christ has not been raised."

If Christ had never, in precise historic fact, risen from the dead then Paul's preaching and the Corinthians' faith were futile: "You are still in your sins." Conversely, if no dead are ever raised, Paul had willfully misrepresented God, had committed perjury by swearing that Christ had risen. And those who had died believing in Him had perished utterly. If it were all a mere shadowy hope, "if our love in Christ is good for this life only, and no more," wrote Paul, "then we deserve more pity than anyone else in all the world."

"But Christ *has* been raised from the dead!" Sheer dogmatic certainty rang through Paul's words, backed by the Corinthains' knowledge of his moral integrity and of his careful examination of the evidence. They knew that no man who so hated deception, who consciously lived as responsible to the all-seeing God of truth, who had taught them new conceptions of goodness and honesty, could propagate a lie as a pious way of explaining that Jesus survived as a Spirit. Paul believed the murdered Jesus had stepped out of the grave.

When Paul turned to forestall the inevitable further question, "How can the dead be raised to life? What kind of body will they have?" he rejected the coarse materialism that supposed flesh, blood, and bones could inherit the kingdom of God. "You fool!" was his reaction to anyone with such an idea. Instead, the continuity and transformation was like seed and crop. "When you plant a seed in the ground, it does not sprout to life unless it dies. And what you plant in the ground is a bare seed, perhaps a grain of wheat, or of some other kind, not the full-bodied plant that will grow up. . . . This is how it will be when the dead are raised to life. When the body is buried it is mortal; when raised it will be immortal. When buried it is ugly and weak; when raised it will be beautiful and strong. When buried it is a physical body, when raised it will be a spiritual body. . . . We will wear the likeness of the Man from heaven."

Paul's contemplation of so glorious a future carried him into another sublime passage, as full of literary beauty as of prophecy. And once again its concluding words, the last of the entire epistle except for a few practical points about immediate arrangements, have never been more finely rendered into English than by the *King James Version*: "Behold, I show you a mystery; we shall not all sleep, but we shall all be changed, in a moment, in the twinkling of an eye, at the last trump: for the trumpet shall sound, and the dead shall be raised incorruptible, and we shall be changed. . . . So when this corruptible shall have put on incorruption, and this mortal shall have put on immortality, then shall be brought to pass the saying that is written, 'Death is swallowed up in victory. O death, where is thy sting? O grave, where is thy victory?' The sting of death is sin; and the strength of sin is the law. But thanks be to God, which giveth us the victory through our Lord Jesus Christ.

"Therefore, my beloved brethren, be ye steadfast, unmovable, always abounding in the work of the Lord, forasmuch as ye know that your labor is not in vain in the Lord."

In the months following his dispatch of the letter to Corinth, Paul himself needed every ounce of that final exhortation and encouragement.

The storm broke. Sometime at the end of 54 or early in 55 Paul was swept into calamity. He had planned to stay in Ephesus until spring, seizing the evangelistic opportunities presented by a great pagan festival and by the public's unhappiness and disquiet after the murder of Silanus, and then to return to Macedonia; he had abandoned his intention of revisiting Corinth immediately, having written instead, and would go there after Macedonia. All this was thrown in the melting pot. A time of terror, such as even the hard campaigning Paul had never known, brought him to the sharpest crisis of his life, ''the affliction we experienced in Asia.''

''We were so utterly, unbearably crushed that we despaired of life itself.'' ''Pressed above measure, above strength.'' ''Completely overwhelmed, more than we could bear.'' ''The things we had to undergo were more of a burden than we could carry, so that we despaired of coming through alive.'' ''Crushed, overwhelmed, and desperate. I feared I would never live through it.'' Thus translators attempt to convey what Paul wrote shortly afterward. It can never be known exactly what happened. He was probably arrested and beaten with rods severely, possibly tortured, for the murderers of Silanus were administrating Asia arbitrarily. Thrown into a dungeon, he probably fell grievously ill with a recurrence of the ''thorn in the flesh,'' for the memory of this terrible time lay fresh in mind on the occasion when he described how the ''thorn'' had buffeted him until he implored the Lord to remove it.

More than this, he passed into mental and spiritual affliction. Research cannot uncover the details, but certain clues are available. Ephesus was the center of witchcraft. No sophisticated modern dare dismiss the possibility that a curse was laid on Paul causing severe mental agony. Those who have known something of the mysterious powers of voodoo in tribal communities or experienced the mystifying exploitation of evil in certain types of western spiritualism cannot lightly eliminate this theory, which would help to explain a choice of words in the famous passage, "Who shall separate us from the love of Christ?" which Paul composed about eighteen months later: "I am convinced that there is nothing in death or life, in the *realm of spirits or superhuman powers* . . . in the forces of the universe, in heights or depths—nothing in all creation that can separate us from the love of God in Christ Jesus our Lord."

Whether or not Paul suffered from sorcery as well as brutality, it seems unquestionable that he descended into a spiritual valley in which his soul endured stresses that nearly shattered him. He had the taut nerves of a genius, on which physical or mental suffering—his own or others—grated with a roughness unknown to less sensitive men. He recoiled from pain, though never fleeing; felt hurt when abused, though bearing no resentment; grew agitated when a church was threatened by those he had won to faith: "Who is weak and I do not feel weak with him? Who is made to stumble and I do not burn with indignation?" In the slime and stench of an Ephesus dungeon, his mind turned restlessly: the problems of Corinth, the problem of evil, the apparently limitless resources of those who hated Christ. "Perplexed; afflicted; persecuted; struck down" are some of the words he uses. As distress increased, he seems to have entered a dark night of the soul and suffered a loss of will.

In a notable section of the letter to the Romans, when the events at Ephesus were still recent, he uses terms about himself which unless purely rhetorical suggest he had been through deep waters of spiritual agony. Though his words are often assumed to describe the period before the Damascus Road, a closer study indicates that they refer to Paul the Christian, and unless he is saying his mental conflict continued endlessly, which the context denies, he would seem to be drawing general conclusions from a particular struggle. "I cannot understand my own behavior," he writes. "I fail to carry out the things I want to do, and I find myself doing the very things I hate. . . . I know that nothing good dwells within me, that is, in my flesh. I can *will* what is right, but I cannot do it. . . . Every single time I want to do good it is something evil that comes to hand." Paul delights in the Law of God; yet sin battles against this and makes him "a prisoner of that law of sin which lives inside my body. What a wretched man that I am! Who will rescue me?"

"O wretched man that I am! Who shall deliver me?" The cry echoed through nights of pain and despair at Ephesus until profound realization of weakness led to a surge forward in the Spirit: "Who shall deliver me? I thank God through Jesus Christ our Lord!"

As Paul slipped into suffering, to a depth he had never previously known, he began to learn more of the power of Jesus: "He said to me, 'My grace is sufficient for you, for My strength is made perfect in weakness.' " "Blessed be the God and Father of our Lord Jesus Christ," he wrote specifically of this Ephesus crisis, "the Father of mercies and God of all comfort, who comforts us in all our affliction," so that Paul could comfort others in any sorrow, with the comfort he had received himself. He realized, as never before, that he was sharing in Christ's sufferings so that he might share Christ's comfort. He saw the purpose of it all, that he might describe to his converts the reality of Christ's extraordinary power and love.

"It has taught us not to rely on ourselves but only on God, who raises the dead to life." God had delivered and would deliver; Paul could never doubt this again, as the future would show. Against the record of calamity, he could write the assurance of rescue. Against the word *afflicted,* he wrote "but not crushed"; against *perplexed,* "not driven to despair"; "persecuted but not forsaken, struck down but not destroyed; always carrying in the body the death of Jesus, so that the life of Jesus may be manifested in our bodies." He repeats it: "Always being given up to death for Jesus' sake, so that the life of Jesus may be manifested." Paul's difficulties and pain actually helped Jesus to show Himself, to spread abroad the aroma of His love, as the scent of rose petals grows stronger when they are crushed.

"So we do not lose heart." Paul had been tempted. Despair had nearly cut him off before some of his finest work. But now he could face whatever might come. "Though our outer nature is wasting away, our inner nature is being renewed every day. For this slight momentary affliction is preparing for us an eternal weight of glory beyond all comparison, because we look not to the things that are seen but to the things that are unseen; for the things that are seen are transient, but the things that are unseen are eternal."

Physical deliverance, the rescue from certain death to unconditional liberty, came somehow through the intervention, at fearful risk, of Aquila and Priscilla. They were ready to die in Paul's place. "Give my greetings to Priscilla and Aquila," Paul wrote after they had returned to Rome next year. "They risked their necks to save my life, and not I alone but all the Gentile congregations are grateful to them." He emerged before the spring of 55, weak in health but purified in spirit.

Almost immediately after release, his life was in peril again. This time Luke could describe the incident in detail, for the riot in Ephesus had nothing to do with Silanus and showed Roman government at its best.

Every spring devotees of the Mother Goddess converged on Ephesus for Artemisia, the great festival which worship, trade, and gaiety made the highlight of the city's year. Processions marched from the Temple of Artemis to the north gate, on below the theater and along the marble way, then up the hill by the city hall and out by the Magnesia Gate. Between excitements the crowds thronged the streets, and this was the coming opportunity which had caused Paul to decide not to leave Ephesus earlier.

It was also the prime sales season for the important guild of silversmiths, whose replicas of the Artemis idol were normally in heavy demand. This year 55, however, the silversmiths suffered a slump, a remarkable testimony to the success of Paul's mission. Hundreds of visitors were refusing to buy; some because, as Christians, they were treating Artemisia merely as an annual outing, a chance to hear Paul again and meet fellow believers but no longer to purchase silver goddesses to take to the temple for blessing; and others because they were converted to Christ during the festival.

The silversmiths had lost sales enough already. One of the biggest employers, Demetrius, in a rage called a protest meeting of his own craftsmen and others, including presumably some Christians who gave Luke an eyewitness account. What Demetrius quite intended to achieve is not clear, for his speech so inflamed his hearers that matters were soon out of his hands.

He made no bones about the chief reason for his fury, whatever lip worship he gave the goddess. "Men," he cried, "you know that from this trade comes our prosperity. And you see and hear that not only in Ephesus but almost everywhere in Asia this fellow Paul has persuaded and turned away masses of people, telling them that handmade gods are not gods at all. And there's danger that not only will this trade of ours fall into disrepute, but the temple of the great goddess Artemis will count for nothing, and her greatness be destroyed, she whom all Asia and the inhabited world worship!"

At that the audience roared the city's worship cry: "Great is Artemis of the Ephesians!" They poured into the street and began to run where citizens instinctively converged in time of emergency—the theater cut from the hillside of Pion, meeting place of the monthly Popular Assembly which every adult male might attend. As they ran up the steep street toward the entrance at the top, shouting, "Great is Artemis of the Ephesians," people dropped what they were doing and joined the rush, certain that a great danger or a great decision must be at hand. Some of the silversmiths seized two of Paul's companions, the Macedonians Aristarchus and Gaius, and swept them along. More and more citizens spilled through the gate at the upper end of the theater and ran down the gangways until tier after tier filled up, while below on the stage Demetrius and his men swayed around Aristarchus and Gaius. On the scaffolding above the proscenium (the theater was being enlarged and improved throughout Paul's period in Ephesus), workmen laid down their tools and looked on astonished.

When Paul in another part of the city heard what had happened, he determined to go to the theater and address the crowd. Apart from intervening to rescue his travel companions, he saw a supreme opportunity to reach the biggest audience of his life. The theater was filling rapidly and it held 19,000. The acoustics were marvelous. Once he had stilled the people, as he knew he could, he could preach about Jesus.

The disciples implored him not to go. While they were still arguing, messengers came from the Asiarchs, the eminent friends Paul had made during his first imprisonment. They too begged him not to risk his life in the theater. His respect for their understanding of the crowd's mood caused him reluctantly to abandon the plan.

Meanwhile in the theater, as Luke dryly describes, "Some cried one thing and some another, for the assembly was in confusion, and most of them did not know why they had come together." Leading Jews feared a pogrom and hastily put up a spokesman, Alexander. Thrusting his way on to the stage, he lifted his hand for silence, meaning to tell them the Jews were not the culprits and hated Paul as much as they.

The crowd recognized him as a Jew. Someone shouted at him, "Great is Artemis of the Ephesians!" "Great is Artemis of the Ephesians" yelled the rest. Mass hysteria swept the tiers. The worship cry came again and again until the entire theater reverberated with rhythmic chanting of four Greek words, "*Megalē hē Artemis Ephesiōn!*"

"*Megalē hē Artemis Ephesiōn!*" The cry echoed across the city and over the water to the ships in the harbor and across to the hills beyond the gulf. They could hear it in the Temple of Artemis. The chant floated to soldiers on the walls along the height of Coressos as they looked down amazed. In the theater itself all but the lowest tiers had a splendid view of the lower city with the wide porticoed street to the harbor gate, and of the gulf, but they had no eyes for these. Work lost, dinners uncooked, the fierce heat of the sun meant nothing. The monotonous and now almost meaningless cry went on and on, "Great is Artemis of the Ephesians!"

The Chief Executive of Ephesus, holder of the highest elected office and responsible for civic order, was thoroughly alarmed. The Romans objected to any irregular assembly. They could treat one that behaved like this as a riot, and punish the city by canceling yet more of what little self-government remained. He was, however, a man of sense. He waited until the vast concourse should exhaust itself. For two hours, while the sun moved steadily along the ridge of Coressos, the chant drummed through his head.

Then he thrust himself forward, put up his hand. The crowd knew him as the one official who rightly should conduct the business of a Popular Assembly. The noise died away.

"Men of Ephesus," he said, his voice sounding back from the specially toned bronze and clay vessels placed round the theater. "What man is there anywhere who does not know that the Ephesians' city is temple warden of the great goddess Artemis and her image which fell from heaven? This being beyond dispute, your proper course is to calm down and do nothing rash. These men who you dragged here are not temple robbers, nor blasphemers of the goddess. If therefore Demetrius and his fellow craftsmen have a case against anyone, there are assizes and there are proconsuls"—a tactful admission that since Silanus' death his murderers were joint rulers, *de facto* proconsuls—"so let them accuse each other there. But if you have something general to discuss, it must be settled in the lawful Assembly. We are in danger of being charged with riot because of what has happened today. There is no excuse for this illegal and uproarious concourse and we shall not be able to give a reason for it."

Having made them thoroughly ashamed of themselves and produced a total anticlimax, he declared the assembly closed.

Twenty-Eight
A TREATISE FOR ROME

After the uproar ceased, Paul knew it was time to move on, as he had always intended after Artemisia. His plan included a return visit to Macedonia and southern Greece, then Jerusalem with some Asian and European converts to hand over the Collection. "After I have been there, I must also see Rome."

Before the riot, being nervous lest his letter to Corinth had been too strong and had discouraged his "children," he had dispatched young Titus of Antioch to investigate the situation, Timothy being detained in Macedonia. Titus was to return, not to Ephesus but to Troas where Paul intended to preach before crossing to Europe. When Paul reached Troas, almost certainly by sea, he found an excellent opportunity for preaching "but my mind could not rest because I did not find my brother Titus there. So I took leave of them and went on to Macedonia" to find Titus, who would be coming up through Greece.

In Philippi, Paul's first visit since the flogging, the church was enduring persecution and deep poverty with remarkable joy, their customary generosity unquenched. But they suffered from false apostles and counterfeit Christians too, so that for Paul "there was still no relief for this body of ours:

instead, there was trouble at every turn, quarrels all around us, forebodings in our heart. But God, who brings comfort to the downcast, has comforted us by the arrival of Titus." Titus brought good news. The Corinthians had taken the punishing part of Paul's letter in the right spirit. It hurt, but they accepted the pain as deserved and were eager to vindicate themselves. They longed to see Paul again. And they had treated Titus with such respect and affection that Paul could write to them, "We have been delighted beyond everything by seeing how happy Titus is: you have helped to set his mind completely at rest. Anything I may have said to him to show my pride in you has been justified."

The situation in Corinth was far from perfect. They still needed rebuke and appeal. Worse, they were disgruntled about Paul himself. They complained that by abandoning his plan to cross direct from Ephesus, he had played fast and loose: they hinted he was untrustworthy. Paul had little difficulty in answering that. "It was to spare you I refrained from coming to Corinth." He had written instead, in order that his third visit should not be as painful as the second.

More seriously, they had been unsettled by the arrival of preachers with impressive panache, carrying apparently impeccable credentials, who seemed all the more superior to Paul in that they charged a stiff fee. Their propaganda was such that the Corinthian church, Paul's very own foundation, actually demanded proof of his commission. The new arrivals had denied him the qualities of a true apostle, pointing out that he carried no letters of commendation from Jerusalem, refused payment, did not live like a genuine Jew, had behaved much too meekly, was contemptible in body and despicable in speech; an apostle should boss his flock, they said. They conceded Paul could write weighty letters.

He was not unprepared for these people turning up in Corinth. He did not scruple to name them, "counterfeit apostles, they are dishonest workmen disguised as apostles of Christ. There is nothing surprising about that; if Satan himself goes disguised as an angel of light, there is no need to be surprised when his servants too disguise themselves as servants of righteousness. They will come to the end that they deserve.'' Paul was astonished at some of their assertions about him, but whereas he had reacted indignantly to similar circumstances in Galatia, his attitude now, ten years later and after the Ephesus crisis, was more one of amusement (''I am a nobody. . . . I will talk like a fool''). Nevertheless, he felt he must answer the Corinthians' inquiries about his status. They forced him to boast, rather wryly, that he indeed bore all the marks of a genuine apostle. He seems aware that they had noticed an overreadiness to vindicate his genuineness, ''but you drove me to it''; and anything he said was to build them up and strengthen them, his very dear friends.

Thus the long Second Letter to the Corinthians, written from Macedonia when Timothy rejoined him, was not so much a defense as a means of demonstrating what an apostle should be like. It contains intimate personal revelations of Paul's life and character past and present, his weakness and sufferings, and is the source of much of the material for his biography; and contains, too, an *apologia* for his motives, and his conceptions of both the task and the message of the true ambassador for Christ.

Paul and the other apostles were not proclaiming their own excellencies ''but Christ Jesus as Lord, and ourselves as your servants, for Jesus' sake.'' ''The love of Christ controls us,'' he wrote, ''because we are convinced that One has died for all: therefore all have died. And He died for all, that those who live might no longer live for themselves but for Him who, for their sake, died and was raised. . . . If any one is in Christ, he is a new creation, the old has passed away, the new has come. All this is from God, who through Christ reconciled us to Himself and gave us the ministry of reconciliation; that is, God was in Christ reconciling the world to Himself, not counting their trespasses against them, and entrusting to us the message of reconciliation.

"So we are ambassadors for Christ, God making His appeal through us: 'We beseech you on behalf of Christ, be reconciled to God! For He has made Him to be sin who knew no sin, so that in Him we might become the righteousness of God.' "

Paul decided not to go to Corinth too quickly. Titus, eager to return, took the letter, and Paul sent two other Christians, one of whom he called "the brother who is famous among all the churches for his preaching of the Gospel." Tradition believed this to be Luke, and that his earliest writings were circulating already.

Paul wanted Corinth to settle down completely before his own arrival. He did not wish to find "quarreling, jealousy, anger, selfishness, slander, gossip, conceit, and disorder." He did not wish to be forced into the role of strict judge. Nor did he want to stir them up in person to complete the contribution they had promised to the Jerusalem Collection. They should have it ready willingly, each according to his means, their generosity measured by the only true gauge: "You know how generous our Lord Jesus Christ has been: He was rich, yet for your sake He became poor, so that through His poverty you might become rich."

At the very end of his letter, after urging them to "Mend your ways, heed my appeal, agree with one another, live in peace, and the God of love and peace will be with you," Paul used a farewell which is without doubt the most quoted sentence of all he ever wrote: "The grace of our Lord Jesus Christ and the love of God and the fellowship of the Holy Spirit be with you all."

The letter dispatched, Paul continued in the north for an entire year. After encouraging the churches of Macedonia, he began evangelizing fresh territory, the neighboring province of Illyricum, the mountainous land bordering the Adriatic which is now Albania and southern Yugoslavia. No word of his exact movements survives, but his activity must have been much as he had described in his recent *apologia:* "Giving no offense in anything, that the ministry be not blamed, but in all things approving ourselves as the ministers of God, in much patience, in affliction, in necessities, in distresses, in stripes, in imprisonments, in tumults, in labors, in watchings, in fastings; by pureness, by knowledge, by long-suffering, by kindness, by the Holy Ghost, by love unfeigned. By the word of truth, by the power of God, by the armor of righteousness on the right hand and on the left, by honor and dishonor, by evil report and good report: as 'deceivers' and yet true; as unknown and yet well known; as dying, and, behold, we live; as chastened and not killed; as sorrowful, yet always rejoicing; as poor, yet making many rich; as having nothing yet possessing all things."

While in the north, Paul nearly crossed the Adriatic to visit the Christians of Rome, but the opportunities of Illyricum left no time before he moved south at last, to spend the three winter months of 56-57 in Corinth. When he arrived in mid-December, their troubles had subsided. No breath of controversy is heard. Instead, in a happy atmosphere, he could give much time to a new project: a letter to the Christians of Rome which should be the distillation of his thought, his nearest approach to the writing of a book, a carefully constructed literary composition which, if he had never written or spoken another word, entitles Paul to rank with Socrates, Plato, and Aristotle among the greatest intellects of the ancient world and, indeed, of all time.

Paul already had several friends and distant relations in Rome before Aquila and Priscilla returned there from Ephesus. Ease of communication in the empire induced constant coming and going to the world's center and he could send greetings to his foster mother from Antioch and her son Rufus, "that outstanding worker in the Lord's service"; to two Jews of his own tribe or family whom he describes as his fellow prisoners, probably when they were in Ephesus, "who were Christian before I was''; to the first convert in Asia; and to others.

He looked forward to renewing acquaintance, and to the fresh experience of enjoying the company of a church he had not founded. Far from being jealous, he had thrilled to hear about their faith and prayed for them regularly, yet his previous plans to visit Rome had yielded in face of unending calls to pioneer where Christ was unknown, to push onward, to watch more and more men and women receiving the grace of God so that thanksgiving and praise flowed ever wider. Paul was determined to go "where Christ was not named"; not therefore to Alexandria and Egypt, or Carthage and other cities of North Africa. He had his sights on Spain, the highly civilized most westerly province of the empire, and he could call in at Rome on the way. He would not stay long. His policy remained never to build on another's foundation. But because his commission was to all pagans, whether civilized or savage, educated or ignorant, "I am eager to preach the Good News to you also who live in Rome," and to win converts there. Moreover, the visit would be of mutual benefit: "For I long to see you that I may impart to you some spiritual gift to strengthen you, that is, that we may be mutually encouraged by each other's faith, yours and mine."

Meanwhile, since he must first take the collection to Jerusalem, and already may have had a premonition that he would not reach Rome as quickly as he hoped, he decided to give them the fruit of his years of experience and learning at the side of Christ. He had now been a Christian for a quarter of a century and was in his late fifties: mature, assured of the supreme excellence of his Master in all the changes and chances of life. In contrast with previous letters, he is not obliged to combat aberrations; or to rebut criticisms except once, when he snubs slanderers who twist his words to "sin away, to give God's forgiveness more opportunity!" Only once too does his tendency to justify himself break through, when he says, "In Christ Jesus, I have reason to be proud of my work for God. . . . What Christ has wrought through me to win obedience from the Gentiles by word and deed, by the power of signs and wonders, by the power of the Holy Spirit''; even then he disclaims personal credit.

Instead, there is a calmness, a magisterial confidence in this letter to Rome, the longest he ever wrote, which distinguishes it from those to Galatia and Corinth. It contains some of his profoundest, most difficult writing and much of his most beautiful. The subject of great commentaries from Origen to Barth, of thousands of pages of exposition and meditation, its every word examined under theological, philosophical, and textual microscopes, it has been also one of the world's decisive books. It formed the seedbed of Augustine's faith and Luther's Reformation. It was reading Luther's *Preface to the Epistle to the Romans* that caused John Wesley's heart to feel strangely warmed. He wrote that he ''did trust in Christ, Christ alone, for salvation; and an assurance was given me that He had taken away *my* sins, even *mine*, and saved *me* from the law of sin of death.''

Paul's words were first heard by one Tertius, his scribe for this letter. With greetings and preliminaries over, the theme rang out in the room at Corinth where they worked: ''I am not ashamed of the Gospel: it is the power of God for salvation to everyone who has faith, to the Jew first and also to the Greek. For in it the righteousness of God is revealed through faith for faith . . .'' and Paul announced his text, a quotation from the minor prophet Habakkuk; six words in Greek which have become familiar in six words of English: ''The just shall live by faith,'' or ''He who is right with God by faith shall live.''

Paul then shows that man has an instinctive awareness of God, and has rejected and excluded him. In consequence, pagans have slipped into the moral cesspool which lay all around Paul in Corinth. Nor could Jews, with all the privileges stemming from God's revelation of Himself, and their pride in their destiny as His people, adopt a smug superiority toward the pagan, for Jews too had stubborn and rebellious hearts which God must punish. Paul cannot offer a condoning God. His burden as a missionary stems not only from delight in displaying the excellencies of Christ but from crystal-clear, terrifying awareness that judgment will come on all men because all have sinned. The whole world is accountable to God, whether consciences excuse or accuse, "on that day when, according to my Gospel, God judges the secrets of men by Christ Jesus."

"But now"—and this was the part Paul loved—"God's way of putting men right with Himself has been revealed. . . . God puts men right through their faith in Jesus Christ." All men have sinned and come short of God's glory, but Jew and pagan alike are justified by receiving His grace as a gift, "by being redeemed in Christ Jesus, who was appointed by God to sacrifice His life so as to win reconciliation through faith." God's justice is thus made plain, in the past by His overlooking sins, in the present "by showing positively that He is just, and that He justifies everyone who believes in Jesus. So what becomes of our boasts? There is no room for them!"

Paul devotes a long section, with special reference to the Jews, to elaborate his thesis that forgiveness cannot be earned; a man can be "accepted as righteous" only by believing "in Him who raised Jesus our Lord from the dead, Jesus who was put to death for our sins and raised to life to justify us." And thus Paul reaches the first great autobiographical passage of the treatise (Romans 5): "Therefore, since we are justified by faith we have peace with God through our Lord Jesus Christ. Through Him we have obtained access by faith into this grace in which we stand, and we rejoice in our hope of sharing the glory of God. More than that, we rejoice in our sufferings, knowing that suffering produces endurance, and endurance produces character, and character produces hope, and hope does not disappoint us, because God's love has been poured into our hearts through the Holy Spirit which has been given to us. While we were yet helpless, at the right time God died for the ungodly. Why, one will hardly die for a *righteous* man! Though perhaps for a *good* man one will dare to die. But God shows His love for us in that *while we were yet sinners* Christ died for us. . . . ''

After a discourse on the origin of sin, Paul turns to a topic which had exercised him grievously ever since he wrote to Galatia, and which Corinthian problems had made the more urgent: the answer to backsliding, how the Christian may overcome the sin that continues to trouble him. He now expounds to the Romans at considerable length his conviction that they must treat the pre-Christian self as dead, and realize that a ''resurrection life'' was created in them when they believed. He switches metaphors and tells them to look at themselves as no longer slaves under orders to sin but slaves of Jesus. Then Paul bares his soul, admitting, ''I fail to carry out the things I want to do, and I find myself doing the very thing I hate''—until he cries, ''Who shall deliver me? I thank God through Jesus Christ our Lord!''

After that he could dilate with zest on the glorious fact that ''if the Spirit of Him who raised Jesus from the dead is living in you, then He who raised Jesus from the dead will give life to your own mortal bodies through His Spirit in you. So there is no necessity for us to obey our unspiritual selves or live unspiritual lives.'' Anyone who does not have the Spirit of Christ ''does not belong to Him. But if Christ is in you—'' and Paul warms to the theme that was his favorite after the cross, the marvel of ''Christ in you'': how Christ's Spirit leads, takes away fear, gives and directs the urge to pray, and creates a consciousness ''that we are children of God.''

Paul's rapture at the glory of the life with Christ, now and in the hereafter, mounts in tempo and glowing language until from the depth of his own experience he cries, ''What then shall we say to this? If God is for us, who is against us? He who did not spare His own Son but gave Him up for us all, will He not also give us all things with Him? Who shall bring any charge against God's elect? It is God who justifies; who is to condemn? Is it Christ Jesus who died, yes, who was raised from the dead, who is at the right hand of God, who indeed intercedes for us? Who shall separate us from the love of Christ? Shall tribulation, or distress, or persecution, or famine, or nakedness, or peril, or sword? . . . No, in all these things we are more than conquerors through Him who loved us. For I am sure that neither death, nor life, nor angels, nor principalities, nor powers, nor height, nor depth, nor anything else in all creation, will be able to separate us from the love of God in Christ Jesus our Lord.''

In a later section of the letter, when Paul urges the Romans to worship God by a manner of life worthy of people whose minds have been renewed, not modeling themselves on the behavior of the world around them, he reveals once again, if unconsciously, many features of his own character. As when he wrote to the Thessalonians during his first stay in Corinth, his exhortations need only to be adjusted to a slightly different focus to provide a pen portrait of himself.

The Paul of Corinth A.D. 57 was determined to use every spiritual gift up to the very limit of his faith, which, too, he recognized as a gift of God. He worked for the Lord "with untiring effort and with great earnestness of spirit," keeping the inward fires well stoked. He was steady in times of distress, gloriously happy in prospect of the future. Prayer was as natural to him as breathing. He was a hospitable, generous man; Paul loved to help people, was cheerful, not doing his acts of kindness sanctimoniously, grudgingly, or smugly. His love was genuine, unsimulated, and he had a marked touch of sympathy, rejoicing with those who rejoiced, weeping with those who wept. Nor did he choose his company with an eye to class, wealth, or position; the humblest Christian found him ready to walk out of his way to do a good turn or share an experience, and Paul had a gift for literally counting every man as better than himself. He loved his fellow Christians;

indeed, was a lovable man whatever his rough edges. He counted it most important to live harmoniously with fellow believers.

As to non-Christian Jews and pagans, Paul did his utmost to live at peace with them however much they disliked him. He hated evil and would not let mockery, discouragement, the malice of antagonists, or impostors loosen his grip on what he knew to be good. Instead he blessed his persecutors, and prayed for them, as the Lord Jesus had instructed in the Sermon on the Mount which he virtually quotes. Paul repaid evil with good: feeding his enemy, giving him drink if thirsty, not seeking revenge but leaving the Lord to look after the question of just recompense.

"Do not be overcome by evil, but overcome evil with good." Paul's aim was to be so full of Christ that no room was left for the unChristlike, in himself or in anyone around.

Part Four

TO THE
OSTIAN WAY

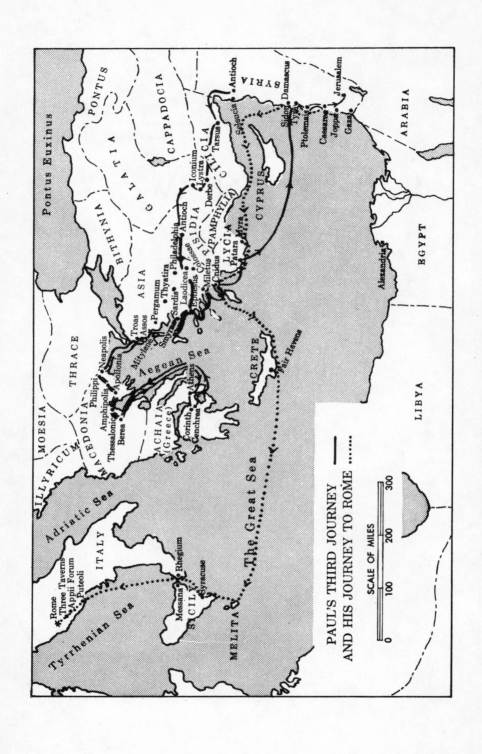

PAUL'S THIRD JOURNEY
AND HIS JOURNEY TO ROME

Twenty-Nine
FACING THE FUTURE

While writing to Rome, Paul in his mind ranged over an acute distress of the past twenty-five years: why should Jews as a nation reject Jesus, refusing to acknowledge Him their Messiah or Christ?

Paul had debated in himself and among friends whether God had rejected the Jews. He concluded forcefully that this was not so, in that he and many other Jews were Christians. On the other hand, if the Jews had flocked as a race and nation to the standard of the Risen Jesus, the Gentiles might always have taken second place in the Christian church. In the letter to the Romans, Paul describes good coming out of the evil of the Jews' refusal, and acknowledges the unsearchable depth of wisdom in God's plan: when the Gentiles have been brought into the kingdom, the Jews will follow in a yet more glorious day.

Yet he could not quite swallow this delay. Not only did he continue to love his own race; this love reached a pitch of extraordinary intensity which could only be compared with the weeping of Jesus as He looked across at the Temple from the Mount of Olives, or His sigh on another occasion, "O Jerusalem, Jerusalem, how often would I have gathered your children together as a hen gathers her brood under her wings, and you would not!'' Paul utters his own longing in terms that, in the context of what Christ meant to him, are almost unbelievable. ''I am speaking the truth in Christ. I am not lying; my conscience bears me witness in the Holy Spirit, that I have great sorrow and increasing anguish in my heart. For I could wish that I myself were accursed and *cut off from Christ* for the sake of my brethren, my kinsmen by race . . . My heart's desire and prayer to God for them is that they may be saved.'' Like Moses, he is prepared to be blotted out of God's book as the price of their reconciliation.

He regarded his coming return to Jerusalem with the collection as a last opportunity to demonstrate his love and to declare Christ to his own people, perhaps before a vast concourse, before going West. He was aware of danger there. He appealed to the Romans, ''by our Lord Jesus Christ and by the love of the Spirit, to strive together with me in your prayers to God on my behalf, that I may be delivered from the unbelievers in Judea, and that my service for Jerusalem be acceptable to the saints,'' so that he would reach Rome happy for his period of rest and refreshment.

Paul originally intended to take passage as before on a pilgrim ship from Cenchreae in March to reach Jerusalem for Passover. Corinthian Jews learned his plans and plotted accordingly: all the sailors in a pilgrim ship would be Jews; sailing at night at the time of new moon, the decks unlit except for navigation lights, Paul was to be tricked to the gunwhale. A stunning blow, man overboard, but no cry raised. . . .

Paul got wind of the plot. He had no intention of dying in a corner. He decided to miss Passover and go overland through Macedonia and sail across to Troas. Troas would be a rendezvous. For at Paul's request, each important church had selected their representatives who should accompany him and deliver the money to the Jerusalem sick and poor, and thus display the essential unity of the worldwide church. Timothy of Lystra and Gaius of Derbe represented Galatia; Aristarchus and Secundus were the Thessalonians and Sopater the Berean. Trophimus and Tychicus, both Greeks, would come from the province of Asia.

Paul and his friends walked north through the unforgettable Greek springtime on roads bordered by wild irises, wild roses and potentillas and poppies, and what later ages would call the Judas tree. But in each city, their foreboding of Jerusalem was intensified by the reaction of Christian leaders. Those who had the gift of interpreting the Spirit's foreknowledge were emphatic in warning.

At Philippi, having dispatched his traveling companions ahead, Paul spent Passover week (April 7 to 14, A.D. 57) with his Philippian friends. Then he and Luke sailed from the nearby port of Neapolis. If the winds had wafted him swiftly to Europe after the vision in the night seven years before, they now seemed to echo the Macedonian warnings. The voyage took five days instead of two.

In the upper part of a tenement house in the middle of Troas, the Christians were gathered together on the Saturday night, the last of Paul's visit. He had found a ship and his party would be leaving next morning.

The little church of Troas, fruit of his two brief previous calls and of the evangelization which had spread from Ephesus, evidently lacked a wealthy member who could invite them to worship on his lawn. They were using the attic, which in a tenement house covered the two or three apartments forming each of the two floors below, and were crushed in, every man and woman, and their children who could not be left at home. Sweaty bodies made the air close, smoke curled from the spouts of little vegetable-oil lamps; the room grew hot and stuffy, for though the night temperature in April was moderate, Troas stood in a sheltered, narrow coastal plain.

A young man called Eutychus had wedged himself on the window sill and listened fascinated as Paul unfolded mysteries of the faith. They had eaten a light meal, their *agapē*, and later would break bread and sip the wine of the Lord's Supper, the beginning of the Lord's Day.²³ Meanwhile Paul and his hearers equally were determined to use this last opportunity. But Eutychus had put in a hard day's manual labor, for his pagan master knew nothing of Sabbath rest, and as he listened his head nodded despite himself. Midnight came and went. All eyes were on Paul, and when Eutychus' head dropped lower on his chest none of the other youths noticed to prod him awake. Paul's voice floated in and out until it was lost altogether.

Suddenly there was a crash and a commotion. Eutychus had fallen right out of the window onto the narrow street below. It was not a deep drop, some fifteen feet, but he fell hard. By the time Paul had followed the agonized rush of the boy's friends and relations down the stairs, Luke had pronounced Eutychus dead. They stepped aside for Paul. He knelt and pressed the body close to his own, and those who knew their Scripture would recall that this is what both Elijah and Elisha did with dead boys. Paul said: "Do not worry. He is alive!"

Whether Paul had consciously used a form of artificial respiration which revived the heartbeat before clinical death had supervened, or was doing as the Spirit moved him without understanding cause and effect, Luke leaves open the question of miracle. Eutychus almost certainly remained unconscious for a time when they took him upstairs again, yet such was Paul's calm and confidence that they were able to resume while the boy lay recovering. Paul talked on and the people listened. They shared the bread and wine. They could not stop asking questions or hearing more of "the Word" until at break of day, without resting, he left.

"They took the boy away alive and were greatly encouraged." And it may be that the hymn Paul would quote in his circular letter to Asia (*Ephesians*) had its origin that night: "Awake, thou that sleepest, and arise from the dead, and Christ shall give thee light."

Paul had chosen a ship not scheduled to call at Ephesus. Hurrying to reach Jerusalem by Pentecost, he did not wish to be sucked into the affairs of the vigorous Ephesus church or risk provoking Jews or pagans into another uproar which might cause arrest and detention. At Troas, however, he arranged that his party should go aboard while he went by road. The first leg of the journey was to Assos, about thirty miles by land and longer by sea as a ship must round Cape Lectrum. Very unusually, Paul insisted on walking alone; he had set off at dawn and could make it in a day at that time of year.

He wanted to face the future. He had been warned in every city that persecution and prison awaited him in Jerusalem. Should he accept these warnings as divine orders to turn on his tracks and go straight to Rome? Could he take what was coming to him in Judea? He climbed from the coastal plain into the low hills, and walked southwest until the road turned east with the land. By midday, from this clifftop road, he had one of the superb panoramas of Asia Minor: on his right hand across the narrow strip of sapphire water, a dark blue of hills, the island of Lesbos. Ahead, the white clouds of springtime made sun and shade dance. Far in the distance at the end of the gulf he could see more distant blue hills in which lay Pergamum. His heart could go out to the Christians there, and to Smyrna, Ephesus, and away to Colossae and Laodicea.

As he walked, he reached the final crisis of his life: whether to turn or to press forward. Undisturbed except by sheep with their bells, and guard dogs to bark at him, and donkeys, and a camel or two, he was able to learn his Master's will and reach the conclusion that would steady him through the tumults to follow.

For the last few hours of the walk, as the sun dropped, the light behind him was full on the fantastic rock of Assos, a great block of granite dominating city and countryside and crowned by a temple.[24] Out of sight at the bottom of the cliff lay the harbor with its breakwater. Here Luke and the others were already waiting, a little anxious that Paul should be out there alone.

When he reached them and went on board, they undoubtedly could see by his face that he was utterly at peace.

Luke's log of the voyage marks where they hove-to each evening when the wind dropped: off Mitylene, capital of Lesbos and once home of the poetess Sappho whose poems gave rise to the word "lesbian"; off the island of Chios, a good run; then another good run to the western side of Samos, the large island southwest of Ephesus and birthplace of Pythagoras, the philosopher and mathematician 500 years before; and then, early on Thursday, April 28,[25] they slipped in past the great marble lions which marked the Miletus harbor, a losing rival to Ephesus yet still a fine port.

Finding that the captain wanted two or three days' wait, Paul leaped at the opportunity of seeing the Ephesian elders once more. A Christian of Miletus sped posthaste the fifty miles. To cross by water that afternoon to Priene, borrow a horse from a Christian, ride over the hills, wake up the Ephesus presbyters in the middle of the night, and get them somehow back to Miletus in about forty hours was good going, but the Ephesians were as eager as the messenger to drop all business at a moment's notice for Paul's sake.

They gathered in a Miletus house, and Luke was there to take down the speech and watch its effect.

"You yourselves know," Paul began, "from the first day I set foot in Asia, how I lived among you serving the Lord the whole time with humility, with sorrows and trials which came on me because of the plots of the Jews. You know I kept back nothing that was good for you." He reminded them how in public and private, to Jews and Gentiles, he had urged repentance, and "trust in our Lord Jesus. And now, look, I am going to Jerusalem, driven by the Spirit. And what will happen to me there I know nothing, except that in every city the Holy Spirit makes plain that chains and rough treatment await me. But none of these things moves me! I do not count my life at any value to myself—provided I may finish my race nobly and fulfill the commission I received from the Lord Jesus, to 'give full witness to the Good News of the grace of God.'

"And now look: I know that none of all you, among whom I have gone in and out proclaiming the kingdom, will ever see my face again! So I declare to you this day that I am absolved from responsibility for any man's blood, for I kept back nothing in proclaiming to you all the whole purpose of God. Be on guard, therefore, for yourselves and for all the flock of God, of which He has made you shepherds." Paul warned them, in words that surely derive from Jesus' warnings about the wolf which scatters the flock when the hireling flees because he does not care, that "after I am gone savage wolves will come in and not spare the flock." Even among these men in front of him some would "distort the truth, to induce disciples to break away and follow them. So be on guard, remembering how night and day over three years I did not cease counseling each one of you, with tears.

"And now I commend you to God and to His gracious word, which has power to build you up and give you your heritage among all who are dedicated to Him. I have not wanted anyone's money or clothes for myself; you all know that these hands of mine earned enough for the needs of me and my companions. I showed you that it is our duty to help the weak in this way, by hard work, and that we should keep in mind the words of the Lord Jesus, who Himself said, 'Happiness lies more in giving than in receiving.' "[26]

Already tears were on some of their faces. Paul knelt and they knelt with him. He prayed in words too intimate for Luke to record (he had probably used a medical shorthand to take down the speech as it was delivered), and when Paul stopped, the men of Ephesus sobbed unashamedly. They hugged him and kissed him, "sorrowing most of all," Luke realized, "because of the word he had spoken, that they should see his face no more."

They went together to the ship and the parting was hard. Luke says, "We tore ourselves away from them."

Thirty
RIOT IN JERUSALEM

About a week later a somewhat similar scene occurred on a beach the other side of the Mediterranean, at Tyre on the Syrian coast.

They had sailed by way of Rhodes and changed from their coaster at a big port in southwestern Asia Minor to a large merchantman, which used the summer westerlies to cross the open sea south of Cyprus direct to Tyre. Here the captain needed a week to unload cargo. Paul and his party sought out the Christian disciples. Once more he was warned against going to Jerusalem, and he recognized that the local church leaders spoke "by the Spirit." He made no comment. Warm affection sprang up between the small group of Tyrian Christians and the nine or ten travelers, and at sailing day all the men with their wives and children came to see them off. Tyre at that time was an offshore island connected with the mainland by a mole, on either side of which sandy beaches had formed. Before the travelers rowed out to their ship, everybody knelt on the sand under the cloudless Mediterranean sky for prayer.

The merchantman sailed twenty miles and put in for a day at Ptolemais (Acre). They again called on the local Christians.

Next morning May 14, 57 another short run round the headland of Carmel completed the voyage to Caesarea, capital and principal port of the province of Judea, where the Procurator's palace, with which Paul was to become so well acquainted, may have caught his eye among the sun-drenched marble public buildings as he landed. At first there were no more warnings. The party were guests of Philip, the notable evangelist whose influence had spread into Africa far up the Nile, once a fellow deacon with the murdered Stephen. Philip had four unmarried daughters; the family later migrated to Hierapolis near Colossae where the daughters were mines of information about the earliest days of Christianity. Each also had the gift of prophecy. But they remained silent about Paul's future.

Some days afterward, the famous prophet Agabus arrived from the hill country. Agabus, whose prophecy of famine when he visited Antioch had been the immediate cause of Paul's return to Jerusalem after the Hidden Years, suddenly pulled Paul's tasseled cord off his waist. The travelers and Philip's family looked on with a premonition that prophetic warning, by symbol and word, was imminent. Agabus squatted on the ground. He tied the cord round his feet and hands. "Thus says the Holy Spirit: So shall the Jews at Jerusalem bind the man who owns this girdle and deliver him into the hands of the Gentiles!"

Agabus had drawn no conclusion or moral; he had stated Paul's future. Luke and others could bear it no longer. "We and those who were there begged him not to go up to Jerusalem." They wept and pleaded. Why should not Paul stay quietly at Caesarea while the rest of them carried the money to Jerusalem and returned, and they could then set out for Rome? They thought he was wrong to ignore the warnings. Many commentators in subsequent centuries have agreed, contrasting Paul's obstinacy now with his quick acceptance when forbidden by the Spirit to preach in Asia or enter Bithynia. Their loud lamentation had an effect. Paul felt (to judge by the word he uses) squeezed and pummeled like the washing under the wrists of an oriental washerwoman. He knew that their urgings sprang from deep affection, from desire to protect him. Yet he had been sure since the road to Assos, at latest, that the higher love of the Lord Jesus called him to Jerusalem. Maybe death there would exert the same decisive influence for Christ as had Stephen's death, perhaps be the linchpin in the reconciliation of Jew and Gentile, the reconciliation of Jews the world over to Christ. If, in passionate love for his people, Paul was ready to be "cut off from Christ" for their sake, he was certainly ready to die.

"What are you doing," cried Paul, "weeping and pummeling my heart? I am ready not only to be bound but to *die* in Jerusalem for the name of the Lord Jesus."

Luke records: "And so, as he would not be persuaded, we gave up the attempt, saying, 'The Lord's will be done.'"

The Caesarean Christians had arranged mules to carry the money bags of the collection, and riding-mules for Paul's party, and had sent ahead to ensure lodging in a Jerusalem overcrowded with pilgrims for Pentecost: they had arranged a stay with one of the earliest disciples, a Cypriot named Mnason, whose background made him sympathetic toward the ex-pagan Christians whom many Jerusalem Christians would despise. All the way up the sixty miles into the hills the bends of the road disclosed parties of pilgrims ahead and behind, for Pentecost drew Jews from every province of the empire. On other roads too pilgrims converged: from Persia, from Arabia and the southern incense countries, from North Africa and the upper Nile, everyone zealous to display devotion to the Temple and the Law of his fathers, and rejoice at the festival of First Fruits.

After a happy welcome at Mnason's, the Christians from Europe and Asia Minor were eager to enjoy the sights. As Paul displayed the beauties of Jerusalem and the outer wall of the Temple, he was seen in the crowded streets by some of his

bitterest enemies, Jews of Asia, who recognized Trophimus of
Ephesus too. If Paul took any of his friends except the circumcised Timothy into the Temple's Court of the Gentiles, he
was not so mad as to let them step through the low barrier,
the "wall of partition," past warning notices that if a Gentile
went farther and defiled the holy courts, he would have only
himself to blame for his death.

Next day Paul and the accredited representatives of the
Gentile churches were formally received by James the Lord's
brother and the Jerusalem elders to hand over the gift of the
alms. Peter and the other apostles were abroad spreading the
Gospel; Thomas, according to tradition, had already reached
northern India. The ascetic James continued to maintain a
cautious policy so that the priests and rulers of the nation
should tolerate those Jews, a large number, who acknowledged Jesus as Messiah while observing the traditions of their
ancestors. Most of the elders were convinced that Paul did his
best to destroy this policy wherever he went. Paul knew their
estimate of him and for months had been nervous lest they
should not accept the gift in the spirit in which Europe and
Asia offered it.

Luke noted the grave kiss of peace between Paul and each
elder; next the delegates brought forward their moneybags.
Then Paul narrated, detail by detail, "the things that God had
done among the Gentiles through his ministry." It was a
missionary speech with a plain implication, that the elders of
the overweighted Jerusalem congregation should spur their
people to go out and follow up the initiative won by Paul
among the Gentiles, until there should be one flock under the
one Shepherd.

The reaction was disappointing. The elders made appropriate noises of praise to God and turned promptly to a much
more pressing affair.

"Brother," they addressed Paul, "you see how many thousands of converts we have among the Jews, all of them
staunch upholders of the Law. Now, they have been given

certain information about you: it is said you teach all the *Jews* in the Gentile world to turn their backs on Moses, telling them to give up circumcising their children and following our way of life." The elders did not venture to suggest they believed the calumny, nor were they concerned with Gentiles, for the letter sent by the Council of Jerusalem had settled that question. But they felt some action by Paul, rather than a pronouncement of their own, must remove the misconception. "What is to be done therefore? You must do as we tell you." Paul must follow a current practice whereby rich men showed their love of the Law by paying the expenses and sharing the vigil of poor men. They had four of their number under a Nazarite vow who had incurred ritual defilement but were too poor to buy the necessary sacrificial birds and animals to purge the defilement and complete the days of the vow. "Then everyone will know that there is nothing in the stories they were told about you, but that you are a practicing Jew and keep the Law youself."

Paul could scarcely be more dashed. Since they knew he had no money of his own they must intend that he should use part of the collection; yet Europe and Asia had hardly supposed their ill-afforded present would be used to discharge ceremonial vows. Besides, he was being invited to dissemble. The elders openly intended to exploit his action to assert that Paul kept the Law. Yet he did not. He honored it; he was ready to be like a Jew to the Jews and "put myself under that Law to win them, although I am not myself subject to it," and he had taken a Nazarite vow himself. But he did not live as a practicing orthodox Jew. Therefore he would be acting a lie.

And such was his love for the Jews that he agreed to the elders' plan, if it might somehow help more Jews to believe in Christ. "Let love be without dissimulation," he had recently urged the Romans. Never do evil that good might come, he had taught; yet now he would reject his own advice. In no way was his love for the Jews more evident than in this error of judgment at Jerusalem at the Pentecost of A.D. 57.

Paul immediately left the home of Mnason to live in one of the inner courts of the Temple with four men he had never seen before for the last two or three days of their vigil. He paid the money, joined the rituals, kept the fasts. And all along knew he was living in the very mouth of the lion. The crowds of pilgrims which milled through the Temple in these days following the Feast were at their most excitable; not many years earlier they had risen in fury when a bored Roman soldier looking down from the citadel of Antonia had gestured obscenely. Jews from Asia and Europe who loathed Paul's very face might see him and resent his presence in the sacred interior of the Temple.

The purification drew to a close. Next morning the four anonymous men would have their heads shaved and the hair burned at the sacrificial fire. Paul would return to Mnason's home and soon embark for Rome.

The continual traffic of pilgrims around him in a Temple and city pulsating with national and religious pride, together with his memory of prophetic warnings, kept him alert for danger. It came suddenly. The Jews from Asia who had recognized the ex-pagan Ephesian in the streets of Jerusalem saw Paul from a distance in the inner Temple courts with four men and at once jumped to the conclusion that they were Greeks like Trophimus.

"Men of Israel, help!" they yelled. "This is the man who preaches to everyone everywhere against our people, against the Law and against this place! And now he has defiled the Holy Place by bringing Greeks into the Temple!"

Those within earshot rushed to lynch a renegade and defiler. The uproar brought others until a milling mass swirled about Paul. Then they were dragging him out of the sacred precinct where no blood might be shed. Pummeled, torn, with screams of frenzy in his ears, Paul was borne down the steps, every yard bringing a bruise. He heard the great doors of the Temple clang to, heard the roar of the mob swelling.

Now if ever was the time to prove his own words, "Rejoice in the Lord always. The peace of God, which passes understanding, shall keep your heart and mind."

He remained on his feet but it was a losing struggle. Soon he would be on the ground and torn limb from limb. Someone had an arm and was twisting it; one ear was split already. His eyes were bruised and swelling. It could not be long. Was he to die without being able to say one word?

He heard above the uproar the metallic clank of soldiers at the double on the flat roof of the portico. Riot had been immediately reported by Roman guards posted for the very purpose to Claudius Lysias, the garrison commander or *chiliarch* (colonel of a thousand), who at once saw from his tower that all Jerusalem was converging on the Temple in that blind oriental instinct which reacts to danger or outrage without knowing the cause. A serious civil disturbance was building up. He took command of the operation himself. With the precision of long training, 200 men doubled out of the citadel of Antonia which dominated the northwest corner of the Temple, and down the steps on to the portico roofs designed for ease of maneuver, and straight to the center of trouble.

The crowd left off lynching Paul and made way for the soldiers. In the last riot, they had resisted, and in the ensuing fight and panic thousands had been trampled to death. Claudius Lysias came up, arrested Paul, and ordered his wrists clapped in double-chained irons. Then he inquired who he was and what he had done.

Some shouted one thing and some another until howling and yelling made inquiry impossible. Lysias ordered his men to take Paul into the citadel. This infuriated the crowd. As the soldiers began to march him, with Lysias at his side, across the court toward the main stairs of Antonia, the mob yelled louder at being balked of its prey. "Kill him! kill him!" they screamed, pressing on the circle of spears and shields, until by the bottom of the steps the pressure was so violent that Paul had to be literally carried up the stone stairway. Lysias had decided the man must be the illiterate Egyptian who had recently led a tragic uprising, inducing thousands to carry hidden daggers and stab political opponents by stealth, then to camp on the Mount of Olives in expectation of the miraculous collapse of the city walls and the defeat of the Romans; the military had routed the armed rabble, hundreds of survivors had been crucified or sent to the galleys, but the Egyptian escaped. He had now returned, and the Jews were venting their rage on the foreigner who had duped their sons.

At the top of the steps, with the howling mob below and with peace and quiet, through imprisonment, a few feet ahead, Paul said to Lysias in Greek: "May I have a word with you?"

Lysias was surprised to hear this panting, bleeding little specimen of matted humanity speak Greek, and asked if he were not the Egyptian. Paul, who could detect by Lysias' accent that, as his name shows, he was Greek by race, replied: "I am a Jew, from Tarsus in Cilicia, a citizen of 'no mean city.' "

Lysias was even more suprised. The battered criminal must be a scholar and a gentleman; he had just escaped death by inches yet had the wit to quote a tag of Euripides. When Paul added, "Please let me speak to the people," Lysias gave permission.

Paul turned, and raised one bruised, chained hand. Lysias was yet more astonished. By some extraordinary force of authority, Paul's gesture quieted the crowd. The yells died to murmurs.

Paul began to speak in Aramaic. Lysias would have a smattering of it but not enough to follow the speech. He had only Paul's word that he was no rebel aiming to rouse the Jews, but Lysias did not interfere. He could marvel to hear a man whose head must throb and every joint ache deliver a powerful extemporaneous speech which held this blood-lusting crowd enthralled, but Lysias could not know of

Paul's tactful choice of words, his sensitivity to this audience, which he was determined to conciliate and then to win. With blood trickling from broken lips, Paul was making one of his most winsome speeches, even if it failed.

"Brethren and fathers," cried Paul. "Hear the defense which I now make before you." The time-honored, respectful formula, together with the realization that he spoke in Aramaic, brought total silence.

"I am a Jew! Born at Tarsus in Cilicia but brought up in this city at the feet of Gamaliel, educated according to the strict manner of the Law of our fathers, being zealous for God. As you all are this day! I persecuted this Way unto death, binding and delivering to prison both men and women, as the high priest and the whole council of elders can bear me witness. From them I received letters to the brethren, and I journeyed to Damascus."

Paul told the story of his conversion. And they listened. Now at last he was preaching to a vast crowd of Jews. The opportunity had come and he had seized it. All pain was forgotten as he described his sudden experience on the Damascus Road and echoed the words that had transformed him: "He said to me, 'I am Jesus of Nazareth whom you are persecuting.'" Paul told of the blindness, of Ananias, "a devout man according to the Law, well spoken of by all the Jews living there," of his baptism, until he reached what must be the hardest part for them to accept. He had more to say, but first he explained why he went to the Gentiles; he spoke of his trance in Jerusalem, recounting his argument with the Lord when forbidden to preach in Jerusalem. "And I said, 'Lord, they themselves know that in every synagogue I imprisoned and beat those who believed in You. And when the blood of Stephen Your martyr was shed, I also was standing by and approving, and keeping the garments of those who killed him.'"

"And He said to me, 'Depart; for I will send you far away to the Gentiles—'"

The word struck like a match in dry straw. The silence exploded. The speech was drowned in yells of "Kill him!" "Away with him!" "He's not fit to live!"

The crowd surged on to the stairway. Others farther back waved their cloaks or threw dust. With the whole place in a frenzy of emotion, Lysias pulled Paul inside the citadel.

Puzzled, not knowing what he could report to his superiors, his respect for Paul destroyed by the mob's violence against him, Lysias gave an order to a centurion and walked swiftly away to his quarters.

Thirty-One
THE TORTURE
CHAMBER

The citadel seemed dark in contrast to the strong sunlight. The noise died as they marched Paul to the lower floor, on down narrower stairs into vaulted cellars lit by flickering torches, through a low archway and into the torture chamber.

They removed his chains, stripped him, then bound his ankles to a bar and tied his wrists to long thongs which they threw over a beam above and slightly ahead of him, and pulled on the thongs until his arms were stretched high above his head and his whole body, leaning forward, hung taut. The position was painful in itself and every blow would fall on tightened nerves and muscles. Paul was not bent over a whipping post for punishment, because the aim was the extraction of information; someone would stand near his mouth, expecting between screams to hear him confess his crimes.

By now Paul knew what was intended. He was to be given the dreaded *flagellum*, a murderous scourge of heavy rawhide thongs loaded with jagged bits of zinc, iron, and bone. Whether to force evidence out of slaves and those without rank, or as the prelude to crucifixion which Jesus had endured, the weight and lacerating of the scourge could kill a man. A survivor would have torn nerves and damaged kidneys; might even be out of his mind.

If Paul went through it, he would never preach again.

When the centurion in charge stepped forward to check that all was ready, Paul said: "Is it legal for you to flog a Roman citizen, and one who has not been convicted?"

The centurion acted instantly. He hurried off to find Lysias. Paul remained stretched from the beam, but the husky slave who held the *flagellum* laid it down and the clerk who must note agonized gasps of confession stepped back; and the garrison commander's alarm may be gauged from the speed with which he came to the torture chamber.

Looking at the naked little Jew in front of him Lysias had a moment's doubt when he saw the scars from whip, rod, and stones.

"Tell me, *are* you a Roman citizen?"

"Yes."

Lysias remembered heavy bribes to intermediaries. "It cost me a great sum to acquire this citizenship."

"But it was mine by birth," said Paul.

Lysias was very distinctly worried. There might be powerful relatives who would cause a fuss and ruin him for tying up Paul to be examined under the lash. He was immediately taken down. The husky slave and the clerk disappeared quickly, for all who were involved could suffer if Paul took proceedings. Paul was helped into his clothes and taken for the night to a cell away from the vermin which infested the general dungeons, and left unbound except for the usual light chain.

Lysias still had nothing to report to explain the riot. Next day therefore he exercised his right as military governor of Jerusalem to order an emergency session of the Sanhedrin to investigate what charge lay against Paul. He had already released him from chains and now conducted him personally to the court, as if to emphasize that Roman citzenship was more honorable than Jewish. He then withdrew from the Hall of Polished Stones but stayed outside. Paul stood in the precise spot where Stephen had stood and the seventy-one judges included a few surviving from the time of Stephen's trial. The president was Ananias ben Nedebaeus, high priest since A.D. 47, one of the most rapacious men ever to disgrace the office. Paul did not know him by sight, and the damage done by the mob's violence made sharp vision difficult. It had not, however, reduced the strength of personality he could exert through his eyes. He gripped the council with the intense gaze which had quelled Elymas the Cypriot long ago, and thereby he seized the initiative and opened the proceedings himself.

"My brothers," he began, "I have lived all my life, and still live today, with a perfectly clear conscience before God. I—"

The president barked an order. One of the court ushers struck Paul a stinging blow on the mouth.

The old Paul flared at such totally illegal behavior. Forgetting his own teaching, "When we are cursed, we bless, when insulted we answer with kind words," he shouted at the indistinct figure of the president: "God will strike you, you whitewashed wall! You sit there to judge me according to the Law; yet you break the Law by ordering them to strike me!"

The ushers were horrified. "You are insulting God's high priest!"

Paul was abashed. "My brothers," he said mildly, "I did not realize he was the high priest. Scripture says, 'You must not speak evil of the ruler of your people.'"

Balked of orderly argument, Paul made a move that was brilliant if reckless. He knew the Sanhedrin was divided between Pharisees who believed in a resurrection at the Last Day and in the existence of angels and spiritual beings, and the party of the Sadducees, who held rationalist, materialist views. Paul was sure that many of the Pharisees would believe in Jesus if only they saw Him as he, a Pharisee, had seen Him on the Damascus Road; belief in the Risen Jesus was the only honest conclusion for a true Pharisee.

He called out to the Sanhedrin: "Brothers! I am a Pharisee and the son of Pharisees. It is for our hope in the resurrection of the dead that I am on trial!"

At that the Sanhedrin erupted, just as it had erupted at Stephen's cry, but instead of rushing at the prisoner the judges began to argue furiously among themselves. "We find nothing wrong in this man," shouted Pharisees. "Suppose a spirit or an angel has spoken to him!" Sadducces, who included the high priest, shouted back angry denials until the judges came to blows, some even leaping into the well of the court intending to seize or protect Paul's person. Lysias heard the commotion, feared that Paul would be torn in pieces between them, and ordered a squad into the Hall who rescued him forcibly and hurried him back to the citadel.

Lysias was no further on. He still had nothing to report. Paul too felt frustrated. His attempts to testify about the Lord to his countrymen had failed and now he might never see Rome. As the day wore on and the patch of June sky through the prison bars turned from azure to red and soon to stars, he slipped into one of his moods of melancholy. His friends had not been allowed into the castle. He felt alone except that he could pray.

Suddenly, as in Corinth at another time of uncertainty, as at other crises, he saw the Lord Jesus. The Spirit, whose constant presence Paul had often mentioned in the letters, revealed Himself for a moment of time to eyes and ears, standing right beside him: "Courage! You have given your witness to Me here in Jerusalem, and you must bear witness in Rome too."

Paul did not doubt that he had seen Jesus, nor that the words would come true. The peace of God flooded into his heart and mind. He knew for a certainty what he had taught as a certainty: that all things work together for good for them that love God and are called according to His purpose.

Next morning the way was opened unexpectly when

the guards brought a visitor, his sister's son whom Paul probably had not see since a child. This young man, who would have been brought up to regard his turncoat uncle as dead to the family, had evidently reached a position of influence sufficient to gain admittance to the citadel. Almost certainly, he had been present, unknown to Paul, in the Hall of Polished Stones and possibly in the crowd which had heard Paul's unfinished oration from the stairs. Admiration had combined with thickness of blood to override the prejudice of years. What is more, the arrival of the nephew seems to have been the first step in a reconciliation which included the release of the patrimony which the family had kept from Paul, for from this point in the story he has money at his disposal again; indeed is sufficiently well-off to be rated a likely source of bribes.

More immediately the nephew's intervention forced the situation. He reported a murder plot. Whether he had been present at its hatching by over forty young zealots, or in attendance when the Sanhedrin approved it in secret session, the nephew risked his future, possibly his life, to betray the plot. A formal request, he told Paul, would be made next day that Lysias should send him down to the Sanhedrin for further questioning. He would be ambushed on the way. Some of the zealots inevitably might die in the scuffle with the escort, but all had taken a solemn religious oath neither to eat nor to drink until Paul was dead: by killing him they would do God service.

Paul did not hesitate. He called a centurion and told him to take the nephew to Lysias. The centurions were already attached to Paul beyond the claims of his Roman citizenship and hurried to do his bidding. Lysias too showed an immediate kindness, taking the young man by the hand where he could talk without being overheard by the staff. Lysias thanked the lad, warning him to preserve complete secrecy, and he took immediate action.

That night at 9:00 a strong force of 200 infantry, 200

spearmen, and 70 cavalry marched out through the new walls. In the center of the cavalry, muffled more for disguise than against the cool mountain air of June, Paul rode on horseback. By next morning, they were at Antipatris at the foot of the hills. The conspirators had been outwitted. The road led on through the cultivated plain peopled mostly with Gentiles, and the infantry could therefore return to Jerusalem, leaving the 70 cavalry to escort Paul to the *praetorium* at Caesarea, where he was immediately brought before the Procurator of Judea, Antonius Felix, the current successor of Pontius Pilate.

The officer commanding the escort handed Felix a letter from Lysias. Its gist was later given to Luke by one of the clerks or published in the government gazette and Luke incorporates it in Acts without comment. His sense of irony must have derived considerable amusement from what was claimed and what tactfully omitted.

"Claudius Lysias to His Excellency the Governor Felix, greeting. This man was seized by the Jews, and was about to be killed by them, when I came upon them with the soldiers and rescued him, having learned that he was a Roman citizen. And desiring to know the charge on which they accused him, I brought him down to their Council. I found that he was accused about questions of their law, but charged with nothing deserving death or imprisonment. And when it was disclosed to me that there would be a plot against the man, I sent him to you at once, ordering his accusers also to state before you what they have against him."

Felix formally asked his province, since if he were from a native state he must be referred to the appropriate jurisdiction. On learning that Paul was Cilician, Felix remanded him in custody, in the *praetorium* built by Herod the Great.

The high priest hurried down to Caesarea despite his great age, and in his entourage brought an advocate named Tertullus. Paul's friends had probably followed too so that Luke was present in court for the hearing. He must have derived further

ironic amusement from noting the florid flattery of the opening speech of the prosecution, for Tertullus knew perfectly
well that since the appointment of Felix in A.D. 52 Judea had
suffered widespread bloodshed from the insurrections he provoked, and from the increase in political murders after he had
arranged for the ex-high priest Jonathan to be assassinated in
the Temple itself. Felix's greed was notorious. He had been
born a slave, had risen to power on the shoulders of his
brother the freedman Pallas, a favorite of Claudius, and his
character is well summed up by Tacitus: "He exercised the
power of a king with the mind of a slave."

Tertullus puffed out his cheeks and hitched his robes in the
immemorial manner of advocates with weak cases.

"Your Excellency," he began, "we owe it to you that we
enjoy unbroken peace. It is due to your provident care that, in
all kinds of ways and in all sorts of places, improvements are
being made for the good of this province. And now, not to
take up too much of your time, I crave your indulgence for a
brief statement of our case." First, Paul had been found "a
perfect pest," fomenting unrest among Jews throughout the
civilized world. Second, he was a ringleader of the sect of
Nazarenes, the implication being that this cult was not legally
recognized by the Romans. Third, by attempting to profane
the Temple, he had broken the Jewish domestic law which
Rome promised to enforce. "But we arrested him—" Tertullus ended rather lamely by saying that if Felix examined the
prisoner he would soon see the force of the charges.

The high priest's party supported counsel vigorously, but
the Asian Jews who had sparked the whole affair were con-
spicuous by absence. Felix called the defendant, appearing in
person.

Paul showed himself entirely at ease, able to offer appropriate courtesies without flattery and to argue with a legal skill
which had not withered in the long years since he had
practiced.

"I know that you have administered justice over this nation

for many years," Paul said, "and I can therefore speak with confidence in my own defense. As you can verify for yourself, it is no more than twelve days since I went up to Jerusalem on pilgrimage, and it is not true that they ever found me arguing with anyone or stirring up the mob, either in the Temple, in the synagogue, or about the town." Paul had deftly shifted the locality of the charge from the "whole civilized world" to Jerusalem only. Even there they could not prove their accusations.

"What I do admit to you is this: it is according to The Way, which they describe as a sect, that I worship the God of my ancestors, retaining my belief in all points of the Law and what is written in the prophets; and I hold the same hope in God as they do, that there will be a resurrection of good men and bad men alike. In these things I, as much as they, do my best to keep a clear conscience at all times before God and man."

Paul described the events leading up to the outbreak in the Temple. He had brought alms for his nation, he had been ritually purified. "There was no crowd involved, and no disturbance. But some Jews from Asia—" Paul broke off in the middle of a sentence, and must have looked around the courtroom meaningfully. "*They* ought to be here before you and make an accusation if they have anything against me. Or else let these men themselves"—indicating the high priest and his followers—"say what wrongdoing they found when I stood before the Council, except this one thing that I cried out while standing among them: '*It is for our hope in the resurrection of the dead I am on trial before you this day!*' "

Paul closed his case.

Felix had already made some investigation of the Christian Way and was probably aware also of Gallio's decision. He could recognize that the Jews had no case under Roman law and that he should acquit. However, he was not averse to keeping the high priest guessing and less disposed to be troublesome; Felix was a prevaricator by nature. He adjourned the court on the thin excuse that he would reserve judgment until Lysias came down.

He ordered Paul to be kept in open arrest, and gave particular instructions that friends should be allowed to visit as much as they liked and bring him all he needed.

Thirty-Two
KING, QUEEN, AND GOVERNOR

The wet Mediterranean winter gave way to the hot summer of 58, made bearable for Paul by sea breezes and by permission to talk on the shore or where he wished, chained lightly to a soldier. Aristarchus of Thessalonica accepted the status of prisoner in order to serve Paul. Timothy had left for missionary travel in Europe or Asia Minor; now about thirty years old, he still retained some of his youthful timidity, but had Paul's single-mindedness. The other delegates had returned to Asia and Europe too except Luke, who took the opportunity for a thorough investigation of the oral and written evidence for the life, death, and resurrection of Jesus and of subsequent events.

It must have been encouraging to Paul each time Luke arrived back in Caesarea after long talks with Mary, the Lord's Mother, or Mary Magdalene if she still lived, or Zaccheus and the once-blind beggar at Jericho; or as they sat together, accompanied by Paul's soldier, while Philip the Evangelist told of the early days after the coming of the Holy Spirit, and described Stephen as he knew him which Paul could confirm from a different angle. Some hold that the Epistle to the Hebrews was composed at this time. The epistle carries no signature and its authorship can never be determined. About 150 years after Paul's day, Clement of Alexandria stated that Paul wrote it in Hebrew and Luke translated it into the Greek which survived; modern scholarship doubts that this version can be a translation. Clement's successor, Origen, believed Paul merely supervised the writing. Tertullian decided it was done by Barnabas. Some other students held it the work of Apollos, a view held by Luther and now increasingly in favor with scholars.

Whatever Paul did in these quiet years, he had at last an opportunity, though unlimited, for reaching his own race. He also had two potential converts of eminence right beside him. Procurator Felix had seduced a member of the Jewish royal family, the very young Herodian princess Drusilla, who divorced the king of Commagene to marry Felix as his third wife. Whether from a guilty conscience, as an adulteress and a Jewess who had broken the Law by marrying a Gentile, or because she had a full ingredient of Herodian curiosity, Drusilla persuaded Felix to send for Paul in private audience.

Paul did not resent Felix's authority. He was not an anarchist. He had urged the Roman Christians, living uncomfortably close to Nero, to regard Caesar as God's servant whose authority had been given by God. Paul's recipe for changing governments was not to foment political revolution but to transform the hearts of rulers, and when Felix offered opportunity he went to it with a will. He talked freely about faith in Jesus Christ without fear of this slave-hearted governor who, like Pilate before him, supposed he had power to release or to condemn but in Paul's view, as in his Master's, had no power except it were given him from above. Felix, with his political crimes and his lust, found that Paul's preaching cut too near the bone. "As Paul," records Luke, "went on discussing goodness, self-control, and the coming Day of Judgment, Felix trembled and said, 'That will do for the present; when I find it convenient, I will send for you again.' "

Drusilla lost interest, but Felix summoned him often, and if he groped toward repentance, he hoped too that Paul would bribe him, after which the case would be settled in Paul's favor. Paul, Luke, Aristarchus, and old Philip and his daughters must have prayed for the Procurator's conversion but Felix was one of Paul's failures.

In the spring of 59, after a riot in Caesarea, Felix was recalled to Rome in disgrace. His brother's influence saved him from execution or enforced suicide, but Felix was never again employed in the public service. Before he left, he could easily have released Paul, but he wished to curry a few last crumbs of favor with Jewish leaders. At least he did not want to give them grounds on which to charge him with maladministration of the case. Mean to the last, he left Paul in custody.

The new procurator of Judea was Porcius Festus, a man of better background and higher principles, whose endeavors to rule the turbulent province broke his health: he died in office after two years.

As soon as he had been installed at the beginning of July 59, Porcius Festus left Caesarea to visit Jerusalem. Inevitably, among many other matters, the high priest and the Sanhedrin raised the question of Paul. They assumed Festus would wish to ingratiate himself, and asked that the trial be held speedily, and in Jerusalem: the young zealots who had rashly vowed neither to eat nor to drink until they had killed Paul, and presumably had walked around for two years under a dispensation, would be waiting to ambush him in a *wadi* or a wood. Festus ruined the plan, probably quite undeliberately. He merely suited his own convenience when he refused to order Paul to Jerusalem, and informed the Jewish authorities that they must appear in Caesarea. He promised to expedite the hearing.

After eight or ten days, Festus returned with his retinue to Caesarea, and next morning took the bench as Chief Justice of Judea. The first case was Paul's. The moment Paul entered, the Jews from Jerusalem converged on him in the pent-up fury of two years' frustration, restrained only by the presence of the procurator. At first they hardly conducted the case in a way likely to impress Festus, for they let it go right over his head. As Festus describes the scene: "When confronted with him, his accusers did not charge him with any of the crimes I had expected; but they had some argument or other with him about their own religion and about a dead man called Jesus whom Paul alleged to be alive." Later they steered the prosecution more on the lines of Tertullus' pomposities before Felix, but called no witnesses; though Luke does not precisely say so, he implies that at each indictment Festus asked for legal proof and none was offered.

Paul simply denied there was a case to answer. "I have committed no offense whatever: against Jewish law; or the Temple; or against Caesar."

Festus saw the force of the defense. But puzzled by the religious quarrel, and not averse to humoring his new subjects, he was ready to hand Paul over to the Sanhedrin. He addressed Paul: "Are you willing to go up to Jerusalem and stand trial on these charges before me there?"

Paul knew that even if he should reach Jerusalem alive, there he could more easily be done away with. The Jews, however, had opened an escape route: had they restricted their charges to the local matter of his alleged profaning of the Temple, he could hardly have refused to be tried in Jerusalem without implying either that Festus could not protect him, or that he would treat the accused less fairly there than in Caesarea. But now the Jews had raised the far wider charge of fomenting disaffection throughout the civilized world. Both charges, the religious and the political, carried the death penalty, but even though the second was the graver, Paul elected to be tried on this, the political issue, which directly concerned the Romans.

Very deliberately, Paul answered Festus: "I am standing at Caesar's tribunal and this is where I should be tried. I have done the Jews no wrong, as you very well know. If I am guilty of committing any capital crime, I do not ask to be spared execution. But if there is no substance in the accusations these persons bring against me, no one has a right to surrender me to them. *I appeal to Caesar.*"

At that appeal, duly delivered in legal form, precedent demanded a short adjournment while the Procurator consulted his advisers whether to give leave. A Roman citizen had an inalienable right of appeal to the emperor, a privilege not accorded other provincials, but a governor must decide whether the case had sufficient weight to be referred to that august court.

Paul's appeal, though unexpected by Festus, was no sudden decision. In the past two years, as the case dragged on, Paul had thought out his next step. He must go to Rome. This offered a way. Moreover, the ruling of Gallio, that Christianity was a recognized cult, might not hold much longer. another governor could rule differently. The only certain freedom for the future was a favorable decision handed down by the supreme court in Rome, the emperor himself. The emperor was Nero. But the young Nero of A.D. 59, despite the dubious way in which he had gained the throne, still remained under the wise influence of Gallio's brother, Seneca, the greatest philosopher of the day. Neither Paul nor any provincial could forecast in 59 the awful degeneration of Nero into the despot whose name has been a byword for lust, cruelty, and bad government. As for the heavy cost involved in an appeal to Caesar, despite its being technically a free process, Paul did not trouble. God had supplied all his needs when wants were simple, and would continue, whether or not it was by the restoration of the patrimony.

All depended on Festus' willingness to grant Paul his right. After that, the wheels of justice would grind slowly but could not be reversed.

The court reconvened. Festus took his seat, then uttered the time-honored legal response.

"Have you appealed to Caesar? Unto Caesar you shall go."

Festus was now in a quandary. He had ruled that a *prima facie* case lay for appeal, yet this first prisoner of the governorship to be referred to Rome had no charges against him which would be clear to Caesar, since Festus could not understand them himself. Fortunately, the Jewish king of the native state which the Romans had set up to the northeast of Palestine, Herod Agrippa II, was due immediately on a state visit. The Herods were proselytes, not full Jews by blood, but Agrippa could act as assessor to advise on the form of indictment.

He was thirty-two years old, the son of Herod Agrippa I, the king of Judea who had sought to execute Simon Peter and died miserably at Tyre shortly after Peter's escape. The son had been considered too young for Judea, which reverted to direct Roman rule, but four years later had been allowed to succeed an uncle as king of the handkerchief-sized state of Chalcis, the narrow plain between the Lebanon mountains and Mount Hermon. This wee kingdom had been extended gradually to a respectable size, totally dependent on the pleasure of the Romans. Agrippa was unmarried but according to gossip lived in incest with his sister Bernice, who was a queen dowager, widow of their uncle whom Agrippa had succeeded. Drusilla, wife of the disgraced Felix, was their sister.

Festus put his problem to Agrippa toward the end of the state visit. Agrippa expressed a wish to hear Paul. A time was arranged for next day. Paul prepared his speech with great care, for he looked on it less as a defense than an opportunity of preaching before an exalted influential audience.

To this state function all the great men of Caesarea were invited, Jews and Gentiles, including the general officers of the military command. Many of the Procurator's household were present in the audience hall, its pillared sides open to catch the air stirring lazily toward the Mediterranean, and Luke would have had no difficulty in securing a seat: his account of the proceedings bears all the marks of eyewitness. He noted the "great pomp" with which King Agrippa and

Queen Bernice were escorted to their thrones, with blare of trumpets, waving of peacock feather fans and the rigid salutes of the generals. No doubt it amused Luke to watch Festus obsequiously giving precedence to a king he could topple at a flick of his finger.

Paul was brought in. Small, bandy-legged, almost stooping, but alert and vigorous in manner; gray-bearded now, a little less thin and wiry after years in moderate comfort safe from stonings or beatings or long treks from city to city, yet with a frailty and a scarred face in sharp contrast to the hearty young soldier who led him, politely enough, by a chain.

Festus opened the proceedings. "King Agrippa! And all who are present with us: You see this man here about whom the whole Jewish people petitioned me, both at Jerusalem and here, shouting that he ought not to live any longer. But I found that he had done nothing deserving death; as he himself has appealed to the emperor, I decided to send him. But I have nothing definite to write to my lord about him. Therefore I have brought him before you—and especially before you, King Agrippa!—that after we have examined him I may have something to write. For it seems to me unreasonable, in sending a prisoner, not to indicate the charge against him."

Festus resumed his seat. Agrippa said to Paul: "You have permission to speak for yourself."

Paul raised his hand, not to command silence but in courtesy, almost as if blessing this young king whose soul he glimpsed behind the incestuous perfumed body, and began on a quiet note.

"I consider myself fortunate, King Agrippa, that it is before you that I am to make my defense today upon all the charges brought against me by the Jews, particularly as you are expert in all Jewish matters, both our customs and disputes. And therefore I beg you to give me a patient hearing.

"My life from my youth up, the life I led from the beginning among my people and in Jerusalem, is familiar to all Jews." They could testify if they wished that he had lived as a

Pharisee, "the strictest party in our religion." And—reverting to the point which had split the Sanhedrin at his Jerusalem hearing—he stressed that he was on trial for his hope in the age-old promise which God had made to their ancestors. "Why," asked Paul, addressing Agrippa but with every one of his audience in mind, "should it be thought a thing incredible with you that *God should raise the dead?*

"I myself was convinced that I ought to do many things in opposing the name of Jesus of Nazareth." Paul described the violence of his persecution of the early Christians. By personal testimony, as the surest way of introducing the Gospel to the great of the earth, he led steadily onward to the heart of the matter. He told of the Damascus Road. He did not mention Ananias, who as an obscure Jew would have meant nothing to Agrippa and Bernice, and he conflated several incidents and divine messages to make plain that Jesus Christ personally had sent him to open the eyes of Jews and Gentiles to turn them from darkness to light, from the power of Satan to God, " 'So that,' " Paul quoted Jesus, " 'by trust in Me, they may obtain forgiveness of sins, and a place with those whom God has made His own.' And so, King Agrippa, I did not disobey the heavenly vision, but I preached this message first to those in Damascus, then to those in Jerusalem and in all Judea, and to the Gentiles also, urging them to repent and turn to God and prove their repentance by their deeds."

Paul's words came straight at Agrippa and Bernice, clearly enunciated: They also should repent and turn to God and prove their repentance by deeds!

Many of the distinguished audience may have grown increasingly embarrassed at this bold discourse which, if taken seriously, must overturn the entire domestic existence of the king and queen.

Paul was in full course: "That is why the Jews seized me in the Temple and tried to do away with me. But I had God's help, and so to this very day I stand and testify to small and great, saying nothing beyond what the prophets and Moses foretold: that the Christ must suffer, and that He, as the *first to rise from the dead,* would proclaim the dawn to the people and to the Gentiles—''

''Paul, you are mad! You are mad!'' Festus shouted, his manners before royalty entirely forgotten. Up to that minute, he had supposed they were arguing about whether Jesus was dead, as the Jews said, or still living. It suddenly broke in on Festus that Paul was actually claiming Jesus had come alive again after being killed; that this was what Paul staked his life upon. The absurdity of it hit Festus between the eyes. ''Paul, you are mad! Your great learning is turning you mad!''

''I am not mad, Your Excellency,'' Paul replied mildly. ''What I am saying is sober truth. The king is well versed in these matters, and to him I can speak freely. I do not believe he can be unaware of any of these facts, for this has been no hole-and-corner business.'' And Paul ignored Festus. ''King Agrippa, do you believe the prophets? I know you do!''

Then Agrippa spoke: ''In a short time you think to make a Christian of me?''

''Short or long,'' Paul echoed, ''I would to God that not only you but also all who hear me this day might become such as I am—except for these chains!''

Agrippa had heard enough. The *Authorized Version's* ''Almost thou persuadest me to be a Christian,'' suggesting the brink of conversion, does not translate accurately a statement which conveyed reproof and refusal rather than fervor. At Paul's dramatic rejoinder, with its tremendous conviction that happiness for king and commoner lay only in the love of Jesus Christ, Agrippa rose from his throne to end the audience. The queen and all the company rose too. Royalty and governor withdrew, and only on reaching the private quarters did they admit how impressed they had been, telling each other that Paul had done nothing worthy of death or prison, and could have been released had he not appealed.

Agrippa and Bernice continued ruling together until the Great Rebellion seven years later, which the queen strove to prevent. They left for Rome, where Bernice eventually became the mistress of the Emperor Titus, the general who had captured Jerusalem, slaughtered its inhabitants, and leveled the Temple and city to dust.

Thirty-Three
SHIPWRECK

Festus handed Paul over to a centurion named Julius serving with the imperial or Augustan cohort, whose officers and men traveled throughout the empire on escort and courier duties. Julius commanded a detail of about a dozen solders: Paul was the only prisoner of rank, permitted to take two attendants who were listed as his personal slaves: Aristarchus and Luke the physician. The other prisoners would be convicts on their grim way to "make a Roman holiday," either as lion fodder at the games or, if burly enough, for training as gladiators. These would all be chained to timbers below decks, but Paul and his attendants could move about freely, though he must always wear a loose chain, symbol of his status.

In Caesarea harbor, Julius found a coastal vessel out from Adramyttium, east of Assos in the province of Asia, about to sail home with a Levantine cargo.[27] He took passage, confident of finding a vessel for Rome at one of the ports where the coaster would call; if she sailed so slowly that the season grew late, he could cross from Adramyttium to Neapolis near Philippi and conduct the party by land, then over the Adriatic to Brindisi. Either way, he expected to have them in Rome by the end of October.

They sailed from Caesarea in the last week of August 59, before a light westerly breeze, and put in for a day at Sidon, sixty-seven miles northeast. Julius let Paul ashore, thus immediately showing a kindness which was more than the respect to be accorded an unconvicted Roman citizen; like other military men, Julius had fallen quickly under Paul's charm and air of authority. The Christians of Sidon gave Paul—and presumably Luke and Aristarchus—warm hospitality and fitted them out with any remaining needs for the long voyage.

The westerly, the prevailing wind of late summer in the eastern Mediterranean, prevented a crossing of the open sea south of Cyprus, the direct route which Luke remembered from the reverse voyage two years previously. They had to keep between Cyprus and the Cilician shore. Once more Paul saw the Taurus range, blue in the distance beyond the plain where he had lived as a boy. When the mountains came closer to the sea, the vessel hugged the coast, using the offshore breezes and the current flowing west, and heaving-to each evening. Luke noted it all. He was not a seaman but described his observations in landlubber's language so accurate that when, in the mid-nineteenth century, a curious Scot with a yacht and great knowledge of seamanship retraced Paul's route, he found that Luke's entire account of this most famous voyage with its disastrous end exactly fitted the facts of wind, sea, and coast.[28]

Tacking along the southern Anatolian shore was slow, hot work. For fifteen days, Paul and his friends never put into a harbor. Calm and pleasant Mediterranean weather meant heat and misery for the chained-up convicts below, and impatience for the soldiers cooped up in this small ship among the sacks of dried fruit which probably made most of the cargo. Julius had plenty of opportunity for getting to know his chief prisoner; if conversion followed, Luke is too discreet to mention it, but Julius' subsequent actions point toward the probability.

They crossed the Gulf of Attalia into which Paul had sailed

with Barnabas on that first pioneering journey long ago. The rough hills of Lycia lay ahead. The weather could be changeable by now, in mid-September, and the mountaintops disappearing into cloud, and the lowland—where it narrowed to a point—etched against clearer evening skies to the west. Paul had never penetrated these mountains, but from his missionary churches to the north and east the faith may have been spreading already into the valleys. When at last the ship put into the great landlocked harbor of Myra, two miles from the city at the mouth of a great gorge, a church could have already been there. Myra, which now is deserted, grew into an important bishopric, and by a peculiar contortion of history and folklore, Saint Nicholas of Myra became Santa Claus.

In the bay among the naval galleys propelled by slave power and the coastal shipping, Julius found a fine large merchantman of the Egyptian corn run, the lifeline of Rome, importing wheat under a system of privately owned vessels commissioned into imperial service. Myra, due north of Alexandria, was a principal port of call in summer, when the wind did not allow sailing direct to Rome.

Julius transferred his soldiers and prisoners. No other military officer was aboard and thus by Roman practice in the corn fleet he took precedence over the captain and the owner or supercargo; in any emergency, Julius would have the last word. His party increased the complement of the ship to 278 souls—Italian and Egyptian merchants, even an Indian or a Chinese; possibly a string of African slaves from the Upper Nile; army veterans returning on retirement, priests of Isis, entertainers, scholars from the great University of Alexandria, together with women and children. With all of these, and a big cargo of wheat, the Alexandrian ship must have been over 500 tons, by no means the biggest known to have been afloat at that period, and no smaller than many merchantmen which plied the Mediterranean at the time of Nelson and the last age of sail.

Paul's, however, differed from a nineteenth-century vessel in several vital respects. She had only one large mast carrying a huge mainsail, thus putting heavy strains on her timbers. Her stem and stern both looked like a modern bow. She was steered by detachable rudders rather like large paddles, and her captain had no compass or chronometer and the roughest of charts, so he never knew his position unless he could see sun or stars to take a bearing by a primitive form of quadrant.

The ship's intended course on leaving Myra was to sail past Rhodes through the archipelagoes, then by the southern tip of Greece (now Cape Matapan) to reach Italy by the Strait of Messina; and so to Ostia, the port of Rome. But when the vessel tacked out of Myra Bay, on about September 16 the wind was still unfavorably northwest and strong. The captain had to work up above Rhodes near the mainland and its promontories, to get smooth water and the shore breezes. "We sailed slowly for a number of days," remembers Luke, "and arrived with difficulty off Cnidus," the spacious port at the very end of a narrow, mountainous peninsula, the westernmost of the southern Anatolian coastline. Cnidus was the last point where they had protection from the full strength of the contrary wind; and "the wind did not allow us to go on." The captain would not enter harbor, though Cnidus had plenty of anchorage, but ran southwest through the Dodecanese toward the mountains of Crete. He rounded Cape Salmone and began to sail under the south of Crete, hoping that the wind would veer before he must turn north. And so "we struggled along the coast until we came to a place called Fair Havens, near the town of Lasea."

They had reached a roadstead well sheltered by the mountains and by islands, which was as far as they could sail into a northwest wind. Immediately beyond Fair Havens lies Cape Matala where the rocky coast turns sharply north for some twenty miles before turning west again, and if they tried to cross that open gulf they would be wrecked on a lee shore. The captain anchored, windbound. Days passed. Fair Havens was pleasant enough but had no port; small parties might go ashore to visit Lasea, but the entire ship's company would need to live aboard if they wintered. October 5 came and went, the Jewish Day of Atonement that year of A.D. 59. The "Dangerous Days," when navigation was feasible but risky, were slipping away. With November 11, all navigation would cease on the open sea because then the sun and stars might be overcast for days on end, with no opportunity for bearings; this, rather than the inevitable hazard of storms, was the factor that stopped sea traffic in winter.

They had lost all prospect of reaching Italy that season. Julius convened a conference to decide the best plan and invited Paul to attend; by now Julius appreciated Paul's judgment as well as his seafaring experience.

The captain urged that they seize the first opportunity to round Cape Matala and reach the port of Phoenix, not far down the coast; probably he feared disaffection in passengers and crew if they wintered at isolated Fair Havens, which had the additional disadvantage, as an anchorage, of being open to nearly half the compass, so that in a heavy gale the vessel might drag her anchors and go aground. If the wind changed to the south, they could just make Phoenix. He was a skilled seaman, as his future actions show, and would know that during autumn in these seas a south wind will often be followed by a violent northeaster, a Levanter. His professional advice was to risk it. The owner backed him, for while the ship lay in Fair Havens, he was responsible for keeping the company from starvation, whereas at Phoenix the passengers would disembark.

Julius turned to Paul.

"Paul gave them this advice: 'I can see, gentlemen, that this voyage will be disastrous: it will mean grave loss, not only of ship and cargo but also of life.' "

Julius decided in favor of the captain and the owner.

About October 10, the captain noted that the wind had changed. Luke disassociates himself from the crew's reaction as if he thoroughly disapproved: "When the south wind blew gently, supposing they had obtained their purpose, they weighed anchor and sailed along Crete, close inshore."

They turned the cape and began merrily across the gulf, the dinghy bobbing behind as was customary on short runs inshore. If the sun shone on them, the clouds were ominously thick on Mount Ida, the highest point of Crete and now full on their starboard bow. Suddenly the wind changed. A tremendous blast roared down from Ida striking them full force; Luke calls its strength "typhonic." The air whirled and twisted; a drenching rain blacked out the coast. Their mast, under full sail, shuddered at the sudden gale, proving the unwisdom of the ancients' practice of sailing single masted: the vibration was so excessive that water began to seep into the hull.

Within a few minutes, the captain knew he could never keep the ship headed into this northeaster: the Levanter was upon them and they must act accordingly. "We had to give way and run before it," to the lee of the small island of Cauda or Gavdos which lay some forty miles off in the exact path of the wind. They had no hope of making its little port, which was on the wrong side, nor could they dare to anchor, but they used the comparatively smooth water and temporary, risky shelter of its cliffs to prepare as best they could for whatever lay ahead. First they secured and hoisted the dinghy, now waterlogged. Passengers helped, and Luke records feelingly, "We managed with some difficulty." Then they used tackle to put cables under the hull in order to brace the timbers, a common precaution in ancient times, and occasionally in Nelson's day, against the strain of wind and turbulent water. The chief fear of all on board was that the ship would either break up or the timbers leak until she became waterlogged: more ancient ships were lost by foundering than by any other cause.

They lowered the yard with its mainsail, for if she ran with this wind under full sail the end—if she did not founder first—would be the shallows and quicksands of the North

African shore, the notorious Gulf of Syrtis Major off Libya. Their one hope was to set stormsails, lay her on a starboard tack (with her right side to the wind), and let her drift slowly to ride out the storm.

Leaving the shelter of Cauda they were soon enduring the full agony of rough seas. Without much weight of sail "We were violently stormtossed"—bobbing about like a cork, with the spray and rain preventing fires, drenching supplies, clothes, everything above and below decks. What little was eaten would be thrown up by retching stomachs. The heaving, slippery boards made any movement painful. Paul, Luke, the convicts now released from their irons, and every able-bodied man would take turns at the pumps, but with the seeping of water through strained timbers the level in the bilge rose remorsely and the ship settled lower. On the second day to lighten her, the captain ordered loose cargo jettisoned: all livestock and much else. On the third, he ordered overboard the spare tackle—cables, spars, anything not essential.

Day after miserable day, night after terrifying night, they rose and fell in mountainous seas. Thick unbroken clouds prevented any reckoning: the captain had no idea of the ship's position. To Luke, it seemed they were tossing on a crazy course but in fact they drifted very steadily at a mean rate of one and a half miles an hour in a direction about eight degrees north of west; had they possessed charts and the means to make dead reckoning, they would have spared themselves much worry, for they could not have set a more advantageous course—provided they did not founder. The main cargo of wheat had become thoroughly water-logged—the sacks too heavy and sodden to move in a pitching ship, and all the time increasing in weight.

The water level rose, the ship settled lower, until by the eleventh or twelfth day of the storm "all hope of our being saved was abandoned." Foundering was inevitable now—a matter of a few days at most even if the storm abated—and would mean the loss of all hands if they abandoned ship.

Luke had not noticed Paul. Little is known of the interior design of ancient ships but all passengers would have been very much on top of one another, sharing their miseries without the slightest privacy. Yet Luke had not seen what Paul saw, until the morning when Paul struggled forward to where the captain and many of the crew huddled dejected. Paul threw his voice above the wind and they gathered round him.

His first words were a chip of the old Paul with the tendency to justify himself, but his hearers respected him too much to notice. "Men," he said, "you should have listened to me and not have sailed from Crete; then we should have avoided all this damage and loss. But now I beg you, take courage! Not one of you will lose his life; only the ship will be lost. For last night, an angel of the God to whom I belong and whom I worship stood by me. And he said, 'Do not be afraid, Paul. You must stand before Caesar. And look, God has given you the lives of all who sail with you.' And so, men, take courage! For I believe God that it will be just as I was told. But we must be cast on some island."

On the fourteenth night since they had left Crete, with no decline of the gale, the sailors suddenly detected the sound of breakers from leeward. They could see nothing, but if they could hear above the storm they must be drifting close to a rocky shore. They took soundings and found twenty fathoms. A little later they found fifteen. At this rate they would soon be wrecked on the rocks. They could see the breakers now but not the shore, for they were in fact off the low point of Koura at the opening of what is now Saint Paul's Bay; Smith of Jordanhill discovered that this was the exact spot which a drifting ship would have reached on the fourteenth night and that the soundings were accurate too.

The captain ordered no less than four anchors to be moved aft from their usual place forward, and dropped through the alternative stern hawseholes with which ancient ships, unlike modern, were fitted. By his seamanlike action, the ship would be prevented from falling on the rocks at night and better positioned to run on shore when daylight allowed a choice. Then "they wished for day." There was nothing else to do.

The sailors thought otherwise. Paul, alert, spotted what they were up to: the men on whose skill the safety of officers and passengers depended were quietly lowering the dinghy, under pretense of dropping anchors from the bow, determined to rat before the ship broke up. Paul said to the centurion and soldiers: "Unless these men stay in the ship, you cannot be saved." The soldiers cut the ropes and the boat fell into the sea and drifted away.

Just before dawn, Paul made another suggestion. The captain had been far too concerned with the crisis to think of it.

Paul addressed the officers and everyone in hearing. "For the last fourteen days, you have lived in suspense and gone hungry: you have eaten nothing whatever. So I beg you to have something to eat; your lives depend on it. Remember, not a hair of you will be lost."

Taking a sodden moldy loaf he gave thanks to God, praying in the presence of all; he broke it and deliberately began to eat. They plucked up their courage and a general meal was organized. The ship's motion being less than for the past fourteen days, the feeding of 276 persons until all had eaten offered no difficulty. With new strength they dumped the rest of the wheat into the sea.

By now it was daylight. The ship lay at the entrance to a bay. No one recognized it; not knowing the rate or direction of drift, they might be anywhere off Sicily or Tunisia. Ahead stood a rocky shore but they could see a sandy beach.

The captain carried out a complicated maneuver. The crew, in Luke's description, "slipped the anchors and let them go; at the same time they loosed the lashings of the steering paddles, set the foresail to the wind, and let her drive to the beach." The captain had her completely under command and half a mile to go. Soon she would be beached and they would wade ashore.

But he could not realize when he gave the order, that the rocky spit of land close on their starboard beam was in fact a little island (Salmonetta) linked to the mainland by a shoal, "a place where two seas meet," as Luke describes it. Because of this the vessel was caught in a crosscurrent and swept on to the shoal until the forepart stuck fast in a bottom of mud and clay while the breakers began to pound the stern to pieces. The company began jumping out. The soldiers reacted instantly, for the convicted felons or Paul might swim off and escape. According to standing orders, they sought leave to slaughter the lot.

"But the centurion, willing to save Paul, kept them from their purpose; and commanded that they which could swim should cast themselves first into the sea, and get to land: and the rest, some on boards and some on broken pieces of the ship. And so it came to pass, that they escaped all safe to land."

Thirty-Four
CAPITAL OF THE WORLD

Seeing a wreck, the natives rushed to the shore. Unlike the Cornish wreckers, they did all they could to help; it had started raining again, and everybody was drenched from sea-water, so the natives lit a great bonfire on the beach, and the ship's company began to dry out.

The seamen had learned by now that this was Malta; the grand harbor of Valetta, with which many would be familiar, was not far away. The wetting had turned Luke rather Greek and superior; he dismisses the Maltese, who "showed us no little kindness," as barbarians because of their dialect and thick accent, though Malta had been Latinized for centuries. He was amused by their reaction to the next incident. Paul had sensibly warmed himself and helped affairs by scavenging around, despite his chain, for brushwood to feed the fire. He threw on a bundle; one of his sticks leaped out at him and fastened on his hand—he had picked up a torpid poisonous snake.

"When the natives saw the creature hanging from his hand, they said to one another, 'No doubt this man is a murderer. Though he has escaped from the sea, Justice has not allowed him to live.' Paul, however, shook off the creature into the fire and suffered no harm. They waited, expecting him to swell up or suddenly fall down dead; but when they had waited a long time and saw no misfortune came to him, they changed their minds and said that he was a god."

Paul had not panicked at the snake, and he was equal to the next call. In the neighborhood of the wreck was the estate of Publius, the chief magistrate of Malta, who at once offered temporary hospitality. The crew and most of the passengers were probably disposed around the huts and cottages of his people, while Julius, Paul, and their attendants were invited to the villa. There they discovered that Publius' father lay sick with dysentery and Malta fever. It was not Luke the physician but Paul who effected the cure. "Paul visited him," Luke records generously, "and, after prayer, laid his hands upon him and healed him; whereupon the other sick people on the island came and were cured."

Paul and Luke were only a few days at the chief magistrate's villa. Julius may have rented a house in Valetta, where the healing and evangelism continued all that winter. Paul, Luke, and Aristarchus became greatly loved so that the people gave them many gifts and on their departure stocked them up with provisions. Tradition in Malta marks Paul's stay as the beginning of an unbroken Christianity; the Maltese kept in memory the site of the wreck for eighteen centuries until Smith of Jordanhill came along to prove them right.

Another large grain ship from Alexandria, sailing under the figurehead of the Twin Gods, Castor and Pollux, had wintered at Valetta. When, early in February 60, her captain decided to take advantage of fair weather to make the short run onward, though the sailing season had not started, Julius booked passages. The voyage was uneventful, and at length Paul sailed into the Bay of Naples, saw Vesuvius with its lazy curl of smoke and the city of Pompeii, unaware that nineteen years later she would be in ruins. The grain ship docked at Puteoli, then chief port of the Bay, where they found Christians. Julius permitted a week's visit as their guests, whether because he knew he was not yet expected in Rome and wished Paul to enjoy a last taste of comparative freedom, or because he had to send ahead to Rome for orders, or because he could not bear to think his days with Paul were numbered.

When at last they set out to join the Appian Way, Paul was a little nervous and depressed at what might lie ahead, both before Nero and among the Christians of Rome to whom he had once written so joyfully and vigorously but who did not owe their faith to him. Forty-three miles out of Rome, at the town of Appii Forum, he met Roman Christians hurrying to welcome him after the news from Puteoli. At Tres Tabernae or Three Taverns, a halting place thirty-three miles out, were yet another group. "When Paul saw them, he thanked God and took courage."

Rome was the greatest city Paul had ever seen. More than a million free citizens and about a million slaves lived on or between the seven hills, some of which had wide gardens and luxurious villas: below Nero's palace on the Palatine a large ornamental lake was being excavated for his pleasure where the Colosseum stands now. Paul had little opportunity to view the forum and the great public buildings; after Julius handed over the prisoners to his superior officer and the convicted felons were taken off to be prepared for butchery by one means or another, Paul was placed in custody in a house rented at his own cost. It was not in the slums, the labyrinth of narrow streets and flimsy dwellings from which the mob emerged for periodical riots. He would have had a home of reasonable size—or small but with a roomy garden—just within the walls near the camp of the Praetorian Guard on the Caelian Hill in the north of Rome.

The rumble of traffic down the narrow cobbled street at night, when the country carts were allowed to bring produce to the markets, the babble of jostling pedestrians by day, the distant roars of excited crowds in the Circus Maximus during chariot races or gladiatorial combats, the stench of a great city even in winter when Paul arrived, and the risk of malaria in summer, did not make for ease or luxury. And the regulations demanded the never-ending presence of a soldier to whom he must be chained. But he was not in prison; he could have friends at his side and invite all whom he wished.

After three days he sent for the local Jewish leaders and they came.

"Brothers," Paul said, "although I have done nothing against our people or the customs of our ancestors, I was arrested in Jerusalem and handed over to the Romans. They examined me and would have set me free, since they found me guilty of nothing deserving the death penalty; but the Jews lodged an objection and I was forced to appeal to Caesar, not that I had any accusation to make against my own nation. That is why I asked to see you and talk with you, for it is on account of the Hope of Israel that I wear this chain."

The Jewish leaders could not tell whether Paul might receive the emperor's favor and protection, and at that period in Nero's reign they lacked influence in the palace. They replied: "We have received no letters from Judea about you, nor has any countryman of yours arrived here with any report or story of anything to your discredit. We think it would be as well to hear your own account of your position; all we know about this sect is that opinion everywhere condemns it."

Since many of the Roman Christians were Jews by birth, the leaders knew more than they admitted, but Paul welcomed the opportunity of carrying out his normal sequence of preaching on arrival in any city: "to the Jew first." On the appointed day, a considerable number came to his lodgings. Paul expounded and debated from early morning until evening, "testifying about the kingdom of God and trying to persuade them about Jesus, arguing from the Law of Moses and the prophets." Some were convinced, others skeptical. When they left him, Paul quoted Isaiah to them, the text used by Jesus in which God rebukes Israel's self-imposed blindness: "The heart of this nation has grown coarse, their ears are dull of hearing, and they have shut their eyes, for fear they should see with their eyes, hear with their ears, understand with their heart, and be converted and be healed by Me." Paul added: "Take notice: this salvation of God has been sent to the Gentiles. *They* will listen!" And the Jews left, arguing vigorously among themselves.

That was the beginning of a period which, despite his sixty years, was as strenuous as any in Paul's life. "He stayed there," wrote Luke in the final words of Acts, "two full years at his own expense, with a welcome for all who came to him, proclaiming the kingdom of God and the facts about the Lord Jesus Christ quite openly and without hindrance."

Luke's words are borne out by Paul's writings. "I have been made a servant of the church by God," he wrote from Rome, "who gave me the task of fully proclaiming His message, which is the secret He hid through all past ages from all mankind, but has now revealed to His people. For this is God's plan: to make known His secret to His people, this rich and glorious secret which He has for all peoples. And the secret is this: *Christ in you*, which means you will share the glory of God. So we preach Christ to all men. We warn and teach everyone, with all possible wisdom, in order to bring each one into God's presence as a mature individual in union with Christ. To get this done I toil and struggle, using the mighty strength that Christ supplies, which is at work in me" (*or* "striving with all energy which He mightily inspires within me").

His days sped by in the same task as at Corinth or Ephesus: winning converts, building up teachers and evangelists who should go out to win and teach others. The church in Rome was numerous and vigorous before Paul, whether or not Peter was there already, which the research of centuries has been unable to fix with certainty; yet there were many ancient hilltop cities in southern Italy awaiting evangelists, and great cities of the northern plains and villages of the Apennines. Rome too was port of call for so many of every race and color in the Mediterranean world and beyond that Paul never knew who might be brought to see him or to what distant land they might take the message. And Romans small and great sought him out. Tradition has it that even Seneca, still powerful as a statesman and philosopher, corresponded with him; but their "Letters" are a third-century forgery and prove nothing.

No one could leave that hired house untouched, if only to "argue vigorously." It had an atmosphere of happiness with the music and singing which Paul mentions in both the chief letters he wrote from it. His character had not been soured or hardened by troubles. To judge by what he thought important, he was kind, tenderhearted, forgiving, just as Christ had forgiven him. He walked in love, the element which bound his qualities together. He was still the great encourager, welcoming a man who was weak in faith but refusing to argue about secondary matters. The Romans learned that he lived as he had taught them when he wrote three years before: "We that are strong ought to bear with the failings of the weak, and not to please ourselves . . . Owe no one anything except to love one another." Like his Master he did not emphasize a man's shortcomings but his potential, and he would not pass judgment on others unless they betrayed their Master by open sin, when he could be severe but with the aim of restoring and strengthening.

In that Roman house, bitter people softened; anger, wrath, clamor died away. Paul had more than ever a sense of his littleness, his unworthiness—"less than the least of all saints"—of the marvel of his being entrusted with a commission "to preach the unsearchable riches of Christ." He seemed to delight in the contrast between the majesty of the message and the insignificance of the messenger: such a gentle little man now, yet with what steel and strength.

The soldiers, turn and turn about, knew where that strength had its chief contact with infinity. In the early mornings, the guard chained to Paul joined willy-nilly the time on his knees and heard the words of thanksgiving and intercession. Paul's heart was far away in Greece or Asia Minor. "Father of glory," the soldier must have heard him pray for the Ephesians, and for the Colossians and "all who have not seen my face": "God of our Lord Jesus Christ, give them a spirit of wisdom and of revelation. May they know what is the hope to which You have called them, what are the riches of Your glorious inheritance, what the immeasurable greatness of Your power. . . . May they live a life worthy of You, fully pleasing to You, bearing fruit in every good work and increasing in their knowledge of You . . . Father, of whom the whole family in heaven and earth is named, according to Your riches in glory grant them to be strengthened by might in the inner man. May Christ dwell in their hearts by faith. May they be rooted and grounded in love, and comprehend with all saints what is the breadth and length and height and depth—and know the love of Christ which passes knowledge, that they be filled with all the fullness of God."

Mentioning many by name, entering into their needs and problems as best he knew them, Paul prayed, sometimes alone except for the soldier, sometimes with Aristarchus and Luke and whoever was with him. His prayers were shot through with praise, and it may have been a soldier, whether Christian yet or not, who first heard in Rome the thanksgiving which would ring out to Asia and thus to the world: "Now unto Him who is able to do exceedingly abundantly above all that we ask or think, according to the power that worketh in us, unto Him be glory in the church by Christ Jesus throughout all ages, world without end. Amen."

Old associates found their way to Paul, joining Aristarchus and Luke "the beloved physician." One was John Mark, whose desertion in Pamphylia long ago had split Paul from Barnabas. Whether Mark had been in Rome with Simon Peter, or had traveled from Cyprus or Alexandria, Paul was completely reconciled and soon described him as "a great comfort to me." Timothy was back at Paul's side in A.D. 61;

and Tychicus too, who had been an Asian delegate on the Jerusalem journey. Another companion, Demas, probably a Macedonian from Thessalonica, would have a regrettable future.

There was also a runaway slave in the household.

Paul one day found himself confronted by the lost property of one of his close friends. The slave, Onesimus, whose name means "Useful," had run away from Colossae in Asia, where he was owned by no less than Philemon, the mainspring of the Colossian church. Like many escaped slaves, Onesimus had drifted to Rome, for in Ephesus or other great cities of Asia he might easily be recognized and hauled back to expect the usual, fearful fate of runaways. Whether Onesimus, in distress and debt, had sought out Paul or had been discovered by one of the companions, Paul "brought him to birth in my imprisonment." He worked as Paul's servant and greatly endeared himself so that Paul described him as "my very heart." More than that, he became part of the missionary team, "a faithful and beloved brother."

Then Epaphras, the original missionary to Colossae, which Paul had never reached, arrived in Rome. He made Paul happy with excellent news of the Colossians' faith in Christ and love for their fellow Christians. But a heresy was troubling and puzzling them. Epaphras, who felt intense desire that they should become mature and "fully assured in the will of God," discussed the heresy with Paul at length. A great man of prayer, Epaphras wrestled in spirit and stirred others to pray for Colossae. Paul speaks of him as "my fellow prisoner," and whether sharing voluntarily or under some sort of similar custody, Epaphras could not return to Asia. Paul determined to write to the Colossians and send the letter by Tychicus. This would deal specially with the Colossian problem; but Paul would send another, more general letter which Tychicus should deliver to the Ephesians for circulation among other churches in Asia, including cities Paul had not visited.

But as he thought about Colossae, Paul knew he must return Onesimus to his owner. Onesimus, well aware what might happen to a slave when recovered by his master, also knew that he must go.

Colossians and the other letter, known as Ephesians, emerged similar in content yet distinctive in style. Thoughts much in Paul's mind are found in both, sometimes in identical phrases so that it is even possible that he composed the letters together, dictating part of one, then part of the other. To Colossae, with a particular church in mind, he included personal messages, while his message to the Ephesians is more formal yet gives intimate autobiographical comments, especially when his mind is with those who have never seen him.

Drawn out of the very depths of Paul's spiritual experiences, containing analogies between Christ's love for the church and a man's love for his wife, Ephesians has proved a mine for Christian mystics which no generation has exhausted. Both letters, in striking sentences, consistent with his earliest writing yet with fresh touches as he works over the themes from different angles, emphasize God's love and its purpose. To the Ephesians: "He destined us in love to be His sons through Jesus Christ according to the purpose of His will, to the praise of His glorious grace which He freely bestowed on us in the Beloved. In Him we have redemption through His blood, the forgiveness of our trespasses, according to the riches of His grace which He lavished upon us. . . . God, who is rich in mercy, out of the great love with which He loved us, even when we were dead through our trespasses, made us alive together with Christ; by grace you have been saved." He repeats it. "By grace you have been saved through faith; and this is not your own doing, it is the gift of God—not because of works, lest any man should boast. For we are His workmanship, created in Christ Jesus for good works, which God prepared beforehand, that we should walk in them."

To the Colossians, he pours out the same theme but must

direct his teaching to answer their special problem. The heretics flourishing in Colossae were saying that they could not know God through Jesus Christ alone but must recast and expand the message in the light of contemporary thought; they wanted to change the very image of God as Christ had revealed Him; to hammer out fresh terms to express His reality; to reach Him by means more reasonable to those among whom they lived. Their theories were peculiarly similar in essence, though not in detail, to the theological ferments of the later twentieth century.

Paul directed the Colossian Christians firmly back. "As therefore you received Christ Jesus the Lord, so live in Him, rooted and built up in Him and established in the faith, just as you were taught, abounding in thanksgiving. See to it that no one makes a prey of you by philosophy and empty deceit, according to human tradition . . . and not according to Christ. For in Him dwells the whole fullness of deity bodily (*or the full content of divine nature lives in Christ, in His humanity*) and you have come to fullness of life in Him." Paul is in no doubt whatever. "*Christ* is the visible likeness of the invisible God. God created the whole universe through Him and for Him. He existed before all things, and in union with Him all things have their proper place. He is the head of His body, the church; He is the source of the body's life; He is the firstborn Son who was raised from death, in order that He alone might have the first place in all things."

The only knowledge of God, the only road to God, whether on earth or in remotest space, is through Jesus: "In Him all the fullness of God was pleased to dwell, and through Him to reconcile all things to Himself, whether on earth or in heaven, making peace through the blood of the cross."

On this foundation, Paul builds exhortation and encouragement, urging the Ephesians: "Walk in love as Christ loved us and gave Himself up for us," and the Colossians: "If you have been raised with Christ, seek the things that are above. . . . You have put on the new nature, which is being renewed in knowledge after the image of its Creator. . . . Put on, as God's chosen ones, compassion, kindness, lowliness, meekness, and patience." Both letters contain advice and direction, grounded in clear spiritual teaching: how a church should be guided and grow; how its different members, including masters and slaves, husbands and wives, fathers and children, should best please God.

When Paul closed his letter to the Colossians, he sent personal messages for particular people, and news of friends in Rome. The letter to Ephesus, being for general circulation, could not close like that. To end it, he hit a stroke of genius, which may have been actually suggested by one of his guards, and certainly was provoked by Paul's interest in the soldiers. He could often watch them at drill on the fields outside the walls near the camp of the Praetorian Guard, and in his traveling days had grown familiar with their service equipment. So now, checking with his soldier of the day, Paul creates one of his famous passages, the Christian's Armor which will enable him to stand his ground when the fight is hottest, deflect the arrows tipped with burning tow, advance wielding a trusty weapon. He went on to describe the belt round the loins; the iron breastplate; the sandals; the shield, the helmet, the sword.

"Take unto you the whole armor of God, that ye may be able to stand in the evil day, and having done all, to stand. Stand therefore, having your loins girt about with truth, and having on the breastplate of righteousness: and your feet shod with the preparation of the Gospel of peace; above all, taking the shield of faith, wherewith ye shall be able to quench all the fiery darts of the wicked. And take the helmet of salvation, and the sword of the Spirit which is the Word of God, praying always with all prayer and supplication in the Spirit, and watching thereunto with all perseverance and supplication for all saints. . . . "

Thirty-Five
THE YEARS OF FREEDOM

A third letter remained before Tychicus could leave for Asia: a note which Onesimus should hand to his master.

The only one of all Paul's epistles to be concerned solely with a personal matter, it shows him in a most engaging light, and without it any estimate of his character lacks balance. Paul, who has just been consciously the authoritative voice of "the mystery of Christ revealed to His holy apostles and prophets by the Spirit," now shows the tactful, diffident, kindly side of him, even the humorous: he makes puns on the name Onesimus meaning "useful" or "beneficent."

By implication, the letter to Philemon displays Paul's total rejection of slavery as a state compatible with the Gospel in a Christian society. Paul was no Spartacus calling slaves to revolt: a sudden end of slavery would reduce the Roman Empire to chaos, and he was realist enough to recognize that to agitate for abolition in his lifetime would be senseless, merely provoking the crushing of Christians as a menace to law and order. But he had taught consistently that "in Christ there is neither slave nor free," since all are equal in the sight of their Master, Christ. Both Ephesians and Colossians (Onesimus and Philemon being surely much in mind as he wrote) emphasize the new relationship between slave and free in which each must look on the other as a brother. And now he was sending back to Philemon not a piece of lost property but a brother Christian, an honored fellow worker.

Philemon had the legal right to butcher Onesimus, to whip or brand him, or put him to hard labor for life. Paul wished to save Philemon from doing wrong. And though Paul may not have expected this personal letter to circulate, its influence and that of his other passages about slavery eventually made the institution so distasteful, as Christianity permeated society, that it withered, slowly enough, and died out in the Christian world, though many Christians were sold into slavery by their Muslim conquerors. It died out, only to be revived in the New World by Spanish and Portuguese Roman Catholics despite the condemnation by the Pope, and by English Protestants, with all the distress and problems that followed.

The incompatibility of slavery with the Gospel is only implied. The letter itself is a window right into the hired house in Rome in A.D. 62. Tychicus was absent when it was penned, and the penman probably was Timothy. Epaphras, Mark, Aristarchus, Demas, and Luke were sitting around (and the inevitable soldier) when Paul began to dictate for Philemon and his family, opening as in the other two letters with warm gratitude and assurance of prayer. "I have derived much joy and comfort from your love, my brother, because the hearts of the saints have been refreshed through you.

"Accordingly, though I am bold enough in Christ to command you to do what is required, yet for love's sake I prefer to appeal to you—I, Paul, an ambassador and now a prisoner also for Christ Jesus, I appeal to you for my child, Onesimus, whose father I have become in my imprisonment." Here Paul made his little play on words: "Formerly he was *useless* to you, but now he is indeed *useful* to you and to me. I am sending him back to you, sending my heart. I would have been glad to keep him with me, in order that he might serve me on your behalf during my imprisonment for the Gospel, but I preferred to do nothing without your consent in order that your goodness might not be by compulsion but of your own free will.

"Perhaps this is why he was parted from you for a while, that you might have him back forever, no longer as a slave but *more than a slave: as a beloved brother,* especially to me but how much more to you, both in the flesh and in the Lord. So if you consider me your partner, receive him *as you would receive me.* If he has wronged you at all, or owes you anything, charge that to my account."

Paul seized the pen and scrawled: "I, Paul, write this in my own hand; I will repay it." He handed back the papyrus and added: "to say nothing of you owing me even your own self! Yes, brother, I want some benefit (*oninemi*) from you in the Lord. Refresh my heart in Christ.

"Confident of your obedience, I write to you, knowing you will do even more than I say."

Paul sniffed the air of freedom himself. The final words of the letter before farewells to Philemon were confident. He would see Colossae at last: "At the same time, prepare a guest room for me, for I am hoping through your prayers to be granted to you." And he added a note to both the other letters about his coming trial: "Pray for me," he asked the Ephesians, "that the right words may be given me, that I may open my mouth boldly to make known the secret of the Gospel for which I am an ambassador in chains: that I may declare it boldly, as I ought to speak."

His plan was to turn his trial into a testimony, whether or not Caesar presided. For the first seven years of the reign when he was still under twenty-five, Nero deputed the presidency of trials to the Praetorian Prefect, the bluff straightforward Burrus or the hated Tigellinus who succeeded him. Yet in A.D. 62, he had begun to amuse himself by presiding, and thus, in the splendid star-domed justice hall of the palace on the Palatine, he may have heard Paul's reasoning of "righteousness, temperance, and judgment to come.'' The red-haired Nero's descent into extravagance and lust was gathering pace. He divorced the daughter of Claudius Caesar to marry Poppaea, the Jewish proselyte previously wife of a close friend, and she encouraged Nero in vice and despotism; had Paul's trial delayed much longer, her influence most likely would have overridden justice to secure his execution.

Instead, whatever their personal reactions to Paul's plain-speaking, the distinguished consuls and senators who sat as assessors apparently gave a majority of votes in his favor, and Nero—who often ignored opinion—acquitted him.[29] The effect of the verdict was to substantiate Gallio's earlier decision: Christianity was ruled in no way an illegal cult. The Gospel could be preached freely throughout the Roman world, little more than thirty years since the crucifixion of Christ. No one then realized how utterly hollow this tolerance would prove.

Paul's fetters were struck off. He left the Palatine palace a free man. The rest of his life, probably about five years, is known only hazily if we discount legends and late traditions. The evidence is fragmentary; three letters survive but the provenance of two of them—the place of origin and the sequence in which they were written—is uncertain, and information about his personal movements slight.

He may have gone to Spain as he had planned when writing Romans. Clement of Rome, in his letter to the Corinthians thirty years later, states that Paul ''reached the farthest bounds of the West.'' Clement must have known Paul but the phrase is vague: it could mean he evangelized as far as Cádiz, the ''Gate of the West,'' and looked out across the Atlantic. Or that he evangelized the Celts: Christianity penetrated very early deep into Gaul up the valley of the Rhône, but no local tradition mentions Paul; nor can a shred of reliable evidence support the romance of Paul landing in Britain.

The belief that he went to Spain was held firmly by several

of the Early Fathers, although again there is no local tradition. Since he had intended to evangelize Spain like Galatia, Greece, and the province of Asia, his time there could have stretched nearly to two years. Then he was back in the eastern Mediterranean: with Titus in Crete; with Timothy in Ephesus (despite Paul's earlier conviction that he would never see the elders again); and surely, if at all possible, he found his way at last up the Meander and Lycus valleys to enjoy Philemon's guest room at Colossae, served by a delighted Onesimus. In his letters to Timothy and Titus, Paul mentions being at Miletus and reveals his plans to spend a winter at Nicopolis in the Epirus of western Greece. The picture now is of constant movement rather than settled work, though slower as if bones were old and rheumatism and arthritis were catching up; and he was slower too in his style of writing.

The sense of urgency is undiminished. For his work was being attacked on all sides.

In the year 64, the favorable legal decision handed down at Paul's trial was turned into a mockery by the whim of Nero after the Fire of Rome, when he deflected the wrath of the populace from his own head by accusing the Christians of arson. In the famous words of Tacitus, then a child of ten and writing fifty years later: "A vast multitude were not only put to death, but put to death with insult, in that they were either dressed up in the skins of beasts to perish by the worrying of dogs or else put on crosses to be set on fire, and when the daylight failed, to be burned for use as lights by night. Nero had thrown open his gardens for that spectacle, and was giving a circus exhibition, mingling with the people in a jockey's dress, or driving in a chariot." His excesses produced commiseration with the Christians despite the unpopularity they had earned for rejecting the gods, because people recognized that they were not suffering for the good of the state so much as "to satisfy the cruelty of an individual."

Praetorian soldiers who had learned to love Paul were among those ordered to torture his friends: former guards who were now Christians were themselves dying in agony. And the way Christians died was in itself a testimony: "In the midst of the flame and the rack," wrote Seneca, "I have seen men not only not groan, that is little: not only not complain, that is little: not only not answer back, that too is little; but I have seen them smile, and smile with a good heart."

Survivors of the persecution took refuge in the catacombs, the warren of caves and burial places deep under the outskirts of Rome. In eastern Europe, Paul too may have had to "go underground" for his travels and preaching as the new imperial policy gained momentum in the provinces. The horrors of 64 certainly give point to his words written to Timothy at this time: "I urge that petitions, prayers, intercessions, and thanksgivings be offered for all men: for sovereigns and all in high office, that we may lead a tranquil and quiet life in full observance of religion and high standards of morality."

Several of his converts or trusted elders made shipwreck of their faith. The unsettled times—persecution in Rome, Judea seething with rumors of messiahs and with unrest about to explode in the Great Rebellion of A.D. 66—led to a ferment of ideas old and new. Leaving for Macedonia, Paul urged Timothy at Ephesus to "insist that certain people stop teaching strange doctrines and taking notice of endless genealogies; these things are only likely to raise irrelevant doubts instead of furthering the designs of God which are revealed in faith." To Titus in Crete, Paul wrote of "many insubordinate men, empty talkers and deceivers, especially the Circumcision party; they must be silenced, since they are upsetting whole families, teaching for base gain what they have no right to teach." Paul emphasized this, in a spark of the old fire, by a choice quote from the Cretan poet Epimenides of Knossos: "One of their own countrymen said, 'Cretans are always liars, vicious brutes, lazy gluttons'—and he told the truth!"

Paul had to warn Timothy against ascetics who disapproved of marriage; and conceited controversialists "with a craze for questioning everything and arguing about words," which all led to jealousy, contention, and mistrust. He had to denounce those who sought to make money by Christian service, and coined his memorable phrase, "the love of money is the root of all evils." "It is through this craving," he added, "that some have wandered away from the faith and pierced their hearts with many pangs. But as for you, man of God," lest Timothy himself should waver, "shun all this. Aim at righteousness, godliness, faith, love, steadfastness, gentleness. Fight the good fight of faith; take hold of the eternal life to which you were called when you made the good confession in the presence of many witnesses."

Paul heartened and guided Timothy. Titus needed advice, but Timothy, the same timid and delicate yet sometimes self-willed Timothy, still very much a young man in Paul's eyes, needed encouragement and care, even in matters of health: "Do not drink water only, but take a little wine to help your digestion, since you are sick so often." "Let no one despise your youth," Paul urged, "but set the believers an example in speech and conduct, in love, in faith, in purity. Till I come, attend to the public reading of Scripture, to preaching, to teaching."

Paul was "in journeys oft." Timothy and Titus stayed longer at one place, but they too were in frequent movement, at Paul's behest, strengthening the sorely tried Christians, rebutting falsehoods, restoring the lapsed. Paul did not resent that far from enjoying a tranquil old age, venerated, uncontradicted, honored, he must battle to the last, for he had expected this trouble. "The Spirit says expressly," he warned, "that in after times some will desert from the faith and give their minds to subversive doctrines. . . . Timothy," he begged, "keep safe that which has been entrusted to you. Turn a deaf ear to empty and wordy chatter, and the contradictions of so-called knowledge, for many who lay claim to it have shot wide of the faith."

It was essential to build up healthy, expanding churches under local leadership, for "God our Saviour desires all men to be saved and to come to the knowledge of the truth." The two letters of this period, the First Epistle to Timothy and the Epistle to Titus, quickly became classics of pastoral wisdom wherever Christianity spread. Timothy in Asia and Titus in Crete were shown how to select and train elders; instructed about church discipline and worship; advised what to do about widows and others in distress or need, how young men and slaves and all other believers should behave so that Christians, however traduced or abused by Nero or their neighbors, might "add luster to the doctrine of God our Saviour. For," Paul reminded Titus, "the grace of God has dawned upon the world with healing for all mankind." The aged Paul was more than ever sure of "the glorious Gospel of the blessed God with which I have been entrusted. I thank Him," he wrote to Timothy, "who has given me strength for this, Christ Jesus our Lord, because He judged me faithful by appointing me to His service, though I formerly blasphemed and persecuted and insulted Him. But I received mercy because I acted ignorantly in unbelief, and the grace of our Lord overflowed for me with the faith and love that are in Christ Jesus.

"This saying is sure and worthy of full acceptance, that Christ Jesus came into the world to save sinners. And I am the foremost of sinners! But I received mercy for this reason, that in me, as the foremost, Jesus Christ might display His perfect patience for an example to those who were to believe in Him for eternal life.

"To the King of ages, immortal, invisible, the only God, be honor and glory for ever and ever."

Thirty-Six
NO KIND OF DEATH

Paul was arrested for the last time probably in the summer of A.D. 66. It may have been in northwest Asia Minor or eastern Macedonia, for he had left his belongings at Troas: his winter sheepskin cloak, perhaps a present from Philemon in the choice wool of Colossae; his papyrus rolls, which would have been handwritten notes of the sayings of the Lord Jesus and possibly copies of his own epistles and Luke's writings; and the vellum parchments, most likely the Law and the Prophets which he had treasured since earliest days.

The immediate cause of arrest may be inferred from Paul's statement soon afterward: "Alexander the coppersmith did me great harm." True to his teaching in Romans, "Never avenge yourselves," Paul quoted a psalm, "the Lord will repay him for what he has done," but warned Timothy against the man because "he strongly opposed our message." To add to Paul's distress, "all who are in Asia deserted me, including Phygelus and Hermogenes." Paul presumably was writing hyperbole rather than a statistical statement, for the context suggests abandonment at the idea of danger, such as Jesus suffered in the Garden of Gethsemane, rather than deliberate and widespread rejection of his teachings.

Opposed, arrested, deserted, Paul would have been hurried by the Via Egnatia and the Adriatic to Rome, and flung into jail. Or he may have returned to Rome before arrest, since he mentions leaving Trophimus at Miletus and Erastus at Corinth as if they had been together on the journey westward. If so, intending a brief visit to encourage the decimated community in Rome, he joined the underground existence of Christians who went about their normal affairs in daytime but gathered for preaching and prayer in the catacombs at night. The walls have several mural portraits of Paul: a long face and nose, unruffled yet eager expression, the beard white and the head nearly bald. They date from the next century, too late for the artists to have seen Paul themselves; but in childhood they could easily have heard old men describe him from their own childhood memories.

Paul was once more seized, shackled, and this time placed in rigorous confinement in Rome, not as an honorable citizen on remand but "chained like a criminal. But the Word of God is not chained," he could add. He was among the felons in the Mamertine or an equally obnoxious dungeon, reached only by rope or ladder let through a hole in the floor above. His weary body must lie on rough stones. The air was foul, sanitation almost nonexistent.

They put him on trial as one of those who had caused the Great Fire. If convicted, he would die as he might have died in Ephesus, as many Roman Christians had already died: driven into the arena to be torn in pieces by lions. The trial of a citizen could not be summary: Paul must appear before Caesar in the great Basilica in the Forum where, besides the senators and consuls on the bench, and the depraved Nero whom all Rome now hated, a large crowd of spectators packed the galleries. Paul confidently expected Christians to testify on his behalf. He looked in vain. The Terror had driven them away. "At my first defense," he wrote to Timothy, "no one took my part; all deserted me. May it not be charged against them! But the Lord stood by me and gave me strength to proclaim the Word fully, that all the Gentiles might hear it. So I was rescued from the lion's mouth." Once again he had turned a court hearing into proclamation of the Gospel, and his voice had carried to the farthest gallery.

He was acquitted of arson but remanded again, to be punished for the less dishonorable offense of propagating a forbidden cult; a capital charge because it implied treason against the divine emperor. Back in prison, possibly no longer the Mamertine, he was lonely. One trusted friend had deserted, and Paul's zeal for the Gospel did not let him keep others in Rome who might visit and comfort: "Demas, in love with this present world, has deserted me and gone to Thessalonica; Crescens has gone to Galatia (*or* Gaul), Titus to Dalmatia. Luke alone is with me."

Then an Asian Christian, who being of some substance in the eyes of the authorities stood to lose much by associating with a criminal, came to Italy. Onesiphorus of Ephesus "was not ashamed of my chains, but when he arrived in Rome he searched for me eagerly and found me," and cheered Paul many times.

Paul was now able to write to Timothy, perhaps by the pen of Luke and the hand of Onesiphorus, urging him to "do your best to come to me before winter," and to find Mark and bring him, "for he can help me in the work," which continued regardless of prison walls. Above all he urged Timothy: "Do not be ashamed of testifying to our Lord, nor of me His prisoner; but take your share of suffering for the Gospel in the power of God, who saved us and called us with a holy calling, not in virtue of our works but in virtue of His own purpose and the grace which He gave us in Christ Jesus ages ago, and now has manifested through the appearance of our Saviour Christ Jesus, who abolished death and brought life and immortality to light through the Gospel. For this Gospel I was appointed a preacher, and apostle, and teacher, and therefore I suffer as I do.

"But I am not ashamed. For I know whom I have believed!'' And I am sure that He is able to guard until that Day what has been entrusted to me.''

He recalled their service and sufferings together in those far-off days in Galatia on the first missionary journey, and encouraged Timothy: "You then, my son, be strong in the grace that is in Christ Jesus, and what you have heard from me before many witnesses entrust to faithful men who shall be able to teach others also. . . . Preach the Word, be urgent in season and out of season, convince, rebuke, and exhort, be unfailing in patience and teaching." Undeflected by those who seek teachers "to suit their own likings," Timothy must "always be steady, endure suffering, do the work of an evangelist, fulfill your ministry."

Paul was not depressed or dismayed at the surrounding stress. Though Christianity might seem in process of extinction by fire and sword, or of being wrested into a different gospel, he could affirm with utmost confidence that "the foundation of God stands sure." The fearful war that had broken out in Judea might be the first portent of the Lord's return to earth; if so, it would mean that all Israel would recognize the Lord Jesus at last and be gathered in. If the Lord delayed, the Gospel would continue to be preached.

The Lord did delay, and Paul's work stood the test of time. Corinth, though always with its difficulties, became an important center, and Ephesus, which the Revelation of St. John commended (with reservations) nearly thirty years later, a great bishopric. When the Roman Empire at last gave Christianity complete toleration in A.D. 313, not one of Paul's churches had disappeared. Yet always, as he had warned, the gold of faith was flawed by dross, and in Asia Minor disputes and political ambitions led to such weakening of what now boasted itself a Christian empire, that 1,400 years after Paul, Islam triumphed. If many of his churches fell to conquerors who denied the divinity of Christ, Paul's writings have survived every attempt to discredit or dismember them. The great thinker, Christ's interpreter, towers above men who would rewrite him or who charge him with twisting and debasing his Master's words and meaning. Paul had expected such activities: "they will turn away from listening to the truth and wander into myths." His own call, in the Second Epistle to Timothy, remains in all its simplicity: "Remember Jesus Christ, risen from the dead, born of David's line. This is the theme of my Gospel."

"As for me, I am now ready to be offered, and the time of my departure is at hand. I have fought a good fight. I have finished my course, I have kept the faith. Henceforth there is laid up for me a crown of righteousness, which the Lord, the righteous judge, shall give me at that Day: and not to me only but unto all them that love His appearing."

Of Paul's final trial, nothing is known beyond a tradition that he was condemned by resolution of the Senate on the charge of treason against the divine emperor. How long Simon Peter and Paul were in prison together before being executed the same day, as an early and strong belief asserts, cannot be fixed: possibly as much as nine months. The date honored in the city of their martyrdom is June 29, 67, Peter nailed to a cross as a public spectacle at Nero's Circus on the Vatican, head downward at his own request, and Paul, as a Roman citizen, beheaded in a less public place.

The ancient tradition of Paul's execution site is almost certainly authentic but the details cannot be fixed. Whereas Christ's Via Dolorosa may be followed step by step, Paul's remains vague. He would have it so. And because Christ had walked that earlier road, Paul's was no Via Dolorosa, for they were walking it together: "Thanks be to God, who in Christ always leads us in triumph." "For to me to live is Christ and to die is gain."

They marched him out through the walls past the pyramid of Cestius which still stands, on to the Ostian Way toward the sea. Crowds journeying to or from Ostia would recognize an execution squad by the lictors with their *fasces* of rods and ax, and the executioner carrying a sword, which in Nero's reign had replaced the ax; by the escort, and by the manacled criminal, walking stiffly and bandy-legged, ragged and filthy from his prison: but not ashamed or degraded. He was going to a feast, to a triumph, to the crowning day to which he had pressed forward. He who had talked often of God's promise of eternal life in Jesus could not fear; he believed as he had spoken: "All God's promises find their 'yes' in Him." No executioner was going to lose him the conscious presence of Jesus; he was not changing his company, only the place where he enjoyed it. Better still, he would see Jesus. Those glimpses—on the Damascus Road, in Jerusalem, at Corinth, on that sinking ship; now he was going to see Him face to face, to know even as he had been known.

They marched Paul to the third milestone on the Ostian Way, to a little pinewood in a glade, probably a place of tombs, known then as Aquae Salviae or Healing Waters, and now as Tre Fontane where an abbey stands in his honor. He is believed to have been put overnight in a tiny cell, for this was a common place of execution. If Luke was allowed to stay by his window, if Timothy or Mark had reached Rome in time, the sounds of the night vigil would not be of weeping but singing: "as sorrowful yet always rejoicing; as dying and, behold, we live."

At first light, the soldiers took Paul to the pillar. The executioner stood ready, stark naked. Soldiers stripped Paul to the waist and tied him, kneeling upright, to the low pillar which left his neck free. Some accounts say the lictors beat him with rods; a beating had been the usual prelude to beheading but in recent years not always inflicted. If they must administer this last, senseless dose of pain to a body so soon to die, "Who shall separate us from the love of Christ? Shall tribulation . . . or sword?

"I reckon that the sufferings of this present time are not worthy to be compared with"—the flash of a sword—"the glory."

NOTES

1. *Cf.* Mark 7:14-23 with Romans 14:14 and Galatians 5:19-22.

2. *Cf.* Matthew 5:14-16, Luke 8:16, with Philippians 2:16.

3. Following Sir William Ramsay, as against many scholars, I place the vision in the Temple which Paul refers to in Acts 22 ("Make haste and get quickly out of Jerusalem") at a later date. See chapter 8.

4. See chapter 19.

5. The *Authorized (King James) Version* translates Luke's term by *Deputy,* the title in use in 1611 for the governor of England's sole major colony, Ireland.

6. English miles. The Roman mile was slightly shorter. Ramsay's estimate for a first-century foot traveler's day is between sixteen and twenty Roman miles.

7. Assuming, with the backing of an impressive array of scholars, that Paul wrote to Christians in southern Galatia and not, as Lightfoot taught, to the actual Gallic tribe of Galatians around the capital Ancyra (Ankara) in the north, whose name the Romans took for the whole province. It is not certain that Paul ever visited them. Biographically, the southern Galatian destination of the letter makes complete sense.

8. Acts 22.

9. The Greek text of Acts has Zeus and Hermes, as in RSV. AV followed the curious Elizabethan habit of translating Greek divinities by their Latin equivalents, to which NEB rather oddly reverts, possibly because the Baucis story is best known from Ovid. In any case, the Lycaonians must have used Anatolian equivalents or Paul and Barnabas would have got wind of it sooner.

10. Luke's statement "they went *down* to Attalia, and from there they sailed to Antioch" is another instance of his extraordinary precision of terms, as any visitor to the delightful resort of Antalya may confirm.

11. Scholars who accept southern Galatia as the epistle's destination are not unanimous in dating it from Antioch and thus as the earliest of all Paul's writings. Evidence for the early date was strongly argued by Ramsay and the discussion is well summarized in Kirsopp Lake: *The Earlier Epistles of St. Paul* (1911), pp. 253-323. As

a biographer, I found that as soon as I rejected my previous ideas and accepted the early date, Paul's life fell into shape.

12. The words *of Jesus*, missing from KJV, were in the Western Text (then known as *Codex Bezae*) and are found in the best of the ancient manuscripts discovered since 1611. See, for example, RSV and NEB.

13. *In God's Underground* by Richard Wurmbrand and Charles Foley (W.H. Allen, & Co., Ltd., London, 1968), pp. 194-95. (Published in the United States as *Christ in the Communist Prisons* by Coward-McCann, Inc., New York, 1968.)

14. The Western Text says the jailer first secured the prisoners before leading Paul and Silas out. Luke is tantalizingly silent about their subsequent fate.

15. 1 Thessalonians 5:2 following Luke 12:39-40; 1 Thessalonians 4:15-16 following Luke 21:27. *Cf.* also 1 Thessalonians 5:3, 6-7 with Luke 21:34.

16. Many scholars, ancient and modern, have held that they went by land. Luke's meaning is not clear.

17. The question whether Paul addressed the Areopagites on this little hill (the Areopagus itself), where they met for formal trials, or in the Royal Portico of the marketplace below, where they conducted day-by-day business, has been much discussed. Most modern scholars tend to favor the marketplace. My choosing the hill may be a case of a biographer's dramatic sense getting the better of his scholarship.

The AV translation of Areopagus (Ares' Hill) into "Mars' Hill" is another instance of converting Greek into Latin gods, Ares being the God of War.

18. The sermon in the synagogue is taken from Romans 10:5-15. Paul's dictation in chapters 9 and 10 of the Epistle to the Romans, which he composed in Corinth a few years later, is held by Professor C.H. Dodd to be very similar to his style of synagogue preaching.

19. I find myself convinced by A.N. Sherwin White, *Roman Society and Roman Law in the New Testament* (1963), that Sosthenes suffered as a Christian, from Jews, and not as an (unconverted) Jew from a Greek rabble. (The word "Greeks" in AV is not in the best manuscripts.)

If the Greeks had assaulted someone in full sight of Gallio, he would have been bound to punish a breach of the peace. If the Jews exercised their domestic jurisdiction by punishing one of their number, the only irregularity was that they punished in public instead of private. However, this theory (which was ridiculed by Ramsay) does not entirely fit the implication of Luke's account, in which he seems to invite a reader's reaction of "Serves Sosthenes right for trying to ruin Paul."

20. The classic statement of the Ephesus theory is *St. Paul's Ephesian Ministry* (1929) by Professor G.S. Duncan of St. Andrews. However, he overstated his case and tried to squeeze *all* the prison epistles, including sections of the pastorals, into the Ephesus years.

21. Or they may have been administrators of the temple dedicated to the honor of the emperor (not the Temple of Artemis). The evidence is inconclusive.

22. Modeled closely on Tyndale's work of the 1550s. For *agapē*, KJV changed Tyndale's *love* to *charity*, a word of wider meaning then, describing any loving action which did not depend on the love being returned, not only "alms" or "charity" in the modern sense.

23. Jewish days were reckoned from 6 P.M. to 6 P.M. The First Day of the week thus began on Saturday evening.

24. The modern traveler approaching ruined Assos by Paul's route sees the remains of a Byzantine fortress on the rock.

25. Sir William Ramsay was able to date the voyage very exactly in *St. Paul the Traveller*.

26. The final paragraph is NEB. For the rest of the speech I worked direct from the Greek, as no version quite conveys the unpolished spontaneity of Paul's words.

27. Adramyttium itself, now Edremit in Turkey, sticks in my memory because as we drove through, a pony carrying a small boy shied at some cattle and bolted. The boy's fur cap flew off. I picked it up and we drove slowly after them. The pony collided with a cow, the boy was thrown and winded, but made me a charming if painful bow when I restored his cap.

28. See *The Voyage and Shipwreck of St. Paul* by James Smith of Jordanhill, 1848 (4th edition, with revisions, 1880).

29. But the evidence is scanty, and many scholars hold that Paul was convicted and executed in A.D. 62. The balance of probability, however, leans toward acquittal, and I adopt this conclusion.